Mass Media
and the Moral Imagination

Mass Media
and the Moral Imagination

Edited by

Philip J. Rossi, S.J.
and
Paul Soukup, S.J.

Sheed & Ward

Sheed & Ward™ is a service of The National Catholic Reporter Publishing Company.

Library of Congress Cataloguing-in-Publication Data

    Mass media and the moral imagination / Philip J. Rossi and Paul A. Soukup, editors.
        p.   cm. — (Communication, Culture & Theology)
    Includes bibliographical references and index.
    ISBN 1-55612-622-0
    1. Mass media—Moral and ethical aspects. 2. Mass media—Religious aspects.   I. Rossi, Philip J. II. Soukup, Paul A.
P94.M33   1994
302.23—dc20

                                                93-30845
                                                 CIP

Published by: Sheed & Ward
                115 E. Armour Blvd.
                P.O. Box 419492
                Kansas City, MO 64141

To order, call: (800) 333-7373

Table of Contents

Preface ix

I. The Context of the Mass Media and Moral Reflection 1

Introduction 3

Section 1. Mass Media as a Site for Moral Reflection 9

   1. The Expressive Face of Culture: Mass Media and the
      Shape of the Human Moral Environment (I) 11
      Gregor Goethals

   2. The Expressive Face of Culture: Mass Media and the
      Shape of the Human Moral Environment (II) 25
      Michael Real

   3. The Democratization of Moral Judgment:
      Moral Leadership and Moral Symbols in Public Culture 34
      William M. Sullivan

   4. Power, Truth, and the Flow of Information 43
      Thomas E. Shanks, S.J.

   5. The Life of the Spirit in a Mass-mediated Culture 52
      Günter Virt

Section 2. The Development of Moral Reasoning
              as Situated in the Mass Media 69

   6. The Formation of Moral Life in a Mass-mediated Culture 71
      Paul J. Philibert, O.P.

   7. Matching the Inner World with Outer Reality:
      Moral Development Domains and the Role of the Media 85
      Michael J. Garanzini, S.J.

II. Moral Dimensions of Public Life 101

Introduction 103

8. Television Images of Work and the Moral Imagination:
Theological Interpretations 107
Lois K. Daly

9. Beyond Necessity:
Toward the Ethics of Entertainment 116
David Eley, S.J.

10. Celebration, Consumption, and the Television Media 123
Joan S. Timm and Henry C. Timm

11. Gender in the Media:
Notes on Profit and Ownership Contraction 130
Christine E. Gudorf

12. Teaching Values:
The Shifting Roles of Women and the Media 146
James A. Capo

13. "And a Third of the Water Turned Bitter": Chernobyl, Truth,
Media Technology, and the Flow of Information 162
Janusz Balicki and Wolfgang Wunden

14. Towards a Solution to the Conflict
Created by Mass Media 178
Ivan Fuček, S.J.

15. The Church as Moral Communicator 197
Paul A. Soukup, S.J.

III. Using the Media for Moral Development 207

Introduction 209

16. Possibilities of Audiovisual Narrative for Moral Formation . . 212
Henk Hoekstra, O. Carm., and Marjeet Verbeek

17. Formation of Moral Life in a Mass-mediated Culture 234
Elizabeth Willems, S.S.N.D.

18. Mass Media and the Enlargement of Moral Sensibility 242
Myrna Reid Grant

19. Mass Media and the Enlargement of Moral Sensibility:
Insights from Theology and Literary History 249
Anne E. Patrick

**IV. Philosophical and Theological Reflections:
The Importance of Moral Imagining** 259

Introduction 261

20. Moral Imagination and the Media:
Whose "World" Do We See, Whose "World" Shall It Be? . . . 264
Philip J. Rossi, S.J.

21. Solidarity and Human Development: Theological Reflections
on Power, Truth, and the Flow of Information 273
James R. Pollock, S.J.

22. Moral Theology as Communication 281
Enda McDonagh

Index 289

About the Authors 299

Preface

These essays, written from the perspectives of a variety of disciplines—communications, education, psychology, philosophy, theology—explore the impact that the emergence and the development of modern communications technology and mass media have upon the shape of the human moral world. They examine the roles that the mass media play in presenting issues for moral discernment, in setting contexts for our moral judgments, and in shaping our moral imagination, that is, the patterns by which we envision a coherent moral order as a guide for our interaction with the surrounding world of persons, nature, and culture.

Moral choices do not arise from reasoned discourse only. Day-to-day reality confronts us abruptly with the necessity to choose the good. The worlds in which we live shape us and call attention to one problem or another deserving our moral reflection. But there is more even beyond this level of moral imagining.

Mark Johnson has recently argued that we come to moral decision more through imagination than through reason.

> Recent empirical research in the cognitive sciences has revealed that both our concepts and our reasoning about them are grounded in the nature of our bodily experience and are structured by various kinds of imaginative processes. Consequently, since moral reasoning makes use of these same general cognitive capacities, it, too, is grounded in embodied structures of meaning and is imaginative through and through. This means that the quality of our moral understanding and deliberation depends crucially on the cultivation of our moral imagination.[1]

Johnson goes on to explain how moral reasoning involves exploring options and explaining values, how it needs to examine possible courses of action, how it must "try on" the futures to which our choices can lead:

---

[1] Mark Johnson, *Moral Imagination: Implications of Cognitive Science for Ethics* (Chicago: The University of Chicago Press, 1993) 1.

> We need to explore imaginatively what it might mean, in terms of pos-
> sibilities for enhanced meaning and relationships, for us to perform this
> or that action. We need the ability to imagine and to enact transforma-
> tions in our moral understanding, our character, and our behavior. In
> short, we need an *imaginative rationality* that is at once insightful, criti-
> cal, exploratory, and transformative.[2]

The workings of imagination serve not only to bring general principles to
specificity, but also to shape those principles. Even were one to reject
Johnson's conclusions, one must still take very seriously the world that
informs our moral thinking, the world we experience, the world we
know, the world in which we live. And in that world the mass media
dominate other voices.

The seven essays in Part I focus on two broad aspects of the interplay between mass media and the dynamics of moral imagination and
judgment. The essays contributed by Gregor Goethals, Michael Real,
William Sullivan, Thomas Shanks, and Günter Virt examine the first half
of the equation: the ways in which mass media function as a site for
moral reflection. The power of mass media to symbolize and express a
moral order is of special concern to these authors. The essays written by
Paul Philibert and Michael Garanzini examine the second half: the processes by which moral consciousness develops within the context of a
mass mediated culture. Both authors utilize the insights of developmental psychology to situate the positive and negative impact of the media
upon the formation of the moral imagination.

The eight essays in Part II move from a broad outline of the dynamics
at play in the interaction between media and moral imagination to analyses
of particular cases and examples. Each essay focuses upon a facet of contemporary life precisely as it involves important public dimensions that
moral imagination and judgment must take into account: work (Lois Daly),
play (David Eley), consumption (Joan and Henry Timm), gender (Christine
Gudorf), teaching moral values (James Capo, Paul Soukup), public truth
(Janusz Balicki and Wolfgang Wunden), and conflict (Ivan Fucek). The
authors do not individually attempt to offer a comprehensive view of the
role which the mass media have in revealing (or concealing) these public
dimensions and their moral import; yet each study suggests how paying
close attention to the structure and function of the mass media in particular
cases may help us frame larger perspectives from which to envision and to
assess the moral significance of the role which the media now play in our
engagement with so many facets of life today.

Implicit in much of the analyses in Parts I and II is the principle that
modern communication and mass media—despite the fact that they have
their own inner dynamic—can be directed to serve, rather than overwhelm,

---

[2] Johnson 187.

the conditions for the discernment of the genuine human good and for the promotion of human moral growth. The four essays in Part III, by Henk Hoekstra and Marjeet Verbeek, Elizabeth Willems, Myrna Grant, and Anne E. Patrick, explore some ways in which this principle can be put to effective use in various contexts in which moral education takes place. They each note how the structural dynamics and the vivid images characteristic of media such as film and television can set moral reflection in motion; at the same time they all underline the need for dialogic processes to keep that reflection focused and to enable its outcome to make a positive contribution to a coherent moral vision and way of living.

The three essays in Part IV, by Philip Rossi, James Pollock, and Enda McDonagh, bring the discussion of the interplay of mass media and the moral imagination full circle by returning to a consideration of some broader philosophical and theological motifs which can be discerned in that interplay. Central to all three discussions is the conviction that our moral imagination is ordered to and serves our ties with one another in human community. Each author articulates a different dimension of the orientation which moral imagination has to enlarging the breadth and the depth of our commitments to one another. Thus they all propose that we understand and evaluate the workings of modern communications technology and mass media in relation to this fundamental dynamic of moral imagination towards inclusiveness, solidarity, and communion.

Acknowledgments

The multidisciplinary and international character of this work has required the assistance and support of many individuals and institutions. The original concept for this collection was developed at a seminar at Villa Cavalletti, Italy, organized and jointly sponsored by the Centre for the Study of Communication and Culture (formerly in London and now located at Saint Louis University) and the Centre for Interdisciplinary Studies in Communication at the Gregorian University in Rome. Many of the essays were first presented at a conference at Marquette University, organized under the auspices of the Psychology and the Theology Departments, with the cooperation of the College of Communication, Journalism, and Performing Arts; funding for the conference came from the Religious Commitment Fund of Marquette University, the Bradley Institute for Democracy and Public Values, and the Institute for Family Studies.

At various stages in this project, as it moved from concept to completion, the following individuals rendered essential support, advice, and encouragement to the editors: Dr. Marvin Berkowitz, Bro. William Biernatzki, S.J., Rev. Peter Henrici, S.J., Dr. John Johannes, Rev. Kevin Kersten, S.J., Ms. Jane Linahan, Mrs. Audrey Martini, Dr. Sharon Murphy, Rev. Leo Murray, S.J., Rev. Patrick Quinn, S.J., Mr. Steven Shippee, Ms. Katherine

Thome, Dr. William Thorn, Ms. Maria Way, and Rev. Robert White, S.J. We also gratefully acknowledge the institutional support received from Marquette University and Santa Clara University.

Finally, we wish to thank Cowley Publications for permission to use material that was first published in Chapters Two and Three of *The Electronic Golden Calf: Images, Meaning and the Making of Religion*, by Gregor Goethals.

We are most grateful for the assistance which all these friends and colleagues have unfailingly provided.

—Philip Rossi, S.J.
Marquette University

—Paul A. Soukup, S.J.
Santa Clara University

I

The Context of the Mass Media and Moral Reflection

I

Introduction

The Context of Mass Media and Moral Reflection

At least two facets of modern life seem inescapable.

First, we cannot avoid moral reflection. Everyday life poses choices, not all of them simple, which demand some reflection on right and wrong. How should one act in the face of violence? What obligations do the homeless impose on the community? Should the state compel political activity? What kinds of medical care do people merit? Are there limits to parental authority? How should we react to drugs in the community? to changing sexual norms? to illiteracy?

We cannot escape these and other issues and the questions they raise. As individuals and as a community we think about them, discuss them, worry about them. And all of this presupposes some kind of moral reflection. Where do we learn this habit of reflection? Certainly, some people study ethics and moral decision making. Some teach methods. Many of us learn a kind of implicit habit of moral thinking from our parents.

At the same time our culture proposes moral practices and norms— usually in unreflective form—which in turn shape our moral reflection. These "rules of thumb" that get passed on often show the influences of Christianity and of past ethical teachers: "Be fair." "Treat others as you would have them treat you." "Don't harm another person." "Love your neighbor." Other, sometimes contrary, norms find cultural warrant as well: "Might makes right." "Defend yourself." "Look out for number one." Children quickly learn these and hold to them, in one form or another, even through to adulthood.

More than these "rules," though, influence moral choices. We also consciously and unconsciously model our behavior on other people who inhabit our moral universe: family members, leaders, religious figures, popular characters. At this point we encounter a second inevitable fact of modern life: the mass media and their products. These, too, propose a pattern of moral reflection by informing our imagination.

3

In moral decision making we reflect on our experience, actual and vi-carious. Because the mass media provide both kinds of experience, they acquire a power over our imagination. On the one hand, the media present us with a wide range of vicarious experiences. Television and film, for example, let us share the emotions, ideas, sufferings, joys, and hopes of people throughout the world. Dramatic presentations enact the death of loved ones, lingering and tragic diseases, various kinds of abuse, family breakdowns, crises of personal identity, as well as falling in love, finding kindred spirits, discovering new continents, triumphing over odds. News reporting brings us around the world to situations of intense suffering, war, disaster, and famine, but also to the dismantling of the Berlin Wall, the rescue of a child, and a look into the depths of space. On the other hand, media experience is real experience—what we watch and read *does* form part of our lifeworld. The dual nature of mediated experience puts in it a special position to influence the moral imagination.

The "moral imagination" serves as a useful shorthand for that process of posing and mulling over issues demanding action and judgments of right and wrong. The moral imagination also refers to the ideas and possibilities that occur to us in judging courses of action. This imagination allows us to safely engage issues and actions in a provisional, hypothetical way: "If such and so were to occur, how would I, how should I respond?" "If thus and so were to demand my attention and action, what course of action would be better?" Imaginatively entering those situations prepares us to decide the all-too-real, non-hypothetical cases of human living.

In this way, the mass media and their products serve the moral imagination and thus serve moral judgment. The authors whose work appears in the first section demonstrate in their various ways how the mass media function as a site for moral reflection.

Gregor Goethals approaches the question through an historical overview of the role of art in culture. Such a perspective might not appear, even to the most highly skilled and educated among us, as the one most immediately relevant from which to examine mass media and their impact on human moral identity. However, Goethals points out that the modern relegation of high art to the function of expressing personal and private meanings manifests the fragmentation of culture that has given mass media a task once proper to art: the fashioning of images and symbols that express shared and public meanings. Goethals argues that, since such public meanings undergird the possibility of ordering the human world into a coherent moral pattern, the "transference of the power to communicate public symbols" into the hands of the media requires critical attention from all who are concerned with the shape of our common moral life. To develop and to illustrate her argument, she sketches the overarching beliefs which the media in the United States, particularly television, legitimate in order to reinforce a sense of identity that is at once, national, cultural, moral, and, indeed, quasi-religious. She focuses our attention particularly on what she terms "authoritative images"—those representations that assure us that trustworthy powers exist who can "address our human need for an ordered universe." Her study provides a look at how the mass media have taken over the symbolic role once associated with art and religion, giving a new kind of popular faith as locus of and justification for moral choices. Advertising, she notes, now defines "the good life."

Michael Real examines the "expressive face of culture" as the place in which both our common and our personal identity takes form. Real's essay provides a range of concrete illustrations of the interactive and constructive dynamic by which media in the United States provide "the clouded mirror in which we see ourselves." How do the media acquire such symbolic power to shape human life? Decades of research into media effects sketch, at least in outline, the process of influence. It works by structuring our existence, by providing images and rituals, by indirectly cultivating values—reinforcing some and ignoring others. Real's five questions for reflection suggest a starting point for any response to the media's power.

For William Sullivan the key issues of moral imagination appear in public and political discourse. Throughout this century the news media have played a strong role in that discourse, at least in the United States. Sullivan draws our attention to a 1920s debate between Walter Lippmann and John Dewey about the role that media play in the efforts of a people to maintain a morally coherent understanding of life in the face of the complexity that exists in the world. Both Lippmann and Dewey saw a positive function for the news media. Sullivan suggests that, while the issue is not new, Americans must deal with it today in a significantly altered context, particularly one dominated by the image. He points to the role that the Pledge of Allegiance played in the 1988 U.S. presidential election campaign and to the media's handling of that issue as illustrative of our lessened ability to sustain public moral argument. In a context in which "Americans are less clear than ever before about what values, what goods they really do share in common," Sullivan sees the need for a reappropriation of the tradition of practical reason, of reasoning about what makes life worth living—a way of thinking about our common culture and public institutions that goes beyond images, slogans, and technological glitter.

Thomas Shanks continues this focus upon the place of news media in public and political discourse but offers the caution that the media themselves bear the traces of their own limits. In analyzing the structural dynamics of information gathering and dissemination by the news media he notes a number of concerns that take added weight when we consider the extent to which we depend on the journalists to inform our moral imagination: the contraction of media ownership; the selectivity of what counts as news; and the reenforcement of the values of "the good life," conceived in highly individualistic terms. Although he sees these dynamics functioning

to establish the authority and power of the media "when they present information of significance to the everyday lives of readers or viewers," he also
notes that these dynamics operate within a context of "interdependent relationships...among audiences, media, and the larger social system." The
news media do have a powerful influence upon our moral imagination, he
concludes, but these media distort what they convey.

Günter Virt places the discussion of the media as a site for moral reflection into a wider context of the tradition of Christian moral discourse.
Examining the activities of sin and redemption within culture, he proposes a
"discernment of spirits" as a response. Even though the media dominate the
location of public discourse, they themselves must become subject to some
criteria. In his application of the language of moral theology to the mass
media, Virt provides a bridge between one tradition of moral imagination
and the contemporary situation.

The second part of this section on the context of the mass media and
moral reflection shifts focus away from the mass media and onto the development of moral reasoning in a mediated world. Given the overwhelming
presence of the media and their products in our daily lives, how does a
moral sense develop? The process involves more than cataloguing media
effects; to fill out the picture we can turn to developmental psychology.

Paul Philibert takes the dual perspectives of psychology and moral theology. He sets the context by identifying an important historical shift in the
dominant cultural understanding of ourselves as moral actors. This shift
leads us to envision our intelligence less as "a capacity for participation in
the reality of another" and more as instrumental rationality: a tool for the
manipulation of objects and persons in service of the aims of our action.
Over against this understanding of intelligence, Philibert sets not only the
classical Greek concept of intelligence as *nous*, "an organ of mystical union," but also Piaget's account of the structure of cognitive development.
For Philibert, Piaget's account serves also as a basis on which to reinterpret
another central feature of our dominant cultural understanding of ourselves:
the "autonomy" that we deem central for responsible moral agency. In contrast to the common understanding of autonomy as "a rational, critical mind
standing over against social conventions," Piagetian autonomy is ordered to
the mutual relation of peers and to the co-construction of a mutually satisfying world. The contrast that Philibert delineates between these ways of understanding intelligence and autonomy enables him to offer an alternative to
the media's role in moral imagination. He proposes a preliminary formulation of countervailing principles that set a quite different moral context—the
life of communities committed to "respect for the integrity of material creation," to "re-appropriation of the sacral tradition," and to the participation of
all in the co-construction of a mutually satisfying world.

Michael Garanzini places the dynamics of media in interaction with
the developing moral consciousness of children. He provides an initial

sketch of the range of important theories on moral development in children to highlight the connection it has with the other domains of childhood growth: physiological maturation, affective development, cognitive growth, and social development. He follows this with a case study to illustrate how interaction with media enters into a child's accomplishment of the variety of developmental tasks involved in growth toward moral maturity. Each of these tasks require the "meshing or integrating the inner world and outer reality." Media can function to help the child "work through struggles and conflicts that are experienced on the inside and in the outside" in the cognitive, affective, and social domains of moral development. He stresses the role of the media in the shaping of imagination and of the imagination in the appropriation and construction of the moral world. While the media's own dynamics, particularly those of image and narrative, offer much opportunity for stimulating authentic moral growth, he concludes that the media's attitudinal stance (in the United States at least) most frequently mirrors a culturally dominant individualism and the competitive ethos of profit capitalism.

This first section describes in some detail the two poles of our inquiry: the media of communication and the moral judgment. Despite the necessity of describing them sequentially, one should bear in mind their interaction in creating and manifesting a moral imagination.

1

Mass Media as a Site for Moral Reflection

The Expressive Face of Culture: Mass Media and the Shape of the Human Moral Environment - I

Gregor Goethals

The British philosopher R. G. Collingwood suggested that in order to understand written or spoken words, it is important to know the primary question that lies behind a presentation. To me the most important question today for media people and for all of us shaped by the mass media is this: How do images function in a democratic, technological, and secular world? In addressing that question, I shall try to show that our society, like others, uses images to construct symbolic worlds which represent beliefs and values.

The high arts today no longer play a significant role in expressing shared public values and myths. Indeed, many people expect artists to present personal mythologies and private visions. In today's world the artist has a special status, not unlike that of the seer or prophet in earlier times. Thus, some envision a career in the arts as a search for liberation and truth, a way of making sense of life. This happens in a culture which is dominated by mass media and technology. Painters and sculptors, for example, are viewed as contemplative free spirits who have rejected the ordinary confining work demanded by highly routinized, computerized society.

By contrast, the arts in pre-modern and medieval religions were integral to ritual at the same time they gave coherence and order to the surrounding culture. Traditional religious images exemplify this synthesis. For example, at the church of St. Mary Magdalene in Vesele, the activities of the ordinary world, the planting, harvesting, celebrating and the movement of the seasons radiated from the Christological drama at the church's entrance. The center is the figure of Christ, but at the outer edges, woven into the sacred story, are the signs and the works of the seasons—the pruning of

Portions of this essay were previously published in Gregor Goethals, *The Electronic Golden Calf: Images, Religion, and the Making of Meaning* (Cambridge, MA: Cowley Publications, 1990).

the vine, the harvesting of the crop, and the cutting of bread. The natural and supernatural orders here were integrated. Today, no such all-embracing, unified vision exists.

To help see why this is so, we need to look at modernity and the contrast we draw in its name between the high arts and popular culture. We associate the autonomy of art with cultural developments of the last hundred years. Yet, its independence is only one facet of what Jürgen Habermas has called the project of modernity. He describes cultural modernity as a fracturing of religion and metaphysics into three autonomous spheres, science, morality and art.[1] Following this disengagement and over time, the visual arts acquired not only independence from the institutional church, but also from the roles once associated with religion. High art emerged as a search for personal symbols.

During the 19th and especially in the 20th century, the quests of spiritually inclined artists have altered not only the content and form of religious symbols, but also their function and location. Traditional theological concerns—the knowledge of God, the world, an authentic meaningful human experience—have been pursued through art. The adventures of the spirit once associated with religious faith and rites have gradually been transposed by artists from religion to artistic creation.

For many, the arts have become an expression of personal salvation. In their passionate engagement with the making of images and objects, some artists achieve a sense of transcendence, fulfilling, to a degree, the human desire for something else beyond the self. In this respect, the practice of art has tended to fulfill human needs once met by religion.

In their reformulations of religious art, Wassily Kandinsky and Piet Mondrian, early 20th-century painters, concentrated on the spiritual symbolism of non-representational art.[2] Similarly, mid-century critics attributed religious significance to the paintings of Mark Rothko and Barnett Newman, which were expected to evoke contemplation in the viewers, even though these paintings were not in a liturgical setting.[3]

To some artists, however, the making of a painting, the direct experience with pigments on the canvas, often took on overtones of ritual action. In the 1950s, a number of abstract artists began to place importance on the

---

[1] Jürgen Habermas, "Modernity—An Incomplete Project," *The Anti-Aesthetic: Essays on Postmodern Culture*, ed. Hal Fasten (Port Townsend, WA: Bay Press, 1983) 9.

[2] Wassily Kandinsky, *Concerning the Spiritual in Art, and Painting in Particular, 1912* (New York: George Wittenborn, 1947) 54-66; Piet Mondrian, *Plastic Art and Pure Plastic Art, 1937, and Other Essays, 1941-43*, (New York: Wittenborn, Schultz, Inc., 1951) 31, 39.

[3] Thomas B. Hess, *Barnett Newman* (New York: The Museum of Modern Art, 1971) 56; Anna Chave, *Mark Rothko: Subjects in Abstraction* (New Haven, CT: Yale University Press, 1989) 197.

physical activity of creating a work, which suggested to some a different religious dimension.

Harold Rosenberg found an analogy between traditional, ritual action and the making of an art object. He identified Jackson Pollock as a painter whose will to make a painting and the ensuing physical activity were central to his creative process. Pollock was, as he wrote, an artist who had a secret—the secret of magic. He was a peer of Navajo sand painters. His art, like theirs, was ritualistic. Rosenberg emphasized, however, the solitary action of a visual artist:

> For this sand painter, the painting was medicine for the artist himself, not for a patient brought out of his tent to be cured for a fee of two goats. Contact was Pollack's salvation. And he tried to make it appear afresh in each painting.[4]

While similarities to ritual are found, especially in action painting, the analogy also exposes a profound difference. In traditional religious settings, images and objects generally accompanied communal religious experiences. But in the later 20th century, artists have tended to explore personal symbols and enact private rituals.

Increasingly, artists, interpreters, and viewers have come to associate the practice of high art with an individual search for salvation. One contemporary painter, Julian Schnabel, has puzzled critics by his comments and titles which sometimes have religious overtones. His references to painting as a way of "mediating reality" and as something that "saves my life" suggests a spiritual, if not a salvific focus.[5] In addition, he has used representational motifs such as saints and crucifixes taken from explicit religious traditions in his work. These themes have caught the attention of numerous critics.

The icons and rituals of most contemporary artists are more private than public, and the authenticity of their symbols rests on individual, not community, experience. While the activity of high art may be redemptive for the artist, the arts themselves are no longer expected to convey common values and meanings. In the marketplace, novelty and lack of meaning contribute to the arts.

Late in the 19th century, secular society transformed art itself into both a sacred object and a commodity. The power of publicity changed the concept of the artist, shifting the attention from art objects to the creator: a celebrated shamanistic court jester. But the courts which artists entertain are not regal or ecclesiastical, but economic—the super rich who appear to be both amused and redeemed by their holy jesters.

---

[4] Harold Rosenberg, "The Mythic Act," *Artworks and Packages* (New York: Dell, 1971) 68.

[5] Grace Glueck, "What One Artist's Career Tells Us of Today's Art World," *New York Times*, December 2, 1984, sec. 2, 1, 6.

In their gradual disengagement from shared symbols, artists have left a vacuum. The public communication of myths, a responsibility and power assumed by high art in the earlier centuries, has been taken over by images of popular culture during the 20th century.

Today, the mass media offer a bewildering array of symbolic worlds and myths which purport to explain and order experience. As 20th century painters and sculptors turned inward to explore individual feelings and to express private visions, American popular culture followed a different course. The representation of social realities, traditionally delegated by state and ecclesiastical authorities to the visual arts, has migrated to the realm of mass media, especially television.

This transfer of the power to communicate public symbols and commonly accepted images has not been sufficiently examined by art educators and historians who look upon television as trivial and even corrupt. I do not wish to discuss here the aesthetics of the medium, but to consider television as public representation. Contemporary American culture is saturated with electronic images, the Super Bowl, the 700 Club, the funeral of a national leader, the nightly news programs, soap operas, countless commercials. These put us in touch with events real and imaginary and attune us to values beyond our immediate experience of time and space. More than simply pictures, the images mediate realities that are otherwise inaccessible to us and at the same time communicate a sense of what is important. They perform, I think, a sacramental function of rendering visible invisible values. Through such images, we not only take part in communal activities but are also indoctrinated with attitudes and points of view.

Traditional religious images in pre-modern cultures rendered visible invisible truths and thus performed a sacramental function. Similarly, in a secular society, television images can give concrete, vivid embodiment to some of the intangible beliefs of a culture and provide a basic framework for knowledge and action.

Bryan Wilson has called the mediation of norms, authority, and information the latent function of religion in contrast to its manifest role of salvation. Contemporary societies, Wilson writes, may operate with little recourse to religion as a social institution: "If modern states are largely secular in operation, this is because social arrangements of humans are no longer dependent upon the latent functions of religion."[6] We no longer look to the church or synagogue for interpretations of all spheres of human activity. Instead, explanations of how things are, are fragmented and diversified, spread throughout various cultural agencies.

In today's world the practice of high art has taken on aspects of the saving dimension of religion, while popular art, especially television, has taken over its latent function, that is, to reinforce a sense of identity and to

---

[6] Bryan Wilson, *Religion in Sociological Perspective* (New York: Oxford University Press, 1982) 45.

perform a legitimating integrating role. This latent function addresses different human questions. According to Wilson, instead of: "What must I do to be saved?," the questions are for individuals: "Who am I?," and for groups: "Who are we?" These questions ask for an account of reality which enables individuals and groups to place themselves in a social, even global scheme of things.[7]

In an advanced, pluralistic society, religion's latent role has been assumed by various authorities—political, economic, and scientific—who provide their constituents with information, values, and identities. In the United States, however, the mass media have become extraordinarily powerful in their capacity to coalesce these several authorities and, in so doing, to legitimate certain basic American values and convictions.

Television, for example, is flooding the nation with pictures of the good life in all aspects of programming—news, sitcoms, and dramas. In its relatively short history, TV's symbolic assemblages of reality have been all too often identified with reality itself. From commercials as well as from entertainment shows come popular mythologies and dogmas that represent social norms and expectations. These programs combine with TV's political and informational images to form a comprehensive and complex environment of symbols. Television's images, of course, are interpreted from a variety of perspectives. Furthermore, we have to acknowledge that all of these interpretations derive from a medium that is itself selective and interpretive in character.

To this assortment of analyses, I would like to add one which builds upon a broad definition of religion and its functions: Bryan Wilson's distinctions between the latent and manifest roles of religion in human experience. Later, I shall emphasize a symbolization of authority that is political, informational, and mythic in commercial television. First, however, we need to explore the overarching beliefs from which these images issue.

During the several decades of the television medium's history, all types of network programming—sports, news, and entertainment—have collectively formed a mosaic of dynamic images and concrete representations of the socioeconomic, political systems. These symbolic artifacts perform a role very much like that of art in previous cultures. Although more fleeting and elusive, TV's electronic images—like those of painting, glass windows, and sculpture in earlier centuries—objectify orders and values of our national experience. Embodying sentiments and aspirations transcending denominational loyalties, television has produced a kaleidoscopic yet encompassing expression of what may be called an American public religion.

In *Public Religion in American Culture*, John Wilson identified mythic materials pervasive in American society. These may be connected with both religious and national identity and appropriated by denominational as well as

---

[7] Ibid. 34.

secular groups. They are shared meanings, which in Wilson's words, were to provide frameworks of self-understanding for individual and collective life. These may be better understood, he says, if we examine the many ways in which they become concrete symbols in a richly complex culture.[8]

John Wilson's analysis of popular piety provides, I think, a foundation for interpreting portrayals of television's faith and values. In a chapter entitled, "Religious Meanings of the American Community," he has tried to pin down elusive, but deeply ingrained sentiments of faith, sources of piety for an American public religion. These shared meanings or "frameworks of intelligibility" operate as if they were religious beliefs. In fact, it might be difficult in a pluralistic culture to distinguish these from religious tenets.

Central to popular faith, he says, are four clusters of meanings:

(1) American society understood as perfected and pure, unalloyed and uncompromised. In contrast to the societies of the old world and antiquity, it requires its members to internalize discipline.

(2) American society as a fulfillment of the dreams and aspiration of the ages, frequently exhibited in historical categories and eschatological symbols.

(3) American society as receptive to the deprived and homeless of the world and promising them new life.

(4) American society as one of opportunity, in which liberty provides the framework for individual and collective development.[9]

While these do not exhaust the list of quasi-religious beliefs, Wilson describes their centrality to an underlying popular piety. Later in his analysis, Wilson shows how these meanings and symbols manifest themselves, not in any one single community but in patriotic societies and lodges, veterans groups and regional groups, civic clubs, and the voluntary associations that characterize our collective life. On special occasions, such as Memorial Day or the Fourth of July, the true believers, he says, symbolically display the roles they believe they bear for the whole community.[10]

Even though there may be tensions among such voluntaristic groups, they all come together with the common conviction that American society and its democratic principles deserve our final loyalty. Throughout the culture, Wilson asserts, there is a primordial attachment to these quasi-religious tenets—in business, merchandising, entertainment, sports and religious denominations. The similarities and sentiments at the sub-strata of our society can help explain, he says, why success in one field proves readily transferable to

---

[8] John F. Wilson, *Public Religion in American Culture* (Philadelphia: Temple University Press, 1979) 94.

[9] Ibid. *96*.

[10] Ibid. Chapter 6. "Social Institutions and American Public Religion," especially 137-42.

another: the athletic star, "becoming a successful businessman or entertainer, the proven businessman finding a ready welcome in politics."[11] Adapting Wilson's insights to television, we see that the piety and symbols of an American public religion are not confined to a particular type of program; instead, symbols are selectively chosen and infused into programs of many kinds.

Let us now consider some examples of political, informational, and mythic symbols which collectively contribute to our understanding of culture and the moral environment. We can begin with the symbolization of various kinds of authority in American television. First, coverage of political leaders, in particular, has created authoritative images comparable to the statuary of the ancient world. Second, nightly news programs map the cosmos with images which define the contours of our reality. Third, American values are personified in heroes and heroines of entertainment programs: sit-coms and soap operas. Interwoven throughout, those litanies of consumer values, the commercials, provide economic support of network telecasting. Unlike ancient priest-kings and medieval clerics, modern American politicians do not participate in rituals nor in acts returning us to the world in the time of the gods or helping us re-experience the first moments of creation or participating in the resurrection. In the mass media however, they address a human need for an ordered universe. They portray themselves as trusted leaders who represent and defend the people's highest aspirations. In ceremonial speeches, politicians remind us of the origins and visions of American society echoing the earliest settler's convictions and views of America as a new Eden. Liberty and equality, the primary themes of this gospel, are frequently used to explain domestic and foreign policies.

Events have become much more than news; they have become, to use the hackneyed phrase, "photo opportunities." But these, indeed, are occasions for the portrayal of political authority. No other American president, including John Kennedy, has been as skilled as Ronald Reagan and his advisers in creating images of leadership, carefully constructed to inform and persuade citizens on matters of public policy.

One of Mr. Reagan's first major victories was a change in the nation's tax laws, ostensibly reducing taxes for all citizens, but relieving most effectively the tax burden on the wealthy. The signing of this bill was presented to viewers on the evening news program. It might easily have been mistaken for a scene out of *Dallas*. The locale was the President's ranch in California, alive with reporters and electronic equipment. A lean cowboy President in jeans and boots strode out of his ranch house and over to an outdoor desk piled with papers to sign. There, pen in hand, he conquered the real enemy—taxes. Meanwhile, on the sidelines, the First Lady, also in western attire, struggled with the family dog, as newspersons scrambled for

---

[11] Ibid. 92, 93.

a better view of the President. Here was one of the best of the American myths: Leader sets people free from taxes as his First Lady looks on admiringly.

Television has made it possible for millions of people to participate to some degree in significant events. In the United States, the media are now indispensable in symbolizing the mythology of the nation as well as the authority of the presidency. When, through an unusual occurrence in 1985, President Reagan's second inauguration was telecast on the same day as the Super Bowl game, the entire day seemed liturgically orchestrated. Viewers were taken from one sacred event to another. As the President was sworn into his second term, millions of viewers shared, through TV, a solemn event in the life of a nation. Later that day, by the miracle of technology, the two sacred spaces were united—the White House and the Super Bowl. In the White House, President Reagan was to toss a coin and start the game across the continent. The newly-inaugurated commander-in-chief ceremoniously opened the event that symbolized to many the value of competition and the importance of being number one. Standing before a large landscape painting of the American west, Reagan seemed to personify the heroic image of a winner. The coin was tossed and the game began.

Later, thousands of miles away, between halves of the game, entertainment reinforced the patriotic sentiments as marching bands and drill teams formed a huge American flag on the football field. Finally, the TV screen offered one more exchange when the President, standing once again before the landscape painting, spoke on the phone to the victorious coach.

For eight years the charismatic Reagan broke the bonds of time, space, and institutional structures and, through the medium of television, addressed the believers, the American public, directly. Magazine and newspaper pictures, combined with those of television, formed a monumental collection of authoritative images that have fashioned a larger than life portrait of a leader. The media mosaic has functioned like the colossal statues of emperors in the ancient world. Through these carefully planned political portraits, this leader became a symbol of a president standing tall, one who revitalized myths of leadership and moral authority. Few other American presidents have enjoyed such popularity.

Political commentator Roger Mudd observed that over eight years, Reagan controlled the public dialogue and set the agenda that would be discussed in the press. His great success as a communicator reinforced the power of mass media as political tools. Moreover, noted Mudd, without television there is no national leadership in the United States any more. He concluded that Reagan set standards for television presidents that will be difficult to match. People now, said Mudd, expect a TV presence from their national leaders that makes all issues seem "firm, round, fully packed...and bland."[12]

For many Americans, Mr. Reagan was attractive because of the good news posture he brought to the presidency. In explaining his policies—economic, military, social—he and his advisers constructed easily recognizable, uncomplicated polarities which work well on TV. Upbeat and positive, he sharply silhouetted oppositional motifs as "we versus they": the free world against communism, freedom fighters against totalitarianism, good against evil, reason against madness. Implicit are metaphors of warfare which are readily symbolic and inspire patriotism; conversely, they may give dissenting individuals a sense of alienation. Complex presentations which entail thoughtful qualifications and adjustments had no place in Mr. Reagan's political rhetoric. Careful thought or scrutiny were seen as slowing down the action.

Even on his way out, Reagan seemed to dominate some of the images of the 1988 Republican convention. In his address to the delegates, he saluted them—and the TV audience as well—and admonished them to do yet one more thing for the "Gipper." Elect Bush.

Mindful of this symbolic power of images, the media managers of both Republicans and Democrats have done their best to create new symbols of political authorities. Both parties employed producers to make the 1988 conventions good show business. The presidential campaign became, as many have noted, the politics of sound and sight bites selected for the nightly news.

Let us now consider a second kind of authority that comprises this moral symbolic environment: the authoritative images presented in the news, which represent the capacity of the news programs actually to shape the reality we perceive.

Traditional religion gave believers fundamental information about themselves and their world. Myths, rituals, and legends shaped the contours of reality, including the time and space of two spheres—the natural and the supernatural. Long before literacy and the mass media, mythological pictures of reality were presented in dramatic narrative enhanced by visual and musical forms. A symbolic world gave significance to personal experience, the community, and the universe. Rituals and myths identified friends, foes, and a communal destiny.

In today's secular, technological, and pluralistic era, no such compact and differentiated pictures of reality exist. Yet amid fragmented religious, political, and economic constituencies, the mass media attempt to portray significant events and provide information which enables us to understand ourselves in this complex society. The nightly news programs present accounts of "reality." Carefully constructed narratives, made up of both words and images, explain what is happening in the world. Although we are not taken back to the primeval hill and dawn of creation, we are taken around

---

[12] Roger Mudd, *The MacNeil/Lehrer News Hour*, January 1, 1988.

the nation and throughout the globe, breaking those bonds of time and space. This modern pseudo-ritual has shifted the explanatory focus from the archetypical past to the ever-changing present and future.

While we have excluded from our ordinary lives the spatial and temporal dimensions of visions, dreams, and illusion, we have nevertheless adjusted our sensibilities to a fantastic movement through the cosmos in a half hour, pausing regularly to enter the illusionary world of commercials. The success of television's ritualistic orientation may be measured by the fact that most of us do not view the news as a symbolic construction but as an essentially believable reality.

Every day, for a limited, carefully orchestrated period of time, our attention is drawn to highly concentrated symbolic reports of events. These 30-minute distillations, unlike detailed lengthy explanations, give us a sense of a totality of things, a selective fabricated canopy of reality. What we actually view are shared symbols of the real world. We may know very little about what is happening in Central America, the Middle East, or Washington, D.C., but we grasp certain symbolic representations which then become the basis of our reading. Without prolonged investigation or reflection, constant viewers of television are indoctrinated through words and pictures into a world view.

When TV words and pictures are our only source of information about the lives of people in distant countries, their land, their government and living conditions, the stakes are high. In a free society, a great responsibility rests on those who produce news programs. Many anchor persons become, indeed, "priests" in the information age. Americans depend on them as special kinds of authority figures, the men and women who lead viewers through intensive, patterned reporting of events. Heralded by ceremonial sounds, silhouetted against global symbols, the anchors introduce the news programs and sustain the connecting link running through the montage of stories. Their familiar faces and voices predominate during a half hour in which viewers get an overview of world-wide happenings. In their commanding roles they appear to sort out the momentous from the less momentous occurrences that go on in the universe. The credibility of the stories and the seriousness to which we respond to them are closely linked to our belief that the information they give us is true.

An extensive investigation in 1986, sponsored by the *Los Angeles Times* and conducted by the Gallup organization, centered on public attitudes toward the American press. A major issue was believability. This study indicated that the veteran anchor, Walter Cronkite, even in retirement, maintained the highest score for believability. Slightly lower were three other network anchors, Tom Brokaw, Peter Jennings, and Dan Rather, whom 90% of the population considered believable. The findings also showed that correspondents such as Sam Donaldson, Mike Wallace, and Diane Sawyer were just slightly less believable than the anchorpersons. The major network anchor persons all scored higher than the President of the United States, and that was prior to the Iran-Contra hearings.[13]

In presenting and symbolizing reality, we sometimes see a clash of authorities, particularly a clash between political and informational authorities. Martin Linsky has demonstrated the authoritative power of the press to frame issues and create perceptions which affect politicians and policy making. In a PBS radio program, Linsky summed up these tensions that frequently arise between the press and the government. He dramatically illustrated these conflicts in recounting the "tripod episode." When Ronald Reagan decided to carry out his trip to Bittburg, a controversy arose between the CBS people and the President's aides over the placement of the tripod for the camera. The spot chosen by CBS would have allowed cameras to frame Reagan against the background of the Nazi SS graves. The administration, however, was adamant that the tripod be placed in a position that would prevent this inclusive perspective.

Finally, let us consider mythic authority, the tales of the good life. News is not the only business of mass media. For most Americans, commercial television is entertainment. We need only look briefly at some of that entertainment to recognize another type of authoritative image. Entertainment programs present mythic sources of order, stories that characterize the American way. The great American dream in both reality and fantasy is the promise of a new life, a second chance. It is real to the deprived and homeless who come to this country; it is also fantasy, especially when one compares the mortality rates of infants in Washington, D.C. with that of underdeveloped countries. Yet on television where mythic themes are emphasized, the aspirations for the good life are often fulfilled.

The *Cosby Show* has drawn criticism for its unreality and for the artificial and misleading pictures of black family life. Critics claim that the plots are too simple and hold out only false hopes and that the portrayal of the Huxtables represents wishful thinking instead of the real situation of black families. It is interesting to note, however, Bill Cosby's own defense of his mythological family: "To say that they are not black enough is the denial of the American dream and the American way of life. My point is that this is an American family, an *American* family. If you want to live like they do and you are willing to work, the opportunity is there."[14]

In these remarks Cosby is not simply defending his show; he is standing fast by the dream itself, a dogmatic, enduring, sentiment that any person, black, white, whatever, can make it in this society with a lot of hard work and some luck. The show is mythological in the promise of

---

[13] *The People and the Press: A Times Mirror Investigation of Public Attitudes Toward the News Media*, conducted by the Gallup Organization. (Los Angeles: Times Mirror Corporation, 1986).

[14] Richard Zogin (reported by Scott Brown, Dan Goodgame, and Jeannie Ralston), "Cosby, Inc.," *Time*, September 28, 1987, 60.

a new life and an opportunity for individual growth and development. Moreover, supporters argue that it presents a much needed counter-image for negative stereotypes.

The new improved good life for most Americans, whatever their race, creed, or social status, is preeminently centered upon the notion of choice; choice is, in fact, the most magical word in American culture. It is an inclusive word applied indiscriminately to decisions important and trivial, ranging from a marriage partner to a deodorant. The steady hum over radio and television about the choices we have is a constant litany to liberty, to the freedom to choose one product over another. Advertising thus becomes a kind of caricature of liberty. It emphasizes buying and selling, neglecting the more profound dimensions of personal freedom. In short, buying has become synonymous with the good life and a symbol of personal development. Whether we are persuaded to buy one product or another, there is in consumption itself an inherent confirmation of freedom of choice. In promoting the general philosophy of consumerism, the commercials repeatedly restate America's faith and freedom.

But to whom are these litanies addressed? If we look at products advertised most frequently in magazines and newspapers and especially television, we find the vast spectrum of consumer goods and services is directed primarily to middle and lower income groups. Watching an evening of television one sees affordable and accessible items for them—food, beverages, insurance, cosmetics and personal items, household goods and appliances, home improvements and financing, over-the-counter medicines, bargain travel packages, and automobiles. Occasionally high priced luxury items are advertised, but generally there is no point in using the mass media to promote what most people can't afford. This means that the persons who command most wealth in this country are not the targets for commercials. Instead, more than $100 billion per year are spent to encourage those with less money to spend more and more.

The construction of symbols that extol these quasi-religious faiths of an American public religion parallels the processes of earlier religious art where, under the auspices of church and state, small powerful groups devised subject matter and empowered skilled artisans to produce images that would reinforce belief. Kenneth Clark has argued that a healthy relationship exists when the elite patrons and craftsmen have fashioned symbols which the majority embrace and honor as their own.[15] Clark, of course, was taking his material largely from ancient and medieval times. His description, however, could be extended and applied to current television as a promulgation of an American public religion.

Diverse special groups—corporate sponsors, ad agencies, and network executives—agree upon basic themes and motifs. They authorize gifted

---

[15] Kenneth Clark, "Art and Society," in *The Nature of Art*, ed. John Gassner and Sidney Thomas (New York: Crown, 1964) 62-64.

writers, artists, and production teams to construct symbols which appeal to the public. Like their medieval and ancient counterparts, these symbol makers attempt to strike a responsive chord in the hearts and minds of believers. Believing, however, is no longer tied to traditional religions but to something we vaguely perceive as the American way of life.

Some media critics warn that democratic principles of the American way may be undermined by this new concentration of authority. As print and electronic media depend more upon advertising, marketing, and business, the opportunities for pluralism and the separation of interests are diminished. Media scholar Ben Bagdikian cautions:

> Mass advertising is no longer a means of introducing and distributing consumer goods, though it does that. It finds its major mechanism in the ability of a relatively small number of giant corporations to hold a disproportionate power over the economy. These corporations need newspapers, magazines and broadcasting not just to sell their goods but to maintain the economy and political influence. And increasingly they are not only needed but they are owned by the corporate giants. Print and electronic media thus are no longer neutral agents displaying consumer goods but are now vital instruments of power for major corporations.[16]

For Bagdikian and other critics, the question is one of genuine freedom: How can the media in America perform their traditional role of an open, true mediator among all the forces in society when they have become a part of one?

Various kinds of institutions in American culture—political, informational, economic, and religious—have tapped the sacramental power of the media. They develop symbolic worlds to generate and encourage a sense of identity and loyalty. In this enterprise, TV myths and rituals represent often superficial and even distorted world views. We must examine seriously the implications of these symbolizations of authority for a pluralistic democratic society. Unless we recognize the power of the media to construct symbolic worlds, we will not even grasp the range of mediated values or choices to be made. Nor will we understand the need for a daring iconoclasm. We will simply stay tuned in. If we do not closely evaluate the mythic power of mass communications, we risk becoming prisoners of illusion like those in Plato's Parable of the Cave, who, in seeing and naming shadows cast on the wall, believed that they understood themselves in all reality.

Let me conclude as I began, with art, or what we now call "high art." As one goes through the great gateway of the Acropolis, one sees the Parthenon, which was Athens' tribute to its major goddess, Athena. Ordinary citizens left the marketplace, the agora, and climbed up high above the polis to pay tribute to the gods. From the base of Athena's temple they could look up and see public representations of beautiful people.

---

[16] Ben H. Bagdikian, *The Media Monopoly* (Boston: Beacon, 1983) 152.

Teaching Art History 101, my colleagues and I find it hard to come up with more perfect images of human figures, Athenian citizens who were assembling for the great Panathenaic procession. But was this "reality"? Not according to Plato and some sophists. Below, in the streets of Athens, life was raw and ugly and only rarely transcended. One sophist fragment reads roughly: "Life, even when it is happy, has nothing great or noble, but in reality is petty, feeble, short lived, and mixed with sorrow; still it is the only life humans have. But oddly enough, there are persons who do not live their present life but they are wondrously active as if they had another life to live and suddenly time runs out."[17]

These images from the Parthenon bear little resemblance to the petty, the feeble, or the life mixed with sorrow. Similarly, I believe that today our friezes, our visual narratives of grandeur and perfection, may be found in popular art. Our beautiful people, heroes, and ideological visions are seen in sitcom, news and sports, and certainly in commercials. Like the ancient idealized people, they may bear very little resemblance to reality.

Today we have a strange and even eerie opportunity to look back and survey the images that have objectified and framed human values over centuries. We observe, through scholarship and technology, the manifold symbols human beings have fashioned to impose meaning on experience, from the hand prints on a paleolithic wall to the pervasive electronic images of today. From this perspective, distinctions between high and popular art fade. In the struggle to impose order on what ultimately defies our ordering, images and materials and forms change. Yet while symbols themselves are fragile and impermanent, it is my conviction that the human sacramental impulse endures: that of rendering invisible values visible. I believe, too, that that impulse is being constantly transformed.

---

[17] Eric Voegelin, *Order and History: The Work of the Polis*, vol. 2 (Baton Rouge, La.: Louisiana State University Press, 1957) 326-27.

2

The Expressive Face of Culture: Mass Media and the Shape of the Human Moral Environment - II

Michael Real

This chapter poses five questions as themes for inquiry into the symbolic power of the media. At heart symbol-making power gives modern media a crucial role in shaping the contemporary moral environment. This chapter draws on what media research and analysis have revealed about our use of communication technologies to give human life expression and shape. To flesh out the five questions, let me introduce little Tiffany, a typical American child, a child of the media. Though imaginary, she represents any contemporary American child, black or white, male or female, from any region or class or ethnic background.

1. How does little Tiffany become herself?
(Our Media, Ourselves)

From her earliest breaths in the crib, little Tiffany forms her sense of personal identity, her emerging consciousness of existence, life, and self through her interactions on three levels. First, she interacts with persons in face-to-face acquaintance: her parents, siblings, relatives, neighbors, and classmates. Second, she interacts with her environment: the crib, the room, her house, the neighborhood, grass and trees, pets, and nature in general. But, third, little Tiffany also interacts with stories read to her, with pictures shown to her, with *Sesame Street* and the Smurfs, with Disney characters and Fisher-Price toys, with ET and Superman. Gradually and increasingly she interacts with all of that vast second-hand experience of television, books, advertisements, movies, posters, magazines, fashion, popular music, newspapers, radio, cassettes, telephones, computers, and the rest of contemporary media.

25

These mediated interactions influence little Tiffany's developing sense of identity as deeply, some claim, as do her interpersonal and environmental interactions.[1] The mass-mediated culture surrounding her becomes her larger frame of reference, just as a small town might have been her frame of reference in turn-of-the-century America or the medieval church, in the Middle Ages. In this frame of reference, she struggles to move from dependency toward a healthy autonomy as Paul Philibert so penetratingly describes in Chapter 6, below.

The media exercise influence not only personally on little Tiffany but also by helping shape those with whom she interacts—her family, her peers, and eventually her fellow workers and her political and social leaders. The media even help shape the physical environment with which she interacts— the architecture, transportation, and products created in the image and likeness of super media. Perhaps more than nature itself or actual people, the mass-mediated culture becomes her psychic and social environment from birth to death.

Little Tiffany is neither unique nor new. Since the first cave paintings, men and women have expressed and found themselves through their symbol-making abilities. The original marvel of human speech and the ingenious development of phonetic writing enable artists and everyone else to communicate effectively and beautifully. In the 15th century, the printing press ushered in a new power of mass multiplied and distributed communication, the "mass" media. In the 19th century, electronic media were born with telegraph, telephone, phonograph, and motion pictures, followed in our own century by radio, television, computers, satellites, lasers, and more, ever increasing the incredible human capability for mediated communication.

Daniel Czitrom has described the challenge modern communication has posed to the American mind in the work of Charles Horton Cooley, John Dewey, Robert E. Park, Harold Adams Innis, and Marshall McLuhan.[2] In a similar way in Chapter 3 William Sullivan focuses this challenge on the provocative debate between Walter Lippmann and John Dewey over the possibilities of genuine democracy in 20th century America. As media technologies pervade all corners of the world, the question of self-determination in a mass-mediated culture challenges all societies.

It is now impossible to conceive of little Tiffany, or anyone else today, developing his or her identity, consciousness, or conscience outside the context of mass-mediated culture. The process begins in infancy and continues throughout human life. Little Tiffany becomes adult Tiffany and finally

---

[1] Joshua Meyrowitz, *No Sense of Place: The Impact of Electronic Media on Social Behavior* (New York: Oxford University Press, 1985); Gary Gumpert and Robert Cathcart, eds. *Inter-Media: Interpersonal Communications in a Media World*, 3rd ed.. (New York: Oxford University Press, 1986).

[2] Daniel Czitrom, *Media and the American Mind: From Morse to McLuhan* (Chapel Hill, NC: University of North Carolina Press, 1982).

aged Tiffany without ever escaping the cultural environment of modern media.

One problem posed by this identification of our media and ourselves occurs through the media's blurring the distinction between fantasy and reality, between fact and fiction. Is what we are seeing on television live or taped? Is it documentary footage or drama? Is the docudrama accurate or distorted for whatever reason? Is the person viewed an actual person or a character being acted? "Real" and "true" become ambiguous terms with conflicting levels of meaning when applied to modern media culture. Prophetically, William Lynch, S.J., dealt extensively with this problem a generation ago in a series of books and articles examining the image industries and the life of the imagination today.[3] A civilization and its members face profound difficulties when there is such a complex blurring of fantasy and reality. The fragmentation of artistic vision today and the complexity of American public religion add to this fundamental confusion, as Gregor Goethals tellingly observes in Chapter 1. So one basic question we are asking in this inquiry is: How can we, individually and collectively, live and grow well, happily, and effectively in this cultural context? To begin answering this question, we need to set down what we know about mass-mediated culture.

2. What does hard science know of the effects of media on little Tiffany? (The lessons and the limits of behaviorist media research)

The empirical media-centered research of hard science[4] has measured how mass media "diffuse information" and bring about the "adoption of innovations," whether in agriculture, medicine, child care, or other areas of human social life. Today the master teacher, a Jacob Bronowski or a Carl Sagan, can teach millions of students on many continents directly, whereas an Aristotle had to be content to teach only a dozen or so students at a time in the classic peripatetic school of ancient Athens.

Even more commonly than acting as agents of change, the media of communication "reinforce the status quo." They can give to cultural oddities—guns and social violence, greed and personal instability—the aura of

---

[3] William Lynch, *The Image Industries* (New York: Sheed & Ward, 1959); William Lynch, *Christ and Apollo* (New York: Sheed & Ward, 1962).

[4] Quotation marks in the text have been used to identify distinct research traditions in mass communications ("adoption of innovations," "two-step flow," "semiotics," etc.). Each of these research traditions is anchored in a series of classic studies and concepts developed by specific prominent researchers. For documentation and details of these traditions, see Michael Real, *Super Media: A Cultural Studies Approach* (Newbury Park, CA.: Sage Publications, 1989).

common sense. Whatever is can be made to seem normal in Tiffany's media world.

With this powerful tool, media professionals act as "gatekeepers," reducing the impossibly vast mass of daily information about all the little Tiffanys starving or thriving everywhere in the world to that simple set of stories available to us each day as what we call "news." The resulting media agenda of reported and emphasized news in turn "sets the agenda" for the public and for individuals: Media may not tell us what to think, but they do tell us what to think *about*. In the words of two famous empirical scientists, Lazarsfeld and Merton,[5] the media "confer status" and "enforce social norms," thus shaping little Tiffany's social world.

In his 1984 presidential campaign Jesse Jackson told a story that illustrates the problem of selectively presenting the range of world events. Candidate Jackson described how one time he and the Pope were out fishing together in a boat and a big wind came along and blew, as Jesse put it, the Pope's beanie off. It flew some 30 or 40 feet off into the water. They sat for a moment dumbfounded, but then Jesse jumped out of the boat, ran across the water, picked up the beanie, brought it back, gave it to the Pope, and the Pope put it on. Reporters sat in other boats observing this. Jackson said, "Do you know what the headlines were the next day in the paper? JESSE JACKSON CAN'T SWIM." The anecdote illustrates how one can find a negative angle even to walking on water. It also illustrates the power of the media to put a spin on a story, negative or positive, penetrating or misleading, in setting agendas, conferring status, and enforcing social norms.

Hard science has also told us that media create effects indirectly as well as directly. Media reach opinion leaders who, in turn, influence the less active segments of the population. This is the classic "two-step flow" of media through personal influence. Media "cultivate values" among the population: Heavy television viewers differ from light television viewers on a number of attitudinal items, especially in their perception of the "mean world syndrome" of crime, violence, police, and victimization. The media "gratify audience needs" by offering an abundance of cultural products to choose from, an abundance but not a true diversity. Little Tiffany can choose her TV program, her movie, her music, her fashion, for her own odd reasons, but always within the given mass-mediated context.

Hard science has also articulated the limits and obstacles to media effectiveness. The credibility of a spokesperson, the personal predispositions of the receiver, the presence of conflicting messages—these and many more factors can restrict the effectiveness of a given message. Yet thousands of

---

[5]Paul Lazarsfeld and Robert Merton, "Mass Communication, Popular Taste, and Organized Social Action," in *Mass Culture: The Popular Arts in America*, ed. Bernard Rosenberg and David Manning White (New York: Van Nostrand Reinhold, 1957).

research monographs confirm what media advertisers bet billions of dollars on each month: that media influence human belief and behavior.

To establish these findings, hard science has favored a dominant paradigm: *Who* says *what* through which *channel* to *whom* with what *effect*? It has often ignored the further questions: In what social-historical context? and For whose benefit? In our commercial media system, well subsidized research has served producers to tell them how a media message affects little Tiffany. This has led to the argument over "powerful" versus "limited" media effects. The argument is a methodological and theoretical trap. The question of specific measurable media effects is too narrow and the methods of hard science are too limited to answer it effectively. Newer approaches, grouped around the label "cultural studies," provide a way out of this hard science impasse, as we shall see in the next section.

3. How do media structure little Tiffany's experience of existence? (Structuralist Understanding of Media)

The study of language and other sign systems has revealed the profound extent to which human understanding is not a given but is a construction. From chaotic experience, we construct meaning and purpose. "Structuralism" shows how, along with language and other sign systems, the media are primary sources of the structure of meaning that is our lives. From her earliest exposures to mediated culture, little Tiffany is provided with "popular genres" and "narrative structures" which she can use to identify the plot structure of her own life, its primary characters and their development, its context and complications, its expectations, its heroes and villains, its peaks and valleys. With such tools, we construct meaning in our life and in all life.

The many-layered or "polysemic" texts of media are tools with which we all express our lives, and therefore they speak to different people in different ways. The same acting that inspired the Academy of Motion Picture Arts and Sciences to award Robert DeNiro a Best Actor Oscar for *Raging Bull* also inspired through a similar role (the title character in *Taxi Driver* under the same director, Martin Scorcese) an emotionally unstable youth, John Hinkley, to shoot and almost kill Ronald Reagan, president of the country, former matinee idol, and symbol of ultimate power and authority. Media texts are multi-layered and complex in how we use them to structure our lives.

To a striking degree, media construct our interpretations of existence and social reality, for example, with regard to gender and ethnicity. Fortunately, Remus, Rastas, and Sambo have been largely replaced by Arsenio Hall, Whitney Houston, and Michael Jordan but the range of African-American roles is still restricted primarily to comedy, music, and sports. The role of Bill Cosby in recoding ethnicity in our generation is a fascinating one.

He has taken one of the most negative stereotypes, that of black males, and reversed it decisively. As faithful husband, involved parent, successful professional, Dr. Cliff Huxtable of *The Cosby Show* has replaced images of unreliable lovers, welfare chiselers, and incompetents that dominated the historical portrayals of black males from vaudeville to Hollywood films.

Similarly, the narrowness of female confinement to hearth and home, to being wife and mother, is changing dramatically in life and media, but male domination of media remains ascendant in ownership and management as well as in portrayals and interpretations. Content analysis of Hollywood films reveals that female-directed films tend to be less violent, more balanced in screen-time for male and female characters, and less stereotyped than male-directed films. But until the 1980s there were hardly enough female-directed Hollywood films to provide a scientific sample for analysis. Women have made steady progress in gaining access to media industries, but media still offer stereotypes and even what has been called the "symbolic annihilation" of subordinate populations.

We construct our image of the family from media as well as personal experience. The television portrayal of the family is of great significance and can play a complex role for viewers. The positive portrayal of *Father Knows Best*, *Ozzie and Harriet*, or *The Cosby Show* may frustrate some while inspiring others. Arthur Bremer, the victim of child abuse who later shot and paralyzed George Wallace, lamented in his diary that he wished he lived in "one of those happy families on television." The revolution of rising expectations that media can set off can later lead to a revolution of rising frustrations.

What is little Tiffany's constructed image of non-whites, of non-males, of the family?

Structuralism and semiotics have taught us a great deal. They raise the consciousness of our expressive capabilities through signs and symbols, and they raise troubling questions about the power and adequacy of media-constructed representations and signifying practices today. There appears an urgent need for the dualities of mind and reasoned judgment that Paul Philibert outlines in Chapter 6 in the context of development psychology.

4. What forces distort little Tiffany's media and thus demand resistance? (Critical analysis of media as social power)

In recent decades critical research has developed an increasing consciousness of the role of media as self-serving institutions: cultural industries colonizing the mind in the service of exploitive political-economic interests.[6] The study of the media industry's political economy and control

---

[6] Herbert Schiller, *Culture, Inc.: The Corporate Take-over of Public Expression* (New York: Oxford University Press, 1989).

reveals a shriveled center of power and interests. Not human justice and growth in a broad humane sense, but economic profit and control tend to dictate the structures and practices of media decision-making.

The resulting ideology shaped through media and reflected in them favors, for example, economic profit-taking over social commitment, abstract corporations over actual workers, consumer markets over struggling populations, negative patriotism over internationalism, opportunism over principle.

As Ted Koppel says, television would have Moses come down from the mountain with "The Ten Suggestions." The media foster a relativism that is less that of situation ethics than that of commercial exploitation. Little Tiffany may be failing in school but she is learning the discourse of super media: brand names, celebrity endorsements, commercial jingles, and corporate logos.

Hegemony of the dominant over the subordinate is maintained through media. It is engineered not through coercion but through a more sophisticated mechanism—consent. We seek at the altar of media our daily bread and learn willingly to accept burnt toast.

Advertising and consumerism serve these interests in constructing our culture. They create commodity fetishes and false consciousness unimaginable even to Marx. In a bad mood? Go shopping. Want status? Upgrade your car, house, and, if necessary, your mate. The once-dreaded Seven Deadly Sins are now the deep structure of a culture of commercials and consumption. Greed, lust, gluttony, envy, sloth, anger, pride—all the once-presumed "lower" urges have been reclaimed from Hieronymous Bosch and made all-gorgeous through the cleverness of Madison Avenue, Wall Street, and their advertising.

In the Olympics, the World Series, the presidential debates, the space shuttle flights, and in the little dramas of our everyday mediated experience, we come together to share moments and motifs that hold us together as a people. As the Milwaukee Brewers rise and fall, the spirit of Milwaukee rises and falls. To the Green Bay fan(atic) "Are the Packers back?" means, "Does my life have a center and purpose?" The solidarity of media ritual may be sentimental and superficial, as Paul Philibert warns, but it may also be a significant expression of values and influence in individual lives.

Each winter some 100 million Americans, perhaps two-thirds of American households, come together at one time in a common ritual celebration, the Super Bowl. This annual rite is the number one media spectacle in the United States in terms of audience as well as cost per second of advertising time. It is a violent, male-only event fought out as pseudo-warfare between organizations with strongly bureaucratic and authoritarian structures. African-American players perform the menial labor while white authorities dominate the power structure behind the game. The competition of football is a struggle for control of property, monopoly control of property, as one attempts to drive the opponent down and off the field. What does this number one ritual say of America as a culture, just as the spectacles in the Coliseum said of ancient Rome or the cockfight says of Balinese culture? Each year Tiffany, her family, and her friends celebrate somewhat unthinkingly but with incredible enthusiasm these revealing rituals accessible through media.

Media raise our place and time in history, our myths and memories past and future, to a higher level for us to see, hear, read, and feel anew. Ritual analysis shows us how the media provide us access to and participation in our collectively shared symbols and acts. These media celebrations reflect and reinforce many of our most cherished values—in the selection of a new president, the landing of a man on the moon, the signing of an arms control agreement.

Ritual analysis of media also shows us the para-liturgical role of "media as a source of liminal experience." Just as a West African adolescent is removed to an isolated location, stripped and scarred, set through trials, and returned an adult to his society, so the media offer opportunities for life, death, and resurrection, aesthetically, emotionally, and culturally. Media ritual helps us face and deal with collective life today, whether a Space Shuttle attempt, an urban earthquake, a summit meeting, or an assassination. Comic Relief, Live Aid, We Are the World—these ambitious media specials not only raise money to aid victims, they also ritually acknowledge the presence of problems and help Tiffany and her friends to relate to them. America first realized the full ritual power of television in 1963 with the shocking murder of President Kennedy. For three days following it, the nation gathered around its tribal campfire—the glow of the television screen—and publicly shared the mourning, funeral, and burial. The average American watched more than 80 hours of television on that unforgettable weekend frozen in time and ritually shared through the wonder of modern media.

Little Tiffany's media from *Amadeus* to *Zorro* can be vehicles of transcendence, sources of "the aesthetic experience" sought by artists and visionaries of all stripes. A powerful book can change a person's life. A moving film can re-awaken our sense of shared humanity. Maturely understood and critically appreciated, the media can take us beyond a threshold, the liminal, and return us more whole and human, more gentle and redeemed.

5. How can little Tiffany find and express her best self through media? (Mass-mediated culture as the human moral environment)

The accumulated knowledge of 70 years of media research and reflection tell us that modern media provide the clouded mirror in which we see ourselves. Through this glass darkly, we live and breath and have our being today.

Each human group and individual inherits a complex network of socio-cultural and moral-ideological traditions. Today's media pass these on to us as if truth is value-free and moral fragmentation is coherence. The resulting public culture is inseparable from the means of its transmission, the public media.

The Tiffany in each of us must struggle to come to terms with responsibility in and for our culture. She learns to use reference groups in the form of interpretive communities to assist in her selection and evaluation of media. She learns to seek media experiences that enlighten, inform, and challenge as well as entertain. She learns the goals of democratizing communication so that each person's life can find expression through media rather than manipulation by media's self-serving commerce.

A grounded understanding of the nature and workings of media in the modern world provides the necessary starting point for sorting out the dilemmas of moral imagination in a mass-mediated culture. This essay has concentrated on an inquiry into that grounded understanding. The five questions which face little Tiffany and her counterparts throughout the world are intended to assist in focusing and directing the search for moral development under the real conditions of the mediated environment of contemporary life. Other essays in this volume extend this task by suggesting aids to working through the confusion, searching out a normative core for a good society and a good life, and recommending guides to evaluate our progress. It is a task as complex as it is necessary. If the process proposed here can serve to improve our mediated vision, to wipe away some dirt from this glass, then we shall have performed one of the highest acts available to men and women, to make ourselves more human, in our own time and place within an awareness of all times and places.

The Democratization of Moral Judgment: Moral Leadership and Moral Symbols in Public Culture

William M. Sullivan

Democracy has become a powerfully catalytic ideology in the contemporary world. Events in the Soviet Union, Poland, Hungary, and China have shown the breadth and power of democracy's appeal. These openings toward democracy, like others of recent years in other repressive societies, ought to occasion serious examination of the nature and meaning of the American commitment to democracy. That the citizens of a democratic society need considerable capacities of moral judgment, and that such citizens can only flourish amid a strong public culture which embodies democratic ideals is not in itself a controversial thesis. More controversial, though often unacknowledged in a society such as ours which prides itself on its democratic ethos, are the questions of whether and how moral judgment can be effectively democratized, and what role leadership and moral symbols need to play in that process.

These are not new issues in American life: The possibility of widespread effective moral judgment in a democracy has been debated several times in the 20th century. However, the issue remains dormant when our institutions seem to be functioning well and no great crisis challenges the basic arrangements of national life. Indeed, after occasioning a sustained and troubling debate during the early decades of the century, the issue of the capacities of the average citizen for intelligent participation in public life receded from attention during the long years of the postwar boom. But beginning with the political and cultural upheavals of the 1960s, the question returned to center stage.

In the succeeding years, it became fashionable to ask whether American society was "governable," or whether the polity was dissolving into such a plethora of "special interest" groups that no larger sense of the common good could emerge unless it was imposed by charismatic or other force. In this context, the Presidential campaign of 1988 provides an interesting point from which to join the issue over the possibility and requirements of democracy.

The campaign of 1988 was characterized by many observers as the least argumentative and most manipulative in memory and, probably not co-incidentally, as a high-water mark of politics conducted through and for the mass communications media. This suggests a situation of a nation whose political business can afford to proceed very much as usual. Yet, in fact, the United States was in the midst of a rare moment of astounding, virtually tectonic change of global dimensions. The United States presidential campaign coincided with the ascendency of Mikhail Gorbachev's reforms in the USSR, a development which had radically altered the world political order, so long dominated by the Cold War.

By 1988, it was also clear to many that the international economic order, in which the United States found itself increasingly hard pressed to maintain its earlier preeminence, was also undergoing fundamental and un-predictable reorganization. It was improbable, to say the least, that the Pledge of Allegiance should have emerged as a central focus of the presi-dential contest at such a time. Yet the Pledge came to play an enormous role in the campaign strategy of the Republicans, and it briefly grabbed a great deal of public sentiment, which in turn ensured that it would also figure in the Democratic campaign as well. But what are we to make of such an event, so seemingly removed from the actual problems facing the nation?

Set in the context of a presidential campaign in which the Democratic nominee claimed to be running on "competence not ideology," the Pledge seemed a symbolic way to signal to a public hungry for moral meaning that the Republican Party stood for something. The electorate's apparent distrust of what many saw as a soulless managerial technocracy was certainly part of the explanation of the electrifying appeal of the Pledge to many voters. Yet there were good reasons for other Americans to be uneasy with having the Pledge of Allegiance serve as a political shibboleth for the campaign. Those with long memories could recall the McCarthy era, the time of loyalty oaths when all kinds of memberships, ethnic identifications, and even associations were made to indicate whether one was in or out of the political nation. That kind of symbolic politics has a long and unsavory history in the United States.

It is probable that the Pledge could not have played the role that it did were it not for the tremendous influence of the communications media on our politics. It was at a political convention planned and organized for tele-vision that it was introduced in a deliberately divisive way. It was clearly intended to telegraph meanings to a vast audience without having to submit those meanings to discussion and scrutiny. A cynic might sug-gest that it was proposed precisely because the emotional reaction to the Pledge, like the public response to the flag, would tend to preempt reflection and argument.

Between those two positions—one, that the introduction of this issue was a good thing, arousing a hunger for moral substance; and the other, that the Pledge really served to divide the "100% Americans" from the less-than-patriotic—lies a less visible, more troubling question. What difference does it make to our political life that so much of its important business is conducted through and by the mass media? In approaching this question, an early 20th-century American debate about the conditions of democracy provides an illuminating perspective on the present. That was a debate which drew into opposition figures of the stature of Walter Lippmann and John Dewey.

It was Walter Lippmann, influential journalist and leading intellectual, who put forward the powerful argument that modern society had grown too complex for ordinary people to understand on the basis of first-hand experience. Human beings, according to Lippmann, nevertheless need some conception of how things hang together in order to conduct their lives. Therefore, he concluded, everyone becomes dependent for the "pictures in our heads" supplied by the media of mass communication, which in his day meant primarily newspapers and magazines. Lippmann argued this thesis in his well-known *Public Opinion* of 1921.[1] There he mounted the charge that American democracy was based upon a false, nostalgic premise, which he called the premise of the "omnicompetent citizen." This was an idea that came from the era of Jeffersonian and Jacksonian democracy. In its origins that idea had rested on the then-reasonable premise that the citizen was able to understand the essential problems confronting him and could decide his— and in those years it was only "his"—own needs for himself. That idea worked in the early 19th century because the concerns of most people were quite local. National government was very small and very distant.

Lippmann went on to argue that under modern conditions most people are far more directly affected by the world beyond their immediate locality than were the Americans of Jackson's time. Yet, modern citizens understand this larger world almost entirely through what he called stereotypes. Lippmann was one of the first to make that term widely current, meaning by it a kind of quick generalization through which we bolster our self-image and our link to our peer group. A stereotype covers our lack of first-hand experience or direct comprehension of the complexities of life. If in the 19th century the average American voter could understand things through talking to fellow citizens who were actually tied into the various realms of life, Lippmann argued that in the modern world this is true for only a small elite.

As an example of such an elite, Lippmann pointed to the diplomats, lawyers, merchants, bankers, and managers of international firms centered on the eastern seaboard who had frequent and first-hand connections with

---

[1] Walter Lippmann, *Public Opinion* (New York: Macmillan, 1921).

Europe, Latin America and Asia. Lippmann noted that such groups had few dealings with average citizens. (One could well extend Lippmann's point to include political insiders or, indeed, those at the center of any important public enterprise.) Most Americans could get access to what this international elite knew first-hand only via an intermediary elite, the corps of publishers and journalists like Lippmann himself who were in a position to move back and forth between the few who were in the know and the many who were not.

Although Lippmann was himself a journalist, he was not sanguine about the implications of this situation for the future of democracy. Lippmann argued that the very structure and techniques of journalism, with its focus on "stories" and dramatic events rather than large-scale and long-term trends, prevented transmitting to the average citizen the kind of knowledge of the world possessed as a matter of course by the active elites. He reiterated this thesis later in the 1920s in a book that also created a wide stir, *The Phantom Public* of 1925.[2] There he pointed out that to have a public in the classic 18th-century sense means to have a body of citizens who are in communication with each other and are able to discuss and rationally shape their opinions. In a world of stereotypes and mass media, such a public was simply not possible on a large scale. Instead, Lippmann proposed reliance upon what he called agencies of "expert disinterested intelligence." He looked to the intelligence operations of the World War as a model of how people who needed to know what was going on for specific reasons could get accurate information. He proposed that the profession of journalism should undertake the provision of such service in the public interest.

The most trenchant response to Lippmann was mounted by John Dewey, the nation's leading public philosopher. Dewey responded to Lippmann in a series of book reviews which in 1927 gave rise to *The Public and Its Problems*,[3] whose title recalled Lippmann's *Phantom Public* of two years before. While Lippmann had been most impressed by the awesome powers he saw in the emerging media culture, Dewey sought as a counterweight the institutions of education with which he had been deeply involved throughout his career. Recognized as America's foremost philosopher, and a participant in many of the cultural and political events of the day, Dewey was well equipped to delineate the shape and needs of a new kind of democratic public.

Dewey acknowledged many of the problems that Lippmann raised. He certainly accepted the obsolescence of the idea of the omnicompetent citizen and its accompanying mythology of the small town. He went on to argue that a properly democratic conception of education would aim to form citi-

---

[2] Walter Lippmann, *The Phantom Public* (New York: Macmillan, 1925).

[3] John Dewey, *The Public and Its Problems* (New York: Henry Holt and Co., 1927).

zens who could grasp the big picture and respond to it through deliberation and action in common. For Dewey, this new conception of education needed to work along with what he saw as the untapped potentials of journalism for interpreting events. Together, the professions of education and journalism could work together to bring into being a new public of attentive and active citizens, even amid complex modern conditions.

The key to Dewey's strategy was his notion of "social intelligence," that through modern communications a whole society could begin to understand its situation and experimentally try to grapple with it. To guide this endeavor Dewey called for a new intellectual discipline to be called social philosophy. This was to be a discipline which would result from forging new connections between the social sciences, which would provide the data (much in the manner of the "intelligence operations" which interested Lippmann), and the humanistic disciplines which would give those data historical and moral interpretation. Journalism would then render social philosophy into an art form, using rhetorical skills to make the complexity of events morally intelligible to citizens. By working together with social philosophers, Dewey thought that journalists would be able to provide the depth of pattern and breadth of connection so missing in the news reporting of his day.

In retrospect, it is clear that neither Lippmann's nor Dewey's conception has been realized in pure form. The disaster of the Depression and then the great American success in World War II precluded the development of the debate as it had been joined in the 1920s. Following the war, the United States entered an era of extraordinary prosperity and world prominence unlike anything in its previous history. This 25-year "American Century" lasted into the early 1970s. Its legacy has been a stereotype in Lippmann's sense, a "picture in our head" which continues to define "normality" and the good life for Americans.

During the postwar decades, dreams of success became a reality: a steadily rising standard of living, suburban home ownership in a crime- and drug-free environment, seemingly unlimited horizons of achievement for the next generation. The stereotype was imaged in a famous ad for suburban Levitown. The advertisement showed a family of four posed in the driveway of their neat, modest home: breadwinner husband, homemaker wife, little boy, little girl. The family was all white, of course, and the woman in a clearly domestic role. Those beneficiaries of the nation's unique economic and military preeminence, often boosted by the GI bill, federal home mortgage and school subsidies, came to think of these achievements as the result of their own hard work. They simply forgot or did not see the vast undergirding structure of national institutional arrangements which had made it possible. The new mass medium of television intensified this focus on what was near and dear, while journalism as a whole failed to convey the sense of interconnection and responsibility, particularly for those left out of the stereotype, which Dewey had insisted it should.

That postwar vision of how life should be was, then, very largely a private vision. The purpose of politics was to elect people who could keep the whole project going while protecting the nation's happiness from marauding, envious foreign enemies. An almost millennial optimism came to suffuse the stereotype. We can find this most powerfully indicated in the elections of 1960 and 1964. In the era of "The New Frontier" there was a strong belief that not only were we going to put men on the moon, but we were steadily improving all areas of social life, including the overcoming of racism and poverty, through the use of our vast power, wealth, and expertise. Politics was expected to take care of itself, and the formation of an informed public opinion that had worried Lippmann and Dewey was also assumed to be taken care of, thanks to the nation's vastly expanded educational apparatus.

The past two decades have seen the painful unravelling of that great postwar stereotype. Regardless of contemporary claims and thanks to the social sciences and a variety of other "intelligence operations," we know that, despite advances for the more affluent fraction of the population, the postwar expectations of steadily growing affluence has been frustrated since the early 1970s. Family life has been radically disrupted, to take but one example, not so much by feminism as by the sheer economic necessity for two incomes in order to maintain a standard of living in a time of stagnant productivity growth. The suburbs were designed to be a good place for children in expectation that someone would always be home. That, for the vast majority of suburban families, is simply no longer true. There is good reason for the fears that something valuable is slipping away. We also realize that the American economy is in a very different position in regard to the world than it was during that 25-year "American Century."

The world, then, has changed. And it has changed in ways that seem painful and baffling to many Americans. American political discourse has had great difficulty in responding with realism. The 1988 campaign exemplified this. That campaign largely avoided addressing the pressing signs of disarray, not only drugs and the growth of an urban underclass, but the enormous economic and political relocations in the midst of which the United States stood like a bewildered, wavering giant. It is as though the very successes of the Second World War and its aftermath had produced a kind of political and moral deficit. We seem less rather than more equipped to take on the difficult matter of negotiating democratic change than we need to be. This is why the concerns of Lippmann and Dewey, which postwar affluence seemed to have rendered obsolete, are back on the agenda whether we realize it or not.

The mass media, like our national politics, still foster the stereotypes of the postwar era. The "pictures in our heads" misinterpret events and so our responses seem ill-timed, out of joint. We are no longer living in the "American Century" no matter how much political leaders or the electorate might wish to vote it back. How, then, are we to escape the tyranny of these now-distorting stereotypes? We must learn to reconceive and rede-scribe our situation, and it is in this connection that those earlier attempts by Lippmann and Dewey to assess the needs and possibilities of democracy take on great relevance.

Our situation is actually much more like the one which Progressive Era intellectuals such as Lippmann and Dewey confronted earlier in the cen-tury than it resembles the postwar era. Like the Progressives, we find our-selves in a world which is clearly changing rapidly though in ways we do not well understand. And, as the Pledge of Allegiance issue suggests, there is considerable anxiety that there may be a vacuum at the center. With all the present talk of values, Americans are less clear than ever before about what goods they share in common and what might be truly common purposes.

By comparison, Lippmann and Dewey seemed confident in their abil-ity to analyze changes in their social and moral world. They were able to maintain a sense of direction because, while equally perplexed by unex-pected, even catastrophic events such as the World Wars and the Great De-pression, they proceeded from a strongly coherent vision of the world that was normative as well as descriptive. Without anything like agreement, Lippmann and Dewey each held a conception of what the good life was, of what a good political leader was supposed to be, and a conception of where American society ought to go. They did not hold these views dogmatically; they were open to argument. Indeed, each changed his views importantly on key issues, such as American involvement in World War I, in response to argument and experience. But Lippmann and Dewey nonetheless shared a traditional belief in personal responsibility for public involvement, a belief which derived from the traditional culture of philosophy and rhetoric. Dewey especially sought to democratize this culture of public responsibility not by diluting its content but by broadening the range of persons who could share its energy.

To democratize moral judgment could mean to proceed from the bot-tom-up, searching for a least common denominator among moral opinions. This is often the implied approach of public opinion polling and the news media's efforts at public service information. It was not Dewey's way. He genuinely sought to enable the people to rule, but he wanted to bring the highest standards of judgment and responsibility to bear on enlarging public sensibility.

There is much we could learn with profit from this approach. It means learning to think about and criticize our often implicit moral and political ideals. This is something which Americans have usually tried to avoid do-ing, with some reason. There is always the threatening possibility that bringing such ideals openly into common debate will so polarize the discussion that deliberation, even compromise, becomes impossible. But there is also an enormous price to pay for trying to get on without such discussion: the price of remaining locked, mostly unawares, inside the prevailing stereotypes held by one's group. In a time of fundamental institutional change, the price of public reticence about political ideals and ends can be quite high indeed. A democracy must be able to formulate a working consensus adequate to the problems needing response.

The old belief in the omnicompetent citizen, beloved in American nostalgia and ferociously invoked in American anti-intellectualism, has melded with the comforting privatism of the "American Century." These stereotypes remain unchallenged by any alternatives comparable in clarity or coherence to the philosophies of Lippmann and Dewey. This makes democratizing moral judgment about the common good very difficult. However, there is in the long-term no substitute for such a working vision if genuine publics of discourse are to form. Therefore, we have good reason to listen to both Lippmann and Dewey and to concern ourselves with the media, with education, and with their interrelation. We need to recover the capacity for practical reasoning. By contrast with 1988, the campaign of 1992, in which the news media explicitly tried to play a more critical role, gave some grounds for hope in this regard.

The capacity for practical reasoning is deeply embedded in the traditions of our liberal arts institutions, not least those institutions with religious affiliation. These institutions are the custodians of the ancient traditions of philosophy and rhetoric. The issue of the age is whether it is possible to combine the understanding that was traditionally the province of education, particularly the education in rhetoric which persons of Lippmann's and Dewey's era still generally received, with the best contemporary understanding of technology, economics, and politics. If we could learn to do that, we would then be in a position to make contact with another important American public philosopher, John Courtney Murray, S.J. It was Murray who defined civilization as "public conversation according to reasonable laws. Here," Murray aphorized, "the word 'conversation' has its twofold Latin sense. It means living together and talking together."[4]

America remains true to itself only if it remains a society, as Murray put it, locked in civic argument, a society whose members are able to argue with each other about the good life. Murray put it this way: "We hold these truths; therefore we can disagree."[5] It is "these truths" that constitute the normative core of political ideals that we have to re-examine and try to articulate and understand. However, it is a normative core that is not so

---

[4] John Courtney Murray, S.J., *We Hold These Truths: Catholic Reflections on the American Proposition* (New York: Sheed & Ward, 1960) 13.

[5] Ibid. 13

much designed to settle argument as to make coherent difference and discussion possible. It is the responsibility to promote such public argument which defines leadership in a democracy. It is that responsibility against which political leaders should be judged. But it is this same responsibility which, in a democracy, defines the calling of each of us to be citizens.

4

Power, Truth, and the Flow of Information

Thomas E. Shanks, S.J.

Wilbur Schramm, a founder of the academic field of communication, once wrote: "Communication is the tool that makes societies possible. It is no accident that communication and community have the same word root. Without communication, there would be no communities; and without community, there would be no communication."[1] From this point of view, we can see society as the sum of relationships in which people share information of some kind; we can judge the strength of a society by the quality of the relationships and the breadth of the information.

The drafters of the U.S. Constitution understood the centrality of information for a democratic society and, in the First Amendment, declared: "Congress shall make no law...abridging the freedom of speech, or of the press...." While it is not clear how they intended the law to be developed, it is clear that they believed truth would emerge if the press were free to disseminate information; they also believed that widespread access to information was one of the best ways to hold accountable those in power, particularly in government. The three words that galvanized our forebears—power, truth, and information—galvanize us today, 200 years later.

In this chapter, I will offer some reflections on how the U.S. press today continues in the spirit of these founders. I will, however, spend more time discussing our current understanding of press power, information flow, and audience self-construction of truth. Each has implications for moral educators.

In many ways, our press is strong in the tradition of the First Amendment. The October 13th, 1988 edition of *The New York Times*[2] provided an

---

[1] Wilbur Schramm and William E. Porter, *Men, Women, Messages, and Media: Understanding Human Communication*, 2nd ed. (New York: Harper and Row, 1982) 2.

[2] "Release Dan Quayle's College Records Now," (Advertisement), *New York Times*, October 13, 1988, sec. A, 11.

interesting example. A full-page ad, paid for by the Independent Committee on Presidential Qualifications, demanded "Release Dan Quayle's College Records Now." Just above the large headline were two questions: "What is he hiding? When will the press get the story?" Just above that were coupons that citizens could send to the President of NBC News, the editor of *The Cleveland Plain Dealer*, and the owner of *The Washington Post* and *Newsweek*, pleading with them to get the rest of the story the Committee judged crucial to the 1988 election.

Of course, we cannot discount venal political motives for this advertisement (or many others that have followed). This may be just another example of what many people considered media Quayle-bashing, begun when 10,000 reporters were captive at the 1988 Republican Convention. Yet, we can see in this ad an appropriate example of the First Amendment search for information and truth in the face of powers that some people judged to be avoiding that truth.

Perhaps better examples of such a search can be found in the media's handling of the Iran-Contra scandal, the impact of deficit spending, Defense Department consultants, and the variety of ethical lapses in virtually all recent Presidential administrations. These cases hold up well as "information," which we will define as Rubin did:

> Information stimulates the intellect so as to encourage education. It consists of relatable knowledge of social, political, or economic value that helps the individual see the real world and take action or make decisions accordingly. Information is the grist that sustains imagination, which is so vital when it is necessary to fill the gaps between the known and the unknown. [It] is not mere data. It is the sum product of data that are evaluated and weighed to fulfill a perceived need for knowledge.[3]

When media present such information, they clearly use the power intended by the Constitution. In this context, social theorist Max Weber's concepts of power, legitimation, and authority are useful. Drawing on Weber, we can consider "power" as the ability to influence others and to overcome resistance; "legitimation" to refer to the acceptance of the exercise of power because it is in line with values held by the subjects; and "authority" to refer to power that is viewed as legitimate.[4] People regard the media as possessing real "authority" when they present information of significance to the everyday lives of readers or viewers. That judgment of significance ultimately rests in the perception of the audience member.

---

[3] Bernard Rubin, ed., *When Information Counts: Grading the Media* (Lexington, MA: Lexington Books, 1985) vii.

[4] Stephen W. Littlejohn, *Theories of Human Communication* (Belmont, CA: Wadsworth, 1983) 241-42.

The news consumer must also make a decision about the truth of the news. James Pollock's description of truth as "onerously personal and inter-personal" and "partial and relative to other truths" (in Chapter 21 below) particularly applies to the media. Most of us know that every news story (and note the use of the word "story") presented to the public is a *reflection* of the truth of the actual event that gave it birth. The story, even if shot with a camera, filters through the frames of reference of reporters, editors, and others involved in its creation. If done well, the end result may indeed reflect much of the truth of the original event, but news always remains *mediated* truth.

As a result, when we think of a reporter's "objectivity," we must judge a story's "balance" and "fairness," rather than expect a mechanical transmission of the facts of the event. Rubin's definition of information even implies the demand, well understood by good reporters, that they actually evaluate and weigh the data on hand because the facts of the event and the truth of the event (i.e., the real meaning of the event) are often not the same. This is particularly the case during political campaigns and at other times when the news is managed by spin doctors" or public relations specialists.

Media "power" concerns us today (as it has since the beginning of communication as a field of study): We continue to ask how much media and media messages influence the way we think, feel, and behave. The concern over negative effects of media messages has led to Congressional action, PTA lobbying, and to nationally-organized letter campaigns.

Among all the concerns about media power, three have important implications for us: media ownership, quality of information sent, and what we'll call (as journalist Walter Lippmann did in 1921) "the pictures in our heads."[5] Ben Bagdikian, long-time journalist, critic, and educator, has been charting a trend in ownership of media corporations. He calls it "The Media Monopoly." By June, 1987, Bagdikian reported that of the country's 1700 daily newspapers, 98% were local monopolies (i. e., only one newspaper in the town or city). This does not include joint operating agreements. When he looked at the circulation of the nation's dailies in 1992, he found that most of it was controlled by 11 corporations.

Using advertising revenues, rather than circulation, Bagdikian analyzed magazines and found a similar concentration. Time, Inc., with its various publications, received more than 40% of magazine revenues. He also found that five companies produce most of the revenue in book publishing. In television, cable has offered more choice, but seven companies have most of the 60 million subscribers.

Contraction of ownership is not new. In 1983, when the first edition of Bagdikian's book *The Media Monopoly* was published,[6] 50 companies

---

[5] Walter Lippmann, *Public Opinion* (New York: Macmillan, 1921).

[6] Ben Bagdikian, *The Media Monopoly* (Boston: Beacon, 1983, 1992).

controlled most of the media businesses. By 1992, that number had dropped to 20. Craig McLaughlin (1988) reports that Wall Street analysts are saying the number could drop to a half-dozen corporations by the end of the 1990s.

The question this raises is one of breadth and diversity of information. In an interview McLaughlin quotes Bagdikian:

> By now the corporations that dominate our media, like alcoholic fat cats, treat this situation as theirs by right....Their concept of a diversity of views is values from center to far right. The American audience, having been exposed to a narrowing range of ideas over the decades, often assumes that what they see and hear in the major media is all there is. It is no way to maintain a lively marketplace of ideas, which is to say it is no way to maintain a democracy.[7]

The Columbia Journalism Review has also explored this issue of corporate ownership. Under the title, "When MBAs Rule the Newsroom," Doug Underwood agrees that technological and economic values to concentration of ownership certainly exist but worries "whether the true value of the business—the craft of writing, the vigor of investigating, the sense of fairness and equity, the gut-level impulse to want to right wrongs—will survive in the new MBA-run, market-driven newsroom."[8] Whether all this does and will survive is the source of study and debate for a great many scholars and practitioners today.

A second concern relates to this one about concentration of media power: the breadth and quality of information sent to America's homes. Specifically, I'd like to discuss coverage and underlying themes.

A marvelous segue from questions of ownership to coverage is the fact that Bagdikian's work was selected as the top under-reported story the year it first appeared by Project Censored. The fact that many readers have probably never heard of Project Censored may justify the existence of this work, conducted annually for almost 25 years by Carl Jenkins and his students at Sonoma State University in California. From a list of 25 nominees, national judges such as Brad Knickerbocker (then national news editor of *The Christian Science Monitor*), economist John Kenneth Galbraith, and linguist Noam Chomsky produce an ordered list of the top 10 under-reported stories each year.

In addition to Bagdikian's work in 1987, other under-reported stories over the years have included reports on biased coverage of Central America, international nuclear accidents, U.S. involvement in torture in Guatemala, the Christic Institute's findings on the Contra-drug connection, an investigation of George Bush's role in the Iran-contra scandal,

---

[7] Craig McLaughlin, "Project Censored: Censored Stories and Media Monopoly," *The San Francisco Bay Guardian* June 8, 1988, 8.

[8] Doug Underwood, "When MBAs Rule the Newsroom," *Columbia Journalism Review*, (March/April 1988), 30.

and a warning that an accident aboard a plutonium-laden space probe could kill millions of people.[9]

Despite this, we should remember that other important stories *were* covered in the national press (and I listed a few of them at the beginning of this chapter). The point remains clear, though: For one reason or another, most people do not have easy access to all the information one would wish they have.

To this, I would like to add the comments of sociologist Herbert J. Gans[10] about the messages behind the news Americans do receive. In his article, Gans examines enduring values found in the news over the last two decades. He defines values as preference statements made in a variety of news media about nation, society, and issues confronting us. He groups his findings around eight clusters of values; I will mention just a few. The first is ethnocentrism—American news values its own nation above all others; stories critical of domestic conditions are almost always treated as deviant cases; American ideals always remain viable. This is particularly clear in war news.

Three values dominate domestic news. The first, altruistic democracy, leads the press to tell us again and again that politics should be based on public interest and service, and that both winners and losers must be scrupulously honest, efficient, and dedicated to acting in the public interest. "Waste" is always an evil; bureaucratic paperwork is a frequent story, as well as stories about paperwork generated by attempts to reduce paperwork. Responsible capitalism is the news approach to the economy—a faith that businessmen and women will compete with each other to create increased prosperity for all, but will refrain from unreasonable profits and exploitation; monopoly is evil, but what Gans calls "the oligopolistic nature of today's economy" rarely is discussed. Economic growth is always positive, except when it causes inflation or pollution, destroys a landmark, or puts craftspeople out of work. That ties in with the value of "small-town pastoralism," that the small town really represents the "good life in America." Gans' other values are individualism, moderation, order, and leadership.

Gans suggests that these values affect what events become news and even help define the news. If that is true, it implies a great deal for those teaching about values and morality in America, and for those of us who use these images (consciously or not) to help make decisions about what is right and wrong. The real concern about media power and the quality of information reaching us, and the point of this collection, results from a concern with how media (and in this case, news) help us understand our environment and

---

[9] McLaughlin 8-9.

[10] Herbert J. Gans, "The Messages Behind the News," in *Media in Society: Readings in Mass Communication*, ed. Caren J. Deming and Samuel L. Becker (Glenview, IL: Scott, Foresman, 1988), 236-46.

how much that understanding influences the way we ourselves deal with that environment and the people in it.

This question, the question of powerful media effects, has been studied from macro-theoretical and micro-theoretical approaches, as Michael Real points out in Chapter 2. The debate still continues about how much effect, in which situations and cultures; however, we can safely conclude, as Comstock and his colleagues did in their 1978 review of the research to date on television effects, that many of these are indeed powerful effects.

My training is in the micro-theories. Research in these traditions suggests that information carried through mass communication has at least two important effects. First, news sets the stage. Here we consider what Vince Price and Don Roberts[11] call the reporting function of the media—that is, the impact of mass media representations on people's perceptions of public affairs. Empirical research on agenda-setting[12] best exemplifies this. Agenda-setting refers to the hypothesized ability of mass media coverage to grant status to a certain problem or person. The agenda setting argument holds that even if media do not succeed in telling people what to think, they "stunningly" succeed in telling them what to think about. Their success is tied to the amount and kind of coverage provided. The hypothesis has been extensively researched, usually in surveys that have provided mixed, but generally supportive results. Price and Roberts report that recent experiments have provided even more convincing evidence of the effect.[13]

Second, news provides a looking glass. We can call this the poll-taking function of the media. Elisabeth Noelle-Neumann's "spiral of silence" theory[14] explains how it works. Based on 20 years of research, she holds that the spiral of silence involves both personal and media channels of communication. The media publicize public opinion, making evident which opinions predominate. Individuals express their opinions or not, depending upon the predominant point of view and the media in turn, attend to the expressed opinion. So the spiral continues.

This means that people who perceive from media reports that trends of opinion run against their views, fearing social isolation, will refrain from expressing these opinions (except to those who share them). So even if these persons constitute a numerical majority, the failure to com-

[11] Vincent Price and Donald F. Roberts, "Public Opinion Processes," in *Handbook of Communication Science,* ed. Charles R. Berger and Steven H. Chaffee (Newbury Park, CA: Sage, 1987) 781-815.

[12] Donald L. Shaw and Maxwell E. McCombs, *The Emergence of American Political Issues* (St. Paul: West, 1977).

[13] Price and Roberts 808-809.

[14] Elisabeth Noelle-Neumann, *The Spiral of Silence: Public Opinion—Our Social Skin* (Chicago: University of Chicago Press, 1984).

municate will lead to the strengthening of the opposition, creating the spiral of silence.

We began this chapter with a discussion of real authority, quality information, and relative truth. We have seen so far that media monopolies have raised questions about the real authority of media; items excluded or included have raised questions about the quality of information we receive; and that, despite the notion of relative truth, media do indeed seem to have some overarching effects.

I would like now to revisit the notion of relative truth, if only because what I have so far presented makes me somewhat uncomfortable. When we step back from media and generalize about content and effects, we run the risk that we can too easily revert to a form of simple stimulus-response theory. "Well," the argument goes, "we have all this negative stuff out there and see, just like we thought, it does all this negative stuff to the people watching or reading."

Years of research have shown that audience members rarely respond in a simple stimulus-response fashion. This heuristic may prove more useful: Any communication "effect" is better thought of as some function of what we can call "content" and "relationship." Content includes the messages and the individuals and organizations that produce them. Relationship includes a host of audience-centered variables: the habits with which we approach messages, communicators, and media; the attentional processes and information-processing abilities we possess; the various motivations to remember and, perhaps, act on a message. If media do indeed act to set the stage and act as a looking glass, this model hypothesizes that all of these audience-variables work to make it so.

A truism in communication holds that the message sent is not often the message received; from this perspective, the real test of communication becomes the transfer of meaning, examining the extent to which an isomorphic relationship exists between the meaning of the sender and the experienced meaning of the receiver. For the communication effects we have described to take place, our heuristic would hold that both sender and receiver must be operating on the message in much the same way. If this is the case then, as Clifford Christians explains, the public should also be held accountable for the current situation: "As responsible beings in public space, we can legitimately be called to account to the extent of our power for effecting change. On those occasions, pointing fingers elsewhere—to media executives or government officials, for example—is unconscionable."[15]

To get a better understanding of the current situation concerning media power, truth, and information, we must understand the interdependent nature

---

[15] Clifford G. Christians, "Can the Public be Held Accountable?" *Journal of Mass Media Ethics* 3, (1988) 56.

of the communication process. This is well-described in the Uses and Dependency Model of Mass Communication.[16]

The model defines "dependency" as a relationship in which the satisfaction of needs or the attainment of goals by one party is contingent on the resources of another party. The model begins with the proposition that there are a variety of interdependent relationships among three integral components of the model: audiences, media, and the larger social system. For example, media are dependent on social systems for legislative and judicial protections; society depends on media for delivery of information; audiences depend on society for values, law, culture, and so on.

Central to the model is the notion that audiences depend on media and media content to meet needs and satisfy goals. As a result, audiences encounter media messages with individual motives, constructed social realities, and numerous dependencies on media for information, entertainment, and so on. The model predicts that when media messages are not linked to audience dependencies or when people's self-constructed social reality is entirely adequate before and during reception, media effects will be minimal. Conversely, when people have a social situation that does not provide adequate frameworks for understanding, acting, or escaping (major needs in a complex society), such messages will have a number of alteration effects. The model predicts that the greater the audience need, the stronger the dependency and the greater the likelihood that media will affect audience cognitions, feelings, and behavior.

The key element in the model is the way the audience consumes and processes information, the experienced meaning we mentioned above. At times of societal change or conflict, or when individual needs and motives are heightened, dependencies and effects will increase. Similarly, the more the audience relies on media, rather than non-media, sources for information, the greater the dependency on and influence of media.

I hope that this model, as well as the chapter itself, has shed some light on the complexities involved in contemporary communication, especially when we consider power, truth, and information flow. If the model does reflect reality, than it points us toward a fruitful discussion about the possibilities of change in the system.

The model implies that a change in any one of the major components will lead to some change in the others. New communication technologies, certainly, are already causing some change, as news consumers begin to gain access to vast on-line computer databases, national editions of newspapers, and cable and satellite information broadcasts. Television networks and local newspapers are beginning to feel the pinch as viewers and readers begin

---

[16] Alan M. Rubin and Sven Windahl, "The Uses and Dependency Model of Mass Communication," *Critical Studies in Mass Communication* 3 (1986), 185-99.

to "vote with their feet," perhaps a reflection of the growing mistrust of media by American audiences.

The real implication of our consideration here remains the improvement of the education process at all levels. Educational efforts must help audiences understand media power, learn to be more critical consumers of news and information, and engage more actively in the construction of their own truth. It would seem appropriate to call for a pledge that we all work toward this end so well described by Christians:

> The goal is conscientization. Only by naming the world, learning to speak a true word about it, will we take the decisive step to liberate ourselves from a state of dependence, and from naive acquiescence in the status quo. This is a theory of non-oppressive praxis; when we gain a critical consciousness—that is, when ideological hegemony begins to break down—the revolution is underway and cannot be halted.[17]

---

[17] Christians 55.

5

The Life of the Spirit in a Mass-mediated Culture

Günter Virt

1. Analysis

1.1 Mass media mirrors culture

This essay deals with the discernment of spirits in a mass-mediated culture. Today the mass media determine and form every facet of human culture. They influence not only *what* we think and feel but also *how* we dream and pray, in other words our whole world view as well as our image of God.[1] This might be the significant characteristic of our present culture in comparison to previous ones: We increasingly make use of instruments which enlarge our range of actions to such an extent that the quality of our actions may change as well. It appears that our moral sensibility for the consequences of actions affecting people whom we cannot see has not yet kept pace with the reach of the technology by which we become aware of those consequences. This essay shall examine this general characteristic of our culture with regard to social communication. Through the media (press, films, radio, television, tapes, records, and so on) this aspect of culture penetrates and interconnects all human ways of thinking and living.[2]

An adequate view of these media reveals human actions as expressions of a specific culture, as achievements of the human spirit and creative power which for their part form the whole of human culture. The aim of this essay is to interpret the media from the point of view of the modern culture that has generated them and to ask what mass media are as phenomena of cul-

---

[1] See P. Soukup, "Communication, Cultural Form and Theology," *The Way* Supplement 57 (1986) 78-79.

[2] See Pontifical Commission for the Means of Social Communication, *Pastoral Instruction for the Application of the Decree of the Second Vatican Ecumenical Council on the Means of Social Communication* (Washington, D.C.: United States Catholic Conference, 1971) no. 1. Hereafter *Communio et Progressio*.

ture, and not, conversely, how and what they effect. Naturally media not only mirror and intensify existing cultural manifestations of life; they also relate different cultures and subcultures so that by means of these various combinations they creatively introduce something new into what previously were relatively isolated cultural complexes. Here the problem of an intercultural ethic poses itself with vital urgency.

1.2 Culture, Spirit, and Holy Spirit

The basis for reflection on the link between culture and spirit shall be people's experience of their own thinking, wishing, and creating.[3] One does not experience oneself as an isolated ego but as a person originating from and being open to a community. Being human means being open to community, to society, to the whole world, to being in general. A thorough reflection inevitably leads to the question of the deepest reason in whose existence and actions the whole world participates, as a result of which human persons find themselves forever united and referred to one another in an original way. From a Christian point of view the essential reason for being ultimately united is the spirit, the Holy Spirit of God.[4] The most decisive experience of the spirit has probably been expressed by Blaise Pascal in his famous saying that the human person infinitely transcends itself.[5] Culture is an outgrowth of this surplus of happenings; "it is a fact bearing on the very person of man that he can come to an authentic and full humanity only through culture, that is, through the cultivation of natural goods and values."[6]

Print media, radio, television, and so on are undoubtedly the expression of a certain culture. But neither the print media nor television were invented because they were needed but they rather are needed because they were invented.[7] There was no necessity for Gutenberg's invention, for the elite who were reading books were sufficiently supplied by the trade of the copyists, and the illiterate masses knew without books what they had to know. In this sense the modern media are likewise not the result of preceding cultural planning after a prior market-analysis but the expression of an

---

[3] See W. Kern, "Vom Geist der Philosophen" in *Christlicher Glaube in moderner Gesellschaft* Bd. 22 (Freiburg im Breisgau: Herder, 1982) 73.

[4] As created by the spiritual word of God (see Genesis 1:2), the structures of the Spirit are to be expected in all parts of creation, including the non-human world.

[5] See B. Pascal, *Pensées*, in *Oeuvres Completes* (Paris: Ed. du Seuil, 1963) 493-641.

[6] *Gaudium et spes* no. 53. [All references to the documents of the Council are taken from Walter M. Abbott, ed., *The Documents of Vatican II* (New York: America Press, 1966).] How difficult a clear definition of culture really is, is mirrored by the multitude of theories of culture which cannot be discussed in greater detail in this essay.

[7] See G. Goethals and M. Real, Chapters 1 and 2, above.

idea. Cultures change through global attitudes, which today we often dif-
fusely call "values." No theory can adequately explain or precisely predict
the genesis of a culture or the conditions under which cultures grow and
create their products. The human spirit is simultaneously—and for the most
part unconsciously—both the creator and the creation of its culture.[8]

Obviously, every culture is ambivalent and, therefore, will find optimistic and pessimistic interpreters. Both optimism and pessimism in the
global estimation of our mass-mediated culture spring from subconscious
prejudices, secret interests, fears, and hopes.

Are such prejudices the final authority for the estimation of our culture? Despite the variety of experiences in differing cultures and times, the
texts of the Holy Scriptures and of the great Christian tradition are inter-
spersed with the conviction that God is active through a power which neither forces nor alienates, a power which is called Holy Spirit, Spirit of
God.[9] Even the spiritual gifts which are given to us as deposit do not necessarily heal the world and human institutions with splendor and glory. The
Spirit rather groans in them as much as in human beings (see Romans 8).
Yet these often inconspicuous spiritual gifts show that even now redemption
is really happening. This Spirit offers a new beginning in the impasse of
human failure, human guilt, and sin, and opens humanity up to a dimension
lying beyond one-sided rationality, an area where reason alone can no
longer gain ground. The Holy Spirit is the gift whereby God presents the
divine self to the person if only the person does not refuse. Only this Spirit
can help humanity to discover the Spirit also in nature, in history, in all the
different cultures including a mass-mediated culture, and in other religions.[10] And it helps to discern this Holy Spirit from other spirits which
obscure it and interfere with its work. Although the church is not simply
the Kingdom of Heaven but always a sinful church, the Holy Spirit operates
in the church in a special and symbolic manner. As it transcends all cultures and their media, the Spirit can always newly inculturate itself in any
culture and, therefore, can be an instance of orientation.[11] For this reason,

---

[8] See A. Huter, *Zur Ausbreitung von Vergnügung und Belehrung...Fernsehen als
Kulturwirklichkeit* (Zürich: Fromm, 1988) 42.

[9] See Y. Congar, "Heiliger Geist in der Geschichte und heute," in *Christlicher
Glaube in moderner Gesellschaft* Bd. 22 (Freiburg im Breisgau: Herder, 1982) 76.

[10] Ambrosiaster, *Patrologia Latina* 17, Sancti Ambrosii, 1866, 258: "Quidquid enim
verum a quocunque dicitur, a sancto dicitur Spiritu."

[11] *Gaudium et spes* no. 58: "But at the same time, the Church, sent to all peoples of
every time and place, is not bound exclusively and indissolubly to any race or
nation, nor to any particular way of life or any customary pattern of living, ancient
or recent. Faithful to her own tradition and at the same time conscious of her
universal mission, she can enter into communion with various cultural modes, to her
own enrichment and theirs too. The good news of Christ constantly renews the life
and culture of fallen man. It combats and removes the errors and evils resulting
from sinful allurements which are a perpetual threat."

Christians can confidently face a change of culture, trying to discern the spirits while trusting in the Holy Spirit.

1.3 Characteristics of a Cultural Change

We are now living in the middle of a cultural change which finds its expression in the media. Because we are caught up in the midst of this change it is very difficult for us to evaluate it: Everybody contributes to this change, even when everyone's room for decision and, therefore, for creativity might be very limited. To divide mass-mediated culture into institutions and communicators on the one hand and recipients on the other and then to ask about the effects of the former upon the latter only limits complex media processes; furthermore, the prejudice imbedded in this kind of asking reduces the person to an automaton. The so called audience disintegrates on closer observation into groups and individuals of society which live in constant exchange of ideas with each other, which act together, voice opinions, make themselves heard. What these partners of social communication say or do is mediated by the printed or the electronic forum of the media. The more complete the information made available by the media, the better will individuals or groups in society be able to make themselves heard, the more freely and independently will they be able to form their opinions, make judgments, decisions, and act.[12]

As the term already points out, one essential characteristic of a mass-mediated culture is that it is a *media culture*.[13] Related to human beings this diagnosis will lead us to the essential question: Why do people use media and how do they use them? According to a current scheme humanity can turn to the modern *"biblia pauperum"* in an affluent society for information, for education, and for entertainment. But this scheme is somewhat abstract: Why shouldn't entertainment also educate or information also entertain? Human beings address the media for various reasons which can by no means be all rationally explained. It is one of the universal anthropological realities that human beings constantly search for fascination and novelty. Sports, for example, become a constant occasion for tension and surprise and offer an occasion for identification with symbolic figures that represent deep-felt desires.

---

[12] H. Wagner, *Einführung und Kommentar zur Pastoralinstruktion Communio et Progressio über die Instrumente der sozialen Kommunikation* (Nachkonziliare Dokumentation Trier: Paulinus, Bd. 11) 41.

[13] See H. Eillensky, "Massengesellschaft und Massenkultur," in *Massenkommunikationsforschung* Bd. 2, ed. D. Prokop (Frankfurt: Fischer-TB, 1973) 116-51.

A second characteristic of our culture is the general increase of leisure time. But the culture of leisure is ambivalent, and many people feel that leisure time has overcome humanity too quickly and that we have yet to cope with it. "The wastage of leisure occasionally has to be offered resistance through a determined engagement of denial."[14] Such a denial will only be possible if humanity can find a meaning in it, i.e., if humanity manages to integrate increased leisure time into its actually experienced meaning of life.

If this integration fails, a kind of curiosity follows which no longer understands what has been seen but, instead, seeks for something new "only in order to leap from it anew to another novelty."[15] Martin Heidegger called the essential elements of curiosity diversion and restlessness, where the person is everywhere and nowhere. As there is nothing worth lingering over, celebrating or marvelling, sooner or later boredom overcomes that person.[16] It is not the media that create that boredom but they are an expression of the need to somehow come to terms with general boredom. This is the drawback and the temptation of a leisure time culture to which cultural pessimists cling. But there is also something positive here; it lies in humanity's increasing endeavor to participate in the goods of the earth. An essential part of these goods is information in its broadest meaning, an urge that itself creates its media in a culture. Democratization, industrialization, administration, wealth, social security, and an increase in leisure time have occasioned change in all cultural fields. Something new developed in history, a *mass culture.*[17] Mass culture, however, is not an elitist culture in a new quantity, for masses have different interests than the various elites. That a mass culture is as ambivalent as an elitist culture shall only be hinted at. Mass media are created for specific contents in which the mass is interested and these are obviously different from those of the elite.[18]

Mass media, especially TV, offer a contrast to our highly specialized abstract and notional culture and thereby to a world that has widely become incomprehensible. Masses want to comprehend the world as well and there-

---

[14] A. Auer, *Ethos der Freizeit* (Düsseldorf: Patmos Verlag, 1972) and lately in R. Bleistein, Ed., *Menschen unterwegs* (Frankfurt: Knecht, 1987) 38-56.

[15] M. Heidegger, *Being and Time*, trans. J. Macquarrie and E. Robinson (New York; Evanston: Harper & Row, 1962) 216.

[16] See W. J. Revers, *Die Psychologie der Langeweile* (Meisenheim/Glan: Westkulturverlag, 1949).

[17] Indeed, there has always been a folk culture, but in each case restricted to a limited area.

[18] Considering the specialization in our society, the phenomenon of elites also has to be differentiated. It is by no means impossible, but rather probable that one and the same person belongs to the elite in a certain field and to the mass in another. Should an elitist existence turn into ideology—even in certain religious groups—serious problems similar to those of racism arise.

fore require adequate measures of help. Thoughts without imaginations are empty for them, as well as for the philosopher.[19] If, according to the wishes of the masses the medium tries to provide everybody with everything, then it must visualize in a well-balanced manner education, information, and entertainment in their seemingly inadequate interaction. And not only visualize correctly but visualize at all. In comparison to a one-sided elitist culture determined by rationality, mass culture turns into *an image and tone culture* (*Bild- und Tonkultur*), with all the consequences discussed in this book. But are spirit and truth only present in abstract notions and not in images, sounds, and rhythms as well? Can spirit and truth only be effective in the rational elements of a culture and not also in a mass culture? Furthermore, can spirit and truth only be effective in an elitist culture?

Every culture has its ambivalence and its drawbacks. Every culture develops its own ideas concerning education and art and perhaps also develops its own myth. The spirit of antiquity and of the middle ages was determined by marvelling at the cosmos and by the awareness of not being able to penetrate its secrets entirely. The spirit of modern times from the age of enlightenment onwards is determined to uncover the secrets of nature by rational and exactly measurable means. This has resulted in a degree of liberation from the dictates of nature but it also presents us with the restraints of rationalization, of excessive mechanization by means of which humanity has already destroyed a great part of its environment as the basis for its own life, and of an increasingly perfected administration. In so far as humanity practices not only a technical domination of the world in all its ambivalence but also secretly practices self-redemption, the Holy Spirit is no longer compatible with the spirit of such a culture.[20] The Holy Spirit of God is transcendent of every Zeitgeist and by critically crossing it the Spirit reveals the tendency to immanence which is at work in a particular Zeitgeist.[21]

Today no one can survey the knowledge of the time. Knowledge has become predominant and on this account members of a mass culture feel to a large extent merely powerless. The surplus of stimuli and information brought about by the media can no longer be digested; it disappears unclarified in the unconscious.[22] There it starts to fight against this one-sided rationality. One begins to suspect that both rationality (and its achievements

---

[19] See I. Kant, *Critique of Pure Reason,* trans. Norman Kemp Smith (New York: St. Martin's Press, 1929) A51/B75. "Thoughts without content are empty, intuitions without concepts are blind."

[20] The question has only to be asked whether Francis Bacon had not already introduced this turn in his famous phrase, "knowledge is power."

[21] See J. W. Goethe, *Faust* (Toronto: University of Toronto Press, 1970) Part I, Scene 1: "What you all call the spirit of the times is just your own spirit with the times reflected in it" (11).

[22] G. Hunold, "Die medienpolitische Herausforderung," in *Die Welt für morgen. Festschrift für F. Bockle* (München: Kösel, 1986) 293.

one would not want to miss) and non-rationality (taken both as a figure for emotional intuition, mainly unconscious interests, and creative urges, but also for fear, hope, and imagination) are in a complementary way each necessary for a full and complete human being. Every culture is an expression of rationality and non-rationality.

Does the historical pendulum now swing in the other direction and bring *a return of myth*?[23] Our lives are widely determined by considerable discomfort about the one-sided concentration on rationality, about an anthropology which divides the *anthropos* into a public intellect and a private heart. In the search for a corrective the mythic in its broadest meaning is repeatedly praised as a remedy. Indeed, not only television but also the modern music of entertainment and the comics now favor that tendency towards the mythic by addressing the person strongly in the pre-rational area. Moreover, they themselves enact myths.

The Old Testament incorporated a number of mythic elements and rites, but it also changed and shaped them considerably until they were consistent with the belief in Yahweh which was founded by the history of salvation. The New Testament sees Christ as the realization of all myths. In the history of this belief on the one hand a positive interpretation of religious myths took place according to the significance of Christ;[24] on the other hand a life and death struggle soon broke out between faith in the fulfillment of salvation history through the Christ-event and the gnostic-dualistic myths. The criterion of distinction in this confrontation was already brought to the point by Irenäus of Lyons: All heretics deny that the word of God really became flesh.[25]

This history of the power of the Christian faith, which after a careful distinction christianized the ancient myths without fear, poses an important two-fold challenge to the present church. The church must not just reject the ambivalent modern media myths in their negative aspects but also acknowledge the unexhausted potentiality of the mass-mediated culture which to a large extent is and will be a mythic one. Furthermore, the church is challenged to help make the media transparent for the one in whom and for whom everything has been created. One cannot see why it should be easier to transform and employ ancient cosmic myths for the mystery of Christ than those which are accessible through modern culture.

---

[23] See K. Hübner, *Die Wahrheit des Mythos* (München: Beck, 1975) and E. Drewermann, *Tiefenpsychologie und Exegese* (Freiburg im Breisgau: Walter, 1985).

[24] See Hugo Rahner, *Greek Myths and Christian Mystery* (New York, Evanston: Harper & Row, 1963).

[25] I. de Lyon, "Contre Les Heresies III," 11, 3. *Sources Chrétiennes 34* (Paris: Editions du Cerf, 1952): "Secundum autem nullam sententiam haereticorum Verbum Dei caro factum est."

2. The vision of a perfectly successful Communio

2.1 Communication and Communio

In its specific human quality communication can only be understood from communication itself. It cannot simply be explained by the behavior that human beings and animals share. But an enormous amount of attempted communication fails. The basic question is how communication can lead to real *Communio*. Communio is that unique reality which can neither be grasped through the worn-out term community nor the abstract term participation. It is a question of longing for being together, for being "in and with each other," for the ways of setting each other free, of mutual openness, of sacrificing and receiving, in sum, for a full and successful unity of life. The desire for this Communio dwells deep in every human being. The ambivalence and ambiguity of the human search for a successful personal Communio receives an ultimate unequivocality from the biblical message that the world has been created by one whose very nature is Communio in an unbelievably perfect manner. "In this Communio of love, in this divine network of relations, there is—metaphorically speaking—a room for man, so that he is able to join the game of divine love."[26]

Even if the immediate experience and perception of humanity's relation to the triune creator is impossible in this world, the direct relation of humanity to God is nevertheless constitutive for being human. This is the meaning of the biblical image of the creator breathing the Divine Spirit into the human being, thereby creating humanity in God's image[27] (Genesis 2:7). The same book of Genesis expresses (1:27) the idea of God's image by depicting human nature as a state of community between man and woman. "That creation becomes Communio: This is the original idea of a communial God. Thereby we mean both the Communio between God and man as well as the Communio among men, for both are inseparably tied to one another."[28] Being related is something deeply marked in human nature by the creation and not something which was subsequently added. This vocation to Communio, however, can be realized historically only by means of communication processes. The vision of a successful Communio of all people can supposedly be realized with concrete conceptions and imaginations in a mass-mediated culture for the first time, in spite of all the problems and ambivalences which may, of course, not be suppressed in the present state of this mass-mediated culture.[29]

---

[26] G. Greshake, *Erlöst in einer unerlösten Welt* (Mainz: Grünewald, 1987) 31.

[27] See I. U. Dalfert and E. Jungel, "Person und Gottebenbildlichkeit," in *Christlicher Glaube in moderner Gesellschaft* Bd. 24 (Freiburg im Breisgau: Herder, 1981) 57-99.

[28] G. Greshake, *Erlöst in einer unerlösten Welt* 32.

[29] See E. McDonagh, Chapter 22, below.

2.2 Menace and destruction of the Communio by sin

If the nature of God is the Communio between God the Father and the only begotten Son in the Holy Spirit and if this communal structure is deeply impressed upon the whole creation, the refusal of such a Communio with God and with human beings is the deepest nature of sin. Thus, the origins of sins are not shortcomings of communication but the refusal of Communio at all, the fact that one withholds oneself from others. Here lies the root of the separation from God: The ego poses itself in the center of all reality and takes over the place that is due to God. The emptiness that emerges from that delusion leads to an attempt to appropriate the various aspects of life as if they themselves were God and not relative, created goods. Consumption, sex, and money as well as prestige, success, and power are seized as if therein being human finds its fulfillment. In a right order all of these things are part of God's good creation. The danger lies in their disintegration and in their being mistaken for ultimate values so that they can no longer be mutually weighed out and integrated into a larger horizon of meaning. It is impossible to love these things wholeheartedly so that longing finds its end. Therefore, sin always signifies a discrepancy between that which we seek and for which we are destined on the one hand and what we actually obtain on the other hand. This gives rise to a selfish struggle for goods at the cost of other people and society. In its tendency sin is always directed against fellow humans and against society. It is especially the mass-mediated culture that illustrates more than ever how much our whole global community is affected by the refusal of Communio and of sharing. Media drastically demonstrate how much the prejudices of rich countries to a certain extent bring about the misery and death from starvation of millions of people in some poor southern countries.[30]

News reports make us especially aware of the frailty of the Communio in the creation with a degree of clarity that was not possible before mass media. This, of course, raises the pressing question how in the present excess of information we handle the evil of life, especially the moral evil of individuals and their consequences in social structures. Many people deplore that men and women readily keep this reality at arm's length by consuming news as pieces of entertainment.[31] Though the media do not create sin they are involved in the power of sin and can increase its range of consequences. Media can contribute to disintegration, insecurity, and stress; they sometimes stir up one-sided life needs and divert humans from reality, leading them to a dream-world; they may hinder rather than support direct

---

[30] Lately, Pope John Paul II has confirmed the preferential option for the poor in his encyclical *Sollicitudo Rei Socialis* no. 42.

[31] See N. Postman, *Amusing Ourselves to Death: Public Discourse in the Age of Show Business* (New York: Viking, 1985).

personal relations; one-sided presentations determined by the autonomy of the media have a strong tendency toward falsification.[32] The many faults that one can rightly enumerate do not, however, hit the nature of sin which becomes obvious through the Spirit (see John 16:8-9). The sin against the Spirit is found in all attempts of self-redemption and of anticipation of the Last Judgment. The biggest temptation put to Jesus is to bring about the Kingdom of Heaven by means of worldly power (see Matthew 4:8-9 and parallels). A centralistic concentration of the media in the hands of only a few would hinder the task of mediating the true discourse of a society which is more and more becoming a global society. The power of those who make their business with the anxieties of the fearful and the naiveté of the simple is an expression of their ultimate lack of faith and hope. Surely, the attitude of the Grand Inquisitor[33] is found not only in religious but also in secular form. The world cannot be redeemed from a central media office, even a religious one. But how can the redemption for which the media constantly raise a desire by their symbols, myths, and news be imagined?

2.3 Redemption as the creation of a new Communio in a not yet redeemed world

True redemption can only happen through a new beginning. And this new start humanity cannot give itself. A new creation is needed that, despite of the history of sin, establishes new Communio. In the history of Israel God is again and again revealed as the one who invites sinful human beings to a covenant by an often surprising divine initiative. In a unique and definite manner Communio comes true as God's intention in the creation and the history of humanity in Jesus Christ. The divine actions which create Communio cannot be missed in the history of humanity. God first addresses the people who are the carrier of the promise of a new covenant in order to collect and unite them, and then addresses everyone with the message of the Kingdom of Heaven, for God's plan is universal. God fights against the separation and division by which people are excluded; by offering a new relationship God cures the sick whose means of communication, namely ears, eyes, and voice, were destroyed. God wins the heart of people who suffer from inner raggedness and disintegration, from disturbance of their inner Communio. "For by His Incarnation the Son of God has united Himself in some fashion with every man."[34] Jesus Christ is the highest possible incarnation of the Father's love who follows the sinner to the last place of this world. At the same time, as brother of all humans the Christ shows how their lives can be fulfilled in total confidence in their Father and in unrestricted love for their fellow creatures. He proved to be "Master of

---

[32] See *Communio et progressio* no. 21.

[33] See F. Dostoevsky, *The Brothers Karamazov*.

[34] *Gaudium et spes* no 22.

Communication."[35] Where relationships are newly created something has to happen on both sides. This also holds true for the new creation where the offered relation has to be accepted and realized on the side of humanity as well. The evil of sin must be totally overcome with the help of human beings. This becomes nowhere more obvious than on the cross where Jesus Christ as a representative of all humanity transforms evil and all suffering into love. In history this permanently marks how the power of sin can be overcome: in a radical engagement for truth, justice, and love which does not shrink back from resulting conflicts. The cross is not only the outer revelation of God's love but also the highest opportunity for the expiatory co-operation of humanity, represented by Jesus Christ.[36]

A pictorial representation of the fact that the Holy Spirit (the Communio between Father and Son in person) is poured out into the world as the foundation of the new Communio between God and humanity is the opening of Jesus' side on the cross (see John 19:34). "In the Holy Spirit the relation between Father and Son is opened to us as well; mankind is somehow re-united, i.e., enabled to final community with God and to a life in mutual peace, justice, and love."[37] This Spirit corresponds both to the deepest human desire and to humanity's vocation. It enables human persons, from within as it were, to participate in community in a new way, and makes them truly a new creation. Thomas Aquinas does not understand redemption as an extrinsic ethic appeal, but as a gift in which the divine Communio itself, the Holy Spirit as an inner authorization, enables the human being to a new practice suitable to God in the middle of a history marked by sin.[38]

Indeed, as long as humans live in the finite world God's love can reach them only symbolically and through human mediation. To the eyes of faith the concrete humanity of Jesus is carried by the infinite capacity of the love of the Son of God himself. His human existence, though limited to a certain point of history, is constituted by the relationship to absolutely all humans and to the whole creation (see Colossians 1:14). He lets himself be affected by all pleasures and misery, of all success and guilt and hopes of humanity and lets himself be hurt by all evil which has ever been and still is performed in this history.

Mass-mediated processes cannot establish such a belief—not even by religious broadcasting satellites reaching the whole world—and cannot re-place the passing on of faith through personal relations, but they must measure themselves by whether they are transparent enough and still open to such a vision. Otherwise media would not only undermine their task of communica-

---

[35] *Communio et Progressio* no. 11.

[36] See G. Greshake, *Erlöst in einer unerlösten Welt* 85-94.

[37] Ibid. 104.

[38] See T. Aquinas, *Summa Theologiae* I-II, 106-08.

tion and in the long run disappoint their audience by replacing the true vision with a false one; they would even destroy the Communio.

2.4 The Church as a sign of intimate union with God and the unity of all humankind[39]

Redemption presses toward realization in the middle of human weakness. Therefore, the community of believers can comprehend itself as the first gift of redemption. It must, however, understand itself at the same time as only an imperfect sign of the redemption effected by Christ. Christ is the light of the world and not the church itself, although He wants to be reflected in the face of his church.[40] The church is not the Kingdom of Heaven, even if in it Jesus's word of the Kingdom of Heaven as well as the intensive sign of this Kingdom is effectively passed on in the Eucharist. The church is not identical with the Holy Spirit, even if this Spirit of Communio is its order. Nowhere, therefore, are totalitarian features and movements and a connected centralism as contradictory as in the church, for they oppose the basic mandate of the church to realize the redeeming Communio given by Jesus.[41]

Despite all dreadful evil that has been, is, and will be done by the faithful and also by official members of the church in the course of history, saints and great spiritual characters especially exemplify that the church is carried by the final word of God and His Promise. In the train of the Second Vatican Council the term "Communio-Ecclesiology" has been given priority as a theological term of orientation. This has consequences for the relationship of the church to communication processes in our global society, which so far are by no means realized on the part of the church. This failure on the part of the church makes us painfully aware of the discrepancy between the actual practice of the church and the challenges put to the church of Jesus Christ in a mass-mediated culture. "The normal flow of life and the smooth functioning of government within the Church require a steady two-way flow of information between the ecclesiastical authorities at all levels and the faithful as individuals and as organized groups."[42] The spiritual values expressed in the church make it necessary, however, that information about its intentions and about all of its actions be given with a maximum of completeness, truthfulness, and openness. If religious offices are not capable of informing or if they deliberately hold back news, they throw the door open to harmful rumors instead of bringing to light the

---

[39] *Lumen Gentium* no. 1: "By her relationship with Christ, the Church is a kind of sacrament or sign of intimate union with God, and of the unity of all mankind."

[40] Ibid.

[41] H. U. von Balthasar, "Integralismus heute," *Diakonia* 19 (1988) 221-229.

[42] *Communio et progressio* no. 120.

truth.[43] Media may and shall take religious functionaries at their word, even when it deals with such concrete matters as finances or conflicts between groups holding different opinions. To leave out such domains would be a Gnostic separation of spirit and matter and deeply unchristian. The struggle for the realization of a "Communio-Ecclesiology" leads to conflicts in the church itself, which can only be settled in a fair and honest way if there is the needed transparency and if every appearance of secret societies in the church is avoided. Not only a mass-mediated culture, but also the church itself needs renewed and increased efforts for the discernment of spirits as a contribution to a culture of dialogue.

3. The discernment of spirits in a mass-mediated culture

According to the New Testament the discernment of spirits was an important gift in the confrontation of the faithful with the heathen culture whose ambivalences had consequences for the parishes living right in the world (see 1 Corinthians 12:10; 1 John 4:1 and 6). This gift of the Holy Spirit had an effect on the spiritual arts throughout the centuries. The great masters of spiritual life more than theologians attended to this charism whose tradition has not yet sufficiently been investigated.

Today the discernment of spirits is essential considering the ambiguities of a mass-mediated culture which poses great opportunities for good as well as serious dangers. This gift is also necessary considering the wealth of opportunities for media consumption which are still expected to increase due to modern technologies. In a mass-mediated culture the individual who can choose among over 50 television channels, order pay-TV, or become independent from the general scheme of programming by videotapes, is even more in need of being able to choose wisely than in former times.

General ethical norms, which sufficiently describe specific actions and then qualify them in terms of the difference of morally right or wrong, do not suffice to regulate all of these many unsurveyable situations of choice. General principles, however, are too broad. The contents of a virtue ethic can best be mediated through images of conduct. But if virtue is defined as the free determination to act right morally in a certain field of action, then such an approach refers back to the question of what is morally right, i.e., back to the logic of norms. Even narrative ethics, as important as its task of mediation may be, does not solve the problem but shifts it; for after the narration the question of the clarity of the spirit that teaches how to part the humane from the inhumane arises anew. What is needed in a mass mediated culture in which more people than ever want to be able to follow the chain of moral reasoning themselves is a middle level of abstraction between general principles and concrete norms. The language most suitable for that

---

[43] Ibid. no. 121.

might be a language formulating criteria and rules of priority which will help moral decisions be made in situations of conflict and upon which norms can be well-founded.[44]

Christian ethics has no other criteria for moral actions than reasonable ones. Christian existence that lives from the gifts of the Holy Spirit, however, has a faith instinct by the help of which integral complex decisions can be made in a highly personal and unique way according to God's will and in the direction of a more intensive Communio. In the domain of an autonomy ethic the courage to act unconventionally but still morally right was known to the great occidental tradition as the virtue of *epikeia*.[45] Such a confidence in the immediate and direct influence of the Holy Spirit in the conscience of the faithful enables one to swim against the current where necessary and thereby contributes a genuine innovation. The Holy Spirit that renews everything has consequences in the ethical field as an imaginative power of conscience.[46] By definition this instinctive awareness of how much the Holy Spirit is effective in a mass-mediated culture resists empirical evaluation. In the following, therefore, my point is to mention some spheres in which the faith instinct reaches further than reasonably surveyable criteriology.

If the Spirit of God has inspired the Holy Scriptures in a unique manner, then surely the most important criterion is whether media processes accord with, or are at least open to, the texts of the Bible. This holds especially true for the parables, those paradoxical narratives told by Jesus which originally encourage the listener to finish the story.[47] In this connection we would especially have to pay attention to the parable structure of many media products. Much the same holds true for modern media myths, which like the ancient myths present representative culture figures. What is needed is a discernment of the degree of authenticity or non-authenticity of these representatives and of their openness to the life concept of Jesus. Considering the number of symbols used in the media, one first must revitalize the human capacity to understand symbols and then attend to what is done with the desires raised by symbols. Are these symbols quickly or directly connected with immanent wishes of consumption? Do symbols unfold larger horizons of meaning and ask for deeper reflections and medita-

---

[44] See G. Virt, "Ethische Normierung im Bereich der Medien," in *Handbuch des christlicher Ethik* Bd. 3, ed. A. Herz and D. Korff (Freiburg-Basel-Wien: Herder, 1982) 546-56.

[45] Günter Virt, *Epikie, Verantwortlicher Umgang mit Normen. Eine historisch-systematische Untersuchung* (Mainz: Grünewald, 1983).

[46] R. Guth, *Das Prinzip Phantasie, Ein Gespräch zwischen theologischer Ethik und Literaturwissenschaft* (Wien: Verband der wissenschaftlichen Gesellschaften Österreichs, 1987).

[47] On the language structure of Jesus's parables see E. Biser, *Die Gleichnisse Jesu* (München: Kösel, 1965).

tion? What is the relationship between the media's symbols and the church's symbols of salvation?

Another very important point is the challenge of truthfulness. Particularly significant in this respect is the autonomy of the media, which has the task of mediating the discourse of society, not dogmatically preaching eternal truths. A demythologization of the media is necessary if our expectations of the media are not to be inappropriate and unrealistic.[48]

A particularly sensitive area is the media's presentation of the negative in its pre-moral shape of evil and in its moral shape of personal guilt and sin.[49] The Holy Spirit of Judgment is active wherever evil is revealed. Of course, this Spirit is identical with the one granted to the disciples to forgive sins and to reconcile. The evil in society, state, and church is meant to be revealed through the media. The discernment of spirits will lie in the way evil is revealed and whether this revelation remains open for reconciliation. It is a characteristic of the media to prefer negative reports. This might give the impression that evil is ultimately victorious. Discernment through the Spirit of Truth, therefore, also means to take care that negative reports are not granted such a privileged position that the public is given the impression that all that works out well is of no importance. The Gospel of the Kingdom of Heaven is the message of a God who takes evil seriously but is determined nonetheless to save the whole world. This is the criterion against which mass-mediated culture must measure itself.

The mass-mediated culture for the first time offers humans the possibility of global participation in the sorrows as well as the values of various cultures. Thereby, the truth about the humane enters our consciousness more colorfully and diversely.[50] The challenges for world-wide solidarity have probably never been as great as today.[51] In this connection the discernment of spirits implies a vigilance on our part, lest our increased awareness of humanity's immense sorrows serve only either to desensitize us or to motivate us for violent short-term actions. The media's task of increasing our awareness of the plight of humanity will succeed only if it is simultaneously realized that our response to suffering is not a perfect solution which establishes heaven on earth. Nevertheless, signs of solidarity are only signs of true humanity if donations are not quick appeasements of conscience but the expression of an increasingly deep consciousness of how we are all involved in the structures of evil in this world. All members of a prosperous country who are informed of the inexpressible afflictions and miseries of

---

[48] Jürgen Habermas, *The Theory of Communicative Action*, 2 vols. (Boston: Beacon Press, 1984 and 1987).

[49] See P. Rossi, Chapter 20, below.

[50] Ibid.

[51] See J. Pollock, Chapter 21 below.

people in poor countries should know that they themselves are also involved and responsible in a larger connection.

Finally, there is a danger of mass-mediated culture that is often difficult to grasp, namely conservatism and mediocrity.[52] Given an abundance of information people tend to perceive only things that confirm their own opinions in order to preserve the status quo. Surely, in a mass-mediated culture we are to some extent always confronted with extremes. The majority of people, however, will tend to mediocrity, whatever the danger of mediocrity might bring about. A mass-mediated culture can also serve and advance centralism in state and church. Such a mass-mediated culture would contradict the spirit of Him who says of Himself in the last chapter of the Bible, "Behold, I make all things new" (Revelation 21:5).

These remarks are in no way complete. They are intended only to stimulate the imagination of conscience for the discernment of spirits and free us from the ultimate fear to venture on mass-mediated culture because of its ambivalences. The nature of sin is not shortcomings in communication but the refusal of Communio. "The People of God walk in history. As they, who are essentially both communicators and recipients, advance with their times, they look forward with confidence and even with enthusiasm to whatever the development of communications in a space-age may have to offer."[53]

---

[52] See T. Shanks, Chapter 4, above and M. Real, Chapter 2, above.

[53] *Communio et progressio* no. 187.

2

The Development of
Moral Reasoning
as Situated in the Mass Media

6

The Formation of Moral Life in a Mass-mediated Culture

Paul J. Philibert, O.P.

This paper is about three topics. The first will be about "mind," the second about "autonomy," and the third about "moral context." My conviction is that we cannot afford to let television create its own moral context. My arguments will include the suggestion that unless we have a moral context within which to receive the media phenomena, those phenomena will somehow generate an implicit moral context of their own. It is imperative for us therefore to create a moral context that can provide a coherent vision of the fitting role of the media, especially television, within our culture.

Before venturing to provide an outline of such a vision, we must first understand the model of rationality most operative in our present culture. A critique of this model and of its implications for understanding the concepts of "truth" and "autonomy" will make apparent the need for an alternative model, one more capable of providing the moral context and vision we seek.

1. The Question of Mind

1.1 Pre-Cartesian and Cartesian Theories of Mind

Let me begin by talking about "mind." There is a story about the painter, Picasso, when he was an old man living in Paris. Coming home one day to his apartment, he found a thief there. As soon as the thief saw Picasso, he disappeared through the window and got away. Picasso was very upset and called the police. When they arrived, they asked all sorts of questions. Picasso tried to describe the thief, but failed to satisfy the curiosity of the police inspector. Finally the inspector said, "Well, Monsieur Picasso, you are a very famous artist. Would you draw us a picture of the thief?" So Picasso did that, the inspector made xerox copies of the drawing, and police throughout Paris received copies of Picasso's picture of the thief.

The next day they apprehended a very elderly woman, a horse, and a mailbox. Naturally, when Picasso was brought in to see if any of them were the man he saw in his apartment, he said, "Well, let me see the drawing...!"

Perhaps the questionable status of draftsmanship in contemporary art is a parallel to the philosophical disorder in approaching the question of mind. Contemporary Western thought uses "reason" to refer to the directive and reflective functioning of self-conscious persons. When we know, we imagine ourselves knowing our own thought. As with Descartes' "I think therefore I am," our primary referent is the "constituting" dynamic that makes the object of our attention real for us. We constitute the real; we think.

Idealist philosophy has always been haunted by the troubling unreality of the undiscovered tree hidden deep in the shadows of an inaccessible forest. In our modern ethos, the psychological has primacy over the ontological: We give more importance to our own act of thinking than to the "thereness" of the object that our thinking turns toward. So the verification of the reality of the real within such a psychological ethos depends upon our human intervention. There is for us no longer a "nature" antecedent to human interest in the object.

Reason in this case can be described as instrumental rationality. Reason is a tool for human action, providing information about the raw materials of action upon the surrounding world, sifting through the alternative options that the material world presents, and finally coming to decision concerning human manipulation of objects or persons. American management philosophy assumes that instrumental rationality defines the nature of responsible behavior because it constitutes the meaning of objects in the world through creative appraisal of their utility for human manipulation. The extraordinary technological capacities of our culture lend credence to such a theory. In fact we often do just what an instrumental theory of reason implies, namely, invent and produce what we imagine to be possible.

The inadequacy of such a vision becomes apparent when we try to apply this meaning of mind to such different moments of cognition as a prayer of radical detachment, or self investment in the Christian mystery through liturgical rites, or selfless obedience to the gospel in humble service. We are forced by quite a number of common instances of the ecstatic mind to find a deeper explanation of the fundamental meaning of mind or reason.

There is a world of difference between our word "reason" and the Greek word "nous" and its derivatives. The Greeks were pre-Cartesians; we are all post-Cartesians. Like Descartes, we say, "I think therefore I am." That is, thinking is an activity I engage in and there must be an "I" to engage in it. The Greeks would say, "I think therefore there is that which I think." What I think is something going on in my head, according to current accounts. Yet what the Greeks think are objects of thought that exist in a world more real than the world of passing reflection. "Nous," the Greek word for mind or intellect, is more a capacity for participation in the reality of another, an organ of mystical union, than it is a cognitive power for symbolic manipulation.

The point of raising this issue of semantics is that Christian theology was born in a pre-Cartesian world. As the First Letter of John affirms, when the moment of eternal transformation arrives, we shall be like God because we shall see God as God really is.[1] This text conveys the sense of the relation between seeing (or knowing) and being transformed into the likeness of that which is seen (or known). Although uncongenial to conventional notions of reason today, "nous" represents a human phenomenon which deepens and grows in contemplative withdrawal, silence, and loving surrender.

Medieval moral philosophers like Aquinas translated the Greek term "nous" into the Latin term "intellectio" or intelligence. This term presupposed the "thereness" of that which is known. Intelligence was imagined by Aquinas as mind's becoming the thing known through the passive potentiality of the mind. Intelligence is molded to the perceptions presented by the senses.[2]

Repeated study leads to more adequate perceptions, which lead to deeper intelligence. Indeed Aquinas remarks that intelligence is derived from the Latin roots "intus" (within) and "legere" (to read).[3] Intelligence occurs when the mind succeeds at penetrating to the essence of the ontological truth of its object.

Such is the Greek epistemological alternative to instrumental rationality. We now turn to the contemporary psychological study of mind for a more recent articulation of reason, truth, and autonomy, one which, like its Greek counterpart, views mind or reason as the organ by which we have contact with a reality greater than ourselves and toward which the appropriate attitude is not manipulation and utility but participation and relation. As such it has more potential for accounting for the importance of genuine, serious public discourse and responsible, communal construction of our social world.

---

[1] 1 John 3:2. For a summary statement concerning "nous" and the Greek idea of mind, see Andrew Louth, *The Origins of the Christian Mystical Tradition* (Oxford: Clarendon Press, 1981), especially the introduction.

[2] See Anthony Kenny, "Intellect and Imagination in Aquinas," in *Aquinas: A Collection of Critical Essays* (Notre Dame: University of Notre Dame Press, 1976).

[3] See Paul Durbin, *Summa Theologiae*, Vol. 12 (New York: McGraw-Hill, 1968), 41: la, 84, 7: "The proper object of the human intellect..., since it is joined to a body, is a nature or 'whatness' found in corporeal matter—the intellect, in fact, rises to the limited knowledge it has of invisible things by way of the nature of visible things."

1.2 Piaget's Stages of Logical Development

Swiss psychologist Jean Piaget is celebrated as the theorist of stages of development in logical thought and as a typical exponent of constructivism in epistemology. His stages are meant to explain the normal way in which any adult gradually takes the sequence of steps that lead to logical thinking. These stages of logical development, discovered by Piaget, are among the most commonly accepted constructs in the psychological study of mind.

Beginning with the cognitive life of the infant, Piaget interprets human cognition as gradually unfolding throughout several periods which contribute to a sequentially evolving structure of formal logic. Piaget's first structure is called sensory motor cognition.[4] This is the knowing of the infant before language who learns the coordination of the body and its organs and muscles. Prerequisite to the vocalization needed for language, this sensory motor learning also leads the child to the mobility needed to explore independently the surrounding world.

Later preoperational cognition is marked by the early use of language by the child of three or four. This period lacks logical understanding but nonetheless provides the child with the capacity to represent objects symbolically with words as well as the capacity to include the self in social exchanges through language. This intuitive or preoperational cognition is filled with fantasy, and some authors suggest that it is at this period that children program their imagination with images that represent a safe and normal world of familiar objects and reassuring persons.[5]

The beginning of logic is called concrete operational thought.[6] Here language is used with an understanding of reversibility, such as that expressed in simple mathematical exchanges. Children can understand the relation of parts to wholes, but only within the framework of their immediately available world of concrete experience. Typically primary education begins at this period, since now children can invest what they learn by rote memory with basic understandings: sums, spelling, facts about the social world of history and geography, and the typical lore and ritual of the culture. This is a period that is tremendously powerful in forming the child's sense of the parameters of the real. (Recent generations of children are the first in history to have grown up through this period under a constant bombardment of media stimuli—where attitudes and values are so often indistinguishable from visual or textual content.)

---

[4] See Jean Piaget, *Six Psychological Studies*, trans. David Elkind (New York: Vintage Books, 1968), introduction and Ch. 1.

[5] See John L. Phillips, *The Origin of Intellect: Piaget's Theory* (San Francisco: W. H. Freeman & Co., 1969) 54-67.

[6] Ibid. 67-90; Jean Piaget, *Six Psychological Studies* 77-98.

The final period for Piaget is called formal operational thinking.[7] At this period the adolescent is able to think about thinking, to entertain "what if?" ideas, and to explore contrary to fact possibilities on the basis of mental fascination with what they have come to know in their concrete experience. Piaget went no further with his stage theory of logical development since he was convinced that all further logical development is an enhancement of the potential of these four stages.

Current research and theory are fascinated with the implications of adult cognitive penetration of sensory motor and preoperational (or intuitive) skills, which will therefore also contribute to more adequate formal thinking as a result.[8] The ability to take a critical stance toward the input of the media and other cultural influences is founded upon the development of the kind of formal thinking described in this last period of Piaget's stages.

In my view, these stages of Piaget's present a picture of human cognitional development congenial to a theory of mind that is broader than instrumental rationality. Piaget's researches underline the essential and enduring role of sensory cognition and imaginative fantasy as mediations of formal thinking. There is never a moment in formal thinking in which you are not at the same time depending upon the lower structures. Although Piaget never used the term "abstraction" (dear to medieval Aristotelian philosophers), nonetheless one can see the abstracted quality of formal thinking relative to the sensory concreteness of intuitive fantasy, sensory connectedness, or sensory motor operations.

Piaget's formal thinking is not thinking that comes out of nowhere—pure cognitive creativity out of the blue; it is rather an increasingly able capacity to delve into the implications of knowledge about objects as related to the self, to others, and to other objects. This growing ability is rooted in Piaget's conviction that human knowing is always expressing a compensatory dynamic which he names "equilibration." This is an awkward term which Piaget coined to express that each new act of knowing renders the knower more apt to get to the bottom of the puzzle, to get at what is real.[9]

Using terminology idiomatically his own, Piaget called the knowing of the prelogical child "centered thinking"—just the opposite of what our characteristic language would do. Centered thinking is thinking that makes the

---

[7] Herbert Ginsburg and Sylvia Opper, *Piaget's Theory of Intellectual Development: An Introduction* (Englewood Cliffs, N.J.: Prentice Hall, 1969) 181ff.; Phillips, *The Origin of Intellect: Piaget's Theory* 93-104.

[8] See, e.g., Robert Kegan, *The Evolving Self: Problem and Process in Human Development* (Cambridge: Harvard, 1982) 225ff. Also, Carol Gilligan and J. M. Murphy, "Development from Adolescence to Adulthood" in *Intellectual Development Beyond Childhood* ed. D. Kuhn (San Francisco: Jossey-Bass, 1979).

[9] Jean Piaget, *Six Psychological Studies* 100-114. See Hans G. Furth, *Piaget and Knowledge* 2nd. edition (Chicago: University of Chicago Press, 1981), Ch. 12: "Equilibration and Development."

child's limited experience its own frame of reference. The child is centered on the child's own way of looking at things. Piaget also referred to this as moral materialism.[10] Centered thinking is due to the child's limited experience and to the relative incapacity to synthesize or integrate fragments of knowledge into a structured whole.

By contrast, children's growing success at integrating their larger and larger experience of the world is called "decentering." Children begin to take a wider frame of reference through education, through exposure to new cultural phenomena, and through their growing native capacity to see the implications that one bit of learning will have consequences for knowing other realities. They decenter in the sense that they take themselves less and less as the center of experience and of reality, and perceive the relationship of what they know to the world around them.

This leads to increasingly adequate intelligence about the way things are. The argument that mind is something broader than instrumental rationality can be seen as germane to Piaget's insistence that "reason" is rooted in a relatedness through sense to concrete interaction with the world. Perhaps more than anything else Piaget was an interactionist. He was convinced that there is a constant back and forth experience of interaction with the world.

This perspective is helpful for us because it suggests that we lose something when we enter a world structured uniquely in terms of instrumental rationality. The Greek idea of mind or "nous" understands a participation of the self in a reality bigger than ourselves, whereas instrumental rationality supposes that there is no objective reality beyond our own manipulation of the material world around us. We lose our bearing on the cosmos and (as religious people) our bearing on God's purpose for the world when we make ourselves the epistemological source of the real within an instrumental theory of rationality.

On the other hand, a theory of abstraction tells us that our on-going capacity to abstract from the reality of the world around us (i.e., to encircle a specified frame of interest and really be in touch with it) gives us only a slice of the real, but still genuine communion with the real. We must maintain a recognition of the modesty of our knowing, but at the same time reverence the authenticity of our contact with reality. Without such a realist epistemology, the concept of "truth" becomes very troublesome.

1.3 The Notion of Truth

The notion of "truth" looks very different from the two perspectives. For instrumental rationality, truth is what works. The verification of the true is the pragmatic output of the researcher or experimental scientist. This

---

[10] Jean Piaget, *The Moral Judgment of the Child* trans. Marjorie Gabain (New York: The Free Press, 1965), Ch. 2: "Adult Constraint and Moral Realism." See Ginsburg and Opper, *Piaget's Theory of Intellectual Development: An Introduction* 99-100.

position remains skeptical about the possibilities for having other than a relative truth. Something of the dignity of the created world is lost when its truth—its relatedness to a transcendent source—is dismissed as an irrelevant or meaningless speculation.

The Greek theory of mind had a much more exalted notion of truth. The Greek word, used by Plato, *aletheia*, means the taking away of a veil.[11] Truth is the unveiling of the real that we take for granted. We take the real for granted not just because of the accounts of our philosophical and religious traditions, but more importantly because of our rootedness in the cosmos. One possible reading of that rootedness is the Piagetian one: No abstract thought is unconnected to sensory and social experience. Truth deals with what is, what is available, but also with what is the haunting hunger of our always creative imaginations.

So it is important in assessing the significance of the media to realize that our understanding of the status of reality as it is negotiated by the media is crucial. I would argue that the status of reality as presented by the media is a notion of reality and truth manipulated by instrumental rationality. We are only sometimes (seldom) invited into concern for *aletheia*—usually in programs carried by Public Broadcasting where, even there, one finds a distant, critical perspective upon the aesthetic, religious, and cultural history of contemporary peoples. Equally important, institutions in our society whose responsibility is the tradition of *aletheia*—the tradition of unveiling or unmasking the hidden depths of life's meaning—such as the churches and the universities, are often coopted by the prevailing media climate into superficial responses to the flow of contemporary life.

2. Autonomy

My second argument is about the notion of autonomy. In a pluralistic world of adults coming from different cultural traditions, we imagine ourselves free, responsible for ourselves, and endowed with the capacity to make meaningful choices on our own. The goal of being an autonomous adult in an adult culture is to form persons who can take care of themselves. Our whole *laissez-faire* economic philosophy is founded upon such a notion of autonomy.

Autonomy is a much used word today and we all presumably understand it. The central notion of autonomy is that the autonomous person's actions become self-generated, or appropriated, or owned by the self—tailored to the self's unique situation. When we say that persons are autonomous we mean that they move themselves to do voluntarily that which they themselves have found meaningful to do. They choose for themselves.

---

[11] See Louth, *The Origins of the Christian Mystical Tradition* 1-17.

A critical look at the term "autonomy" in the literature of psychology, however, shows it to be something very different. There is a startling diversity in the meanings assigned to the term by three authors who have worked with autonomy as a central concept: Erikson, Piaget, and Kohlberg. For Erik Erikson, autonomy arrives when the child learns the minimal physical self-control represented by successful toilet training. This is linked to the child's ability to walk, to explore the world, to reduce somewhat its dependency on nurturing parents and to become something other than an automaton. The child is no longer the morally insignificant automaton picked up and put here and there by parents, but begins to become autonomous.[12] Thus autonomy for Erikson focuses upon the early inception of an interior self-determination by the small child and its foundations in such rudimentary dimensions of self-control as muscular development.

By contrast with Erikson, Piaget places the dawning of autonomy somewhere around seven or eight years old. The child who has been in a certain sense constrained to enter socially profitable modes of interaction with adults begins to understand what these modes of interaction are all about and begins to appropriate them.[13] It is instructive to observe that Piaget understands the development of peer cooperative behavior to be the seed or germ of the development of autonomy. When peers, i.e., persons of equal moral status, cooperate, they create a new moral environment based not on constraint, but on shared energies. This moral synergy is at the very heart of autonomy for Piaget. Children begin to experience this in childhood play, where they escape from adult constraints as companions on a shared journey to spontaneous, original meanings.

Finally, Lawrence Kohlberg (whose six stages of moral reasoning achieved wide attention before his tragic death a few years ago) always had the tendency to assign his understanding of autonomy to an adult (post-conventional) posture. Kohlberg saw autonomy as the attitude of a rational, critical mind standing somehow over against social conventions. The autonomous individual, therefore, would take some distance from the conventions of the social order and utter conscientious *sed contras*, personally conceived moral judgments. Such a person, then, knows what the social order wants, but under these circumstances judges that something else is more reasonable.[14]

Of these three approaches to the notion of autonomy, Piaget's is the most useful, since it is tied to a dynamic theory of the transformation of moral vision through relational development. Piaget's two terms—"heteronomy" and "autonomy"—have been normative in all consequent work in

---

[12] Erik H. Erikson, *Identity: Youth and Crisis* (New York: Norton, 1968) esp. 107-114.

[13] Jean Piaget, *The Moral Judgment of the Child* 70-71 and 341-342.

[14] Lawrence Kohlberg, *Essays on Moral Development.* Vol. I: *The Philosophy of Moral Development* (San Francisco: Harper & Row, 1981).

childhood and moral development. These terms, dear to the heart of any student of Immanuel Kant, are related directly to two forms of relation. In heteronomy there is an authoritarian relation. Piaget calls it also a unilateral relation: Someone is one up; the rest of us are one down. We are not peers; we do not cooperate. Rather we acquiesce to the person who calls the shots. The very meaning of heteronomy is structured so that the sense of morality is based upon inequality. We all start life as children in a posture of heteronomy, for we all have to be directed through nurture, language acquisition, and socialization.

We all start off dependent and gradually move into a more and more cooperative posture. None of us ever leaves the condition of heteronomy altogether, because throughout life we are in various ways dependent upon the expertise of specialists with whom we cannot stand as peers in the area of their expertise. If you are not a brain surgeon and you need brain surgery, you are going to be heteronomous vis-a-vis that particular expertise. You are not going to tell the brain surgeon how to perform your operation. We willingly depend upon our experts in this complicated society.

Autonomy is directly related to a different form of relation, namely, peer or mutual relations. In this bilateral or peer relation of mutual support, one begins to "co-construct" a mutually satisfying world.[15] Using this Piagetian notion of autonomy, the term begins to take on characteristics that have implications for the quality of social world that one shares with others. Autonomy is no longer an asocial or individual trait, but more an ethos mutually created with peers and constructive of a framework which conditions the quality of moral discourse and interaction.

For Piaget then autonomy means collaboration in a spirit of generous mutual interest, whereas in Kohlberg's writings autonomy is always somehow suggestive of the isolated individual standing over against the community. In Piaget's sense, then, autonomy is community; it is cooperation.

In my view, Piaget's understanding of autonomy is helpful in analyzing the role of the media in our society. The tenor of this sense of autonomy is a respectful, cooperative, and mutually sensitive attitude that holds others' values in esteem and asks for reasonable respect for one's own values. The autonomous individual is self-determining not in isolation, but rather in dialogue with other points of view. The autonomous judgment is not the Olympian power of a separate, arbitrary outsider, but rather the socially sensitive co-construction of mutual benefit, arrived at through peer interaction. This sense of autonomy, demanding as it is, is more verifiable than other notions (say, Kohlberg's, for example) in that it implies that autonomous interaction produces a state of cooperation and concomitant mutual satisfaction.

---

[15] James Youniss, *Parents and Peers in Social Development: A Sullivan-Piaget Perspective* (Chicago: University of Chicago Press, 1980), esp. Ch. 1.

Other contributors to this volume have made it clear, however, that the *raison d'être* of the television industry as it exists in the U.S. today is for-profit merchandizing. The entertainment components of the industry are subsidiary to the networks' corporate money making. Advertising drives the industry. Capturing a mass audience's attention drives advertising. Consequently, the first principle of the television industry is to capture the audience—no matter how.

How might we deal with that?

One possibility is to imagine ourselves impotent before the enormous social machinery of the television industry in a morally heteronomous situation. To some degree we factually do remain in a heteronomous situation economically, in terms of access to the technological tools of the industry. But there is always the possibility that some form of autonomy can be created in the peer, mutual co-construction by people who will band together to address their value concerns to the industry.[16] It may be a mini-community, but it will be a community of autonomous discourse.

The fruitfulness of a notion of autonomy based upon peer relation and cooperation is that it offers a form of analysis that at least suggests possible approaches to remedy the present impossible predicament of people from traditional value communities in a mass-mediated society. As Thomas Lickona has repeatedly insisted, people from such communities need to find that one possibility for responding to the world of television is quite simply to say "no" to it. That would be saying "no" to a partner in discourse who will not take the stance of a peer, who will not extend respect to the traditional value community's interests, and who will not engage in a dialogue of mutual support. Other avenues that may prove more productive in the end would make their way along the difficult path of securing the technological means to become something of a peer in a television world. The Catholic Television Network of America and other similar religious media groups are moving toward the realization of this possibility. This is painfully difficult, since it entails competing in an increasingly expensive technological medium (television) without the backing of limitless financial means made available through advertising.

3. A Moral Context for the Media

My final point deals with the question of moral context. This is probably the most salient ethical question for both moral education and ethics in the media. A prudential weighing of what is fitting within a given context is at the very heart of discovering what is moral. What do we mean by

---

[16] This is, in fact, happening in the evangelical churches in this country. Religious viewers are going straight to advertisers and controlling the industry through the financial pressure that their boycott potentially represents.

moral action? We mean an action that upon reflection can be rationally identified as more prudent in weighing what is fitting within the social structures and the value principles of a community.

It is, therefore, important for a community to have an explicit repertory of principles against which to measure media phenomena. The general public in the U.S. has become so passive in the face of what television offers that the idea of insisting upon contextualizing principles may sound like madness. In my view, however, the madness is that we have allowed ourselves to be so easily manipulated by so powerful a force without programmatically analyzing its influence upon our foundational sense of what is moral.

We have, by and large, allowed the media culture itself to create its own context. I will argue against the rationality of accepting complacently such a situation for there clearly are principles that order the media culture, even if these principles are tacit and implicit. Before bringing Piaget's communal understanding of autonomy directly to bear upon the media culture, therefore, let me state plainly how I read the principles that order the media culture in the U.S.

The first principle is consumer manipulation: Generate artificial hunger for products in a profit-driven ethos. If, indeed, we receive the media phenomena within the context of the profit-driven ethos, we will find ourselves disabled. We will not be able to defend ourselves against the manipulation of our feelings and our fantasies. The consumer ethos strives to identify "whims" with "needs." The most humble products of simple convenience are sold in TV ads through identification with inane dramatic moments. Paper towels save a hostess embarrassment when the boss comes to dinner; a deodorant is the decisive factor in a romantic relationship. But this dramatic energy charges the commonplace with passion. Then passion itself becomes a quasi-moral principle. To exist for very long without passion is to know a certain kind of emptiness. The corruption of the natural human capacity to live a certain kind of emptiness named solitude productively may be one of the most negative contributions of the television ethos.

Another aspect of the media culture is its contentious tone: Presume the hypocrisy of any elevated value—especially religious values. Oddly, I think, we are still operating in a media climate in which there exists a presumption that we must dislodge smug complacency. That might have been an interesting function for the media in 1963 and 1968; but in the 1990s, it's odd. There is something offensively self-congratulatory about the newsroom stance of the networks when everyone, in every social role, is presumed vulnerable to the charge of hypocrisy. The networks have never been forced to try to articulate what their positive social vision and social principles are. Yet it is not hard to see that any statement of those principles would have to include an unhealthy zest for muck-raking.

In the entertainment sector, television implements the principle: Sexual titillation and sexual stimulation of the viewer engages attention and promotes continued viewing. So much of television entertainment, not just soap operas, indulges voyeurism, and in doing so corrupts young viewers to become habituated to such a stance. It is not sex that is wrong, but the trivialization of sex as entertainment. Rare indeed is the network program that renounces cheap sexual titillation as a plot energizer.

Television also appears to maintain the principle: Evoke superficial, sentimental solidarity with the underdog. Often this principle makes possible the trashing of obvious social values that are part of the legal structure of our governmental system. Robbers, thieves, adulterers, or fraudulent entrepreneurs are made to appear as victims of their unfortunate upbringing or circumstances and are portrayed by beautiful or handsome actors apt at conveying the pathos of a conflicted human situation. This attitude is hostile to critical thinking, not supportive of it. Television would often have us believe that the legitimacy of issues is far less important than the generation of emotional sympathy for troubled persons, whatever their values may be.

Finally, the media culture in the U.S. holds for a zero taboo ecology. We are asked to demystify each and every nonrational allegiance, to reduce every value to some uniformly simple, reasonable explanation. As we do that, we disempower our poetic vision as well as our religious ritual world. The term "taboo" connotes the powerfully felt symbolic limits that a society places upon its objects of reverence. Reverence for sacred ritual objects is an expression of taboo. Refusal to discuss certain things in polite conversation is another. Such symbolic limits help to define the context of our ritual exchange with God. Intuitions of conscience, mystical solitude, engagement with sacred ritual—these are privileged sources of religious experience, yet they are not privileged by the media. They are often the object of ridicule.

Piaget's insights into the nature of autonomy have much to offer us in our quest for the principles of a moral context for the media, particularly the alternative context which I would call principles of Christian humanism. I do not in the slightest way want to suggest that I am in a position to come up with an adequate statement of such principles. But I do want to call for a serious effort of concerned social participants to co-construct this principled agenda. If we choose to take an autonomous stance (in the Piagetian sense) before the manipulation of the media culture, then we will have to have a substantive dialogue that engages sympathetic viewpoints and that is aimed at generating principles that would promote analysis of present discontents and potential future remedies. The nature of the relation upon which autonomous morality is built will demand difficult but productive dialogue that will reinforce the relation of respect at the same time that it generates moral insight. That is the nature of "autonomy" properly understood.

Some traditional statements of principles representative of Christian humanism, however, would be clearly appropriate here. One of these is re-

spect for the integrity of material creation. We need to discover and acknowledge natural rhythms and natural needs and their relation to the least
favored of our society. This is directly opposed to the consumer manipulation that generates artificial hungers for products in a profit-driven ethos.
What is natural? How do we provide access for every participant in society? There is a huge literature on both of these questions. What are lacking
are not resources to explore these questions, but rather a recognition of the
relatedness of such questions as these to the moral context of the media.

Another positive principle of Christian humanism is critical realism:
Honor the sensitive balance of social wholes. Co-construct and celebrate
mutual commitments. Demand critical depth and get to the bottom of
things. Let's not be manipulated by the trivialization of issues that appears
normal for public discourse when public discourse is coopted by instrumental rationality. We must demand historical, philosophical, and wholistic approaches to the moral dilemmas of our times.

Finally, we also need a principle for on-going reappropriation of sacral
tradition. Here is where the argument for autonomy comes together with the
argument for moral context. At bottom, the base community of any value
tradition becomes responsible for the articulation of its principles and for the
implications of those principles in the lives of the members of the community. We must be able to articulate what we believe in. Do we know what
it is? If we do, we need to say it. And once we've said it, we need to
compare it or contrast it bravely to the world that surrounds us.

The issue of what we do about the media culture, especially about
television, is an urgent question. I agree with Michael Real and Elizabeth Willems that television offers us the potential to process information and to appropriate experience in ways that have phenomenal implications for our growth as a people and as individuals.[17] What we earlier called "decentering"—taking a society-focused perspective rather
than an egocentric one—is promoted by the cognitive stimulation and
breadth of experience that TV provides.

But if we are really going to grow into the autonomy that is a mutual
recommitment to the co-construction of our deepest values, then we have to
have some kind of standard with which to agree and to dialogue. We need
the articulation of a core set of truths (of the kind proposed by William
Sullivan[18]) that we can invest in. I am less optimistic than Sullivan about
our being able to do this out of our current understanding of American republican principles. I have lost hope in our being able to bring about the
renewal of values in the general culture in the short run on the basis of
present, established habits. I think our renewal will have to come out of
base communities.

---

[17] See Michael Real, Chapter 2, and Elizabeth Willems, Chapter 17.

[18] See William Sullivan, Chapter 3, above.

If we are able to build commitment to base communities (parishes, voluntary associations for self-help, economic cooperatives, etc.), we will be articulating the values that unite us as peers, we will be building agendas for meaningful interaction and thereby spelling out a fruitful vision of living in a new way. The base community concept (so congenial to our origins as a republic) makes possible the stance of an autonomous community that can hold its own against the manipulation of the media industries.

4. Conclusion

To talk of base community is to revisit in sociological form the quality of relation that underlies true moral autonomy. Autonomy can not authentically be represented simply as the power for influence of an individual in a competitive, capitalistic, for-profit economy. Human dignity demands better of us. In the Piagetian theory of logical and human development, there is the potential for understanding the essential foundation of adult morality in a relation of peer, mutual respect. We have seen at least the principal lines of development of such an argument.

What is so offensive about the ethos of the mass media is that it so often substitutes for mutual respect the gross emotional manipulation of the media audience. When they operates out of their own competitive context, the mass media (especially television) substitute aggressive promotion of artificially generated consumer values for peer dialogue (or for appeal to reasonable reflection). In a society created for the possibility for genuine autonomy, the media abuse social freedom and often restrict rather than extend moral sensibilities.

In the face of the unilateral domination of the extraordinary social means of communication in our vast communications culture by greedy networks, some form of "autonomous community of moral discourse" will have to be created in order to repossess a forum of genuine social communication. If it takes new structures of voluntary association—base communities—to achieve such a goal, so much the better for us and for our future as a people.

7

Matching the Inner World with Outer Reality: Moral Development Domains and the Role of the Media

Michael J. Garanzini, S.J.

This chapter attempts to explore both the positive and negative aspects of media as agents for helping develop the moral consciousness of children. A case study will be used to illustrate aspects of the developmental tasks of integrating the inner world and outer reality in the affective, perceptual, and cognitive domains related to moral development. Key theories in the psychology of moral development help to illustrate media's potential usefulness or harm. Because of the general bias in the literature focusing on the harmful effects of excessive exposure to violence, aggression, and sexually explicit materials in media, an emphasis on possible benefits will be stressed.

Our interpretation of the influence of television in the moral development of children has been shaped by our conviction that multiple transformations are always at issue. We are concerned with three aspects of moral transformation: perception, affect, and social cognition.

1. Three Domains of Individual Moral Development

Moral development is not a developmental process in children which is somehow unrelated to development in a variety of other areas. Physiological maturation, especially of the nervous system, affective, cognitive, and social development are all aspects of moral development and contribute to a child's growing appreciation of the ethical dimensions of the universe. The development of the capacity to reason about moral problems and come to ethical judgments involves capacities to perceive moral implications of a situation and to have an emotional investment in the outcome of human interaction, especially if those outcomes do not directly involve the perceiver. From a psychological perspective, the development of moral consciousness is especially concerned with the development of capacities to perceive, to feel, and to reason around moral situations.

No single theory of moral development has been able to explain satisfactorily the child's development in all key areas. Rather, psychodynamic psychologists have contributed insights to the domain of affective and emotional development as it relates to the moral sphere. Cognitive or structural developmentalists have outlined the process of moral reasoning and judgment. Social learning theorists have stressed the child's growing capacity to take on roles and to perceive the moral dimensions of a given situation.

1.1 Psychodynamic Psychologists and the Affective Domain of Moral Development

Psychoanalysts have traditionally stressed the intrapsychic world of the child. Conscience development is, in this school, the result of the child's introjecting parents' values and beliefs. If instinctual urges (to possess or take the place of one parent) are gratified, the child fears repercussions. This view sees the superego developing, for the most part, in the Oedipal phase, when the child is between three and four years old.

The development of an individual ego ideal is essential in this process as well, since it functions as a model for what is good. Freud's own view was that a child set up an ego ideal as "the substitute for the lost narcissism of his childhood in which he was his own ideal."[1]

Psychoanalytic theorists see the ego ideal as arising from three sources: from the idealization of the parents, stemming from the child's attribution of omnipotence to them; from the idealization of the child by the parents which the child erects from their approval and disapproval; and from the idealization of the self, which brings on feelings of well-being and self-satisfaction when living up to the ego ideal, but feeling shame and worthlessness when this goal is not achieved. Thus, the ego ideal functions as a guide to behavior; the child can turn against impulsive behavior in socially, personally, and morally acceptable ways.

More recently, object relations theorists, building on the strengths of the Freudian approach, have rejected the emphasis on the intrapsychic processes to the exclusion of interpsychic processes. The child is understood as embedded in relationships with important caregivers and motivated, not by desire for instinct gratification, but by a need to maintain affectional ties or bonds.[2]

---

[1] S. Freud, "The Ego and the Id," in *The Standard Edition of the Complete Psychological Works*, Vol. 19, ed. and trans. J. Strachey (London: Hogarth Press, 1961).

[2] J. Klein, *Our Need for Others and its Roots in Infancy* (London: Tavistock Press, 1987).

Emde for instance, in his review of the infant observation research, examined the earliest manifestations of moral development.[3] He traces the first two years of life to the rise of prosocial, cooperative behavior. The mother-infant bond that rules for communication and turn-taking is established. These early-functioning capacities for reciprocity are central to moral development. The control of aggressions (apparently more difficult for boys) in addition to comforting and caring behaviors begin at about 18 months in normal children.[4]

Good parenting—not too good nor over-intrusive and not too bad, that is, not too neglectful or punishing—motivates the child to internalize rules of conduct and become independent of adults who are not always capable of meeting the child's needs and wants.[5]

By ages four to seven, a triadic structure evolves in the child's parent relationship which replaces the previous dyadic bond. This initiates a new dimension of prosocial concerns. Thus, jealousy, envy, gratitude, and affective reactions to external environmental cues and situations force re-evaluation of motives for interpersonal behavior. Internal world and outer reality, the giving up of fantasies of omnipotence and egocentrism are brought into check.

How do media affect the growing moral development of the child on the affective plane? Tactics available to the child for managing frustration or stress are three: The child can take it out on someone else, can talk about it, or can develop a strategy for dealing with it in fantasy in order to master the circumstances. Beside providing useful information to the developing child in the four to seven age bracket, media can aid interpersonal and intrapersonal affective processes by offering opportunities to vent aggressive impulses, fears, and worries, by offering models of impulse control and by identifying feeling states and dramatizing their sources or counterparts in the real world.

Early fantasies (ages four to seven) often involve taking a parent's place while later fantasies will often involve mastery fantasies of social situations, whereby self-esteem is restored after some humiliation or setback, and passivity fantasies. In passivity fantasies children demonstrate their objection to parental influence and intrusions.[6] By imaginatively handling parents, a child can shift energy from more inward-turning fantasies toward those with a greater correspondence to the outer world, which is making more demands on the child. A punitive and harsh parental introject is

---

[3] R. N. Emde, "The Prerepresentational Self and its Affective Core," *Psychoanalytic Study of the Child* 38 (1983) 165-92.

[4] J. Kagan, *The Second Year: The Emergence of Self-awareness* (Cambridge, Ma.: Harvard University Press, 1981).

[5] D. W. Winnicott, *Deprivation and Delinquency* (London: Tavistock Press, 1984).

[6] C. Sarnoff, *Psychotherapeutic Strategies in the Latency Years* (New York: Jason Aronson, 1987).

paired off against a real parent, hopefully one who is kind and insightful. If the real parent is actually punitive and harsh, the child is overwhelmed by the threat of the real world and will retreat into less and less "productive" fantasy-making. A punitive and uncontrolled parent may leave the child without a model for handling impulses, while a punitive but self-disciplined parent may leave the child with stoicism and sternness.

In later latency, ages seven to 10, fantasies concerning sexual awakening and sexual identity, right and wrong in social interaction, and the birth process are typical. Parents who provide adequate modeling help the child deal with fantasy life and the opportunity to check these fantasies against the real world. Media offer representations of possible models and information regarding topics which inhabit the child's fantasy world. More important than the images they offer, however, is the availability of adults the child can compare with images of adulthood offered by media. But before going further, it may be helpful to discuss a case example.

1.2 The Case of Mario: Inner World, Outer Reality, and Media Images

Let me describe a client with whom I worked for over five years, from the time the child was nearly five until about his 10th birthday.

When I met Mario, he was beginning kindergarten in a Catholic grade school. His mother felt he was "spiritually gifted," as she put it, but that he also had a "difficult streak." That he was sometimes hard to manage and that she sometimes felt overwhelmed soon became the focus of the sessions between Mario's parents and myself. The sessions with Mario alone, however, revealed a complex child struggling to make sense of his mother's erratic behavior and mixed messages. After a very short time it became clear that the mother has a borderline personality. She functions fairly well most of the time, but under stress she will regress to more pathological forms of behavior. Her own inability to handle ambiguous feelings, to tolerate frustration, to manage cognitively and handle emotionally the complex situations often leads to unnecessarily harsh behavior, usually in the form of cruel verbal assaults on the child. When she becomes more calm and feels better about herself and her situation, she represses almost everything she said that might be termed abusive. In other words, Mario's mother is one who splits good and bad, and who "splits off," that is, denies that part of herself which she cannot tolerate: the cruel or bad mother, when such a "personality" has taken over.

For the greater part of a day or week, she is able to control herself, to feel adequate, and to enjoy mothering. The good mother is able to function as the caregiver she prefers to be. Her chief coping strategy is to somatize. She develops migraine headaches, colds, pre-menstrual syndrome, asthma, or whatever will relieve her of responsibility for her punitive or withdrawn attitude, which may run for periods lasting several hours to several days.

Mario is unable to accept his own less attractive feelings because he has introjected his mother, who has herself "split" them off and buried them in her unconscious. Both mother and son were excessively religious and pious. For a period of several years, Mario was able to win regular praise from his mother for his religious insights and mirror her own success at impulse control. Her own religiosity grew out of an intense hatred of her abusive, drug-dependent parents. Religion has kept her from "splitting apart." Piety kept Mario from being the object of her displeasure and allowed him to be the mirror of herself, the good mother.

Mario himself began to show evidence of minor forms of "splitting" behavior when in school. In the third grade he was caught stealing from a fellow student but denied he had taken anything that did not already belong to him. He had problems with peers, who found his piety uncomfortable and unusual for a child of their own age. He denied his own outbursts of anger. But a strong desire to fit in, to make and keep friends, and to win the affection of teachers have motivated Mario to attempt to master the internal world of his conflicting feelings—including both love and rage at his mother. Mario was also attempting to master desires to be indulged and also to be punished for disappointing her. His desire to master the demands of reality included the unpredictable world of his home, the autonomous world of his peers, and the more fair-minded world of the school.

Given the enormous need for genuine affection and care, for both coddling and for fairness, plus the desire to master appropriate tasks for a child his age, Mario was often left torn and bewildered. At times, Mario suffered intense depression. Such depression in a 10 year old is relatively unusual, but these bouts served as both a sign of the almost impossible task of making sense of inner world and outer reality, as well as an opportunity to retreat from the world of home and school in order to assess and grapple with issues and problems. They have allowed him the chance to indulge in self-pity over a home situation which he sometimes finds unmanageable and unpredictable. During an intense and nearly suicidal depressive episode following the birth of a second sibling, Mario was hospitalized. While in a child treatment unit, he vented enormous amounts of anger and pain but also reasserted his own independence from his mother and renewed his interest in academic activities and peer relationships.

This depressive episode led to a respite from his home and a chance to recoup some recent developmental losses. It also initiated a renewed investigation into the nature of his split world. Helping him tolerate his own ambiguous feelings about his mother and his "self," which she has damaged by her erratic parenting style, has been my goal for therapy with Mario, while other therapists have insisted his mother and father remain in family counseling.

Telling stories and the creation of works of art have been two effective therapeutic techniques in my work with Mario. Mario watches a great deal of television and he loves action movies, which his father rents for him. The way this child uses these media in his therapy offers us an opportunity to see how a child constructs and builds the needs and demands of his inner world in relation with outer reality. The cartoon character, Garfield, and films such as "Indiana Jones and the Temple of Doom" are his favorites. Art produced during the course of his therapy regularly reverted to images and scenes from either his favorite cartoon or a clash between forces of evil and good taken from a movie. Stories told in therapy and the line drawings he produced are actually projections of the inner world into an acceptable artistic form shared in the therapeutic setting, which Winnicott called "the safe and holding" environment.

For instance, during a period of intense conflict between Mario and his mother, he produced a description of a cartoon episode which he said was particularly entertaining. The character of Garfield, a lazy cat who talks slowly and dispassionately and has an air about him of being unaffected or unnerved when in crisis, occupied half the page. On the other half, Garfield is confronted by a large buxom woman dressed in Viking helmet and carrying a sharp spear. Garfield smiles wryly at the woman, who is commanding him to perform some slave-like task. What followed was an elaborate story of how the cat outwits her and escapes her wrath at the same time. Clearly the child was using a cartoon episode to work out his own wished for ability to outwit an intrusive mother. Power and autonomy are momentarily achieved to relieve this child of the burdens of his real world. Unfortunately, the selection of Garfield, a relatively passive character whose talents are used in the service of avoidance, mirrors Mario's own lack of initiative and industry.

During another period, when he was particularly worried about getting along at school, Mario produced a story designed around a Peanuts episode he had seen on television prior to his weekly visit. In the Peanuts episode, Lucy wants to exclude Charlie Brown from playing baseball because his abilities are so poor that they will only cause the team to lose. Charlie accepts her accusations gracefully but insists he can help out in the outfield, where he will be less likely to harm the team's efforts. The actual outcome of the story was not a concern of Mario in our conversation because he used the plot to examine his own situation. He explained how he would attempt to convince his fellow-students that there must be a place for everyone, no matter how poorly coordinated or distractible. The story offered him hope by hinting at solutions. In the Garfield episode, the unconscious affective life with mother was being worked out, while in the Peanuts story, a more conscious effort at problem-solving was being examined. The significance for Mario's moral development can be inferred. In order to acquire an autonomous morality he needs to individuate from his mother, which is something therapy and his own fantasy life are working to accomplish. In addition, lessons in cooperation, in accepting limitations (Mario is not a well-coordinated boy), and an abandonment of a strategy of revenge and retaliation are important moral tasks learned with the help of Peanuts characters. This second example is related more directly to aspects of perceptual and cognitive development to which we now turn.

2. Media and the Domains of Moral Development

2.1 Media and the Perceptual Domain of Moral Development

How the child is able to use media, especially the entertainment media, to work through struggles and conflicts experienced on the inside and outside becomes evident in the artistic productions they triggered. But media also bring a world which Mario has not met, a world of ideas, people, and affective experiences not necessarily part of his world—inner or outer. Despite his home life and despite what his parents and school are teaching him, Mario is taking in certain messages about the way the world beyond home and school operates. He is introduced to a variety of cultures, dilemmas, and motives he could not have imagined in his Hispanic home and inner city Catholic school.

The stories he sees and the dilemmas he watches played out in hundreds of scripts sometimes relieve him of his unpleasant world but at times play into his rather harsh experience of reality. This further sours his perceptions and frightens him. Their messages, both implied and explicit, in morals and dramatic conclusions, have filled him with the following beliefs—all themes taken from projective stories told in therapy:

- If you cannot succeed by cooperation, try coercion;
- Violence and aggression are common in the world;
- Few people have control over what happens to them;
- You can count on certain things from some types of people, such as cops, businessmen, and minorities;
- Families (stereotypes) on television are always consistent and parents are always helpful;
- Drugs are "out," but what is "in" is not clearly indicated; and
- Sex is a confusing topic because of the many conflicting references to it and because his mom is so uptight about it when the subject arises.

No doubt hundreds of additional subtle messages are harder to detect or make conscious. As Mario develops, he will use the media's representations of his peer group and the adult world as clues to understanding the way it is outside his home and immediate surroundings. Research into children's perceptions of media messages confirms these negative "metamessages," as they are called. Mario, like all children, looks at media to tell him what it is like beyond his own world and to help him understand the "meanings" of his immediate experiences.

Because of his affective problems, Mario's psychosexual development remains slow. His moral consciousness is not completely dependent on his relationship with his mother, and while this primary bond is crucial, the vicissitudes of its development do not predetermine progress in other areas. It may, however, make these other fronts difficult to negotiate. If Mario is to develop a healthy moral consciousness, he will have to grow in various ways, on several levels.

2.2 Social Development and the Perceptual Domain of Moral Development

We have seen that media help Mario deal with the affective component of his moral life. The unpredictable home life of this child could diminish his ability to perceive the moral aspects of situations.

Because his home life is overwhelming, his affective poverty could obstruct perceptual and cognitive aspects of moral development. To some extent, this happens to all children. But media help Mario in important ways in his perceptual abilities. Pre-moral and early moral abilities lay the foundation for recognition of the moral aspect of complex situations. Research in infancy and early childhood has helped delineate these pre-moral capacities. Media's obvious role can be easily inferred from the necessary tasks moral competence requires.

The child must:

- acquire the ability to focus and select important interpersonal aspects of a story for reflection;
- develop the capacity to sustain attention as more and more facts become evident;
- learn to assess a situation for its satisfactory or unsatisfactory aspect and to see the difference between normalcy and conflict;
- learn to care about outcomes of social situations, even those where the child has no part to play;
- learn to recognize legitimate caregivers and legitimate authority in specific situations; and finally
- develop an ability to reflect on fairness, given plot capacities, competing needs, and duties.[7]

Media such as television and movies help children like Mario achieve these pre-moral and early moral capacities which are the fundamental building blocks for perceiving moral dimensions of human interactions.

Social learning theorists have also stressed the media's positive value for teaching children how to infer motives. Bandura has stressed the impor-

---

[7] L. Kuhmerker, "The Antecedents and Beginnings of Moral Behavior," *Moral Education Forum* 12/3 (1987) 1-14.

tance of social models, over and above the perception of elements in a story, for the moral development of the child.[8]

We are spared the tedious, haphazard, even dangerous trial and error experimentation in the area of social life by emulating competent models. Media present competent models which can be compared with available models in the environment. No doubt this is the case with Mario, whose own mother is unable to model behavior that leads to socially productive interactions. Bandura focuses on attentional processes, retention processes, and motoric reproduction, that is, symbolically acting out what one has perceived. Both positive and negative reinforcements play a significant role in acquiring these abilities, according to Bandura. When conflicting models of behavior occur, a child relies more heavily on the emotional source. That is, as parents decrease in importance and peers become more important, peer behavior is imitated more often. As parents and peers become less emotionally satisfying, we can presume media's models become more important sources of modeled behavior.

2.3 Media and the Cognitive Domain of Moral Development

Cognitive developmentalists, especially Piaget and Kohlberg, have focused on the moral world of the peer and the school. A movement away from moral imperative that comes from without, especially from authority figures, transfers over to autonomous moral behavior which recognizes the need for respect for others' rights.[9] In recent times, Kohlberg has dominated this school of thought and stressed the world of the school with its duty to aid the development of moral reasoning. Justice, he maintains, is the most adequate of moral deals and so justice must be the aim of moral education. Kohlberg had a strong feeling that families are by nature partial and protective, and therefore not good agencies for inculcating the virtue of justice.

Kohlberg's six stages fall into three levels: a preconventional or presocial level, a conventional or social level, and a post-conventional or principled moral autonomy level. Children at a preconventional level act out of self-centered interests—avoiding punishment or wanting to please parents and adults who are important in the child's life for the sake of their "reputations." Young people at the conventional level should be able to take into account the needs of others. At stage three, the post-conventional level, concern for the group dominates moral reasoning.

Tied as it is to the epistemology of Piaget, this moral reasoning scheme has had appeal for educators in need of curricular materials and programs. Media presentations of moral dilemmas are absorbed by the

---

[8] A. Bandura, "Social Learning Theory of Identificatory Processes," in *Handbook of Socialization Theory and Research* ed. D. A. Goslin (Chicago, IL.: Rand-McNally, 1969).

[9] J. Piaget, *The Moral Judgment of the Child* (New York: Free Press, 1965).

child's cognitive structures, which allow insight into moral implications that operate on the characters. Moral development progresses as the cognitive structures of the child mature.

Conn's book on conscience, Likona's work on child-reading, and the work of Kegan and Gilligan all attempt to account for inadequacies of the cognitive developmental approach by looking at the issue of feelings or affect. Each of these authors takes a somewhat different approach to filling in the missing pieces of the moral development puzzle. Kegan, for example, concentrates on the world of the self. Gilligan addresses the problem of affect and the role of self-concept. Conn tries to show by his analysis of virtue that a child who seeks to do the just thing can do so only if there is affective consonance. Finally, Likona stresses the role of parents as even more crucial in moral formation than the school and emphasizes the family's role in forming this moral universe.

Turiel, who has advanced and critiqued the work of Kohlberg, reminds us that children are often aware—perhaps more aware than adults are—of the arbitrary nature of rules and conventions.[10] When adults treat infractions for such things as impoliteness, lack of punctuality, or disobedience in the areas of dress codes in the same manner as a cheating infraction, aggression against another child, or even stealing, they blur the distinction between moral and social domains. The lesson taught to children in such cases is that the will of authority is more important than the nature of the infraction. Also, we are reminded that children naturally vacillate between an acceptance of codes of convention and a questioning of them. This is normal and healthy. The best strategy in school or in the home is to enter into negotiation with social conventions from time to time and distinguish those codes from properly moral codes. Media, as for example television situation-comedies, are quite good at this point. They regularly show individuals bending the rules of social convention. They can be quite insensitive, however, to the gray area where social convention and morality are linked.

Gilligan's work is helpful in alerting us to the possible variances in perception of moral and social problems arising from a difference in self-perception and self-definition.[11] While the chief concern and governing principle for many may be justice, for others care will be a more compelling principle. Certainly justice, tempered by care, can be upheld as the ideal in moral decision-making. It was Thomas Aquinas who postulated an array of moral virtues and who insisted that the moral life is a matter of balance between competing demands. When acting out of a sense of care, one must keep prudence, fortitude, and temperance in balance. The more conscious

---

[10] E. Turiel, "Domains and Categories in Social Cognitive Development," in *The Relationship of Social and Cognitive Development*, ed. W. Overton (Hillsdale, NJ: Lawrence Erlbaum Associates, 1983).

[11] C. Gilligan, *In a Difference Voice: Psychological Theory, Women's Development* (Cambridge, MA: Harvard University Press, 1982).

media become of this divergence and variety, the more beneficial they are for socializing children on these points. Children's programming should be quite sensitive to this point.

Television and movies which help children grapple with issues of convention and morality from the perspective of different roles, different genders, and different social classes are enormously important in raising a generation of citizens who are affectively attuned, perceptually sensitive, and rationally articulate in the moral sphere. To the extent that our media neglect these multiple perspectives, they contribute to the formation of morally immature citizens.

Because media research has focused on short-term results on a narrow range of issues such as aggression and sex, and because it has not accounted for the complexity of issues of moral development, it has not produced knowledge for furthering the potential of modern media as a force for good.

Other forms of media are even less studied. Recently Mario has become interested in music and has gravitated toward what is called the "heavy metal" style. Little, if anything, is known about the subtle or not-so-subtle messages of some forms of pop music. As modern poetry, music has great power to persuade, inspire, and relax but can also falsely present the world, even as it resonates with inner desires felt by a young man who has spent his life struggling to keep the inner or outer world from overtaking him.

3. The Role of Imagination in the Development of Moral Consciousness

One often neglected area in the discussion of the impact of television and movies on the lives of young people is the role imaginative stories play in the formation of the creative life. In his book on the function of fairy tales in the psychic economy of the child, Bettelheim has stated: "Fairy tales help children with the task of meaning-making, helping them transcend the confines of self-centered existence...." He faults much of modern media's emphasis on "true stories" because they have the effect of making tragedy a *fait accompli* and fail to stimulate and nurture the resources needed for handling anxiety. As Bettelheim sees it, imagination is fundamental in the moral life.[12]

Infancy studies have pointed out that the emergence of the self occurs in the process of communication with another. A child develops because an "other" posits a self that is "not yet but almost visible." For example, a mother may talk to her infant as if the baby will talk back. If the mother does not treat the non-talking baby as capable of using language, the infant will never come to know itself as a talker and so will not speak. By speak-

---

[12] B. Bettelheim, *The Uses of Enchantment* (New York: Vintage Books, 1975).

ing to the baby, cuddling, cooing, and encouraging every attempt made in the "right direction," the mother creates a child who speaks.

In the beginning of life, the child relies almost exclusively on others to posit a "self" that is not yet. The child incorporates that vision and creates a new self over time. As more information is received about the inner and outer world, the child modifies, analyzes, and looks to others for confirmation and new information. Parent's images of who the child is are corrected because peers' opinions count more heavily. The child then begins to view the self as a member of an institution, such as a school, and eventually as a member of a society situated in historical time. Images of who and what the child is need to include a familial self, a social self, an institutional self, a cultural self, and an inter-individual self.[13]

In other words, the child creates a self from that which is already given and that which has not yet occurred. Eventually, the child takes over the job, formerly done by caretakers, of creating a self that is "not yet." The raw data for the project include all the above, plus memories, talents, physical attributes, and will.

The child's first practice with this capacity occurs in the activity of fantasizing. As inner and outer worlds are brought together and reconciled, the life of fantasy is changed and modified for purposes other than the containment of anxiety, especially for creative endeavors. Creativity does not depend on intellectual ability to the same extent that rational abilities do, nor on affect. Intellectual, affective, and perceptual abilities aid the development of creativity but one can be creative without having special gifts or being especially well developed in them. In play, suspension of the "actual" leads to creative activity whereby a self is sought and found.[14]

The poet, Wallace Stevens, called creativity the faculty of our poverty. It is our weakest and poorest developed capacity; we tend to downgrade it and squelch it so as not to have too many "different" people within us or outside us with which to contend. Creativity tends to destroy predictability.

In the realm of the moral, creativity and imagination are mistrusted, as Philip Keane has pointed out.[15] They lead to the testing of hypotheses, to making changes in one's life, to taking chances. The danger lies in placing oneself outside the herd, outside of a tradition of moral belief. Moral advance—be it the kind advocated by Jesus, Ghandi, King, or Mother Teresa—requires the courage to envision a different world and a different self within it. It requires the courage to create that world from the fragments of available conditions. And, as every artist knows, the canvas will resist the brush, the stone will resist the chisel. This project then requires dogged

---

[13] R. Kegan, *The Evolving Self: Problems and Process in Human Development* (Cambridge, MA: Harvard University Press, 1982).

[14] D. W. Winnicott, *Playing and Reality* (London: Tavistock Press, 1971).

[15] *Christian Ethics and Imagination* (New York: Paulist Press, 1984).

determination, the ability to withstand criticism and ostracism and the ability to compromise. Stories of moral virtue are needed to feed the creative process and the moral life, since without examples of such insight to call us out of our complacency, we would be helplessly tied to our present state, like a child with parents who do not talk because the child cannot talk back.

We rely then on the imaginative process for comprehending a past we may or may not have participated in, for understanding its meaning, and for analyzing how it may have affected us in the present. We rely on the imaginative process for selecting out of the present the options open to us. We rely on the imaginative process for creating a vision of the end product that will pull us forward. Those without imagination are hopelessly limited to a former way of seeing, feeling, and reasoning about moral dilemmas. This amounts to moral poverty related to sin when this poverty is preferred.

Media's ability to present a world that is beyond the child's experience, to bring stories of individuals who creatively exercise their freedom, to influence the child's budding ability to posit a "me" and a world that is not yet, serves the development of moral imagination. Imaginative presentations of individuals with moral courage lead the way for the child from feelings to thoughts, from thoughts to analysis and reasoning, and on to deciding and willing. By wanting to see things differently, the child re-thinks, re-feels, and re-perceives both former and new moral dilemmas. In the process, a self changes and re-forms.

4. The Contribution of Media to Awakening Moral Sensibilities

Media presentations, especially network television, contribute two things to the cauldron of children's moral development: narrative materials and attitudinal stance. The media invite us inside the stories and the drama of others' lives; these narratives become raw materials for the search for meaning and significance in our own lives. Television narratives have the potential to provide a lessening of stress and even a resolution of tension because of the penetrating interpretive osmosis created by the dramatic climate. Theories of poetics have explored the phenomenon of catharsis since the age of Greek theater. One essential component of any theory of catharsis is a similarity between two stories: that of the drama and that of personal experience.

Because of a similarity of narrative materials, TV drama can be morally dynamic of itself, in the sense that it shows a way out of an alternative solution to a painful or restrictive life situation. The drama's raw materials are not just its story line, but also its modelling of feelings, responses, and ways of relating. In many subtle, indirect ways, television offers images of human significance. It shows viewers roles and options for work and expression that may have been utterly foreign. It provides a way to glimpse diverse personality structures interacting with others. It also frequently proposes images of heroism, exceptional generosity, or success—not always exalting values a Christian community would esteem as authentic.

The power of the media's capacity to intrude into deeper territory within the substratum of moral consciousness is enormous. Events powerfully evoked by TV drama can motivate, even when viewers remain aware of the fictitious distance from their own life situations. We all hunger for more existential meaning, more significance. As teenage fads show, young people find energy in imitating what is modeled for them by the mass culture. This power of TV can serve as a narcotic or a symbolic resolution of psychic tensions. But the media message itself is not the only dynamic at issue.

The other dynamic force which the media contribute is their attitudinal stance. No story or event is ever seen neutrally but is always seen from some perspective. There is a huge difference of perspective between detached indifference and committed sympathy. Further, the object of one's sympathy is revealing. Quite often one value that dominates the perspectives of the media's offerings is the sanctity of individual will. The multiplicity of divergent ethical traditions in our country makes a strong endorsement of any common vision suspect or controversial.

The television media especially reflect the perspective so often manifested in American mercantile life: Any means is fair game to corner a market. We have seen television degenerate in its use of vivid sensationalism. Sex and violence are two of the most powerful forces for creating this vividness. The disappearance of sacred space and sacred feelings are the usual consequence of this perspective, and this is disastrous for any deep religious vision.

What we must do as communities founded upon and nurtured by a religious vision is to celebrate our common vision as a context which influences all three areas of moral transformation: perception, affect, and social cognition. We are far from the day that church-based communities will be in a position to influence mainline entertainment with critical values consistent with their religious vision. Perhaps that will never or should never be the case. But in the present, we do need to be able to call attention to the harmony or contrast between media emissions and Christian values.

In a world in which television is such a powerful shaping force of childhood and adolescent consciousness, we need to engage children in reflection upon the narratives they see. We do this often enough in therapeutic sessions with troubled young people, since their reflection upon TV drama engages the unresolved dilemmas of their own emotional life. On rare occasions, classroom teachers also refer to TV narratives to summon up a shared base of experience among students. In both instances, the results can be dynamic.

Such moments allow teachers, therapists, or parents to evoke a common vision of Christian moral values, often by way of contrast with the media's perspective. We value the common good, not just individual aggressiveness. We value the sacredness of human life as gifts of a loving Creator, not just random opportunities for individual self-interest. We value non-violence as a gift from our God, not the vain glory of domination by main force. Sometimes the media do arrive at promoting values more Christian than materialistic. But even when that is not the case, the raw materials of human narrative can be penetrated by moral reflection. What is needed is a network of human belonging to promote a positive selective perception, benevolent affect, and social cognition in harmony with Christian vision.

A real challenge for moral development in our TV age, then, is to generate for young people a two-fold capacity. We need to help them find a moral ground to stand on. TV ordinarily presupposes no value structure in the viewer; anything at all can be grist for the mill of voyeurism and vivid stimulation. Even if the Christian moral vision cannot always contain the products of the industry, it can serve as a point of reference. This capacity of being able to recognize limits in legitimate human expression and feelings provides a base from which to view the meaning of the surrounding world. Meaning gives significance by binding us to others who share a common world shaped by a common vision. Without such a base, life experience must be either pointless or anomic (dizzying)—precisely what one picks up from TV emissions like MTV telecasts directed to the alienated young.

The second capacity is to be able to dialogue with the attitudes represented by the media. Here again the young need to be initiated into the skills needed to obtain a critical purchase on media events. TV is a deeply emotional medium and it is not easy, especially for the young, to rise above the spontaneous reactions elicited by a dramatic presentation. Positively, however, when persons do achieve a critical ability to engage the meaning of television stories, they can often find powerful new meanings in elements of their value tradition in the process. Teachers who have used film for moral discussions know how true this is.

5. Conclusion

Our analysis yields the following judgments. First, television has great power to engage moral attention and move moral feelings. As such, television is a strong potential tool for moral education. Probably children are not aware of this potential until they are drawn into moral reflections with teachers or parents. Such reflections can be important for engaging deep feeling on almost any ethical issue.

Second, television tends not to be a proponent of any consistent moral stance. It is fundamentally a tool of profit capitalism. In selling air time, the industry is fundamentally selling advertised products. Indifference to fundamental human values and its frequent endorsement of sex and violence as stimuli for gross human attention are negative dynamics in the field of contemporary culture. If we are to address the attitudinal stance of TV, we must unmask the emotional manipulation so common in the industry.

Our discussion in this chapter has illustrated how, in a context of therapeutic reflection and analysis, even television violence and the trivialization of human narrative serve as dramatic materials that allow children to re-work their own experiences of repression, violence, or frustration. This is a tribute to the resilience of the human psyche, but it is also a recognition of the dynamic power of the ever-present TV drama to intersect with volatile emotions and moral feelings in each of our lives.

As we acknowledge this resource for engaging moral issues and psychological needs, we also want to alert readers to recognize that we have hardly begun in this culture to provide reflective resources that would assist viewers to identify the moral base needed to lead their responses into the channel of moral growth. Happily, the unmanageable abundance of moral development means that spontaneous and fragmentary moments of human interchange help us process the dynamic transformation of perception, affect, and cognition that are at the base of our development. But we hope our essay can also help set an agenda for responding more adequately in the future. Parents, schools, and churches need to know that their input in interpretation can be vital in helping resolve the tensions and ambiguities of conflicting values that their clients experience. The time has come to look for the means to facilitate that ministry.

II

Moral Dimensions of Public Life

II

Introduction

Moral Dimensions of Public Life

Despite the fact that moral decisions apply to both private and public life, heated discussion often focuses on the private side of issues like bioethics and sexuality. The Unites States Supreme Court's stance that sexual morality (as manifest in cases dealing with abortion and homosexuality, for example) falls under "rights of privacy" reinforces this interpretation. Public issues, which affect people with equal force, often fail to merit the same kind of attention. Again, government policies of deregulation and privatization (regarding broadcasting, banking, housing, and so on) tend to support the perception that moral issues are private issues.

Yet public life bears its own share of moral uncertainty. Even apart from the public side of "private" issues, which impinge on public life—issues in bioethics, for example, affect the common good more than they do private individuals—public life itself has its own issues. Thinkers of past generations examined areas dealing with powers of the state, church-state relations, business and commerce, education, journalistic and governmental truth, work, and so on. Some tried to delineate the differences between moral norms binding individuals and moral norms binding the state;[1] others proposed a theoretical model balancing ethical claims among competing powers.[2]

However they are considered, public moral issues affect everyone's lives. And, as the essays in Part I demonstrate, the mass media and their products play a role in public moral discussion. They can highlight and explain issues, shaping a public consensus; they can, perhaps more easily, ignore issues. They can also, in their day-to-day functioning, influence the moral imagination of their millions of followers. Apart from the obvious moral issues noted above, what public moral dis-

---

[1] Niehbur, Reinhold. *Moral Man and Immoral Society: A Study in Ethics and Politics.* (New York: C. Scribner's, 1941).

[2] John Courtney Murray, S.J., *We Hold These Truths: Catholic Reflections on the American Proposition* (New York: Sheed & Ward, 1960).

course do the media enter? How do they help define those issues? How do they limit the issues?

This section turns to public morality, not through definition but through examples and case studies. The essays here examine various dimensions of public life and its moral demands. Not meant as comprehensive, they concentrate on seven, somewhat interrelated, areas whose moral demands do not always receive scrutiny: work, play, consumption, gender, teaching moral values, public truth, and conflict.

Lois Daly considers the portrayal of work in typical situation comedies as expressive of a vision of "the good life" defined in terms of money, the material possessions money can buy, and status. Work functions rarely, if at all, as a mode of satisfying self-expression or as a fundamental form of human social relatedness; rather, television limits work to a means of gaining prestige. In contrast to this constricted view of work and its concomitant vision of the good life, deficient in its sense of human relatedness, Daly proposes the alternative found in the theologies of work developed by Dorothee Sölle and by Pope John Paul II. Bringing work back into discussion as a public moral issue serves to acknowledge human social relatedness and to restore public argument about what constitutes "a good society."

David Eley poses the obverse: what of play and leisure? For Eley, the primary moral domain consists in how we human beings use our time. He argues that an adequate moral understanding of media's role in the use of time for leisure requires investigation of two questions: What do people use television for? What is the nature of the pleasure that television affords its viewers? Such study would help to develop a "discernment of spirits" for our experience as viewers and users of media, which in turn would allow us to understand better how these forces of pleasure recreate our spirits and affect the human community. His argument demonstrates how, when the media enter the picture, one can begin with seemingly private events and end with public life.

Joan and Henry Timm approach the public/private dichotomy in yet another way: through the dichotomy of celebration and consumption. Their analysis begins with the impact that the commercial television industry as a medium for advertising has had upon the possibilities for genuine public celebration within culture in the United States. Commercial television has turned leisure time into entertainment that serves consumerism. The Timms particularly note how such programming effects an ironic privatization of culture: "The medium which transmits a so-called common culture into our homes also renders unnecessary an active involvement in that culture." This privatization has debilitating consequences for our imagination because it trivializes the images and myths that express our culture's most fundamental belief system.

Christine Gudorf asks a more disturbing and potentially more far-reaching question: How do the media and their products construct gender?

In the light of a growing awareness of inequality in gender relations, the mass media's portrayals of gender take on greater significance. Gudorf argues that, despite changes in the media's treatment of gender roles during the last two decades, the for-profit nature of the media and the process of ownership contraction constrain them to base screen portrayals and hiring practices on a theory of gender arrangements that limits rather than promotes gender justice. In consequence, media representations of gender symbolically reinforce and legitimize a division into masculine public spheres and feminine private spheres. Gudorf identifies a number of the strategies by which media influence the public to accept this view of a divided reality; she also suggests courses of public action to balance that influence.

James Capo calls attention to a consequence of the unbalanced gender roles which Gudorf has identified. How do shifting roles and increasing media exposure affect the teaching of values? In the amount of time people now spend using mass media, Capo sees one indication that media have started to displace previous value inculcators; the indications that the media also transmit values, (e.g., that money and technique are goods and ends in themselves), which contrast with traditional values, concerns him. Capo argues that this shift in the locus of value inculcation exacerbates a prior separation of responsibilities between men and women, one that had placed the burden for the transmission of values within women's "domain" of home and family. Such a separation reflects a sharp division between private and public worlds. Capo calls for a reexamination of the gender separation of value inculcation roles, particularly in view of the media's unwillingness to acknowledge "their own engagement in value laden communication" or the social and cultural metamorphosis that has placed this responsibility in their hands.

Janusz Balicki and Wolfgang Wunden propose one specific case of reporting as a vehicle to analyze the dynamics of the media in the processes of social change. Looking at news coverage of the Chernobyl nuclear disaster, they focus on identifying the factors that make moral principles and moral judgments credible in a society that claims open discussion as one of its fundamental characteristics. The contrast they draw between Soviet and Western reporting and accompanying notions of truth illustrates the need for a moral examination of the performance of the news media. They argue that the very public nature of reporting calls for a wider involvement with the media by the whole community.

Ivan Fuček chooses a different case study but reaches similar conclusions. His analysis turns on the issue of conflict in media in order to explore the possibility that, even within a culture of pluralism, the resolution of conflict must come to rest upon an appeal to a shared and common moral base.

Paul Soukup returns to the theme of teaching moral values but in some ways stands the discussion on its head. Looking at the Church as a moral communicator, he argues that its moral teaching has its greatest effect, not when the media amplify it, but when ordinary people live it out. The various characteristics of the community as teacher provide the force of this kind of moral teaching. The moral dimensions of public life take shape in individual actions open to a moral imagination enriched by a narrative and artistic tradition.

The eight essays in this section provide eight different perspectives on public life, the media, and the moral imagination. They invite, first, reflection and, second, action.

8

Television Images of Work and the Moral Imagination: Theological Interpretations

Lois K. Daly

It is nothing new to assert that human beings are image using animals. We do so as a means of interpreting and organizing our experience, as individuals and as communities. As a result, it comes as no surprise to hear that human culture is an "image culture." The claim that the more we are immersed in such a culture, the more difficult it is to think conceptually about those images may surprise us, however.[1] Yet, we must think about precisely those images if we wish to explore the development or shape of the moral imagination as it is manifested in contemporary culture. For the purposes of this essay, I will use a common-sense definition of the moral imagination: The moral imagination includes that range of options that individuals and communities have available which provides resources or strategies for working out both immediate and long term plans and goals. In other words, the moral imagination involves those images appropriated by individuals and communities which, as judged by those groups themselves, appear to provide the means for self-realization and self-fulfillment.

An obvious place to begin looking at the images which populate the moral imagination is television because television programs focus attention on the full range of human activities, including education, family life, work, and sex. Although television is certainly not the sole factor in shaping the moral imagination, we must recognize it as a very important contributor if only because of its magnitude. For example, experts estimate that there are roughly the same percentage of households in the United States that have at least one television as have indoor plumbing. Moreover, America exports a

---

[1] Michael Warren makes just this claim in his "Images and the Structuring of Experience," *Religious Education* 82 (Spring 1987) 247.

huge volume of programs to virtually every part of the world and, judging by ratings, these programs are extremely popular. One of the clearest examples of this is the popularity of *Dallas* in over 90 countries.[2]

Given the pervasiveness of television, its portrayal of so many activities, and the need to come to grips with the images which prevail in the moral imagination, I will explore the image of one human activity, namely work, that is commonly portrayed in one of television's most popular genres, the sitcom. I will follow the procedure suggested by Michael Warren for thinking conceptually about images. In "Images and the Structuring of Experience," Warren proposes a three step process: (1) naming the image, holding it up for analysis; (2) finding a hermeneutical key which assists in evaluating that image; and (3) renaming the image in light of the evaluation, that is, identifying its inappropriateness in light of alternatives.[3] The first part of the paper, then, describes the image of work commonly portrayed on sitcoms. The second part uses the theologies of work provided by Dorothee Sölle and Pope John Paul II as a key for interpreting this image, and the third part draws some conclusions about the image in light of those theologies of work.

1. Naming the Image of Work in Sitcoms

As most of us know, the situation comedy or sitcom, one of the staples of television, typically runs 23 minutes with two acts and an epilogue. Episodes, usually self-contained, revolve around a single situation and involve a regular cast of characters. These characters usually engage in repetitious behavior from episode to episode.[4] Since the beginning of sitcoms on television with *I Love Lucy* in 1951, four "kinds" of situation or domestic comedies have appeared. Three–the suburban, rural, and urban comedies–depend on the location in which they take place. The fourth kind, the social critical comedy, was developed much more recently. Despite these differences, a single dominant image of work emerges in each of them, an image described by Hal Himmelstein as the myth of the Great American Dream.

According to Himmelstein, this Dream is "the 'good life' as described in the myth of eternal progress and characterized by the perpetual economic expansion of the society and the growth of personal material compensations."[5] In some cases, Himmelstein allows, eternal progress may transcend

---

[2] Ien Ang, *Watching Dallas: Soap Opera and the Melodramatic Imagination*, trans. Della Couling (London: Methuen, 1985) 1.

[3] Warren 251-55.

[4] Hal Himmelstein, *Television Myth and the American Mind* (New York: Praeger, 1984), 77.

[5] Ibid. 14.

material possessions to include the desire for personal fulfillment.[6] More important, however, is that part of the American Dream which says that "personal freedom transcends the notion of social responsibility"; in fact, a key aspect of the Dream involves freedom from responsibility.[7] The Dream calls attention to easy progress available to anyone who has some talent, some luck, a willingness to work hard, and the self-confidence to grab an opportunity.[8] This myth, then, divorces its adherents from the social reality in which persons live, a reality filled with structures which curb or make possible individual accomplishment. It insists that all individuals can achieve whatever they set out to achieve, and they can do so by reason of their own efforts alone.

All four kinds of sitcoms evidence this Great American Dream. A brief look at examples of each will help clarify this myth, its pervasiveness, and its power. The first kind includes those domestic comedies located in the suburbs. These illustrate an attitude toward work shaped by the Great American Dream without actually portraying the workplace itself. Classic examples of these include *The Adventures of Ozzie and Harriet, Father Knows Best, Leave It to Beaver, The Donna Reed Show,* and *My Three Sons.* As Himmelstein describes them, these programs paint

> an idealized vision of suburban living...a place of full employment; [featuring] conventional white, white-collar corporate families;... Success was measured by its visible material manifestations.... [P]rinciples of fair play prevailed;...everyone had a right to freedom of speech; everyone was entitled to the best possible education; the able, hardworking person would, with a bit of luck, do well financially.[9]

In these shows work provides the means for material success and comfortable family life. It is something fathers do to provide for their families and not because they enjoy it or because they want to improve the conditions of others. Furthermore, television's suburban life idealized the lifestyle of upwardly mobile white Americans without showing its underlying structure: "We see the results of progress limited to the privileged, but we are denied access to the broader social reality in which that progress occurs."[10]

The rural areas sitcom also focuses on family life, but this time on a family life which holds to more traditional values, eschewing the suburban "keeping up with the Joneses" mentality. Despite this apparent divergence from the values of the Great American Dream, these shows ultimately do not threaten it or even call it into question. Shows such as *The Real*

---

[6] Ibid.

[7] Ibid. 26.

[8] Ibid. 29.

[9] Ibid. 87-89.

[10] Ibid. 88.

McCoys, The Beverly Hillbillies, Green Acres, and *The Andy Griffith Show* portray their characters "outside the mainstream of contemporary technicized culture." In this way, their actions react to a society they neither understand nor participate in. As a result, Himmelstein concludes, they are "rendered both quaint and unthreatening because one operates outside the guiding myth of eternal progress. We can therefore laugh at the hillbilly without heeding his or her warnings dealing with questions of morality and ethics in advanced capitalism."[11] In other words, despite the outward appearance of conflict between traditional rural values and the Great American Dream, these comedies ultimately reinforce that Dream by portraying those rural characters as unable to deal satisfactorily with contemporary issues or by ending with the adoption of aspects of the Dream itself. As Himmelstein reminds us, "Andy Taylor did eventually move to the city."[12]

The third type, the urban setting comedy, includes both domestic and work oriented sitcoms. In both there is more direct portrayal of and discussion of work with the myth of eternal progress at their heart.[13] Consider, for example, Ralph Cramden's continual quest, in the *Honeymooners,* for the successful get-rich-quick scheme. Ralph does not enjoy work; he is intimidated by his boss and only grudgingly goes to work. Ralph is not committed to the bus company or to the effort to provide transportation for people who need it. Instead, he always seeks a way out, another way in which he can provide for his wife, but his schemes always fail. With each failure, his attitude to work declines. Or, consider the more recent example of *Taxi.* This program features a group of taxi drivers who would all rather be doing something else. While waiting for their big chance, they drive taxis to support themselves. Their only camaraderie occurs in the garage; while they may be loyal to each other, they make no effort to contribute to some larger good. They are isolated and alienated.

Consider, finally, a more recent example: *The Cosby Show,* one of the most popular versions of the urban sitcom. In one episode, the two principal story lines both relate an attitude toward work implicit in the Great American Dream. In the first, Theo has failed to reserve a dorm room for himself and so attempts to find housing around New York University. He comes home triumphant because he saw the perfect place: a $400,000 condominium with health center and seven-day-a-week cleaning service. Theo proposes that his parents buy this condo in which he will then live without cost to them; after he finishes school, they can sell it at a profit. Theo even offers to allow his parents to use it as a weekend getaway. Cliff and Claire reject the plan immediately. Notice Theo's emphasis on this condo not costing his parents anything–beyond the initial investment, of course–yet bring-

---

[11] Ibid. 98.

[12] Ibid. 112.

[13] Ibid. 113.

ing them a great profit after a few years. This way, housing for Theo, complete with maid service, will be free. This is the Great American Dream: something for little or nothing.

The second story line is even more telling. Denise has decided to quit college and take a job, without telling her parents. When her sister and brother-in-law offer her a minimum wage job in their wilderness store, she astounds Cliff and Claire by refusing even though she has no money and is living with them. Denise confidently announces that she will take a job only in the fashion and music industries. Cliff, in particular, looks at her in disbelief. Sondra and her husband, however, do not seem surprised. We might recall that when they, as college graduates, wanted to open the store in the first place, Cliff and Claire did not initially support them. The parents were more interested in jobs with higher social status and financial returns. Later in the show, Denise proudly announces that she has achieved her goal; she has a job as an assistant to the executive in a record company. After she explains her duties, her father summarizes them by saying that she gets coffee and answers the phone. Denise does not agree. Then comes the clincher. Denise's salary is $25 a week.

In her case, unlike Theo's, Cliff's and Claire's reactions reinforce the values of the Great American Dream. They think Denise (and Sondra before her) ought to take the best possible job she can find, and they measure the best primarily in financial terms, not by what the children enjoy or feel enables them to contribute to society. Success or the possibility of success matters. Of course, this is tempered by the fact that, although they may be disappointed, Cliff and Claire will not disown their children or stop providing for them until they are able to support themselves. As Cliff says repeatedly, "No one's going to tell me when I'm going to kick them out of the house!"

Clearly in this the example of *The Cosby Show*, some of the elements of the Great American Dream have undergone a transformation since the days of the so-called ideal suburb of *Father Knows Best*. In the late 1980s, images of the Great American Dream did not apply only to white families or to families where the mother stays at home smiling throughout the day. *Cosby* successfully includes within the Great American Dream some of those who were previously excluded. And it does so in a way that undermines stereotypes of black families as well as black men, women and children. For that, *The Cosby Show* is to be commended. At the same time, however, it puts the new black family squarely in the context of the Great American Dream, a Dream that still requires evaluation.

Before turning to that evaluation, though, one more kind of sitcom remains. The fourth in Himmelstein's typology, the social comedy, consists of shows like *All in the Family* and *M*A*S*H*. Both contain some measurable criticism of the Great American Dream but carry out the criticism in such a way that the Dream remains unchallenged. For example, despite the level of criticism of "the way things are," Mike (the Meathead) pursues an education as part of the dream.[14] No matter what the pressures of the moment, he refuses to give up his conviction that if he can finish his degree, he will be able to support his family the way he wants to. And before the show ends, Mike succeeds in getting an academic job.

In the case of *M*A*S*H*, war is the social issue in question, yet the war becomes a mere setting or backdrop "for the personal struggles which unfold. Ideology, as it directly impacts on the modern question of the justifiability of wars of national liberation as opposed to wars of foreign intervention, is conspicuous by its absence."[15] Both shows, then, have a critical edge, but the underlying message does not take on the entire mythology of the Great American Dream. Instead, the myth is powerful enough to transform criticism into an acceptable form, a form which ends by assuring us that if we just hang in there long enough, we will succeed.

In sum, the Great American Dream fosters an image of work that focuses on success in terms of money and status. Workers do not, and perhaps should not, like to work, but resign themselves to it as the means for assuring the "good life." Material goods supply the content of that "good life." Furthermore, the programs portray workers as primarily isolated individuals unrelated in any fundamental way to other workers; they have little or no responsibility to others, especially to those who appear to be below them. Finally, anyone who makes the effort can achieve this dream. Social mobility is not an unattainable ideal; anything is possible.

2. The Theology of Work as Hermeneutical Key

The theologies of work developed by Dorothee Sölle in *To Work and to Love: A Theology of Creation*[16] and by Pope John Paul II in the encyclical *Laborem Exercens*[17] provide quite a contrast to the image of the Great American Dream. Both Sölle and the Pope emphasize our role as co-creators with God. Both build this from an interpretation of the creation of human beings in the image of God. We participate in God's creative work through human work, which begins with tending and keeping the garden.[18] If we understand work as our co-creativity with God, then we must unmask, criticize, and transform alienating labor and images of alienating labor. In this way, the theology of work can become what Warren calls the hermeneu-

---

[14] Ibid. 131.

[15] Ibid. 137.

[16] Philadelphia: Fortress Press, 1984.

[17] Gregory Baum, ed., *The Priority of Labor* (New York: Paulist Press, 1982) 95-152.

[18] *Laborem Exercens* 102 and Sölle 72.

tical key, the key which provides a way to evaluate and transform the image of work.

For the most part, Sölle and the Pope agree on the content of the theology of work. The heart of the matter for each of them is the priority of labor over capital. This priority, something which each identifies as critical of both western capitalism and eastern collectivism or state socialism, means at least two things. First, both insist that work ought to be the self-expression of the worker. According to Sölle, "through work we not only give of ourselves, but simultaneously create and sustain ourselves."[19] For the Pope, work "corresponds to [hu]man dignity [and] expresses this dignity and increases it." Through work we achieve our fulfillment as human beings.[20] Notice that work itself, and not the exchange value of work, fulfills and expresses human dignity.

Second, Sölle and the Pope both insist that social-relatedness is a dimension of human work. As Sölle explains, "work is the activity that relates a person to her society."[21] In this way, work mediates our relations with others, and for that reason, "it should epitomize our relatedness."[22] However, because of our western emphasis on commodity exchange and value assigned according to the number and quality of material goods, the notion of competition prevails over constructive and positive relatedness. This emphasis overlooks the fact that work is communal in space and time. "We must produce in order to survive, and in order to survive we must produce together," says Sölle.[23] Instead of a communal sense, workers increasingly feel unrelated to each other. This results partly from the constant threat of job loss; without a job, the worker loses contact with the larger society.

Both Sölle and the Pope advocate a combination of a planned economy and a decentralized government as a solution. On the one hand, workers need government for protection; but on the other hand, as the Pope points out, collectivizing the means of production will not in itself protect or defend the rights of the worker. The proper balance is achieved only "when on the basis of his work each person is fully entitled to consider himself a part owner of the great workbench at which he is working with everyone else."[24] One solution suggested by the Pope is a closer association between labor and the ownership of capital.[25] As Sölle sums it up: justice *and* solidarity are required.[26]

---

[19] Sölle 73.

[20] *Laborem Exercens* 112.

[21] Sölle 93.

[22] Ibid.

[23] Ibid. 95.

[24] *Laborem Exercens* 124.

Although Sölle's and the Pope's positions contain these similarities, there are two important differences. First Sölle also includes as a dimension of human work the need for reconciliation with nature. She argues that people need to "reconceive" production and technology so that human work stops spoiling the planet. As she explains, the "hope for reconciliation with nature through human work amounts to a rejection of the traditional, masculine aspiration to dominate the earth."[27] Here Sölle discusses the relations between the First and Third worlds with respect to capital intensive work. For Sölle, good work promotes self-sufficiency and not dependency both on the domestic and the international levels.[28] Although the Pope also raises the question of the Third World, he does not do so in the context of how human work affects the environment.[29]

The second difference between Sölle and Pope John Paul II centers on his refusal to reinterpret the situation of women in terms of human work. This is reflected, according to Sölle, in his sexist language and in his discussion of women's role in the home.[30] According to the Pope, "the true advancement of women requires that labor should be structured in such a way that women do not have to pay for their advancement by abandoning what is specific to them and at the expense of the family, in which women as mothers have an irreplaceable role."[31] In addition to Sölle's comments, one might also point out that the Pope here neglects the indispensable role that fathers play in rearing children.

Despite the seriousness of these differences, their theologies of work do offer a clear alternative to the understanding of work implicit in the Great American Dream. In contrast to the "rat-race" of consumerism and the drudgery of mindless work that workers have no control over, Sölle and the Pope describe work in terms of self-expression and social relationship. Their view does not divorce personal responsibility from the conditions of the wider society nor measure human fulfillment by material consumption. And both Sölle and the Pope are aware that this theology requires a substantial transformation of the economic systems now dominant in both east and west. Such a transformation will also require, however, a transformation in the culturally dominant images of work, images that television transmits and reinforces.

---

[25] Ibid. 125.

[26] Sölle 100-01.

[27] Ibid. 103-04.

[28] Ibid. 105-06.

[29] See *Laborem Exercens* 124.

[30] See Sölle 91 n.12.

[31] *Laborem Exercens* 134.

3. Evaluation and Renaming the Image

In brief, when we accept the theologies of work articulated by Sölle and the Pope, and are convinced that genuine human work corresponds to the dignity of human beings as co-creators with God, then the Great American Dream does not fare very well. In fact, as a result of using our new hermeneutical key, the Dream needs to be renamed. A fairly obvious candidate for this is the Great American Nightmare, since it denies what it offers. It holds out for us the hope that with work will come the answer to our dreams: the security of status, comfort, and happiness. In fact, however, for the majority of us, work is more likely not what we would prefer to be doing all day, every day. We may enjoy aspects of it, or even most of it, but it does not provide the opportunities for self-expression and connections with others that Sölle and the Pope describe.

Does this mean, then, that we ought not watch television sitcoms? I, as a child of television and proud of it, could not seriously recommend that for a number of reasons. First, we need to keep in touch with the images of life that appear on television because they reveal much about the moral imagination (as I indicated at the beginning of this essay). Knowing something about those dominant images gives us an idea about how much transformative work we need to do—work, by the way, that is also self-expressive and related positively to others.

Second, there are moments even on the sitcoms and perhaps especially in the more recent development of the "dramedy" that suggest some wrinkles in that Great American Dream or some signs that not everybody in "Hollywoodland" is convinced that "audienceland" believes in the Dream anymore. I am thinking of shows such as *Frank's Place*, which, I should point out, the network quickly canceled. Nevertheless, the appearance of such shows suggests the possibility of more like them, and therefore the possibility of diverse images of work appearing on television. The value of diverse images lies in the expansion of our moral imagination, of the scenarios we can visualize as a result of seeing, vividly at times, someone else's experience.

Third, after examining the image of work fortified by the Great American Dream, we may watch the same old shows differently, that is, with a critical awareness. This awareness will help us to appreciate just the slight differences of approach or definition that do appear from time to time even on those shows which are usually most stereotypical. In fact, that critical edge will help us to identify stereotypes more easily and to unmask them as such. In that way, the Great American Dream will command less attention; as more of its content is revealed as stereotype, the less compelling it will be. At least we can hope so.

9

Beyond Necessity:
Toward the Ethics of Entertainment

David Eley, S.J.

The key words I want to stress in this essay are "leisure" and "entertainment," particularly mass media entertainment. I shall start with leisure and end with entertainment. I take this path to get to a critical question of ethics: What do individual people and groups do with their time? The ethical domain examines human action; if it asks what people do with their time, consequently, within that domain, it must ask how they orchestrate their leisure.

To get us on this path, consider the four following human activities in terms of what I have just called the ethical domain: (1) getting out onto the playing field on a beautiful sunny afternoon to play baseball. Think of the costs involved, the time involved, and the materials needed; (2) getting tickets to go to Toronto for the opening game of the World Series. Think of the costs involved, the materials involved, and the opportunities people have to do that; (3) watching the World Series on television or listening to it on the radio. Again, think of the time and the costs involved, and the opportunities people have to do that; and (4) reading the results of the game in the Sunday morning paper. Each of these four activities involves us and our leisure in a different way. I particularly want to note how the mass media (options 3 and 4) take on a greater and greater leisure role in the guise of entertainment.

In the context of reflecting upon the ethical dimensions of these four activities–i.e., upon how time and our other resources are orchestrated within them–consider leisure: the nature of leisure, how we use our time and what all this means to us. This, it seems to me, is the other side of the discussion of work introduced by Lois Daly in Chapter 8. To carry on the baseball image and to lead us further into consideration of notions of play and recreation, I shall quote a little poem from Rilke, which Gadamer places at the very beginning of *Truth and Method*—an ontology of the nature of

116

play and culture—and, in Gadamer's mind, the key to the "human" in living human lives together.

> Catch only what you've thrown yourself, all is mere skill and little gain;
> but when you're suddenly the catcher of a ball
> thrown by an eternal partner
> with accurate and measured swing
> towards you, to your center, in an arch
> from the great bridge building of God:
> why catching then becomes a power—
> not yours, a world's.

1. Leisure

Where do we begin? All of us might reflect on the patterns of work and leisure in our own lives. We cannot deny that working can bring certain forms of satisfaction and pleasure to us in addition to its more obvious result of producing income and resources for ourselves and our families. Work can bring us the pleasure and satisfaction of our contribution to worthwhile projects and efforts. This satisfaction can result from the nature of the work itself, be it educational, building bridges, or building cities. But leisure has its own necessity: No matter how much we might like the work we do and involve ourselves in it, there simply comes a point at which we have to crash down and stop. It is built into the structures and institutions of our contemporary societies just as it has been in nearly every society humans know.[1]

In our culture the understanding of "leisure" has Greek and Biblical origins. The Greek word for leisure is "*skole*"; the Latin, "*scola*"; and the English, "school." Leisure originated in the activity of education: a time for reflection and critical thought on poetry and on language, activities that we now relegate to school. Most of us who work and study in schools, colleges, and universities today do not usually think of our activities as any form of leisure at all, so we are well away from what the Greeks did with their leisure time. They also ran marathons and other forms of activity for recreation and recuperation of the body.

---

[1] There is a peculiar exception to this: the pre-contact Innuit people, the Innuks in northern Canada, apparently did not have a concept of play or leisure. All the tasks of their life were somehow integrated: The beading of costumes, the making of blankets, and all the basic necessities of life were integrated into rituals of work and play. They never took time off. They took journeys, they were nomadic, and they went out on hunts. The journeys may have functioned as a break. But before the white man came, which was only as recently as 1938 for some of the communities there, they did not have that distinction. Nor do they have the distinction of night and day, because it's night for months and it's day for months—so when you work and when you rest is also arranged quite differently.

We have lost their sense of leisure. What, then, does leisure mean to us? We have turned many activities that in other times were forms of leisure into forms of work; we often turn our physical exercise into work. How many of us strap ourselves to exercise machines—an activity that reflects how far we have introduced notions of the rational, the organized, the productive into our leisure time.

We find the Biblical root of leisure in the narrative myth of Genesis— the creation story—and watch it played out in other sections of the scriptures. It is "shabbat": In the Genesis text, the commission to take rest was probably based on something that already existed in the society mainly for the treatment of slaves. You could not work slaves seven days in a row–six days was enough. Babylonian society had a system in which every 10th day was the day of rest. There is something very pragmatic and obvious about that. However, in the Ten Commandments the command differs; it tells the people to keep the "shabbat" holy. It adds a religious dimension to the rest that it commissions for the people: The time of rest is returned to them with a commission which defines the nature of leisure. While definitely rest, it was time spent with family, time to reflect upon the work of the other days and on the traditions of "shabbat," time to be conscious of God's covenant with the people. So it had a very religious sense.

Perhaps we exaggerate if we think "there is nothing left of the Biblical sense of rest or leisure in what we do today." Do we not have the weekend–the two days in between the five days of work? Each of us has to look at our own situations to measure sociologically the patterns of leisure and the industries of leisure in our own societies. First, little patterns of leisure fit into every day: when we get home from work and go to eat and before we go to bed. Second, as I noted, the weekends have patterns of leisure. Finally, there are additional holidays like Thanksgiving.

2. Television: From Leisure to Entertainment

Television's structure follows the patterns of leisure in people's lives. It is segmented to grab little bits of leisure time: If you have only 30 seconds of leisure time, television has a 30-second segment to give you; if you have an hour or a half hour to fit in between supper and whatever else you are doing, you can have a little news; and if you have three and a half hours, you can watch a ball game on a Saturday afternoon. And people have responded by giving over their leisure time to television. Consequently, television has become the most frequent, the largest leisure time activity. Television literally occupies leisure time.

Because the orchestration and organization of time forms one of the chief limited resources of both personal life and collective life, we need to take a close look at television and its relationship to leisure and leisure time. We should explore what television programming offers the viewer in return for the leisure time that the viewer gives to television. We can then see whether or not television fulfills the purposes that leisure has in its reciprocal relation to work.

I particularly want to stress two points as important for the exploration of these issues. First, we need to do studies to find out more about what people use television for; second, we need to understand better the kind of pleasure that television affords, since people watch television chiefly for pleasure.

Conrad Lodziak, in *The Power of Television*,[2] reports one of the few studies that opens the door on the question of how people really use television. He details a study of the way lower middle-class families use television and what they do while they use the television. With video cameras the researchers recorded all the other domestic activities and relationships into which television came as a player. The study showed that domestic work goes on, eating goes on, certain levels of intimacy go on, parental relationships go on. In sum, life goes on, somewhat in interaction with television, somewhat ignoring what happens there when, for instance, commercials come on.

Whatever set of measures we use, we have to agree that there is an immense amount of time being spent with television. We need to find out more about what people are really using this time for. Nielsen ratings, broadcast ratings, and semiotic studies of image construction and narrative cannot tell us whether the process of communicating is in fact finding its target. These ratings and studies do not measure whether or how people actually invest their attention, interpretive powers, reflective powers, and gathering powers in what they see on television, nor do they determine whether or how people bring television content to discourse in the family. It is quite possible to have a very elaborate technological structure of communication, including encoding and decoding and satellites and messages, but if that final human person at the end does not participate in the television act, then nothing has really happened in that chain of communication. Counting the number of sets on and which channel they are on really has not told us anything about that act. We need answers to the question of how people actually use television in order to explore adequately the role of television within the ethical domain. How does it fit within what people do with their time and the ways they orchestrate their leisure?

The second point I want to stress is that if we want to do an adequate ethical questioning and examination of television we need to understand the reasons why people watch television and why they watch so much of it. The fact is that 30 years ago people did not do this, and now they do. We have to try to answer the question why they do.

---

[2] Conrad Lodziak, *The Power of Television: A Critical Appraisal* (London: Frances Pinter, 1986).

The question is difficult to answer. From among the variety of possible answers I would like to propose one very much in need of extensive discussion by moral theologians: We watch television for pleasure. We have to understand the nature of the pleasure television affords to come to any significant ethical assessment of the role of television in people's lives. People—we—watch television because it is enjoyable to do so. People have been shocked for generations now that even the most poor in any society—including Third World societies—make their first large acquisition a color television set, even if they have to endure great hardship and go into debt to have it. That relationship with the tube is bringing something to those lives that we have to understand.

What is the nature of this pleasure? John Fiske has a section on this question in his book, *Television Culture*,[3] which gives pertinent sociological and psychological views. Roland Barthes' fine small book, *The Pleasure of the Text*,[4] also enters into this question. I suggest that we should be doing ethical examinations of it too.

The pleasure of television is, first of all, a pleasure of the eye and of the ear. It is an aesthetic pleasure as well as an experience. The images that we see refer to things perhaps elsewhere—the Challenger tragically blowing up in the sky, a nation burying its president—but the experience for the viewer is sitting in a chair and looking at an image. In our examination of the pleasure television affords, we need to focus on entertainment television because that area bespeaks the key to pleasure more so than other kinds of television. It is the area of the junk: the soaps, the sitcoms, the game shows; yet entertainment television has also begun to transform television's coverage of news and sports and other events.

One element of the pleasure of television, the pleasure of the eye and the ear, has to do with the pleasure of recognition; that is why there are so many repetitive elements in the programs. The pleasure comes not from seeing or hearing something fresh or new for the first time but from seeing and hearing it again; such repetition deepens the pleasure of seeing and hearing.

A second element of this pleasure involves the affirmation of our identity: In our bodies we feel good and that gives affirmation to our identity. On television, it doesn't matter what is being said–what is being felt matters. The content of television is *our* emotions. The shaping and the form of television happens as it does in order to give articulation to our emotions. So many dramas, even the better ones, are very predictable at the cognitive level. It is the pleasure of seeing old J. R. or Don Johnson in *Miami Vice* do the same thing again and again. We have to gain a focus on the ethics of

---

[3] John Fiske, *Television Culture* (London: Methuen, 1987) 224-239.

[4] Roland Barthes, *The Pleasure of the Text*, trans. Richard Miller (New York: Hill and Wang, 1975).

emotions, the ethics of the body in the experience of viewing and hearing, to come to an understanding of how this affirms our identity.

Although this may sound all very positive so far, as if entertainment television by providing all these wonderful pleasures has been the best thing that has happened to our culture in the past 30 years, many a troublesome area also lurks in this domain. Neil Postman, *Amusing Ourselves to Death*,[5] unfolds the negative side of this notion of amusement and entertainment: It does not provide the recreation of the spirit, the firing of the imagination, or the participation and coming together in community to which the nature of leisure calls us and which the nature of work demands from us. It is not accidental that the more rationalized and factory-like work becomes for most people—the same people who watch television—the more the pleasures of this entertainment and the amusement and diversion of television have grown and developed.

Pleasure has always been a demanding element for any society to control. The church as well as civil society have traditionally had a difficult time in dealing with the experience of and the purposefulness of pleasure. Sexual pleasure has certainly concerned them because of its obvious connection with family making and baby making; but other forms of pleasure have concerned society, too. One particularly troublesome area in the pleasure television affords is that, from its visual perspective, the greatest pleasure of looking takes the form of a man's looking at a woman. Most visual media build on this relationship of men and women. It should not surprise us that a gender factor would be very central: As John Berger and his colleagues[6] have told us, the possession of a woman through looking at her has formed one of the themes of art in Western culture since the Renaissance. It still dominates as the theme of the cinema and remains one of the main themes of television. Directors and writers orchestrate dramas so that the camera—acting as the male regard—comes and finds the woman in distress or the woman of desire. Even women join this male gaze. Although a few have experimented to find a non-patriarchal presentation of image and drama, for the most part the mainstream remains this masculine pleasure.

The voyeurism in this pleasure still troubles us, too. We become peeping Tom; through our television sets we see something that we ordinarily don't get to see: the inside of a mansion in Texas or the inside of the White House. Through that looking we fetishize certain objects, notably the female, but also other objects. In this sphere advertising also plays powerfully with the icons and objects of desire that it orchestrates throughout.

---

[5] Neil Postman, *Amusing Ourselves to Death* (London: Heinemann, 1986).

[6] John Berger, Sven Blomberg, Chris Fox, Michael Dibb, and Richard Hollis, *Ways of Seeing* (London: Penguin, 1972) 47ff.

In this pleasure we find an empirical residue as Bernard Lonergan calls it,[7] and what Roland Barthes calls the grain in the voice.[8] It is the pleasure of hearing and recognizing the sound of somebody's voice, Pavarotti's for instance, and simultaneously noting the difference between that voice and Domingo's. At that level of hearing and only in these experiences do we know the determination and the distinction: a form of resonance within our own bodies for pleasure.

We need a moral guide through all this. The body has a constant: It instinctively chooses pleasure and avoids the hurtful and the unpleasant. Within this context we must start measuring proportional purposes and aims. The domain at which we should look is the game of the text, the game we ourselves play with the images. We need a form of discernment of spirits on these experiences. As we are taught in Galatians 5 and through holy writers of many ages, by our behaviors we will know the movements and directions of the spiritual energies and forces upon us. We have to understand better how those forces of pleasure lead and cooperate in the recreation or the deadening of our spirit and in the making or in the destroying of human community.

3. Conclusion

I have touched on two or three key ideas only, which form part of a much larger theory of mass culture, in order to focus specifically on the experience of the viewer–rather than on the programmer or the structure of the image–as being an important place in the ethical domain. Our evaluation of that experience takes place in the context of the necessary nature and function of leisure time. That leisure time and all its uses must in turn find a place in the moral universe.

---

[7] Bernard J. F. Lonergan, *Insight: A Study of Human Understanding* (London: Darton, Longman, and Todd, 1957) 25.

[8] Roland Barthes, *The Grain of the Voice: Interviews 1962-1980.* trans. L. Coverdale (New York: Hill & Wang, 1985).

10

Celebration, Consumption, and the Television Media

Joan S. Timm and Henry C. Timm

Social celebrations help form the moral imagination. Long associated with religious events, celebrations both reflected the religious mysteries and shaped the consciousness of the participants. In the modern world, the media of communication not only play a role in cultural celebrations but have changed them, noticeably through a strong reinforcement of patterns of consumption. In this sense the media now help fashion people's moral judgment.

Celebration and consumption. As two themes of this reflection, we can ask what those terms mean and whether these processes contradict each other within the context of a mass mediated culture. What moral issues does their conjunction raise today?

According to *Webster's Seventh New Collegiate Dictionary*, the verb "celebrate" means "to perform a sacrament or solemn ceremony or...to honor by refraining from ordinary business."[1] "Celebration," therefore, refers to collective participation in such ceremonies. "Consume," on the other hand, means "to destroy, use up, squander...or to spend wastefully."[2] "Consumption," therefore, refers to actions which satisfy personal interests or pleasures. The dichotomy is clear. The one orients us toward group cohesion; the other orients us toward our own desires.

Celebrations originated in relation to holidays or "holy days" and involved both religious and cultural beliefs. These beliefs emerged from myths that symbolized the tribe's most profound world view about human experience, and the rituals surrounding them re-presented these views in dramatic form. The tribe, therefore, acted within a public context which cre-

---

[1] *Webster's Seventh New Collegiate Dictionary.* (Springfield: G. & C. Merriam Company, 1969) 134.

[2] Ibid. 179.

ated, in Suzanne K. Langer's term, a "virtual space" in which their celebration made both a social and spiritual statement. Langer writes,

> the mark of a genuine myth is its power to impress its inventors as literal truth...in complete defiance of argument. It appears to be so sacred a truth that to ask in what sense it is true...seems like frivolity.[3]

Thus, the beliefs and the rituals were inseparable—the dance and the dancer were one. The forms of celebration involved movement, sound and vision and the dynamics of celebration united the whole tribe in a common archetypal psychological experience of which union, healing, and redemption were a part. The integrity of this archetypal process was crucial for celebration and called for a special space set aside for such purposes. The church or the theater held the everyday world apart—and business was temporarily abandoned for the world of the spirit.

What happens to celebration, however, if it is no longer separated from the world of business? What happens if it is confused with entertainment?

In the United States business implies consumption, leisure implies entertainment, and all four converge in the media. Television, in particular, has become a powerful force in American life. Exactly what impact has it had?

Many people outside the television industry blame it for being "too commercial." For example, in telecasts of the Olympic Games, the number of commercial interruptions annoys many viewers who perceive these games as a celebration set apart from daily routine. But the plethora of commercials should come as no surprise because the networks announce that they pay millions for the broadcast rights. Even the athletes cannot resist commercial pressure. When, for example, a gold medalist had his medal rescinded, he lost several million dollars in product endorsements for advertisers.

Criticism of the commercials overlooks television's historical roots. When the Federal Communications Commission was established in the early days of radio, the airwaves were viewed in the capitalistic sense as a resource to be used for commercial purposes. This perception reflected a fundamental change in the bourgeois ethos in the United States which began around the turn of the century. T. J. Jackson Lears[4] has described this ethos as shifting from a work ethic involving saving, civic responsibility, and a morality of self denial to a new set of values focusing on leisure, compulsive spending, apolitical passivity, and a morality of individual fulfillment. The new culture viewed magazines such as *Good Housekeeping, The American Magazine, Harper's,* and the *Saturday Evening Post* and, to some extent

---

[3] Suzanne K. Langer, *Feeling and Form* (New York: Charles Scribner's Sons, 1953) 81.

[4] T. J. Jackson Lears, "From Salvation to Self Realization: Advertising and the Therapeutic Roots of the Consumer Culture, 1880-1930," in *The Culture of Consumption: Critical Essays in American History, 1880-1980,* ed. R. W. Fox and T. J. J. Lears (New York: Pantheon Books, 1984), 3-38.

newspapers, as advertising media. Radio, at its inception in the 1920s, was also viewed by those in the industry as an advertising medium. Television, the child of radio, inherited its parent's legacy.

Great Britain and other countries took a contrasting view. They regarded the airwaves as a public trust to be used to *celebrate* their society. It is no accident that programs imported from England focus on English culture, whether in the form of Cromwell's civil war or the old Empire theaters.

In the United States, the media are not separated from the world of business—they *are* the world of business. Those controlling the media do not seek to celebrate life in the American scene. Their primary goal differs dramatically. Let us, for a moment, examine how their industry works.

If I were to offer you an opportunity to purchase stock in an industry which sells a commodity it does not own, manufactures a product which it views as a throw-away, and promises to deliver a product which it does not manufacture, would you buy? Probably not, but this is precisely how the television industry does work. A network aims to sell *time*—time on the air—to sponsors who wish only to lure the audience into buying their products. The programs, or the things which the network produces, function simply as bait which entices the viewer to watch the channel long enough to receive the advertiser's message. Networks perceive the audience as the product—a product which the networks deliver to the advertiser or sponsor every time an advertised item is purchased. Thus, viewed from inside, *consumerism* justifies the industry's existence; viewed from outside, *entertainment* does. The public tends to confuse an advertising medium with entertainment. We need to ask, "To what extent are those in positions of power—those who control the networks—held accountable to their audiences for the claims made by their sponsors and for the programs they produce?"

While the concept of "caveat emptor" dates to Roman times, we can still ask at what point an assumed sales pitch undergoes a transformation into chicanery. For one of us the first shock involving the ethical dilemma at the center of television advertising came in her first job after college when, as a young advertising executive, she asked a merchandising manager whether the claim he made for a product were true. He looked at her with disbelief and said "Truth? What has truth got to do with anything? Who cares what's true, so long as it sells?"

A serious consequence follows this sell-no-matter-what attitude, however. Commercial television becomes subject to the cynicism of the hucksters, and the audience receives *that* message. George Felton observed this trend among his college students: They claim to have learned a cynicism which seems to transfer into other areas of experience from the exaggerated claims of television commercials. As a result, the students show a tendency not to believe *anything* heard or seen. This implies, in Felton's words, "they don't have to make any commitments,...and most important, they

don't have to believe anyone."[5]   Such an attitude of indifference strikes at
the heart of a democratic society. Without belief and participation, we have
nothing and therefore no culture to celebrate.

Aside from the message of lies contained in commercials, what messages does television convey in its programs?   Dramatic form requires
movement, sound, and images. The only change in this form since the Renaissance has been technological advances surrounding the drama itself. We
have the capacity to cast images of movement and sound over vast dis-
tances, but the choice of images seems to reflect a fascination with surface
action and icons of commercialism, egotism, sex, and cruelty. Why? Whatever sells the program sells the products advertised during the station
breaks.   Some entire programs become commercials, glorifying consumerism in general.

Even broadcast news must compete with other programs conceived of
as entertainment, and therefore it must become entertainment as well. Responsible newscasters are deeply concerned about the necessary condensa-
tion of important events into 30 seconds or a minute with the inevitable
over-simplification of issues. But some view sensationalism as more important than substance. When a person causing a disturbance in a crowd gains
more air time than the presidential candidate's message, the network's message is clear: What the candidate has to say does not *entertain* as much as a
trivial peripheral action.   Importance has nothing to do with it.   Felton's
observation of cynicism starts in the broadcast studio.   Try to imagine a
newscast of the events surrounding Oedipus the King or King Lear. What
30-second images would be shown?   A blinded king and a dead daughter?
For what purpose?

Even public broadcasting does not escape the pressures of consumerism.   For example, Exxon announced a decision to stop supporting *Great
Performances* in favor of other "charities"—perhaps to enhance more effectively its public corporate image. It seems ironic that more programs celebrate English culture than American culture on American public television,
primarily as a result of lack of funding for the support of American play-
wrights and artists.

Another area of moral and media concern clusters around the term,
"icons." Icons are images originally meant to convey a profoundly spiritual message. All image makers employ their "imagination"—the word
literally means the "making of images"—and they create visions which
will most effectively convey deeper meanings to the viewer. Some popular images have succeeded in expressing concern for the human condition. Photographs of medical waste washed ashore on eastern beaches
are testimonials of such powerful messages. But other popular images in
magazines and on television convey little more than a preoccupation with

---

[5] George Felton, "Students of 'the pitch': To them, the world's an advertisement,
and in class nothing is funnier than irony," *Newsweek* 112 (September 26, 1988) 10.

sex or life in the fast lane. Ironically, it is sometimes impossible to determine exactly what some commercials advertise. Headless torsos in bikinis, rock bands, and even scenes of family life all lure the viewer into buying a variety of products from cars to sodas to hamburgers. What messages do these images convey? Underlying sexually alluring bodies, so-called designer clothes which have no famous designer behind them, or fast and expensive toys lies the lure of a chance at the life-style of the rich and famous.

What results from the imaginative process which created these images? Popular use of the term imagination generally refers to the creation of a fantasy or untruth. Certainly this definition fits many commercials and programs as well.

Imagination, however, may also refer to the act of creating images which express a world view. Is there a danger that the trivialization of human experience portrayed in the dominant television images has become our world view? Today less than one family in three actually conforms to our idealized concept of the American family. When a newscast program cuts from a story about the homeless in America to a commercial showing affluent neighborhoods, some interpret the message as plain indifference. In one recent news program a report about the recall of an unsafe automobile was actually followed by a commercial for that very same automobile. It makes one wonder whether network executives pay any attention to such ironic contradictions.

We suggested at the beginning of this essay that celebrations are public and social events. Television provides private spaces where individuals view images of sound and movement alone, separated from others. Ironically, the medium which transmits a so-called common culture into our homes also renders unnecessary an active involvement in that culture. Where does this isolation leave us as a society? In the absence of collective participation, who in the crowd can cry out that the images most resemble the emperor who has no clothes? That there is often *nothing* there? Who is there to hear? Trivialization produces a trivial world view but not trivial results.

Celebration in a mass mediated culture? Perhaps, but we need to address a profound question. In such a culture, have we altered our most fundamental myths? Popular use of the term "myth" generally refers to imaginary objects or events, but Joseph Campbell claims that myth acts as a metaphor for what lies beyond the surface or visible world—that it refers to life itself. Thus myth refers to a culture's most fundamental belief system. Myths also represent universal or cross-cultural truths which share the same insights into the nature of human experience in relation to the divine.

Campbell has further pointed out that a society's architecture represents a profound statement about its belief system—about its mythology.[6] In a medieval town, the cathedral stood as the tallest building. In an 18th century town, the political palace dominated. In a modern American city, the most imposing structures are corporate office spaces and hotels that provide meeting rooms for business. They also provide spaces for commercial ceremonies. The question arises, "To what extent have our social events now merged with the business of doing business?" Historically, ceremonial buildings were temples where imagery and pageantry joined to unify the group in celebrations of joy. Where is our joy—our enjoyment?

What are our American myths? One of our most firmly held myths embraces individualism but, as Bellah and his colleagues have so eloquently pointed out, the roots of individualism in America grew out of both classical republicanism, evoking "an image of the active citizen contributing to the public good" and Reformation Christianity, "inspired [by] a notion of government based on the voluntary participation of individuals."[7] Bellah places these roots in a context of "moral and religious obligation" but he goes on to indicate that "modern individualism has pursued individual rights and individual autonomy in ever new realms...[and that] it has come into conflict with...biblical and republican thought."[8] De Toqueville used the word "individualism" to describe his observations of "the restless quest for material betterment" and upward mobile status in American society in the 19th century.[9] "Individualism," however, originated as a derogatory term which implied putting one's self interests ahead of social concerns. Americans have turned this self-orientation into a virtue. Today consumerism depends on this later cultural interpretation of individualism. Does this transformation endanger our national spirit?

Images, imagination, and myth. How can we know whether viewpoints embodied in images are untrue, imaginative, trivial, or mythic in the spiritual sense? We know by the degree to which they resonate through human experience across time and space throughout history: The story of Gilgamesh remains as true today as it was in ancient Mesopotamia. Concerns of the human spirit are both universal and universalizable, and true myths are inextricably tied to morality and ethics. They concern the human condition and the issues of love and justice. They concern heroic deeds—not merely what people usually do but what they *should* do. They concern heroes.

---

[6] Joseph Campbell with Bill Moyers, *The Power of Myth* (New York: Doubleday, 1988), 95-97.

[7] Robert N. Bellah, R. Madsen, W. M. Sullivan, A. Swidler, and S. M. Tipton, *Habits of the Heart: Individualism and Commitment in American Life* (New York: Perennial Library, Harper & Row, 1986) 142.

[8] Ibid. 143.

[9] Ibid. 147.

We must ask ourselves as consumers in a mass-mediated culture whether we shall admire celebrities or heroes. A celebrity–that is a strange word in the context of this discussion for it literally means a person who is celebrated or famous. But what do celebrities celebrate? Themselves? Campbell has claimed that, among the many possible distinctions between the celebrity and the hero, celebrities are not models so much as objects of gossip.[10] Heroes, however, act to redeem society.

Television usually fails to distinguish between celebrities and heroes. If its producers either cannot tell the difference or are not interested in the difference, we as consumers, nevertheless, have choices. We can demand higher quality by holding network executives accountable for their broadcast decisions. We can resist the tendency toward trivialization. We can support programs which probe into substantive issues including a variety of formats from news to talk shows, from drama to dance. We can demand aesthetic quality. Network executives often make the mistake of underestimating their audiences. A late adolescent said recently, after he had seen his first Shakespearean play, "I cannot believe how dependent I have been on television for my own imagination. It's like junk food. That's why I am so hungry for real food now."

We need not buy advertised items whose images degrade or stereotype and we need not "buy" the programs they support. We can demand human values. For example, letters written to the Sears Roebuck Corporation by admiring parents helped to save the Fred Rogers show at a time when the only other significantly prosocial program for young children was Captain Kangaroo.

As audience members, we can resist seductions based on selfishness and we can respond to our own heroism. Recently our son participated in a church youth group conference in which guitars, song, dance, and symbolism were brought together into a pageant. The image was of a world filled with caring—with *caritas*. When he returned home he said "I used to think that art was what came out of television. I see how wrong I was. *Art* really has something important to say about life." His belief and his participation had unified compassion and aesthetics into a new world view. His celebration was complete.

If we, as audience members, demand no less of ourselves or those in positions of media power, then our public ceremonies can and will celebrate our most cherished collective American myth—a belief in the dignity and value of each and every one of us.

---

[10] Campbell 16.

11

Gender in the Media: Notes on Profit and Ownership Contraction

Christine E. Gudorf

Among the moral problems facing contemporary culture, the complex phenomenon of gender justice looms large. Whether or not they choose to, the
media play a very public role in the struggle for gender justice. At the same
time, the media are extremely limited in contributing to gender justice.
Gender justice entails the socialization of both men and women in ways that
allow the greatest possible freedom and creativity in the construction of personal identities and gender roles. Gender justice presents a problem for the
media because our society lacks gender justice in many ways, locked as it is
into slowly changing the restrictive gender roles which limit personal identity formation. People usually hold the media responsible for both reflecting
our social reality and presenting social reality as it should be in order to
influence persons toward that ideal society. With gender roles, as in many
other areas, it is usually impossible in any given instance to represent both
what is and what ought to be. If the role of the media were accepted as
primarily educational, the task of supporting gender justice in the media
would be simpler, though it would still be difficult to satisfy many whose
interpretations of both reality and ideal society differ. If the media were to
focus on research and information, documentaries and interviews, they could
explain how the present gender situation developed and what forces change
it.

But given that the media do not focus on education but on entertainment, the task of supporting gender justice becomes very difficult. In a
television sitcom, for example, does one represent the most common situations, including men's higher salaries, women's concentration in lower paid
pink collar work, sexual double standards for teens and adults, and the failure of most divorced men to honor child support agreements, or does one
attempt to change attitudes by presenting a society in which these situations
no longer exist? To present the real risks reinforcing the underlying atti-

tudes; to present the ideal risks encouraging complacency in a public which does not know how far social practice is from that ideal.

There can be little doubt that the last two decades have seen significant changes in the treatment of gender roles by the mass media. We see women as reporters for television and newspapers, as anchors for television news, as stars of their own television series. In book publishing, women's fiction, poetry, and feminist non-fiction have become big sellers. Many smaller, specialized presses actively seek out women's writing. On television we see women depicted as doctors, lawyers, police officers, and government officials. We read newspaper and magazine stories about women business executives, judges, and politicians. A whole new type of news story has developed: the account of a woman who has broken into a previously all male occupation. We have also begun to see a few men depicted in roles of nurturing parent, even positive roles of men as single parents. But the recent news flap over President Clinton's withdrawing support for Attorney General candidates Zoe Baird and Kimba Wood because of their illegal alien babysitter problems raised new issues of gender discrimination.

At the same time, it is very clear that some media areas are still not entirely open to women: Tradition by and large excludes women from covering sports, unless the players are women.[1] Also sports coverage, with the exception of the Olympics, features almost exclusively male sports. Television shows have fewer female than male leads. Within the ranks of the media industry, women seldom rise to the top executive positions.[2] Media companies, like many other organizations in our society, seem to imitate class elections in schools of the past: Women can be officers, but only secretaries, or at best vice-presidents to male presidents and treasurers.

In general, the changes made in the media regarding gender reflect an explanation of our society's gender arrangements based on liberal sex role theory.[3] This theory assumes that traditional gender roles just happened historically, that they can be changed by our deciding to act in different ways and teaching these new ways to the next generation, and that the obligation to change derives from the limitations placed by traditional gender roles on women's freedom. The mass media seem to take for granted the organizational structures of our society, and to assume that society satisfies gender

---

[1] John Leonard, "One Hand Clapping," *Ms.* (March 28, 1988).

[2] Janice Castro, "Women in Television: An Uphill Battle," *Channels: The Business of Communications* (January 1988) 42; "Study: No Strides for Women Execs," *Variety* (2 December 1987) 38; Jean Gaddy Wilson, "What It Takes To Be a Pro," *Working Women* (October 1985) 130; Elvis Mitchell, "Prime Time Players: But Will They Ever Break Through to the Top?" *Savvy* (April 1988); Kevin Goldman, "ABC Newswomen on the Warpath," *Variety* (22 January 1986) 39.

[3] Carol Robb, "A Framework for Feminist Ethics," in *Women's Consciousness, Women's Conscience: A Reader in Feminist Ethics,* ed. Barbara Andolsen et al. (San Francisco: Harper and Row, 1985).

justice when it admits women to occupational roles on the same basis as men. The burden falls on women to fit into the existing structures according to their desires.

This essay explores how the media have responded to the challenge of gender justice. First, it critically examines the sex role theories that the communication industry uses to justify its actions. Next, it proposes two alternative explanations for the industry's actions: its economic structures and its ownership structures. Finally, the essay concludes with a listing of methods for obtaining a more adequate treatment of gender in the media.

1. The Media, Gender Differences, and Sex Role Theory

Seldom do the media probe the issue of sex differences. Traditional assumptions about sex differences remain largely unchallenged despite an openness to new roles for women. For example, the portraits of men in the media demonstrate these traditional assumptions by portraying men in one of three patterns. (1) Men can appear as sensitive and compassionate as women, but then they are also depicted as either weak, pitiful objects of fun, often under the thumb of women, or as androgynous but asexual beings. (2) Men can appear forceful, vain, stubborn, stupid roosters not so subtly manipulated by women, the Al Bundys of the world. Or (3) men can appear as strong, silent, relationally isolated, competent leaders who get things done but who seem, upon careful probing, to live rather shallow emotional lives hedged around by impenetrable walls: the traditional romantic hero. Not so surprisingly, this last hero type often becomes a male sex symbol who demonstrates his desirability by the number of women he goes through every year.

Many television reviewers have noted that for all the problems the media have presenting women, they do a far worse job on men. Their overall message seems to indicate that real men—namely those not like women or dominated by them—are emotionally stunted.[4]

The gender problem from the media perspective is women, not the masculinist pattern of the public world. At their best the media demonstrate the difficulties women face in trying to compete in a public world formed to accord with masculine socialization: in competitive, impersonal enterprises which demand total commitment, compartmentalization of public and private selves, where the self-disclosure which makes intimacy possible is understood as dangerous vulnerability. At worst, the media depict the traditional values, commitments, and habits of women as impractical and inefficient in this public world, belonging rather to the domestic hearth which supports the public realm by serving as a refuge from it, a place of healing

---

[4] Tim Appelo, "Who's the Boss? In the Brave New World of TV Sitcoms Women Are Calling the Shots," *Savvy* (February 1988) 38.

which restores those who labor in the harsh public world and prepares them to return to it.

This perspective accords very well with an approach to gender based on liberal and democratic sex roles. It claims that we all reflect whatever understanding of sex roles society conveys to us. Society changes, conveys new sex roles to us, and leaves us with the task of making peace with the new roles. Attacks on these roles are defended with reference to liberal views on individual freedom: All persons are free to choose what roles they want, and the majority has chosen these. Furthermore, this is often understood to mean that whatever roles the majority has chosen are thereby not to be opposed, for the majority is always right. There is little understanding that majority support, while sufficient for determining social policy in areas where pluralism cannot exist, says nothing about the appropriateness or rectitude of the policy chosen.

Two major problems exist with the media's use of sex role theory to explain gender arrangements. First they inadequately present sex role theory and, second, the theory itself inadequately accounts for the phenomena. The media, which make only partial use of sex role theory, do very little to explain the very complex process by which we socialize our young into gender roles. The media, by failing to show the extent to which gender is a learned construct, convey the impression that biology dictates most of the content of gender roles. For example, much of the public has no idea that even the pitch of men's and women's voices is artificial: Men learn to pitch their voices lower, and women higher, than natural biological differences dictate.[5] The media convey the idea that aggression is natural for men and unnatural for women. While research indicates that aggression directly responds to levels of the male hormone androgen, different levels of androgen in both men and women produce situations where, though men as a group can be expected to be more aggressive than women as a group, some women will act more aggressively than some men.[6] Furthermore, the effects of teaming can overcome even the predisposition to aggression due to high androgen levels. We know societies with negligible levels of violence and even aggression among both women and men. We also know of societies which so encourage violence and aggression that women behave as violently as men.[7]

Nor do the media represent to the public the extensive ways in which we socialize males and females differently. Media examples of gender so-

[5] Nancy Henley and Barry Thom, "Womanspeak and Manspeak: Sex Differences and Sexism in Communications, Verbal and Non-Verbal," *Beyond Sex Roles,* ed. Alice Sargent (St. Paul: West, 1977) 201.

[6] Robert Crooks and Karla Baur, *Our Sexuality* (Indianapolis: Benjamin Cummings, 1987) 57, 63, 68.

[7] The classic research here remains Margaret Mead's *Sex and Temperament in Three Primitive Societies* (New York: Morrow, 1963).

cialization tend to be the most extreme and obvious: giving girls dolls and boys erector sets, the double sexual standard for males and females, and job discrimination against females. They make little attempt to convey the absolutely central role sex differences play in our understanding and behavior. We treat babies differently from the moment of birth onward, based on sexuality. Parents, even nurses in hospital nurseries, talk more to girls, hold them more often and more gently, and allow them to cry less than they do boys.[8] Such behavior occurs almost exclusively non-consciously. Most of us cannot touch or talk to a child until we know the sex of the child, whether the child is three days or three years old. We simply do not know how to respond to the child without knowledge of its sex.

In addition, the media act as if all segments of our society—much less all the other societies in the world—understand gender roles in the same way. In fact, gender roles differ greatly between white, black, and Hispanic societies in the U.S. The women's movement has learned this since black women in particular began to speak out to protest the white assumption that oppression of black women followed the same pattern as that of white women. The failure of the media to represent minority communities in general, and the complete failure to represent them truthfully, includes a failure to represent their understandings of gender roles. For example, a 1971 study of the inclusion of black women in U.S. children's encyclopedias—a prime source for school children—found black women severely under-represented. A 1987 replication of the study found that major encyclopedias failed to have entries for such persons as Maya Angelou, Ida Barnett, Angela Davis, Nikki Giovanni, Fannie Lou Hamer, Rosa Parks, Nina Simone, and even Sojourner Truth. Furthermore, black women entries received pictures at only 13% of the rate at which other groups' entries were pictured. Many of the entries failed to mention that the person was black.[9]

Nevertheless, perhaps the inadequacy of sex role theory itself matters even more than the adequacy of the media's use of it. Sex role theory fails as an explanation for gender arrangements because it cannot predict or derive an effective strategy for making gender roles more just. For even when sex role theory includes a recognition of the injustice of our gender arrangements arising from the restrictions imposed on the developments of both males and females, it fails to move beyond descriptions of the present reality. Sex role theory remains ahistorical to the extent that it fails to describe what historical groups and forces created and change these arrangements, which groups benefitted from them, and whose interests these arrangements continue to serve. Sex role theory implies that these arrangements just happened in history, served a function in the past, and now can be changed

---

[8] Crooks and Baur 77.

[9] Henrietta W. Smith, "Missing and Wanted: Black Women in Encyclopedias," *School Library Journal* (February, 1988).

because they are no longer functional. Since sex roles affect all people, the theory presumes that all support change in gender arrangements.

This explanation ignores the fact that, while sex role socialization has stunted the development of both sexes, this stunting has not had the same effect for both sexes, since other cultural and class variables significantly affect sex socialization. Males and females do not equally share an interest in changing gender arrangements. Women as a group would benefit much more from changing gender arrangements, since the present gender arrangement operates much more in the interest of men. For although men may be equally stunted by sex roles, the present arrangement compensates them with much greater social, economic, and political power than women have. Eliminating sex role distinctions therefore entails both gains and losses for men in general, while only gains result for most women. Yet even among women we find some individuals whose personal stake is at odds with that of the rest of their sex due to class and status differences among men. These women, by virtue of their connections to men of great power and wealth, share more of men's benefits from gender arrangements than they do women's restrictions. To be the wife or daughter of a powerful wealthy man may gain a woman a good job, allow her to share his prestige and respect, and at the same time allow her to escape many of the burdens experienced by ordinary women through hiring other women to do those tasks for her. For such a woman, equalizing gender roles will usually mean a loss of privilege.

Why is sex role theory the dominant model for understanding gender arrangements within the media? I want to sketch two structural aspects of the media which support the choice of sex role theory for explaining gender arrangements. These are the for-profit nature of the media and the process of ownership contraction within the media industry.

2. The For-Profit Motive within the Media

The for-profit nature of newspapers, combined with their need to compete with television for the media dollar of consumers, dictates that newspapers stake out a specialized share of the newspaper market and try to satisfy the desires of that market segment. If the readers of a metropolitan daily have more interest in sports or gardening than what happens to the diverse Soviet peoples after the disintegration of the Soviet Union, then that newspaper prints more sports and gardening stories. Specialty newspapers, such as the *Wall Street Journal,* construct their coverage to attract the largest possible audience interested in business news. News coverage is not about creating a well-informed general public but about supplying to a particular audience news for which it has already developed an appetite and which it demands to be fed. If the majority of the readers of a major city daily find complex economic or political news unfathomable, then instead of efforts to make the complexity intelligible, the paper simplifies the news by restricting itself to headlines followed by a few details. Such treatment has the double attraction of appealing to the greatest number within the newspaper's audience, which makes the newspaper more competitive, and of substantially cutting costs. Newspapers can afford to cut back on numbers of reporters, since news stories no longer require any real background expertise. Papers can replace news specialists with a reporter pool. Most major dailies commonly switch reporters' beats at the paper's convenience: If a paper need provide no real explanation or analysis of the news, then it can switch the reporter who has covered religion to cover the elections, and shift another from covering the courts to covering society. (Perhaps the only area still regarded as requiring expertise is sports.) In the use of reporter pools, papers' desires to cut costs and to meet readers' desires coincide.

Hard news has not only shrunk in terms of the amount offered by newspapers, but its character has changed as well. Newspapers have especially curtailed coverage of foreign news, with many relying almost exclusively on the wire services to the point where it has become almost impossible to follow what is happening in foreign countries by reading the daily newspapers. Increasingly those truly interested in news must subscribe to specialty papers and magazines to remain informed. Foreign countries may not make the general news even when extraordinary events occur unless those events touch national U.S. interests as those are popularly understood. When stories of coups, assassinations, widespread riots, or wars do hit the general news, the reader seldom has enough background information to enable an understanding of the meaning of the news. And since newspapers rely on the same few sources, the reader has little variety in what little news analysis does appear. The same thing increasingly happens in regard to domestic news: Plane crashes, hurricane damage, sex scandals about political figures and similar events take precedence over any attempt to understand trends in politics, economics, or society.

The for-profit nature of the media which dictates that news organizations limit coverage to what already interests or can be made to quickly interest the majority with their preselected audience works against the interests of those working for changes in gender roles. For it means that there is little coverage of minority movements and trends in any depth. TV, in particular, learned that its visuals, especially action tape, grabs attention, and so TV focuses on stories for which visuals are possible, especially video clips of dramatic action. Groups and organizations with counter-cultural messages concerning gender obtain little coverage in the news (or in entertainment programming for television or radio) until they learn to stage dramatic action accessible to TV crews—and such coverage as can be gained through such tactics conveys little useful information about their issues. What in-depth coverage special interest groups do get before they become mass movements tends to focus on individual personalities who warrant attention (movie stars who support feminist causes, for example) or who are considered entertaining freaks. Thus general coverage of the women's movement in this nation for years conveyed the movement in terms of isolated incidents of bra burnings, with no attempt by the media to cover the rather rapid infiltration of all the academic disciplines by women scholars, challenging and changing long-established understandings of both method and content in history, education, literature, philosophy, religion, and communications itself. Only when women's organizations began to have impact on the business world through court victories and on political organizations through lobbying and organization did the women's movement began to get dignified media coverage. Still today the impression given by the media is that affirmative action aims at non-exclusion of female bodies rather than at the inclusion of different, typically female perspectives and approaches to ideas and to reality itself.

This tendency of the media to focus only on what can grab the immediate attention of large audience blocks deprives members of society of the ability to decide for themselves, just as it prevents the many sectors of the society from working through the process of forming a deliberate social consensus. The purpose of knowing about special interest groups and movements in one's society is to inform one of choices offered for ongoing social development, to give one the opportunity to evaluate the proposed options, to stimulate one's ability to imagine yet other options, and to gather support for the option of one's choice in hopes of building a social consensus around that option. But the media often presents social change as something to be reported and adapted to, seldom as something to be probed and understood so as to be able to responsibly influence future change. The media thus encourage audience passivity.

This trend in newspapers also applies to television and radio news as well. Human interest stories play a large part in both local and network news. National news stories on television are largely headlines, with brief TV videoclips/30-second soundbites, reporting statements by government officials or those in opposition. When TV does attempt to analyze these statements, television news strenuously aims for "balanced" treatment of any disagreement, with little or no effort to demonstrate truth or falsity, even when it could easily find such information. The "balance" achieved is often more artificial than real since the institutional (Presidential, congressional, UN, etc.) position is most often presented as the center position which must be balanced by a view from the right. During the Reagan-Bush years, for example, family leave was treated so that any provision of family leave was leftist, the Administration veto was centrist, and the right advocated allowing employers to decide whether or not to include coverage of reproductive health care in worker benefits, as well as *allowing* sex/age discrimination likely to affect worker absenteeism. That spectrum is really a center to right spectrum masquerading as a left-to-right spectrum. There is no place on that spectrum, for example, for the paid maternity leaves that laws in Western Europe and even some Third World nations provide to women. The same problem exists with related issues, such as child care provision. In the liberal economic framework of the U.S., the spectrum of political views on child care has been presented as extending from a conservative position calling for legal/tax incentives for mothers of young children to be full-time mothers, to a moderate position in which government ends incentives for women to remain at home but does nothing to encourage mothers of young children to work, to a left position under which the government offers tax credits for child care and/or subsidizes child care for the lower working class. Again, there is no room to consider a system such as found in other developed nations whereby government makes child care accessible to all families at sliding scale rates, in neighborhood settings, subject to educational and health standards consistent with those in the public schools.

Most radio news, with the exception of programs such as NPR and some all-news radio stations, similarly lack news analysis. Again, those who desire any real knowledge of current events constitute a special audience. One might think that with radio stations gearing themselves to narrow specialized audiences,[10] some in-depth news stations would appear. But the general trend is to entertainment formats; within that general trend there are divisions of radio stations into call-in talk shows, country music, 50s music, 60s music, 70-80s music, hard rock, easy listening, and classical variety.

The special weekly news programs on television offer more background and analysis of selected news stories, but most of these include at least as much soft news as hard news and tend to avoid foreign news. Furthermore, in order to make real news more palatable to the broad public, television's hard news stories are likely to be exposés because the general public will follow, not the workings of our society, but scandal of various forms. We are more likely to turn on a show whose advertised lead story is pedophilic priests in the Catholic Church than we are a story on injustices and strains within the German reunification process or the medicinal riches being discovered in the Brazilian Amazon. This tendency, together with targeting special groups, leads to a splintering of the public not only in terms of the sources of information but also in terms of the ability to discuss, plan, and decide social policy. The different audiences might as well speak different languages for all they have in common.

What do these trends in media coverage have to do with media treatment of gender? A great deal. All these trends affect media coverage of gender. The exclusion of foreign news from the lives of most Americans means that they have no ability to compare gender roles in the U.S. with patterns in other cultures/societies for purposes of changing gender constraints. Clearly, for example, changes in understandings of women's roles

---

[10] David L. Altheide and Robert P. Snow, *Media Worlds in the Post-journalism Era* (New York: Aldine de Gruyter, 1991) 58.

in the U.S. arose from an acceptance of women's demands for equality in terms of their sameness with men. Women now have opportunities to take on male occupational roles. However, those demands of women which emanate directly from women's *differences* from men, remain controversial. Demands for adequate and affordable day care, for paid maternity leave without prejudice, for improved infant-maternal health programs, for the inclusion of reproduction options under both health insurance and Medicaid— all of these demands are made for women *as women,* not because they are already rights of men to which women demand equal access.

This differs from the pattern in many Latin nations, where women enjoy benefits premised upon their differences from men—their reproductive role. Peru, for example, has a law requiring employers to give a pregnant woman two months paid maternity leave before the birth of a baby and two months paid leave after the birth of a baby, followed by six months in which she has one paid hour of released time each day to go home and nurse her baby. Similarly, women in many traditional societies constitute a major workforce of manual laborers-farmers, water carriers, food gatherers, and even industrial workers. In Africa, for example, women perform more work than men, especially in agriculture. This contrasts with the U.S. understanding of women as appropriate workers only in light work, and thus challenges our prevailing notions of gender roles and traits. Without information about other societies, it is easy to accept U.S. patterns as both normative and "natural."

While prime time television still sometimes features women in traditional roles of homemakers or sex symbols, much more common is presentations of women in terms of stereotypical feminine characteristics: as naturally more compassionate, less violent, more sensitive, and more nurturing than men in the same occupational roles. A male attorney who treats clients brusquely or a male police officer who develops a hard shell against emotional involvement in tragic situations is only being professional. However, a woman who behaves in the same manner has serious "character flaws," or has allowed personal problems to interfere with her work. For example, liberal popular shows such as *The Simpsons* or *Cheers* present the women characters as more sensitive both to victims of various types and to nuances of relationships than even the most sensitive of the men. Similarly, the main characters in *Northern Exposure* speak much more openly about their emotions and are much more openly in pursuit of self-realization than most TV characters, but while both men and women are presented as having quirks and idiosyncrasies, the women are consistently presented as more relational, self-disclosing, and sensitive. In many ways, the traditional assumption that woman's role is to humanize the world has merely shifted from its traditional locale in the home where women ministered to husband

and children, to the public realm, where women must minister to all, with some men requiring a great deal more ministry than others.

3. Ownership Contraction in Media Industry

Another reason for the pattern of media support for existing gender arrangements comes from ownership contraction. In 1986, the top 25 newspaper companies controlled almost 60% of daily papers.[11] Similar trends appear in book publishing and in ownership of television and radio stations. But perhaps more alarmingly many companies own many different kinds of media. "In 1981 there were 46 corporations which controlled most of the business in newspapers, magazines, television, books and motion pictures. By 1986 there were 29."[12] For example, among the top 15 group owners in radio in 1980 were CBS (#1), ABC (#2), Metromedia (#4), NBC (#6), RKO (#7), Taft (#11), and Gannett (#12).[13] The percentage of group-owned television stations has steadily risen from 35% in 1954 to 73.3% in 1983 and continues to rise. In television program production, the leading 20 firms during the 1970s increased their audience share from 59 to 74% in prime time programming, and from 97-100% in daytime programming. The top firm controls 25% of daytime programming; the top four, 67%; and the top eight, 85%.[14]

Not only does contraction in media ownership continue, but that ownership does not reflect the general population. Minorities or minority companies own 1.7% of television stations and 1.9% of radio stations.[15] Minority or minority companies seldom own large stations.

Ownership contraction has severe implications for gender. When ownership contraction occurs, it means that large enterprises put a squeeze on the smaller, weaker owners, and that would-be-owners find it difficult to break in and stay in. Economies of scale as well as the ability of large corporations to use profits in one part to absorb losses in another for purposes of undermining competition both operate to continue the contraction of ownership in favor of the strongest, best established companies. This process now threatens the progress made in founding small women's presses during the last two decades. Publishing giants, who often refuse to order from small presses, own more and more bookstore chains. To sell books,

---

[11] *The World Almanac and Book of Facts 1988* (New York: World Almanac, 1988) 359. See also Thomas Shanks' treatment of this in Chapter 4.

[12] John A. Williams, "Prior Restraints," *The Nation* (23 April 1988).

[13] Christopher H. Sterling, *Electronic Media: A Guide to Trends in Broadcasting and Newer Technologies 1920-1983* (New York: Praeger, 1984) 57.

[14] Ibid. *66.*

[15] Ibid. *56.*

small presses must conduct direct mail advertising, which raises their costs and therefore their prices, making them less competitive.

Television stations owned by major companies buy much of their programming from either the networks or their own parent companies. It becomes more and more difficult for small companies which offer alternative messages about gender, or any other subject, to get a hearing in this medium.

Philip Green summarizes the compelling description of what Edward S. Harmine and Noam Chomsky in their book *Manufacturing Consent* call the "propaganda model" of the media:

> Structurally, of course, "the size, concentrated ownership, owner wealth, and profit orientation of the dominant mass-media firms," together with the historical development of advertising as their primary income source, necessarily define "mass media" (i.e., those capable of reaching millions every day) as central institutions of corporate capitalism. Since reporters and news gatherers are—and for the most must be, if they wish to be securely successful—no more than employees of the media giants, and since only governments and other corporate giants can systematically afford to provide "news" in an easily usable form, individual behavior is chiefly determined according to the simple workings of rational choice in a free market. In any event, the powerful did not get where they are by being inattentive, and the media market is therefore not really free; it is what Harmine and Chomsky call a "guided market." This "guidance" comes from employers and from the governments on which all depend for their continued "freedom"; it also comes indirectly from other "filters." These include the need of reporters and news gatherers to rely on information provided by governments, business and especially the "experts" funded and approved by them; the subvention by big business of an industry for producing "flak"—in the form of organized letter-writing campaigns and pressures from media "watchdog" organizations—as a means of disciplining media employees; and, at the ideological level, the careful cultivation of anti-Communism "as a national religion and control mechanism."[16]

A variety of factors largely obscures from the public the fact of ownership contraction in the media and its implications for social change. The data are not easily available, and corporations are faceless. The faces and voices on the media represent media to the public, and the phenomenon of tokenism gives the impression of gender revolution in the media. Women appear in anchor news spots, as reporters, as stars of series, as writers, and even as producers and directors. There are so many that few consider them tokens. But tokenism does not end merely by an increase in the number of tokens. The exclusion of women from executive positions in media companies and therefore from policymaking roles means that women in the indus-

---

[16] Philip Green, "The Commissar's Command," a review of Herman and Chomsky's *Manufacturing Consent: The Political Economy of the Mass Media* (Pantheon, 1989) in *The Nation* (15 May 1989) 670-671.

try function not to represent the experience and perspective of women (which is the message which comes across) but rather to represent the experience and perspective of male policymakers as if those were characteristic of women. Women in media, as women in any other male-dominated area of society, must conform to expectations of their employers who are the final arbiters of their skill and talent.

Ownership contraction in media means that a smaller and smaller number of powerful wealthy white men control the chief avenues of information and consciousness formation in our society. The self-interest of this group opposes any major shift in gender arrangements because this group represents the power and success of the dominant model of gender structuring. Emphasis on equality, on equal parenting roles and career opportunities for men and women, on equal responsibility for social and political decision making and housekeeping, threatens them both personally and professionally. Emphasis on the limits that the common good places on competition threatens their position.

The self interest of media owners compels them to promote a particular view of gender and gender roles that represents a social construct. An analysis of gender in our society discloses that gender has come to have a meaning apart from individual human persons: It can refer to dimensions of society independent of the gender of persons involved in that aspect of society. Such an analysis of gender discloses that masculinity and femininity exist as social constructs, and that we have structured our reality into masculine public spheres and feminine private spheres.[17] These spheres utilize wholly different values, which correspond to the differences between male and female experience. For example, both our understanding of politics and the structure of our political system reflects a predominantly masculine outlook. Both build on an understanding of human beings as separate individuals in competition with each other for survival, success, power, and wealth. Groups, while based on shared self-interests, are understood to exist without great stability because individuals within groups compete for influence and success against each other; further, all groups compete with other groups on the basis of self-interest. Order comes from balancing the power of these competing groups and individuals. Our governmental system incorporates a system of checks and balances based on this same understanding of competing interests. The different branches of government balance each other's power, preventing tyranny, just as competing interest groups within the country balance each other by exerting opposing pressures on government offices and officials. Thus no one group becomes dominant. Within this system failure to compete to protect one's own interest damages the whole by failing to check the power of the opposing force and allowing its domi-

---

[17] Anne Wilson Schaef, *Women's Reality: An Emerging Female System in White Male Society* (New York: Harper and Row, 1986); Ann Douglas, *The Feminization of American Culture* (New York: Knopf, 1977).

nation. Those who fail to complete not only lose, but create injustice. In fact, our criminal justice system uses this same understanding of reality—that truth and justice proceed from a competition between opposing forces, with the judge and jury deciding the winner. Cooperation between the two sides evinces a miscarriage of justice: One side has failed to represent its interest.

The feminine private sphere operates very differently. In the home, in personal relations, in families, and in religious communities the human person is not understood as essentially alone, an individual connected to others by self-interest, but as essentially social and relational. Order comes from supporting relationships between persons, from cooperation in the interest of the weaker. Parents cooperate to protect and instruct the young; families help out members faced with trouble such as sickness, death, job loss, and other tragedies. Religious and charitable communities work to provide emotional, economic, and political relief for persons and groups in need, whether they be dying members, local hungry or homeless people, politically powerless groups such as refugees, or foreign populations requiring assistance.

Analysis of reality as divided into gender spheres challenges the legitimacy of the masculine sphere in and through which media owners have achieved their power and wealth even more than it challenges the feminine sphere. For even those who defend the masculine sphere do not wish to see it universalized. They, too, need a place where they can be intimate not competitive, relational not isolated, and where they are loved for who they are and not for their status, power, or achievements. Defenders of the masculine sphere have, then, a double defense task: They must defend both the existence of the masculine sphere and the overall division of society into masculine and feminine spheres.

If media owners are to protect their self-interest, they need to use the powerful tool of the media to influence the public to accept the division of reality into these two spheres. This includes a number of subtasks, which I will list for convenience. They must

- Reject any responsibility for educating the public; instead propose media responsibility as limited to providing what the public already wants.
- Address products to the composite profile of the particular market. Accept no responsibility to respond to the desires of those outside the market or to the conflicting desires of segments of the market. (Programming thus exaggerates similarities and diminishes particularity within the audience, homogenizing it, erasing roots and histories, and obscuring particular situations as well as separating and differentiating the audience from other audience markets within the whole society.)
- Minimize the flow of information which stimulates comparisons of gender arrangements either cross-culturally or historically.

- Give women equal access to traditional male roles so as to mask the masculinist nature of the media and the public sphere in general. Emphasize the presence of women in the media organization.
- Stress "realism." Emphasize existing problems such as crime, violence, war, and international terrorism as complex and unsolvable, requiring tough handling by powerful experts.
- Encourage a need for leisure and entertainment as relief from the harsh and depressing reality of work and the public sphere. The media can both increase profits by selling products marketed as improving the quality of leisure time, and shape and control leisure time through such marketing.[18]
- Present religion as a private concern, a source of personal comfort and hope for individuals. Give support to this kind of religion: Give Sunday morning television and radio time, and print schedules of Sunday services in the newspapers. Depict those religious movements attempting to illuminate and change the nature of the public realm as dangerously fanatic and idealistic.

These are, of course, exactly the trends we see operating within the media. It requires a great deal of naivete to believe this is a coincidence. At the same time, the elite group of media controllers has not needed to shape the American public to the mold which best suited their interests. The historical character of the American public fits extremely well into that mold and continues to operate in more or less content acceptance of the wishes of the controlling class. The American public has tended, since its very beginning, to isolationism from the rest of the world, to extreme individualism, and increasingly to the privatization of religion. The for-profit nature of the media works to strengthen these tendencies, and the shrinking group which controls the media uses these tendencies to consolidate and preserve its own power. In many ways, the entire process serves the preservation of gender arrangements which benefit the few at the expense of the many.

4. An Alternative View

Things do not have to stay this way, however. Methods for obtaining more adequate treatment of gender in the media include

- Greater use of legally mandated processes for evaluating licensed media's performance in serving community needs.
- Legislation to reverse the contraction of media ownership, legislation that would raise women and minority ownership of media.

---

[18] Eli Zaretsky, *Capitalism, the Family and Personal Life* (New York: Harper and Row, 1975).

- Organization of women and pro-women organizations (such as women's professional associations, and unions with high female membership) to own and direct public media.
- More watchdog groups able to organize letter and telephone protests aimed at specific newspapers, magazines, stations, and their corporate sponsors over gender treatment.
- Continuing efforts at incorporating critiques of gender treatment within educational curriculum, especially in professional training, job training, and continuing education programs.
- Organization of small publishing houses in order to (a) enter the retail bookstore business, (b) press anti-trust cases against major publishers owning largest bookstore chains, and (c) press the large bookstore chains to accept books from small publishing firms.
- Continuing efforts of women-identified women to move into executive positions in the media.
- Increased efforts at cross-cultural exchange at all levels of society and more educational stress on foreign language, history, international politics, and social history.
- Public demands for better analysis and background in news treatment in television, radio, and newspapers. (Calls and letters have an effect, especially if a whole office, PTA, or neighborhood group calls or writes.)

It should be obvious at this point that inadequate treatment of gender in the media shares both its causes and its solutions with other symptoms of dysfunction in our social system. We need a movement to focus on including all presently marginalized groups in the educational, decisional, and structural functions of society. The churches should be an important part of such a movement.

12

Teaching Values: The Shifting Roles of Women and the Media

James A. Capo

Over the ages different groups have served as the major bearers of a culture's values. In agricultural and early industrial societies institutions like family, religion, and education carried a major responsibility for such inculcation. In this essay I wish to explore how electronic media function as a conveyor of our culture's value heritage, and whether their activities threaten or counter the responsibilities once exercised by more traditional institutions and individuals, particularly women.

To clarify this exploration we need definitions; let me propose what I mean by values and value inculcation. Values consist of, at least, deeply held and enduring ideals about the principles for a full human life and for the highest forms of community. They might include ideals like love, freedom, justice, equality, loyalty, courage, and so forth. "Values" differ from "mores," which refer to the everyday customs or habits of people. Value inculcation, as I use it here, refers to the process of introducing, transmitting, and reinforcing the culture's most deeply held ideals.

The idea that media inculcate values goes back at least to Harold Lasswell, one of the founders of media theory, who viewed media as more than just information transmitters or sheer entertainers. He included among the social functions of the media: first, the surveillance of the environment to disclose threats against community values; second, a convocation of activities in groups in society to make a response to those threats; and third, a transmission of the social inheritance.[1]

Media communication in this view operates as both a transmission process and as a process of "sharing, participation, association, fellowship,

---

[1] Harold D. Lasswell, "The Structure and Function of Communications in Society," in *Mass Communications*, ed. W. Schramm (Urbana, IL: University of Illinois Press, 1960) 117-130.

and the possession of a common faith." The media engage "in the construction and maintenance of an ordered, meaningful cultural world which can
serve as a control and container for human action."[2] Media power results
not only from their messages but also from the constant ritualistic process of
reinforcement of the cultural world. Even the act of regularly watching television or reading the newspaper, for example, form part of that ritual. For
Moore and Myerhoff, media are emerging as forms of "secular ritual" that
attempt "to bring some particular part of life firmly into orderly control"
and "to structure the way people *think* about life."[3]

Fiske and Hartley similarly offer a number of inculcation functions of
media. Media articulate an established cultural consensus about reality; they
locate persons in terms of the dominant value system of a culture; they celebrate and justify those representing the culture; they assure the culture at
large of its practical adequacy; they expose any inadequacies present; they
convince the audience that the culture as a whole guarantees their status and
identity; and they transmit a sense of cultural membership.[4]

However, we cannot restrict the exploration only to the phenomena of
media. For the last century, at least, American families viewed women as
inculcators of personal and social values. Women also played important
roles in value inculcation through education and religion. Now that media
increasingly convey values through their orchestrated social rituals, what
happens to traditional value inculcation and the role of women in it? And
how, if at all, does a medium like television address these matters? Teaching values emerges as not just a communications issue; it also confronts the
culture as a whole.

Therefore, I shall devote my attention in this essay to an exploration of
four questions:

- How do media, particularly electronic media, play a role in value
  inculcation?
- Do the media diminish the effectiveness of those previously under-
  taking such inculcation?
- Have the media had an impact on the gender-specific roles of
  women in the United States changing and thereby diminishing their
  importance in the value inculcation process?
- How do the media portray this metamorphosis in roles?

---

[2] James W. Carey, "A Cultural Approach to Communication," *Communication* 2
(1975) 1-22.

[3] Sally F. Moore and Barbara G. Myerhoff, eds. *Secular Ritual* (Assen, The
Netherlands: Van Gorcum, 1977) 3-4.

[4] John Fiske and John Hartley. *Reading Television* (London: Methuen, 1978) 88.

1. Media as Value Inculcators

Media teach values in two ways. From the perspective of media communication as a transmission process we see the media convey certain values and not others. Researchers have suggested that dominant American media do not regularly convey matters like care and love, mutual service, sharing goods, joys and sorrows.[5] As Michael Real pointed out over 15 years ago, American media stress action, measurable achievement, materialism, property, progress, optimism, competition, and individualism. That contrasts, for instance, with what Real's study of Peru found emphasized in that particular culture: feeling, subjective involvement, idealism, qualitative experience, tradition, acceptance, cooperation, and sociality.[6]

The media values closely align themselves with the values of the dominant American social system in which we live—the ones that we see all around us. Those underplayed also fail to find an echo in the dominant social system. The research suggests that media have taken an increasingly greater role in the presentation and inculcation of values of the dominant culture.

Second, media teach values more subtly—by the way they proceed and by the way people use them. Even "objective" (i.e., "value-free") news engages in the inculcation of social values that support that nation's socioeconomic profile.[7] Dahlgren classifies these persistent "ways of seeing" as agencies of "ongoing socialization."[8] Gitlin calls them "hegemonic frames" that legitimate mainstream institutions as mediators of cultural and social conflict.[9]

For Goethals, broadcasting operates as a daily, secular ritual that reenacts events thought to be crucial for the community, renews the citizen's faith in a center of values in America, and confirms his or her place in the larger social and symbolic order. Television provides contemporary national icons (sacred images) and rituals (enactments of myth) as substitutes for the symbols and creeds of other mythic traditions and ritual practices.[10]

---

[5] Mary L. Schropp, ed., *Platform for Action: The Electronic Media, Popular Culture and Family Values* (New York: United States Catholic Conference, Department of Communication, 1985) 13-21, 41-47.

[6] Michael R. Real, *Mass Mediated Culture* (Englewood Cliffs: Prentice-Hall, 1977) 208-230.

[7] Gaye Tuchman, *Making News* (New York: Free Press, 1978); Herbert J. Gans, *Deciding What's News* (New York: Pantheon, 1979); W. Lance Bennett, *News: The Politics of Illusion* (New York: Longman, 1983).

[8] Peter Dahlgren, with Sumitra Chakrapani, "The Third World on T. V. News: Western Ways of Seeing the 'Other'," in *Television Coverage of International Affairs,* ed., W. C. Adams (Norwood, N.J.: Ablex, 1982) 45-48.

[9] Todd Gitlin, *The Whole World is Watching* (Berkeley: University of California Press, 1980) 51, 66.

[10] Gregor T. Goethals, *The T.V. Ritual: Worship at the Video Altar* (Boston: Beacon Press, 1981) 125-144.

Thorburn makes the same point, although his concern is aesthetic and he focuses solely on American network television. The programs of such television operate as a

> consensus narrative...a chief carrier of the lore and inherent understanding of...society's idealizations and deceptions about itself. That inherited understanding is...a matrix of values and assumptions that undergoes a continuous testing, rehearsal, and revision in the culturally licensed experience of a consensus narrative..., where the deepest values and contradictions of society are articulated and, sometimes understood.[11]

One former television producer suggests that media and God function in similar ways–as all knowing, all present entities, capable of changing the course of world events. Americans have become almost wholly dependent on media for news and now imbue television actors with angel-like qualities. Americans have not abandoned religion–many now find it on television.[12] Critics have called television the successor of conventional faiths and a new religion.[13] Yet this medium propagates values at odds with traditional religions observed by Americans.

Mass mediated values matter because, as most of the research suggests, people increasingly use media throughout the day. Radio, for example, enjoys its highest rating during time periods when it is difficult to watch television: during commutes and at work. In greater New York, for example, AM radio now invades the work place with talk formats; decades ago, music radio penetrated elevators, retail locations, and assembly lines through Muzak. The media play a greater role because of their greater use. Consequently, other means of communication such as the interaction and symbols one might encounter through education, religion, and family life have correspondingly less impact on value inculcation.

2. Diminished Effectiveness of Traditional Agents of Value Inculcation

Our second question asks whether the effectiveness of those previously engaged in value inculcation has diminished. While recognizing the difficulty of the question, I maintain that their effectiveness has decreased.

---

[11] David Thorburn, "Television as an Aesthetic Medium," *Critical Studies in Mass Communication* 4 (1987) 171.

[12] Tony Schwartz, *Media: The Second God* (Garden City, N.Y.: Random House, 1983) 3-9.

[13] George Comstock, Steven Chaffee, Natan Katzman, Maxwell McCombs, and Donald Roberts, *Television and Human Behavior* (New York: Columbia University Press, 1978); Michael Novak, "Television Shapes the Soul," in *Television: The Critical View*, 2nd ed., ed. H. Newcomb (New York: Oxford University Press, 1979) 303-318.

Various signs point to the emergence of values different from those conveyed by traditional inculcators. One is the rise of consumption as the single good in society; another is the alteration in understandings of time and
space; and the third is a loss in a personal sense of power and imagination.

Media operate as the most widely used exponents of today's prevalent consumer clutter which validate some relationships at the expense of
many others:

> Money is the be-all and end-all of every television minute.... There is
> no issue, no matter how serious and complicated, that cannot be boiled
> down to a 30-second spot. Any programming is justified that will at-
> tract and hold viewer attention inexpensively between commercials.[14]

Whatever else transpires in the privacy of American homes, media often
reflect or focus attention on values and behaviors inadvertently at odds with
those that traditional American society has espoused: "Media elites are
imagining our lives and world for us in ways that run counter to the fundamental commitments in my life." Audiences accept media images "because
they fit in with a culturally produced ethos, with a way of life and habit of
thought that has merged among a people over time."[15]

The invasion of the home becomes especially significant for youth
when so many adults must earn outside income: "Children are more likely
to be familiar with the total pattern of life of television families than with
that of their own parents." They may emulate adults from their favorite TV
dramas "or young entertainers whose linkage to the world of work is only
through their art, and those private lives are the subjects of the fables of
stardom." Meanwhile, commercials idealize "products and styles of life that
may be far different from the patterns developed in the local community. In
many ways, then, young people learn to see the world through the eyes of
Hollywood and Madison Avenue."[16] When television presents activity, it
often emphasizes conflictive or consumptive resolutions of problems facing
dramatic agents. An early governmental study of media violence found that
physical violence served as an important part of entertainment plots.[17] Subsequent studies uncovered continuation of the pattern. Competitive sports
programs, with variations on personal aggression and intimidation, also manifest

---

[14] Everett C. Parker and William B. Kennedy, "On Control: A Discussion of the
Ethical and Moral Issues Arising from Current Communication Policies and
Practices," *Religious Education* 82:2 (1987) 211.

[15] Michael Warren, "Images and the Structuring of Experience," *Religious Education*
82:2 (1987) 247.

[16] Barbara Hargrove, "Theology, Education, and the Electronic Media," *Religious
Education* 82:2 (1987) 221.

[17] Robert K. Baker and Sandra J. Ball., *Mass Media and Violence: A Report to the
National Commission on the Causes and Prevention of Violence* (Washington, DC:
U.S. Government Printing Office, 1969).

this phenomenon. Even news emphasizes conflictive relationships.[18] Robinson called heavy television viewers an "inadvertent" news audience, deeply frustrated about real-life displays of continuous, evenly-matched conflict.[19]

Meanwhile, advertisements portray people turning to products to resolve human problems of love, social acceptance, parenting, etc. Game shows construct money and luxury products as goals worthy of interpersonal feuding or ridiculous, dehumanizing behavior. Popular prime-time programs in the 1980s like *Dallas* and *Dynasty* gave paramount importance to money and acquisition for families embroiled in bitter conflict.

A second factor suggests a decrease in the impact of traditional inculcators of values: our new understandings of time and space. Through a VCR and a remote control device a child now has the ability to change time and space in ways previously unavailable. This new technological power externalizes imagination through which the child will experience different realities—the home at one moment, the school the next, "Fantasyland" the next, and so on. The media too often provided a fragmented view of the world. Meyrowitz argues that in recent decades electronic media have greatly impacted Americans' sense of place and ushered in a new order. Social groups once defined by their isolated location in "kitchens, playgrounds, prisons, convents" have become part of the social (i.e., media) landscape. The world now seems "senseless" to many because it is "relatively faceless." Electronic media disintegrate "distinctions between here and there, live and mediated, and personal and public." Consequently, controlling media content "will not maintain old forms of social organization. Even conservative content may be revolutionary when disseminated in new ways."[20]

While traditional value inculcators stressed a rich past, a transcendent future, or both, electronic media emphasize the present. As both Boorstin[21] and Bennett[22] argue, modern media convey fragmented and ahistorical views of experience. These media provide a breeding ground for "radical" freedom, thereby isolating individuals and making them susceptible to social control where managers and therapists in the name of value-free knowledge gain ominous control.[23]

---

[18] Bennett 9.

[19] Michael J. Robinson, "American Political Legitimacy in an Era of Electronic Journalism: Reflections on the Evening News," in *Television as a Social Force: New Approaches to TV Criticism,* ed. D. Cater (New York: Praeger, 1975) 105-110.

[20] Joshua Meyrowitz, *No Sense of Place: The Impact of Electronic Media on Social Behavior* (New York: Oxford University Press, 1985) 307-313.

[21] Daniel J. Boorstin, *The Image: A Guide to Pseudo-Events in America* (New York: Harper & Row, 1961) 11.

[22] Bennett 18-21, 99-100.

[23] Robert N. Bellah, "The Sociological Implications of Electronic Media," in Schropp 15.

Fixed time and space held positions of permanence in traditional value systems. But modern media highlight disconnected, ephemeral change–a forever and ever with neither pause nor eternity. In such an environment, no value enjoys lasting importance. No enterprise requiring personal persistence seems worth doing. The associative miracle of juxtaposing electronically visual images of problem with solution (usually a consumer-oriented or behavioristic one) can make audiences bored with anything that lasts more than a few seconds.

Third, for persons perpetually in the incessant media flow, personal alienation and fragmentation can occur. Losses also take place in imagination and in a personal sense of power as people fail to stay abreast of the flood of mass mediated data of the moment. In the face of the media onslaught users relinquish attention to the past and future, to memory and foresight, and to an in-depth encounter with experience or self. Media usage facilitates union with the ever perishing present at the expense of reflection and action.[24] When a media user displays silence, it too often "signifies passivity..., hypnosis..., alienation..., surrender to the immediate instead of the transcendent, and a moral life dominated by rhetoric but not ethics."[25]

A similar passivity seems to operate in the generation of college students I teach. The so-called "electronic generation" seems more interested in being entertained than in controlling information or personal imagination. Too often electronic "others" do the imagining and the controlling for us. Television often generates mechanistic passivity or predictable behavioral responses.

> If we live in a global village, it is a strange village indeed, though we live in it, we are mute and powerless.... [W]e cannot even decide what portions of the village or aspects of its life we will see, or the points of view from which we will see it. These decisions are made from the frame of a television screen, by the values of a television director, according to the biases of a television network.[26]

Since audience numbers still determine the economic success of most television (commercial, public, cable, VCR tapes), little incentive exists to alter the sheer behaviorism of passively staying tuned. This orientation has become so commonplace that, for example, TV journalists portray political

---

[24] Jacques Ellul, *The Political Illusion*, trans. Konrad Kellen (New York: Knopf, 1967) 56-63.

[25] James A. Capo, "The Shallow Silence of the Media World," *Media Development* 29:4 (1982) 4.

[26] National Council of the Churches of Christ in the U.S.A., "A Report of the Study Commission of Theology, Education, and the Electronic Media," *Religious Education* 82:2 (1987) 171.

campaigns as spectator sports watched to ascertain the winner, rather than as occasions for public debate about important issues.[27]

For Boorstin, modern media fabricate the illusion that people enjoy a power once held only by God, while in actuality, they are worse off than the chained human in Plato's cave.[28] Gerbner and Gross characterize the response of heavy television viewers toward violence in terms of increased, paralyzing fear about personal safety and decreased involvement in the outside world.[29] Instead of a healing, transcendent silence, television engenders a homogeneous passivity and respite from daily frustrations, even as its messages reinforce the authority and necessity of routine.[30]

> Even, constructive, educational programs like "Sesame Street" do not escape the criticism of engendering passivity. By helping the viewer learn the proper letter or experience through a camera zoom or cut, the picture, not the person achieves the answer. This can discourage individual imagination in learning: the tendency to search, and find for yourself what is important and hone in yourself, which we would otherwise cultivate in children, is in fact not being cultivated because the camera is doing the mental work for you. So your own tendency to do that mental work atrophies.[31]

The passivity reinforced by the media experience connects to other cultural value shifts. Capitalism's subordination of "being" to "having" entered a new stage with electronic communication. Now appearance subordinates possession as the major criterion for behavior. Narcissism, a way to cope with this environment, rejects both sacred and profane temporality in favor of the present.[32] Life resembles a constant look into the imaginary camera poised to record and replay every blemish of one's performance.[33] The electronic media amplify this cultural trend.

If urbanized, industrialized, capitalistic civilizations have already embraced functions carried out by modern media, what singles the media out

---

[27] See Paul Weaver, "Is Television News Biased?" *The Public Interest* 26 (Winter 1972) 57-74; Michael J. Robinson and Margaret A. Sheehan, *Over the Wire and on T.V.: CBS and UPI in Campaign '80* (New York: Russell Sage Foundation, 1983) 144-151.

[28] Boorstin 239-261.

[29] George Gerbner and Lawrence P. Gross, "Living with Television: The Violence Profile," *Journal of Communication* 26:2 (1976) 172-199.

[30] Capo 5.

[31] Robert Liebert, and William B. Kennedy, "Understanding Media: An Interview with Robert Liebert," *Religious Education* 82:2 (1987) 196.

[32] Christopher Lasch, *The Culture of Narcissism: American Life in an Era of Diminishing Expectations* (New York: Norton, 1979) 28-33.

[33] Michael J. Arlen, *The Camera Age: Essays on Television* (New York: Farrar, Straus, Giroux, 1981) 9-17.

for special concern? Too many media, it would seem, relate the intimate affairs of others to large audiences without generating public space or facilitating discussion about their social implications. Television, for example, provides a feeling of intimacy without any sense for community. Its social message emphasizes consumerism (a private activity) as an appropriate response to problems which may have civic significance.

If television simply transmitted information or reflections of the "real world," critics would not single it out for attention. But as *celebrator* of a certain cultural inheritance, it may lead to illusions of intimacy and lasting values,[34] even as it denigrates both and destroys the possibilities for public space.

> As one critic notes, "These images, these things that are being named into my life, these do not reflect the true me. They do not come out of me. They are thrown at me.... If I let them, they will turn my life around or even inside out. Rather than operating from an inner core, my life will be moved almost entirely from the outside, by norms and fashions concocted by those who care nothing for me or for my life."[35]

The confusion of public and private realms extends to the family as well. Television's invasion of family life has resulted in its becoming a dominant educator of the young (especially through programming not intended for young viewing)–in areas where the child has few or no "counterviewing sources of information by which to compare and evaluate television messages, and his or her developing intelligence and social skills may not be able to assess and evaluate adequately what is seen on television."[36]

The developing educational role includes a corresponding rise in television's importance and effectiveness in the transmission of social values to children. Citing Bandura[37] and the findings of numerous mass media effects studies, Comstock reports that television appears to have become a major agent of socialization, capable at least of influencing the behavior and evaluation of youth in a variety of areas.[38] As an influence on socialization, television "to some degree has replaced more traditional agents–home, school, and church," although the relative importance of these "alleged

---

[34] Goethals, *T.V. Ritual* 125-136.

[35] Michael Warren, "Some Reflections on Religious Media," *Catholic Library World* 53:10 (May/June 1982), 424-427.

[36] George V. Coelho, "Introduction," in *Television as a Teacher: A Research Monograph*, ed. G. V. Coelho (Washington, DC: National Institute of Mental Health, 1981) 2.

[37] Albert Bandura, "Social-Learning Theory of Identificatory Processes," in *Handbook of Socialization Theory and Research*, ed. D. A. Goslin (Chicago: Rand McNally, 1969) 213-262.

[38] George Comstock, "Television and Social Values," in *Television as a Teacher: A Research Monograph*, ed. G. V. Coelho (Washington, D. C.: National Institute of Mental Health, 1981) 135-163.

agents of socialization" has not yet been empirically assigned.[39] The extent of its influence in younger children probably rests on the "degree of abdication" of authority "indulged in by" parents and other adult educators.[40]

3. Impact on a "Traditional" Role of Women

For the last 100 years, American society has divided responsibilities in the area of value inculcation between men and women. While this separation may have existed before, men were wrenched out of the household as America industrialized: They lost face-to-face interaction with children and women during weekdays. As industrialization removed work from the household, the woman's functions began to focus increasingly on bearing and nurturing children, while providing physical and emotional support for the males now working in industrial settings. This division of "labor" in the post-agrarian age left to women the specialized activity of value inculcation and created a new consumer role for them. While sexism had existed for many years before that particular shift, the rise of industrial America placed greater responsibility on the woman to deal with value inculcation of those standards that traditional societies held in highest esteem. Now that the mass media play a role in inculcating values, what is the impact on women?

The contemporary rise of media in the value inculcation process along with the changing roles of women may threaten the values that had operated in the so-called "private" sphere and undermine the social meaningfulness of a "traditional" role for women who still engage in it. The gender division that occurred about a 100 years ago was reinforced, at the time, with a greater division of the private from the public world which reached its peak when men left the agrarian work place (the homestead) and society no longer viewed women as "workers."

In our contemporary situation, media (electronic media to be sure, but all media) re-invade domestic space and blur distinctions between private and public spheres. Rakow, for example, found out that telephone usage in smaller communities have helped women hold onto positions of power in relation to men through the conversion of the community from a public world of men to the private sphere of women. Through its combination with another private and media related activity, shopping, electronic communications technology has contributed to the maintenance of woman's economic, political, and social status.[41] And Spigel has argued that, although broadcasting "offered a grand illusion of the outside (i.e., public) world,"

---

[39] Ibid. 137.

[40] Ibid. 147.

[41] Lana F. Rakow, "Not Just Another Piece of Data." Paper presented to The 38th Annual Meeting of the International Communication Association (New Orleans, May, 1988).

women "recognized the discrepancy between the everyday experience of domestic isolation perpetuated by television and the imaginary experience of
social integration which television programming constructed."[42]

Spigel's analysis of magazines in the early 1950s indicates that women
were shown as isolated from this new electronic theatrical experience in the
home because they still had to carry out traditional chores. If their households were able to purchase the latest appliances (for example, an electric
dishwasher), they too could engage in the new family activity.[43] Needless
to say, the consumption of commodities in order to reenter family life (now
reorganized around the television set eventually located in a space called the
"family room" separate from the "living room") contributed to role shifts in
the domestically inclined women—if not value shifts as well.

Television brings to the private sphere a consumer value system dominated by images of the popular culture, and similar to the ones that operate
in the competitive economically driven "public" world. When we invite a
Dallas, the evening news, sporting events, or any commercially sponsored
American television program into our home, we may be introducing value
inculcation system and message that counters the ones previously there. We
may actually be transforming what might be called "private space." Increasingly, people at home are being defined socially—as consumers. Once these
people/consumers appear as demographic numbers and statistical bits of information, different kinds of domestic interaction and value transmission
grow in importance. One merely needs to look at advertising portraits of
family interaction to get the media answer.

The exodus of American women from the home, or at least from the
private and domestic activities assigned to them in the 19th century, has
accompanied (though the two do not necessarily directly correspond) the
invasion of domestic space via electronic media. Factors like modern technology, the rise of feminism, readily available college education for both
sexes, the need for women to earn money in order for families to maintain
their standards of living, the consumer message of media, and other changes
in contemporary life[44] have all contributed to this exodus with an inevitable

---

[42] Lynn Spigel, "Installing the Television Set: Popular Discourses on Television and
Domestic Space, 1948-1955," in *Private Screenings: Television and the Female
Consumer*, ed. L. Spigel and D. Mann (Minneapolis: University of Minnesota Press,
1992) 1.

[43] Ibid. 3-15.

[44] For some of the "other" changes, see: K. Davis, "Demographic Foundations of
the Sex Role Revolution," *Social Science* 71:1 (1986) 1-5; J. Cross, "Social Issues
Affecting Women," *Dulwich Centre Review* (1985) 60-63; H. S. Strean, "The
Psychoanalyst: An Agent of Social Change," *Current Issues in Psychoanalytic
Practice* 2:2 (1985) 29-37; J. I. Roberts, "Changing Roles of Women: Birth of a
New Reality," *Women and Therapy* 4:1 (1985) 41-51; and A. Cherlin, "Changing
Family and Household: Contemporary Lessons for Historical Research," *Annual
Review of Sociology* 9 (1983) 51-66.

shifting of roles for women. A relative change in the process of value inculcation has resulted as one of the unplanned, (and, perhaps, unconscious)
outcomes of shifting roles in contemporary American society.

When a social institution like television infiltrates personal, intimate
space with a message that celebrates anti-personal and anti-community values, it requires ethical responses that are more "social" in orientation. We
cannot approach electronic media as simply matters of personal choice, any
more than we can issues of race relations, natural resources, or urban living.
As institutional celebrator of important communal values, television becomes common property.[45] We cannot simply view it as a neutral instrument available for responsible private conveyance of traditional communal
values. For many media critics, any simple instrumental appropriation of
television in the name of the good family, a deeply held faith, or the just
society will not resolve the complex societal problem that the institution of
American television poses. Cultural researchers thus need to determine who
now takes responsibility for value inculcation, how much of it rests with the
media, and how important the inculcation role of women and other more
traditional sources of value really is.

4. Media Portrayals of Role Changes in Value Inculcation

The fourth question for exploration in this essay is whether or not
media themselves portray this metamorphosis in roles. Do media acknowledge their own engagement in the value-laden communication and do they
portray satisfactory alternative social roles for women? My observations
suggests that for the most part media ignore the change in value-inculcation
roles and do not depict their own engagement in this process. Meanwhile,
their current representations of women suggest insensitivity to women and
the complexity of their current situation.

According to researchers, print media before the recent feminist movement relegated women to special sections (like "fashion," "home," and
"women's"). Visual media emphasized stereotypical features of domesticity,
sexuality, and limited intelligence. Then media caricatured feminist efforts
in demeaning ways and later treated the feminist movement as a series of
discrete events all concerned with a single issue Overall, Tuchman and her
colleagues found media treatment of women through the mid-1970s as inadequate and insensitive to the social changes underway.[46]

---

[45] National Council of the Churches of Christ in the U.S.A. 179.

[46] Gaye Tuchman, Arlene K. Daniels, and James Benet, eds., *Hearth and Home:
Images of Women in the Mass Media* (New York: Oxford University Press, 1978)
3-38.

While adjustments in media treatments have occurred over the last 15 years, the changes are not considered sufficient by a number of researchers and critics as Christine Gudorf pointed out in Chapter 11.[47] Entertainment and advertisement producers now portray women as engaged in an expanded variety of social roles.[48] While some female characters engage in social or economic activities outside the domestic world,[49] a greater number are still depicted in places associated with traditional roles of value inculcation–often in "family" settings at home or the work place. Others appear to be struggling with the tension between inculcation roles and other responsibilities they have assumed. Still others are portrayed as threats to the enhancement of traditional values–particularly physically attractive and sexually alluring creatures.[50] Finally, some represent victims of cultural evils and violence.[51] The media depict working women as increasingly active and skilled. But in the domestic world, they engage primarily in consumption and the exercise of technique. Like men, they enjoy negative freedom ("freedom from" or "liberation") but they do not engage in positive freedom (to imagine or create new forms of relationship). The "new woman" has too often been depicted as a symbol of American male-dominated myths of material progress and ethnocentrism rather than as a living challenge to and reformulator of these myths. Increased portraits of females in the media will do nothing to reconstitute these myths if the women's roles portray predominantly conflict or consumption behavior.

---

[47] See also, for example, Muriel G. Cantor, "Feminism and the Media," *Society* 25 (July-August 1988) 76-81; C. L. Ferrante, A. M. Haynes, and S. M. Kingsley, "Images of Women in Television Advertising," *Journal of Broadcasting and Electronic Media* 32:2 (1988) 231-37; D. Chavez, "Perpetuation of Gender Inequality: A Content Analysis of Comic Strips," *Sex Roles* 13:1-2 (1985) 93-102; C. M. Lont, "It's Not What They Play, It's What They Say: A Content Analysis of D.J. Chatter," Paper presented at the 11th annual meeting for the Study of Communication, Language, and Gender (San Diego, 1988); C. Berg, "Sex, Violence and Rock 'n' Roll: The Manipulation of Women in Music-Videos," Paper presented at the 70th annual meeting of The Speech Communication Association (Chicago, 1984); or S. Steenland and L. Whittemore, *Women Out of View: An Analysis of Female Characters on 1987-88 TV Programs* (Washington, DC: National Commission on Working Women, 1987).

[48] D. J. Bret and J. Cantor, "The Portrayal of Men and Women in U. S. Television Commercials: A Recent Content Analysis and Trends Over 15 Years," *Sex Roles* 18:9-10 (1988) 595-609

[49] S. Steenland and L. Whittemore, 1987. See also S. Steenland and P. Fujita, *The Picture Improves: A Look at the 1984 Television Season* (Washington, DC: National Commission on Working Women, 1984).

[50] A. C. Downs and S. K. Harrison, "Embarrassing Age Spots or Just Plain Ugly? Physical Attractiveness Stereotyping as an Instrument of Sexism on American Television Commercials," *Sex Roles* 13:1-2 (1985) 9-19.

[51] C. Berg, "Sex, Violence and Rock 'n' Roll".

With the exception of those women shown as experiencing tension between traditional (domestic) and liberated (professional) functions, the media give little attention to changes in the woman's role in value inculcation. (Even fewer portraits of men who experience this tension make it in the media.) And when changes do appear, media ignore larger historical or social causes and offer no insights about consequences. Often, responsibility for ultimate resolution rests solely on the individual female character.

Media have continued to argue that they are *not* engaged in value-laden communication. Objectivity is one touted "strategic ritual" employed to avoid assignment of responsibility.[52] But claims that media give "the public what it wants," provide "mere entertainment," or simply "reflect the current culture" seem insidious and incorrect defenses against the mythic, ritualistic, and interpretive activities in which media engage. More than enough media research exists to demonstrate the value-laden selectivity process involved in all media communication. The fact that the shibboleth of value-free communication continues to dominate so many conversations about media testifies more to the media's dominance and pervasiveness in American society than to the legitimacy of the claim.

Too many of the portraits of "non-traditional" women emphasize "new" roles that replicate male-stereotyped characters. These women often appear as successful professionals in the masculine social world or as aggressive consumers and technology users in the capitalistic, domestic world. The value inculcation that once took place at home finds itself left behind at the office, factory, or shopping center.

5. Conclusion

What does all this do for value inculcation of the sort that women and traditional value inculcators tried to advocate? It would appear that media emphasize the economic and political change of "liberation" and ignore cultural value transmission and inculcation.[53] Now that media successfully accentuate certain social rituals and ignore or alter others, the role of the American woman as a value inculcator diminishes and changes significantly in character.

---

[52] Gaye Tuchman, "Objectivity as Strategic Ritual: An Examination of Newsmen's Notions of Objectivity," *American Journal of Sociology* 77 (1972) 660-679.

[53] New, improved brands "replace" earlier versions of the same product. Successful entertainment characters, correspondents, etc. attract audiences from year to year based on their predictability, not on their development. Successful underlying plot structure stays about the same, thereby destroying the possibilities for real growth through commitment to certain values and then application of those values to our life as it changes.

Traditional domestic and religiously informed holidays like Thanksgiving and Christmas, for example, have been restructured to permit the intrusion of sports media into the celebration's routine. No longer are these days organized solely according to traditions in a specific family–until recently passed on from female generation to generation. Now, many families accommodate their schedules to that of televised sporting events and permit even in these highly private domestic rituals the intrusion of the social, commercial, male values and rituals. Meanwhile, media-generated events such as the Super Bowl, Olympics, national political conventions, and presidential debates have become highly visible rituals of American life which change the domestic landscape and require women to alter their nurturing and value inculcation roles to fit in with these emotionally impoverished, male commercial rituals.

In short, too many mediated revisions of women portray a more liberated but not necessarily more humane being. When combined with a serious lack of change in media portraits of men, the shift decreases the opportunity for representations of traditional value inculcation and for androgynous responses to emerge in either the domestic or the social world. And media can't be expected to help the situation. They do other things better: activities that tie in with their own structures as Gudorf describes them in Chapter 11. In general, media affirm an impersonal order and undermine efforts to inculcate the values of a personal society. They constrict pluralism, and thereby prevent the use of media by others who want to celebrate or convey alternative values. Third, media tend to inculcate a resigned relativism and determinism–generating a sense of powerlessness in individuals who accept the media culture. Media generally present conflict or consumption as the best solution for problems. They demand habitation of the present and discourage reflection.

Trends in media content, policy, and structure threaten the possibility of open channels through which celebrations different from those of the dominant culture can be readily communicated. Traditions that reject a consumer-oriented ideology must evaluate and debate these tendencies in media within every forum. Groups with alternative enduring value commitments can serve as centers for developing a well-defined public philosophy that exposes and opposes such practices. In such an approach, "eliciting moral distaste for sexist images and teaching persons how to mitigate the effects of their invasion into the living room is not enough."[54] Actions must also be aimed at the policies and structure that constitute the media industry.

Audience term-setting of television's meaning and practices has been receiving increased theoretical and research interest. White, for example, argues for new understandings of mass media as aculturators to replace simple information transfer and sender-receiver models with a "receiver-cen-

---

[54] National Council of the Churches of Christ in the U.S.A. 179.

tered" paradigm. He suggests beginning research with "individuals and groups that are attempting to make sense out of" their situation and relations between structural conditions and communication patterns, sociocultural and technological change, and movement from innovation to institutionaliza-tion.[55] All groups seeking a greater pluralism of images and messages over the media should overcome their differences to work together to diminish the communal privatization tendencies of media and to transform govern-ment from its current manipulation of interests, "divorced from any specific moral community," to its original role as "a servant of the public will."[56]

Notwithstanding the importance of television in today's world, women as a specific group in the audience should actively determine its limitations. Media rituals cannot replace those that women have carried forward for so long. This does not imply that women should simply adopt television in their cause. Adoption of television without gender analysis can lead to inadvertent embrace of the values the media now inculcate and of the culture they reflect. When any group unconsciously adopts TV, it may successfully "package" itself for acceptance by an identifiable audience, but its message will likely be perverted, contradicting some of the very values it seeks to convey.

Under such conditions, concerned men and women might better help focus attention on the media situation, develop a transformative approach to learning about renaming, reacting to and utilizing the media, and work to-ward sound strategies for media criticism, transmission and public action.

---

[55] Robert A. White, "Mass Communication and Culture: Transition to a New Paradigm," *Journal of Communication* 33 (Summer, 1983) 279-301.

[56] Hargrove 224.

13

"And a Third of the Water Turned Bitter": Chernobyl, Truth, Media Technology, and the Flow of Information

Janusz Balicki and Wolfgang Wunden

Just as water is necessary for the biological existence of every human being, so true information, made available for the whole of society, is an indispensable element of public life. A high ethical standard, therefore, is demanded of those who make information public, just as it is from those responsible for the institutions of media and the political, economic and cultural systems of which those institutions form a part and on which, to a certain degree, their achievements depend.[1]

Water as a symbol for truth corresponds to another important idea of our times, namely that information is an abundant, vital substance moving quickly and mightily from one point to another without ceasing—hence the term "information flow." However, with this goes the fear that the flow may be unduly restricted or that it may be manipulated so that it becomes dangerous. It is not enough, therefore, to speak of a "flow of information"; we must also speak of a "just flow of information."[2] This will be a key concept in our discussion on a new world order of information and communications which is a consequence of modern media technologies with their

---

[1] For the issue of truth in the media, see Otto B. Roegele, "Gibt es Wahrheit in den Medien?" *Internationale katholische Zeitschrift* 16:4 (1987) 320-33. For a general overview of mass communication theories, see Elisabeth Noelle-Neumann, Winfried Schulz and Jürgen Wilke, *Publizistik, Massenkommunikation* (Frankfurt: Fischer, 1989) especially the article, "Kommunikationstheorien" 123-33.

[2] Herbert I. Schiller, *Die Verteilung des Wissens. Information im Zeitalter der großen Konzerne* (Frankfurt; New York: Campus, 1984). Elisabeth Noelle-Neumann, et al., "Internationale Kommunikationspolitik" in *Publizistik, Massenkommunikation* 93ff.

abundance of programs—words, sounds, and pictures—that have a profound influence on society.[3]

This article is an investigation of how messages can be truthfully transmitted. We will use the concept of "media technology" to consider the inner structures of media, independent of the political, economic, or social environment in which they are used. Seen as technology and according to its inner possibilities and structures, media mediate between an event and the public. The actual technical means of that mediation and the inner diversification of responsibilities and services within a media institution belong to what we call "media technology."

As information flows through media channels, these channels imprint their own characteristics on it; in the process of transmission, the truth changes from the event perceived by someone, through its handling by the agencies, to its reception by the viewer, reader, or listener. Ideally and ethically, therefore, the process should be aimed at mature men and women who are able to make their own unbiased judgments.

The coverage of the Chernobyl nuclear disaster presents a valuable opportunity to discuss the connection between truth and the use made of it by the media technology of different political and economic systems.

1. The Chernobyl Disaster and Its Ethical Implications

In the Ukraine, on the night of April 25, 1986, an incident began in Block IV of the nuclear power plant at Chernobyl. A large amount of radioactive material was released into the atmosphere and transported by the wind over a great part of Europe. The radioactive fallout differed in concentration from one area to another, but all people were warned about air, ground, and food pollution—such was the information given in a "Resumé Report of the Radiation Protection Committee" in the Federal Republic of Germany.

To understand any event, one requires an intellectual framework in which to place it. The word "Chernobyl" means "bitterness" or "wormwood." When the nuclear plant burst, the Ukrainian people, whose intellectual framework is the Bible, saw it as a sign from heaven that God's day was near, the sign given in Revelation 8:10-11:

---

[3] Frederick Williams, *The Communication Revolution* (Beverly Hills: Sage, 1982). Gerhard Maletzke, *Kulturverfall durch Fernsehen?* (Berlin: Spiess, 1988) 47-51. With regard to the "knowledge-gap-hypothesis," see Ulrich Saxer, "Zur Theorie der wachsenden Wissenskluft und ihrer Tragweite aus politischer und sozialer Sicht," in *Media Perspektiven* 5/1988, 279-86. On the general effects of media exposure on the perception of reality and on reality itself, see Joshua Meyrowitz, *No Sense of Place: The Impact of Electronic Media on Social Behavior* (New York: Oxford University Press, 1985).

> Then the third angel blew his trumpet. A large star, burning like a torch dropped from the sky and fell on a third of the rivers and on the springs of water. (The name of the star is "Bitterness.") A third of the water turned bitter and many people died from drinking the water, because it had turned bitter.

However, the majority of the European people, living as they do in secularized societies, had no such framework in which to place the strange disaster. For them to be directly threatened and yet to have no real evidence of what the media were telling them was an entirely new experience. There was nothing they could do but rely on the media for information and help.

Two ethical considerations arise therefore from the Chernobyl disaster: First, what are the advantages and risks in using nuclear technology? Can the use of nuclear energy be justified when one considers the immense threat it poses to the life, not only of the present generation, but of future generations, too? Second, what was the use made of media technology in reporting the Chernobyl disaster? Was true information given or was the "flow of information" turned into "waters of bitterness" so that the human spirit's proper environment of truth and integrity was damaged—just as the natural environment was corrupted by radioactivity? These considerations are linked in an ethical reflection on the role of technology in the development of humanity.

In creating human beings, God ordered them to subdue the earth (Genesis 1:28). This means that human beings, in their endowments of mind and intelligence, received the proper tools to live and develop here on earth. However, in the process of deepening their knowledge of the forces of nature they have gained not only more and more excellent and powerful tools, but also more dangerous and harmful powers, the application of which brings even greater risks and threats to themselves and their world. Our human standards of morality, in consequence, must keep pace with technological development in order to ensure the appropriate application of such power. The Chernobyl case is an example of the many dangers involved if the development of technology is not accompanied by the development of human ethics.[4] Such moral development and progress is important in our era of vast technological advancement.

Without excluding other moral considerations, we will look at the question of truth in the media's treatment of this incident. This calls into question, first, the basic ethical issue: What does human life really mean

---

[4] For a general review of the different systems within society and their inability to solve the major problems existing today, see Niklas Luhmann, *Ökologische Kommunikation. Kann die moderne Gesellschaft sich auf ökologische Gefahrdungen einstellen?* (Opladen: Westdeutscher Verlag, 1986). On the connection between media and politics, see Frank E. Böckelmann, ed., *Medienmacht und Politik* (Berlin: Spiess, 1989).

and how are we to live it responsibly?[5] Second, in dealing with truth in the Chernobyl case, we must consider media coverage as it reflects the political, economic, and social structures of a given society because these structures determine to what degree information given to the public can be true.

2. The Marxist Interpretation of Truth

In reporting the Chernobyl disaster, the information services of both the Soviet and Western governments, where they informed the public at all, tried to minimize what had happened.

In the Soviet Union, the incident was the first big challenge for "Glasnost," the policy of open information on important issues in the many nations under the centralized Russian government. However, it proved to be too big a challenge. At the beginning of 1986, the poet, Andrej Wosnessenski extolled "Glasnost," the promise of Secretary General Gorbachev, with these verses:

> Finish old lies!
> Only Truth
> Only Truth
> Only Truth
> is now new.

In the Stalinist version of the Marxist totalitarian system, the duty of being truthful was not taken into account either in internal relations or in external ones.[6] The principle that "the end justifies the means" was applied in the everyday reality of the state control of society. The state was regarded as the private property of the ruling establishment which felt no obligation either to consult the people or to inform them about decisions made. The populace was not informed of any event which could tarnish the idealistic image of "the most perfect system in the world"—the myth of the Communist paradise had to be maintained at all costs. Information policy was directed solely to presenting the authorities themselves and their system of government in a favorable way.

Propaganda about economic success was spread, despite actual economic failure. The release of information about railway accidents, air crashes, and accidents at work were forbidden and even news of natural disasters like earthquakes and their aftermath was withheld.

---

[5] Hans Jonas, *The Imperative of Responsibility: In Search of an Ethics for the Technological Age* (Chicago: University of Chicago Press, 1984). Alfons Auer, *Umweltethik: Ein theologischer Beitrag zur ökologischen Diskussion* (Düsseldorf: Patmos, 1986).

[6] Peter Dittmar, *Lob der Zensur. Verwirrung der Begriffe, Verwirrung der Geister* (Köln: Kölner Universitätsverlag, 1987) 72 and passim.

It is not strange therefore, that, at the moment of the Chernobyl disaster, the same mechanisms for the suppression of news swung into place and information was denied not only to the Russian people but to the rest of the world. The first information about a raised level of nuclear activity came from the Scandinavian countries, but even then the Soviet Union did not announce the incident or give information about the release of radioactive material into the atmosphere. It was only at a conference called "The Post Accident Review Meeting of the Chernobyl Accident" held in Vienna from August 25-29, 1986, by the Atomic Energy Agency, an organization of the United Nations, that members of a delegation of Soviet scientists gave details of how the accident had happened and on its effects in the Soviet Union.

The Russian authorities had not realized that in today's world it is no longer possible to hide great events within the boundaries of one state. Satellite communication enable us to observe the whole world, to monitor such fundamental matters as radioactive concentrations and their sources. The Chernobyl case proves both how difficult it is to hide the truth and how important the independent flow of information across state boundaries is for humanity, irrespective of political systems. Achieving this degree of openness, however, is not easy. Even in the best climate, the fact does not change: In the Eastern Bloc, information has been not only a tool in the exercise of authority, but also the condition of keeping the ruling powers in control.

Moreover, East and West have had different ideas of how mass media ought to function and how to control it. The Eastern Bloc complained about Western media coverage of events and situations in the countries of Eastern Europe; they believed that such broadcasting is too diverse and too free. However, even if the democratic governments of the West were to concur, there is little they could do because Western media policy is not dictated by the State but by market forces. Such a model completely excludes external control of the objectivity or reliability of information. On an open market, it is customer choice which decides what is accepted and what is rejected.

This is not an ideal solution, but for Western societies and governments it seems less harmful than that envisaged by the Eastern Bloc. These think that not market forces, but a "sense of responsibility for the word" should decide the content of information flow. Its contents should coincide with aims such as "preserving peace," "strengthening confidence between nations," and "battling against injustice and exploitation." These governments maintain that freedom of mass media cannot be a freedom to spread "rude ideas...initiating hatred or provoking disagreement,"[7] all of which they believe Western media does. However, there is no agreement between East and West as to what truth, freedom, and responsibility mean. The East-

---

[7] Censorship as exercised by Church authority is not a good example for secular societies. See Herman H. Schwedt, "Kommunikationskontrolle durch den römischen 'Index der verbotenen Bücher,' " *Communicatio Socialis* 20:4 (1987) 327-38.

ern countries give their own interpretation to these words in an attempt to protect themselves from external criticism.

3. News Coverage of the Chernobyl Disaster in German Mass Media.

At first glance, in the liberal and pluralistic countries of the West the situation seems to be quite different from that which prevailed in the Soviet Bloc. Information can flow freely and liberty of opinion and of commentaries in the media are taken for granted. The state is prevented by law from hiding the truth or from controlling the media. Yet even under these totally different conditions, questions must be asked, for example: Did the information which the West Germans received in news coverage of the Chernobyl disaster give them the truth? How far did media technology, because of its inner "laws" or because of the use made of it by others, change the truth of the incident? How far did "the waters turn bitter" in the flow and overflow of information on Chernobyl?[8]

From the wealth of materials analyzing this news coverage, we focus on two research papers, one by Will Teichert, the other by Günther Rager with Elisabeth Klaus and Elman Thyen.[9]

We will consider first, the more extensive research of Will Teichert.[10] His first step involved interviews with responsible journalists from different broadcasting stations and regional newspapers in which questions were raised about internal information policy and about the individual experiences of journalists in connection with Chernobyl.

The second step was a quantitative content analysis of the actual coverage of events between April 29 and May 15, 1986, in the main news services of the First German Television (ARD, National Public Service) at 8 pm *"Tagesschau"* and 10:30 pm *"Tagesthemen"* and of the Second German Television (ZDF, National Public Service) at 7 pm *"Heute"* and 9:45 pm *"Heute Journal."*

Teichert then analyzed the national edition of the *"Frankfurter Allgemeine Zeitung"* (FAZ) and the *"Basisdienst"* of the biggest news agency in the Federal Republic, the dpa (Deutsche Presse Agentur), and divided the

---

[8] Klaus Traube, et al., *Nach dem Super-GAU: Tschernobyl und die Konsequenzen* (Reinbek: Rowohlt, 1986).

[9] We limit ourselves to the news. It goes without saying that there are science magazines with very good information—but they do not reach a wide, general audience. Thus, the limitation is justified.

[10] Will Teichert, "Tschernobyl in den Medien. Ergebnisse und Hypothesen zur Tschernobyl-Berichterstattung," *Rundfunk und Fernsehen* 35:2 (1987) 185-204. See also Gertrud Linz, "Experten, Experten...Industriekatastrophen in den elektronischen Medien," in *Weiterbildung und Medien* 12:1 (1989) 6-9.

material into types.[11]   He also noted the country where each article originated, which agency presented each statement, with what political system,
industrial or economic lobby each system was associated, and if the facts
reported were connected to evaluative statements.

It is not possible here to present the details of all of Teichert's results.
However, those which shed light on the connection between the information
media's reliable transmission of information and the media technology operating in a given political, economic, and social-cultural context deserve special attention.

Information services, of necessity, reduce a complex event to the
shortest possible form, and this obtained in their reporting of the Chernobyl
event.   Nevertheless, it is surprising that more than 50% of all television
spots were no longer than one minute. The briefness of that reporting presents difficulties, particularly as one news bulletin can contain many items.
In view of the seriousness of the Chernobyl disaster, one would have expected whole news bulletins to be devoted to it alone. However, Teichert
discovered that, in the TV news coverage, one third of the information units
presented three or four subjects as well as Chernobyl. Only each fifth unit
dealt exclusively with Chernobyl.

For many years, newscasters on both TV and radio have been criti-
cized for providing an "overflow" of information which leads to disorienta-
tion and information-overload for listeners and viewers. Why then was
there such a scarcity of news coverage in the case of the Chernobyl disaster?
Because of its seriousness and wide-ranging effects people were in need of
both an interpretive framework by which to understand the disaster and assistance in coping with the emotions which it evoked. People felt deeply
threatened by Chernobyl, and the condensed presentation of the facts surely
served only to strengthen these feelings.

The chaotic nature of the media coverage of the Chernobyl disaster
was due, in part, to the confusing technical and scientific language used to
report it. Teichert's study indicates, however, that the chaos and confusion
was only heightened by such factors as the incompleteness of the information given by the Soviet authorities, the high degree of politicization of
every aspect of the event—the debates about "levels of nuclear radiation,"
"radiation tolerance levels," "the security of reactors in the Federal Republic," etc.—and the conflicting judgments and evaluations of scientific experts. Because of the unclear reporting of information, calming statements

---

[11] Teichert used the following categories: statements referring to the Chernobyl
disaster itself, statements referring to the load of nuclear radiation, information
about the reaction of the population, information about measures of precaution taken
by the administration, statements referring to the measuring and fixing of radiation
tolerance levels, statements referring to Soviet and German information policies,
information about nuclear energy in general, statements about the abandonment of
nuclear energy as a source of power, statements about the security of reactors, and
statements about alternative energy sources.

about the levels of radiation were not heard. They were reduced to the level of informative statements about nuclear fallout.

Another important finding of Teichert's study was the high degree of politicization of all aspects of the Chernobyl disaster. Public complaints like that of the Chairman of the German Radiation Protection Committee proved to be valid. People recognized that two thirds of all the news was given by agents of the political and administrative sectors. Because Chernobyl called into question the legitimacy of using nuclear energy, those sectors who had a vested interest in its use had to react. However, in May, 1986, the acceptability of the use of nuclear energy was considerably reduced in public opinion. The percentage of its advocates sank from the earlier constant percentage of 52% to 29% while the percentage of its opponents grew from 46% to 69%.

Within this context, it is interesting to note that certain important themes owed their "career" to the fact that political controversies raged around them. The theme "limit values" was at the summit of its career on May 12 when the Radiation Protection Committee raised the limit of cesium for fresh vegetables from 100-250 Bequerel per Kg. The state governments of Hessen, Bremen and Saarland retained the lower level while in Bayern a dispute arose about the "right" measure, hence the political vulnerability of presumably scientific data was publicly revealed and discussed. The fact that the majority of statements about the fixing of limit values, exposure to nuclear radiation and the security of reactors were made in a polarized political context undermined the scientific truth of such statements. Everyone was able to see that objective scientific truth was used and interpreted in accordance with people's political intentions so that it lost its neutral function. Scientific experts were virtually silenced and the people were denied their right to scientific truth. Teichert concluded that the loss of credibility of political and social institutions deeply affects the credibility of the media which on many occasions in the Chernobyl case could do nothing more than quote opposing statements.

4. Use of Media Technology in East and West

Media coverage of the Chernobyl disaster exemplifies very clearly our thesis that media technology is embedded in political structures from which it finds it difficult to free itself. In the West as well as in the East, states and governments can use these technologies for their own purposes and for propaganda.

Selected or generated items of information are released to the media to create or confirm certain popular opinions and convictions in order to gain the people's conformity to the political system. While media in the East is directly integrated into the state system, in the West the situation is different. For example, in the Federal Republic of Germany, broadcasting is predominantly public but private broadcasting has already gained one third of the market. Print media is private, but radio, TV, and newspapers are not free of influences from the political and economic sectors.

On the whole, the situation of Western media is more complicated than in the East. While the right of free access to all information is granted by all constitutions, actual truth is not so easy to attain because those who produce broadcasts and newspapers are subjected to many pressures. First, they are dependent on their sources of information and they cannot vouch for the knowledge, sincerity, or discernment of such a variety of authorities and experts. Second, they must tread the minefield of the vested interests of political parties, powerful economic lobbies, and other pressure groups. Where media coverage is expensive and financial backing frequently provided by such groups, it is often a matter of "he who pays the piper calls the tune." Third, in the West, it is often the case that no one can declare with authority what the actual truth of an event is. In principle, the media has access to almost all sources of information as, for example, the Watergate case exemplified. But there is often such an excessive flow of information that the media seems incapable of rendering its complexity intelligible to readers and listeners.

Western democracies seek to safeguard the truth through the ideals of full disclosure and free comment. Full disclosure denies to anyone the right to admit certain information to the media while withholding other information. Information is, in principle, freely available. Furthermore, freedom extends also to the opinions and commentaries expressed in the media upon that information.

However, in practice, selection of issues and their evaluation in commentaries and other forms of coverage are dependent on who is at the top of the media institution and which form of control over media content has been chosen. It is within these limits that the honest media worker must strive to mediate a true and objective picture of events to the consumer, while avoiding professional deformation and corruption. Acknowledging the nature of this task within the given structure, media research is able to verify how different media respond to the criteria for an objective coverage of events.

Günther Rager, journalism teacher at the University of Dortmund, together with Elisabeth Klaus and Elman Thyen, analyzed how often which issues of the Chernobyl disaster were treated in daily newspapers, weeklies, and TV coverage.[12] They confirmed the findings of Teichert that the confusing proliferation of perspectives on the political and economic questions connected with Chernobyl resulted in the disaster itself being almost forgotten. Rager and his colleagues noted that the various media had very different patterns of argumentation. *Spiegel* mentioned the arguments of the advocates of nuclear energy as frequently as those of its opponents in order to

---

[12] Günther Rager, "Kommentar ohne Meinung," *Journalist* 10 (1987) 36-38.

refute them. *Taz* predominantly reported the argume
order to confirm them while *Welt* quoted above ?
advocates and agreed with them. Researchers note
media there was no distinct separation between fa
tary articles on Chernobyl. Speaking with journalisto
of the Chernobyl coverage, Rager also discovered that beic
occurred owners and chief editors of print media had been insisting
journalists only write articles favoring the use of nuclear energy. There
was, therefore, a lack of public information on the possible consequences of
nuclear disasters. This meant that journalists as well as readers and viewers
had to be provided with basic information. Finally, the coverage brought to
light a structural problem of journalism: the lack of journalists who are able
to represent so complex and controversial an issue to a broad public.

5. The Ethics of Information and the Mission of Mass Media

As a result of the analysis of media coverage of Chernobyl, ethical
reflections and the findings of media research must be put together to form
some guiding principles; in other words, there must be an ethics of information. Such an ethics forms a part of an overall ethics of communication
which, though first developed in a time when mass media did not yet exist,
must now be developed further to take into account the special features of
modern media technologies.

The Chernobyl case shows precisely how important truth is in the flow
of information. Only in truth can human beings safely and creatively make
the world subordinate to themselves; only by living in the truth can they act
in accordance with their full dignity in all the spheres of their activity. A
lie destroys the moral authenticity of human existence, forming a contradic-
tion between internal belief and external expression. It deforms interpersonal communication, and therefore threatens to destroy society. Every system of social communication should tend to an ethical ideal which demands
a proper attitude towards the truth. However, as Pius XII said in his encyclical *Miranda Prorsus*:

> To serve truth means more than simply to refrain from falsehood, lies,
> and deceit; it means shunning everything that can encourage a way of
> life and action that is false, imperfect, or harmful to others.[13]

Moralists dealing with the flow of information point out that the right
to true information is written into the essence of human nature. It is not
rooted merely in profit but is a moral imperative, a human value, and an
absolute necessity if the human being is to live and develop. Because it also

---

[13] No. 47. This translation is found in Claudia Carlen, *The Papal Encyclicals
1939-58* (Wilmington, N.C.: McGrath, 1981) 352.

...tes the opportunity for responsible participation in social life, the giving ...d receiving of information is a way in which each person willingly ac-cepts his or her great responsibility for the fate of society. Such responsibility demands that all members of society be informed about problems and events. It implies that information must be properly differentiated in order to be at the service of socially and culturally deprived communities. Moralists insist that because society depends upon information to make decisions such information must provide the most objective image of events that it is possible to achieve. Since the right to true information is rooted in ethical foundations, legislation must regard it as an essential, not as a privilege.

Moralists also draw attention to the media's responsibility for the recipient of information. It must not entangle human persons in the inner spheres of their emotions and imaginations by proposing and suggesting standards of life and behavior far removed from ethical ideals.

Because moral theologians aim at helping human persons in their unending quest to understand the deeper truths about themselves, they must often criticize the new media technologies which do not serve this moral reflection. The media can inculcate attitudes of passivity and egoism which prevent people from reflecting on the crucial problems of life. Truth is frequently distorted by advertising which creates artificial needs and panders to the lowest instincts. Pseudo-values are often lifted to the level of laws and are never evaluated or discussed.

Truth means harmony between external expression and internal belief.[14] It is the right application of the living word in a dialogue and in individual situations. Truthfulness guards not only the material precision of expression but first of all the real meaning of a word, a conversation, a gesture, a general attitude arising out of a person's intellectual and emotional predispositions, whether conscious or unconscious, and it transmits these faithfully to that person's audience. These dimensions of truthfulness are of vital importance in our technological civilization, which often applies the most sophisticated means to manipulate human thought.

In our era of widely developed mass communication the phenomenon of manipulation poses a more serious threat than the conscious lie which is often so evident that it is more easily recognized and rejected. The various types of linguistic or psychological manipulation are very dangerous; for example, often repeated false judgments which finally convince the recipient that they are true; emotive or expressive narratives which cloud the judgment of the hearer; unintelligible modes of expression which paralyze recipients' minds, rendering them unable to reflect calmly about the true content of the message. Also included are instances of modern disinformation

---

[14] Hermann Boventer, *Wahrheit und Lüge im Journalismus* (Köln: Bachem, 1986). See also Roegele, "Gibt es Wahrheit in den Medien?" 320-33.

which results not from lack of information, but from a surplus of it. This arouses feelings without understanding and prepares a fertile soil for further manipulation. Another example is any process of over-simplification which results in an advanced selectivity of information, giving it a one-sided character. Manipulators use knowledge of human psychology to make others extremely vulnerable; it reduces people to function as means rather than ends. It is a process which replaces the moral dimension of interpersonal relations with the pragmatic. Moral criteria of good and evil are replaced by profit motives.

Moral theologians and mass media specialists are in agreement that there is an urgent need to improve the flow of information because of its social and psychological power to spread ideas and to influence standards of group and individual behavior. Rapidly spreading and developing information technology must try to cover all information, thus helping to form public opinion. Information cannot be treated as a commodity and sold according to economic rules because it is meant to promote the common good and thereby serve society.

This does not imply, however, that information has to be solely in the hands of the state. Public authority must treat information as property common to all, and protect it by law to ensure that it is used for the good of all. Giving it such a status not only ensures the free flow of information, but guards the quality of that information, taking into account the actual cultural and historical conditions within any given society. The crucial role of the state is not only to allow, but also to favor the participation of all spiritual and cultural forces in the flow of information. Such broad participation cannot occur without tension, but amidst this tension the goal must be a dynamic balance which makes criticism possible.

6. Professional Ethics and Media Politics

Even a short history and development of the theory of mass media shows us the difference between the media specialist (in the widest meaning of the term) and the moralist, and also how necessary is the existence of both of these disciplines. They have a common field of interest as both are concerned about the freedom of the media to express the truth. At first, the role of the moralist was not commonly appreciated and despite the rapid development of media from the beginning of the 20th century onwards, intensive research on the ethics of mass communication was not undertaken until after World War II. Until then, handbooks dealing with mass media were dominated by technological and legal problems. The law replaced ethics which was limited to a specially formulated code and relegated to an appendix.

Attention was paid only to the duty of fidelity to the law, but not to the responsibility to further human moral development. Only in the 1970s did this attitude to the ethics of mass communication change.[15] The Watergate affair and the Vietnam War helped people realize that the media are not morally neutral tools because the social, cultural, and political information which they carry brings in its train a whole range of moral questions which cannot be solved without ethical reflection. Since the 1970s, therefore, there has been much moral reflection on the whole field of mass media. This is evident, for example, in the U. S. where between 1930 and 1970, no handbooks on ethics were published, and now two to three such books are published each year. Similarly, in Western Europe, only in the 1970s was there such evidence of systematic ethical reflection.

The essential difference between media specialists and moralists or moral theologians is their perspective on the role of information transferred via media. The media specialist is interested from the professional point of view in information transfer, the possibility of reaching the greatest number of people, and positive public acceptance. The moralist, on the other hand, treats information transfer as an agent intended to serve personal and social development. Hence, when the media specialist pays attention to "transfer," the moralist takes care of "communication." "Transfer" means the one-way flow of information from the communicator to the recipient, whereas "communication" takes into account a response from the recipient, thus leading to "*communio*," the formation of a community of persons. Such community is possible only when we deal with a true transfer of information which forms human beings.

The moralist is interested in the activity of information experts and of institutions propagating information as they form and create public opinion. The moralists emphasize that this great responsibility of dealing with information requires not only technological competence, but, first of all, a well-formed conscience and moral code.[16] They demand from all journalists great sensitivity to human problems as well as a critical attitude towards the ideological influences of governmental systems.[17] Information must

[15] Hermann Boventer, *Ethik des Journalismus. Zur Philosophie der Medienkultur* (Konstanz: Universitätsverlag Konstanz, 1984). Alfons Auer, "Verantwortete Vermittlung. Bausteine einer medialen Ethik," in Heinz Glässgen and Hella Tompert, eds., *Zeitgespräch. Kirche und Medien* (Freiburg: Herder, 1988) 63-84.

[16] Hans Jürgen Schultz, *Warum wir schreiben* (Stuttgart: Radius Bibliothek, 1988).

[17] That leads to harsh controversies and open fights. For the battle between journalists and economic enterprises in the United States, see Holger Rust, *Entfremdete Elite? Journalisten im Kreuzfeuer der Kritik* (Wien: Literas-Universitätsverlag, 1986). On the other hand, corruption cannot be excluded. See Peter Christian Hall, "Alltägliche (Un-)Moral. Über schleichende Anpassung und strukturelle Korruption," in Wolfgang Wunden, ed., *Medien zwischen Markt und Moral* (Stuttgart: Steinkopf, 1989) 101-110.

be characterized by objectivity and reliability to enable the collecting, ordering, and transferring of the true image of world events, their evolution, and their importance.

It is well-known that information can be neither completely neutral nor provide an anonymous photograph of reality. Since the interpretation of facts is essential, there must be criteria to guide choices in the information process such as which facts are to be emphasized, and how they are to be contextualized and interpreted. These criteria, moreover, must become visible in the doctrinal or ideological position adopted in commentaries. To achieve information objectivity, there must be a clear differentiation of the double function of mass media: the collecting of information and the moral or ideological orienting of public opinion.

According to moralists, the ethical ideal to which each information system should tend requires simplicity of interpretation criteria and fidelity to a code of values. Events which are the object of information are critical for society only when they are associated with matters of importance and interest to at least a part of that society. Hence, the precise determination of the criteria for objectivity is reached by uniting two elements—facts which are to be faithfully reported, and the social significance of these facts for the whole or majority of the society. However, the sensational press, for example, bent as it is on exploiting primitive curiosity, cannot agree with this ideal.

Moralists underline the fact that mass media must use truth in the service of humanity to build, form, and improve the human condition. The responsibility for truth falls on individual people working in the field of information. Journalists must be people of truth; in the words of John Paul II:

> The attitude of journalists to the truth is a kind of identification card and what is more, a certificate of their professional skill as workers in the domain of information. It should lead to a double fidelity—first of all to their own missions and further to their obligation to those they serve.[18]

Moralists postulate the dignity of truth itself in opposition to subordinating it to other interests. In this, they maintain that the personal attitude of a journalist is of the utmost importance. When mass media is used for lying, inciting hostility, or spreading immorality, the authenticity of a journalist's service is seriously compromised and a grave threat is posed to the dignity and freedom of those whom the media ought to be serving.

The ethics of information also concerns the political, economic, and cultural systems in each country.[19] It depends upon the moral quality of each individual system, on the autonomy and forms of democratic participa-

---

[18] John Paul II, "Ad quosdam diurnarios in aula supra porticu Sancti Petri coram admissos," *Acta Apostolicae Sedis* 78 (1986) 1012.

[19] Manfred Rühl, "Ordnungspolitische Probleme eines künftigen Rundfunks in der Bundesrepublik Deutschland," in Florian H. Fleck, ed., *Zukunftsaspekte des Rundfunks* (Stuttgart: Kohlhammer, 1986) 77-101.

tion within the society in which it exists. Information, with its own proper function in society, is always and essentially the dialectical result of action linking in itself all the dominating forces and overwhelming influences of the social and political system.

Moralists insist that mass media should always remain in the service of the general good of society. This means that state authority has certain obligations. First of all, it should organize mass media and give it a legal status. Further, it must ensure the quality of information; it must allow and approve pluralism of information and communication. For this reason it should support various individual and social initiatives useful for the general good. State authority should also take care that citizens are not manipulated by the media, since manipulation endangers individuals and social progress. State authority should therefore defend against the spread of harmful material which undermines authentic values; it should protect youth in particular against harmful influences. However, authority does not always fulfil its obligations. It sometimes usurps to itself a monopoly in the domain of mass media, harnessing it for its own political or economic ends. In this way, authority becomes the oppressor of its citizens.

Finally, all fields of human activity constitute the interest of the moralist but in every area he or she needs the cooperation of specialists within the field. Hence mutual cooperation between media specialists and moralists is an imperative; their functions are complementary.

7. Truth as an Aim for Media Education

Truth, the vital material and prime value of every human society, deserves the common effort of moralists and media people. The coauthors of this essay tried to find some initial answers to the following questions: How can truth be achieved in pluralistic societies? What factors in media technology itself, in the media structures as far as they are embedded in social, political, and economic systems, and in the individuals involved in the process of information, hinder the achievement of truth?

The biblical imperative not to lie and manipulate the truth, originally directed to individuals, becomes a broader and much more complicated question which could be formulated in the following manner: What can be done to make available to all members of society more of the true information which they require if they are to live and act in accordance with the reasonable life demanded of them?

The dignity and freedom of the human person demands that the information mediated to society be objective and true so that it can form the basis of well-informed choices with the potential to lead to authentic personal and communal life. How, therefore, can the person's dignity and freedom be guaranteed and media forced not to manipulate? How can media be given the enormous funds it needs and yet retain its freedom? How can a sense of responsibility for truth in the sense defined above be awakened not only in the media but in viewers and listeners?[20]

While moral theology postulates the value of truth and puts it in the perspective of the whole of human morality, media research shows the overall dimension in which that value can be achieved, shifting attention from individual morality to the structural and political planes.

8. Conclusion

Our analysis of the media coverage of the Chernobyl disaster has taken into account the fact that the situation of the media varies greatly between East and West. While freedom and plurality of information have begun to be granted in the East, western societies must learn that an overwhelming flow of information is not identical with truth—that much of the "water is bitter." Authorities in the West also keep information secret without reasonable cause, in order to keep people quiet. Most political information comes from propaganda institutions of governments, of political parties, of industry, and of service institutions and should, therefore, be critically evaluated.

In both East and West, the media were able to provide much information about the Chernobyl incident. However, in order to tell the truth, it is not sufficient merely to provide information. Truth requires that information be presented in ways that are credible, understandable, and which show the implications of the material for everyday life decisions. There is an urgent need for media education aimed at the critical and competent user of mass media who is able to check the sources of information and compare them with one another, and who, as a citizen and participant in political elections, demands that "clear water" be granted by the political system concerned.

---

[20] On media education and ethics, see Dieter Baacke, "Zum ethischen Orientierungsrahmen der Medienpädagogik," in *Medienpädagogik im Informationszeitalter*, ed. Ludwig J. Issing (Weinheim: Deutscher Studien Verlag, 1987) 53-71; Rudolf A. M. Meyer, "Neue Medienpolitik oder Die Frage nach der Verantwortlichkeit für den Innenweltschutz," in *Entfesselte Forschung: Die Folgen einer Wissenschaft ohne Ethik*, ed. Anton-A. Guha and Sven Papcke (Frankfurt: Fischer, 1987) 174-199; Wolfgang Wunden, "Medienethik-Medienpädagogik" *Zeitschrift für Evangelische Ethik* 30 (1986) 60-73.

14

Towards a Solution to the Conflict Created by Mass Media

Ivan Fuček, S.J.

We may begin by asking ourselves whether the posing of the question of conflict in the context of mass media is a helpful one. In fact, in all facets of human life there have been conflicts of every type, and it is obvious that there will always be. It is also clear that these conflicts can be resolved neither through highly speculative moral theology, hermeneutics, epistemology, nor even by a moralist. Given the structures of evil in which people are continuously involved, conflicts of conscience are inevitable, whether they be subjective or objective, in the personal or social order. Is this not a valid argument rather in favor of the permanence of conflict than of conflict resolution, one which human reason and the story of humanity continuously offers us?[1]

By saying this, we do not want to prejudge the possibility of useful discussion of the theme of conflict in this work on Moral Theology and Mass Mediated Culture; our intention is, above all, to call attention to the difficulty, seriousness, and complexity of the problem before us. Having said this, our first question is: What do we intend to do and what can we do in the treatment of the current study? What is our approach or, better still, what kind of general approach can a moralist of today take in confronting this theme of conflict and its resolution? We live in a pluralistic society and in a culture governed by mass media that seems not to favor the solution of conflicts but rather to encourage the opposite. How do we, then, face conflicts that make manifest the diversity between lived ethos and systematic ethicality? In other words, there are moral norms on the one hand, and

---

[1] See Stuart Hampshire, *Morality and Conflict* (Oxford: Basil Blackwell, 1983) 140-69. His treatise ends with the following words: "My argument has been that it is for us natural to be unnatural in these spheres, following both reason and history, and consequently it is natural for us to be involved in repression and conflict; these are the costs of culture and of the balance between reason and memory" (169).

concrete life on the other, which in many respects harmonizes neither with these norms, nor with morality as a normative discipline.

The intention here is not to provide a universally applicable proposal to be accepted as a definitive solution to a problem; this would be unrealistic and utopian. But we can and must indicate possible ways of lessening this condition of conflict, of facing adequately from a philosophical and theological vantage point a problem which is both ancient and new; the problem is gathering in strength, not without influence today from the media. For this more modest and realistic goal, it is worthwhile to use the document of the Pontifical Council for Social Communications titled, *Pornography and Violence in the Communication Media: A Pastoral Response* (hereafter referred to as PV), published May 7, 1989, on the occasion of the 23rd World Day of Communication.[2]

Why have we chosen this document? Is it so important? Does it solve our problem? According to critical remarks of lay communicators, the document is inadequate. But it is not difficult to guess why. Among other reasons, the ethical parameters of today vary greatly according to the preferences of individuals or the groups to which they belong. These ethical parameters often enough become ideologies corresponding to philosophies and cultures or to the vision of metaethics which becomes a measure of the lived ethos and human ethics.[3] Thus, it is evident that the media programs are not neutral, but "colored" according to the attitudes and interests of those concerned.[4] We are dealing with a problem in which many people of different ideologies are interested.

---

[2] I make use of three texts that are slightly different: (1) The original text: Pontifical Council for Social Communications, *Pornography and Violence in the Communications Media: A Pastoral Response* (Vatican City, 1989), signed by Mons. John Foley, President of the above-named Council; (2) the Italian, and (3) the German translations.

[3] Exhaustive information on "metaethic norms" can be found in E. Chiavacci, "Il morale come supremo problema dell'uomo," in E. Chiavacci, *Teologia Morale 1/Morale Generale* (Cittadella, Assisi, 1977) 7-26. Chiavacci discusses here "metaethic norms" of morality in different ethical systems: in analytic philosophy, in ethnocentrism, in heteronomous ethics, in Marxism, in existentialism, in the Frankfurt School—in connection with the problem "science and philosophy," in "political liberation and emptiness of values." To examine further the metaethical norm in the morality of revelation, see pp. 27-48. The results show that "every ethic" has its value of ethicality that would legitimize itself as uniquely valid. From here, it becomes clear that the foundation is the human person, the image of humanity, the anthropological project which "every ethics" has and follows. This, however, suggests another question: Are there elements common to all ethics? Which are they? The whole of the present work is an attempt to give an exact response to these questions.

[4] See Willard D. Rowland, Jr., *The Politics of TV Violence: Policy Issues of Communication Research* (Beverly Hills: Sage Publications, 1983) with a detailed bibliography, 308-19.

PV has two characteristics of which it is important to take account. In the first place, the text gives evidence of serious scientific preparation, being based on studies "conducted throughout the whole world on the negative effects of pornography and violence in the media." PV recognizes that specialists at times hold divergent opinions about the extent of the phenomenon of pornography and violence and the way people are affected by them; but, as it says, "the broad outlines of the problem are stark, clear, and frightening" (PV 9).

Secondly, PV is somewhat timidly formulated; the main theme running throughout the document is the challenge for a "continuous dialogue" (PV 30), that could lead to a rethinking and revision of the media programs affected by the pornography and violence phenomenon, which tend to create and reinforce conflicts in many people. This second point (challenge to dialogue) is our main consideration here.

Although PV does not enter directly into our theme,[5] it does provide some elements for a scientific and moral-theological approach, even if it must be admitted that these are at times insufficient. The document offers some positive elements on which a plausible base could be constructed for a moral approach to conflict in the media. While more or less implicitly rejecting some ethical models as inadequate for a solution to our topic, it recommends other models as plausible and certain. Only after a detailed study could PV rightly be regarded as a serious model or a new ethical paradigm that could be used to tackle the problem of conflict in every field of lived and Christian ethos.

In relation to the ethical foundation of PV, we intend to examine, first, the concept of conflict, second, the ethical models which are opposed to the spirit of PV and which are incapable of treating and solving the problem of conflict. Third, we will examine the ethical models which are more accessible and advisable, although PV never takes any stand on them.

1. Conflictual Reality

We now come to the concepts of "conflict" and "conflictual reality." First, there is the individual case of conflict. In the past, individual cases of conflict were described and resolved by the traditional schools of moral theology, such as those of Alphonsus, Bucceroni, Noldin, Merkelbach, Prüm-

---

[5] PV never explicitly uses the terms "conflict," "conflict of conscience," "conflicting situation," "conflicting mentality," and so on. In this sense, the document is incomplete regarding an explicit formulation of a moral approach to the theme. Still, PV in its entirety is nothing but a narrative description of the actual conflict strengthened by the pornography and violence of the media. To this end, PV describes the effects and causes of the phenomenon and attempts to provide observations on how to tackle the problem, with what means and what remedies. Thus PV implicitly speaks of conflict in our own sense of the word.

mer, Hurth. The most modern concept of conflict, that is, of "a relation of opposition between two or more units of action of which at least one tries to impose itself," also ultimately resolves itself into individual cases of conflict.[6]

Secondly, from the individual case of conflict, it is necessary to pass to a broader idea of conflict because today in many situations one does not think of only the individual case "right here and now," but rather of a conflict situation which has a broader application in time and space. We can now speak of "conflict" in a general sense, since the entire human race is caught up in it, and not merely a single person, family, or group. Today we speak of the whole of humanity living within a conflictual mentality, set up and situated in such a way that it has become a new "aeon," in which contemporary humanity realizes itself and without which it is not able to do so, whether on the personal level (the level of conscience) or on the objective level (of language, of thought, of decision and choice). All of our modern life revolves around this new "aeon" of conflictual structures, which often are simply structures of sin.[7]

Thirdly, if it is said that our total capacity to think, and all our morality, our lived ethos, and our systematized ethic have and must have their basis in conflict, this is to be denied, although all these things are realized in conflictual situations.[8] Earlier we stated that in the history of humanity

---

[6] D. Mieth, "Conflitto," in B. Stoeckle, *Dizionario di etica cristiana* (Cittadella ed. Assisi, 1978) 104-06, where the author tries to describe and define different types of conflict. For a different opinion, see M. Forschner, "Conflict des devoirs," in O. Hoeffe, ed., *Dictionnaire de Morale* (Univ. Fribourg Suisse - Cerf, Paris, 1983) 28.

[7] John Paul II, *Sollicitudo Rei Socialis* (1987) mentions ten times "structures of sin" (nos. 36a, 36b, 36c, 36f, 37c, 37d, 38f, 39b, 40d, 46e). It is for the first time that this term appears in a papal document. The reasons are economical, political, and moral: "If the present situation can be attributed to difficulties of various kinds, it is not out of place to speak of 'structures of sin' which, as I stated in my Apostolic Exhortation, *Reconciliatio et Paenitentia*, are rooted in personal sin, and thus always linked to the *concrete acts* of individuals who introduce them, consolidate them and make them difficult to be removed. Thus they grow stronger, become widespread, and become the source of other sins, and so mold the behavior of people" (no. 36b). S. Bastianel, ed., *Strutture di peccato. Una sfida teologica e pastorale* (Piemme, Casale Monferrato, 1989) 15-38; F. Biffi, "Cinque letture dello sviluppo dei popoli. Guida introduttiva all'Enciclica 'Sollicitudo Rei Socialis'," in *Le ragioni della speranza. Studi sull' Enciclica Sollicitudo Rei Socialis*, PUL, ed., (Lib. Ed. Vaticana-Lib. Ed. Lateranense, Roma, 1988) writes: "These structures of sin [it is interesting to note that John Paul II does not hesitate in repeating a typical expression from the 'Theology of Liberation,' while until now he spoke of 'social sin,' for example, in his Apostolic Exhortation, *Reconciliatio et Paenitentia*, see also the no. 65 of SRS], in the case in point of development, are distorted and betrayed, if they are reduced to the non-observance of the 'second table' of the Ten Commandments" (161).

[8] Stuart Hampshire, *Morality and Conflict* 151: "My argument repeatedly returns to this starting point: that the capacity to think scatters a range of differences and

there were conflicts, not only in the sense of single cases, but also of prolonged conflicts and situations of continuous conflict. It cannot be denied that we live today in a conflictual reality that is both powerful and reinforced. From a human point of view, it seems that a future without conflict and in perfect harmony is not to be conceived of. This would be utopian for a humanity full of contradictions and sin.[9]

There is no doubt that contradictions could be partially resolved. But today it seems almost normal and natural that our existence be constantly and in every situation embroiled in conflict of all sorts. Thus, in the continuous struggle to do good, amid numerous and fearsome dangers, moral persons of goodwill continue on their weary journey, and the whole of humanity pays a dear price for moral development. Undoubtedly, reason and history demonstrate the permanence of conflict and the impossibility of a definitive solution, even in individual cases, whether in a particular field or a particular time.[10] Thus, the existence of social conflictual structures and a conflictual mentality cannot be denied. Objectively, it can and must be said that contemporary humanity lives in a new "existential" social ethic: It is an ethic of conflict—or reality become conflictual through human activity.

---

conflicts before us: different languages, different ways of life, different specializations of aim within a way of life, different conventions and styles also within a shared way of life, different prohibitions."

[9] Ibid. 152: "There must always be moral conflicts which cannot, given the nature of morality, be resolved by any constant and generally acknowledged method of reasoning. My claim is that morality has sources in conflict, in the divided soul and between contrary claims, and that there is no rational path that leads from these conflicts to harmony and to an assured solution, and to the normal and natural conclusion." There are elements undoubtedly true and rightly formulated here which refer to the circumstances in which the human person lives. However, we are far from the author's affirmation "that morality has its sources in conflict" and "in the divided soul." If the author with "its sources" is thinking of the foundation of morality, then he needs to say that the ultimate foundation is *God*. If with "divided soul" he is thinking of an anthropological dualism, then it is necessary to state that the human person is a duality and not a "dualism," neither in a Platonic sense, nor a Cartesian, nor any other sense, because humanity is *unity* in duality. See Ivan Fuček, "L'Unità e la dignità della persona nell' antropologia sessuale cristiana," *Medicina e morale* 39 (1989) 465-89.

[10] Stuart Hampshire, *Morality and Conflict* 169; see also M. E. Roloff, "Communication and Conflict," in *Handbook of Communication Science*, ed. C. R. Berger and S. H. Chaffee (London: Sage Publications, 1987) 484-534; L. L. Putnam and J. P. Folger, "Communication, Conflict, and Dispute Resolution: The Study of Interaction and the Development of Conflict Theory," *Communication Research* 15 (August 1988) 349-59; E. Diener and L. W. Woody, "Television Violence, Conflict, Realism, and Action," *Communication Research* 8 (July 1981), 281-306; H. Adoni, A. A. Cohen and S. Mane, "Social Reality and Television News: Perceptual Dimensions of Social Conflicts in Selected Life Areas," *Journal of Broadcasting* 28 (Winter 1984) 33-49; P. J Tichenorr et al., "Community Issues, Conflicts, and Public Affairs Knowledge," in *New Models for Mass Communicator Research* (December 1988), 45-77.

Fourthly, in the course of history, what was once evident only in sporadic cases now permeates the whole of our free activity which, now obscured, even if not determined by this conflictual reality, has developed into a new social existential: a new nature imposed upon contemporary humanity from outside, a new "way of being," a reality immersed in the conflict of this historico-spatio-temporal "aeon."

The conclusion? Conflictual structures, which are often the structures of sin, and the intensity of moral conflict prevent any flight from this reality, even in cases in which responsibility is not attributable to any acting subject.[11] But is it at least possible to mitigate this universal situation of conflict? Is it not possible in many cases and situations, with the proper and prudent means, to be successful? The answer of a moralist can only be the following: It is obligatory for one who wishes to lead an ethical and religious life to strive with renewed effort to effect, as much as possible, upright human actions and to maintain moral values. Morality is a process of wisdom. It obliges us profoundly, always, and in every situation. In the final analysis, it is based on the one and only human anthropology which is valid for all, although it is not recognized as such. This human anthropology has, in the historico-phenomenological perspective, a conflictual aspect which is continuously elaborated by people of every time. But Christian anthropology, which recognizes that humanity is fallen (Genesis 3) and ensnared in conflict, is not without redemptive hope (Genesis 2:15), as will be seen below.

Where does PV see the basic ethical criteria by means of which the problem of conflict could be tackled, not only in the situations of pornography and violence emphasized by the media, but also in conflict in general? There are various biases which PV considers, which point to various ethical criteria: the tendency to eliminate ethical considerations altogether, whether these be human or theological; the ethical models of tolerance and facile legalization; an ethic of conformism and individual pleasure; and a new ethic of "total opposition."

---

[11] See M. Alcala, "Pecado social y pecado estrutural," *Razon y Fe* (Septiembre-Octubre: 1985) 125-43; I. Camacho, "El cristiano ante las contradicciones de desarrollo," *Proyeccion* 35 (1988) 201-17; D. E. Cooper, "Collective Responsibility," *Philosophy 43* (1968) 258-68; J. Idigoras, "Nuestros pecados culturales," *Revista Teological Limense* 17 (1983) 17-38; E. Lopez Aspitarte, "El tema del pecado en la Reconciliatio et Paenitentia," *Proyeccion* 33 (1986) 55-69; M. Vidal, "El misterio de inquidad en las estructuras. La categoria teologico-moral de pecado estructural," *Verdad y vida* 44 (1986) 383-404.

2. Ethical Models Criticized by PV

2.1 Optimal Functionality

The first model of thought, while not explicitly mentioned in PV, is implicitly presumed and rejected. We are alluding to that kind of nonethical "scientific" thought emphasized by those who advance the theory of maximum functionality in today's world. They argue that the industrial and media culture and all of its subcultures must be judged exclusively according to the criterion of maximum functionality. That is, every such culture—whether it be industrial in character or specifically media-related—must be conducted according to purely rationalistic considerations of cost-effectiveness and profit-making on investments. Thus, it is these purely rationalistic considerations—and not rationality itself—which leads to the attainment of earnings and maximum possible profit. All the best technical means are directed to the achievement of this optimal objective; every other method that could possibly diminish or delimit such an outcome is eliminated in advance. In such a school of thought, an ethical principle, or worse still, control by way of norms or moral regulations, has no place because it has no meaning.[12] With this elimination of serious axiological reflection any honest attempt at dialogue on the ethical level makes no sense.

Unlike any putatively "neutral" rationality, axiological reflection is already of itself non-neutral. It is an ethic that touches upon human action under the aspect of human dignity and which realizes that human dignity can never be renounced, much less eliminated, from any ethical reflection which would not reduce the person to a mere machine. More than that, persons can never understand themselves, nor their work, nor any other reality whatsoever, without attentive reflection. The model of optimal functionality presupposes a rational procedure—that is to say, it presupposes a line of action which is thought out, analyzed, detailed, and systematized. But such a process cannot be developed in a day, by a single individual, even if the person were brilliant and ingenious. It requires, rather, a combined meeting of minds, in continuous dialogue, which gradually leads to the discovery and selection of means to procure optimal results. The point is that all of these operations are always linked with concepts, reasonings, and ethical judgments and therefore already belong to the ethical sphere.

2.2 Tolerance and Legalization

PV mentions elements of two other models of ethical thinking. The first manifests a "certain tolerance in regard to pornography" (PV 20b). This "certain tolerance" has already been imposed on all by the current situ-

---

[12] J. Mittelstrass, "Wirtschaftsethik als wissenschaftliche Disziplin?," in *Ethik und Wirtschaftswissenschaft. Schriften des Vereins für Sozialpolitik* , ed. G. Enderle, Neue Folge Bd. 147 (Berlin, 1985) 17-32; H. Schabl, "Editorial," *Universitas* 41 (Juli 1986), Heft 7, 669-72.

ation and the conflictual mentality. All the same, that "certain tolerance" which PV mentions cannot be allowed at "the cost of the moral welfare of the young and of the right of all members of society to privacy and to an atmosphere of public decency" (PV 20b). There exists, of course, that tolerance which affirms the natural right to "freedom of religion," connected with the dignity of the human person in a transcendental sense, and this has implications in the ethico-religious and socio-juridical sectors.[13] But as a personal attitude in the encounter with others, tolerance is not to be construed as a noetic, religious, ethical, political, and ideological indifference or as a uniform standardization of values. In the theoretical sense, tolerance means "to admit" the equal right of other opinions, even if these are contrary to one's own and even erroneous—but it does not mean permissiveness. In the practical sense, tolerance means forbearance towards those who, for reasons that seem to them overwhelmingly convincing, profess and maintain error; it does not mean to permit error, evil, corruption and moral evil themselves. Tolerance opens the door to freedom in which conflicts and the situation of conflict do not aim at a forceful oppression, but have a chance to express themselves objectively. This makes it possible that the dialogue undertaken in the midst of a situation of conflict be maintained on a reasonable level. Along these lines, we arrive at a contemporary discussion about tolerance understood as a moral virtue.[14]

The second model proposes legalization as a more expedient way of combating pornography and violence. It is argued that, as in the case of drugs, legalization would drive prices down, thereby paralyzing the profiteers and reducing consumption. This "legalization model," like the "tolerance model," is proposed, according to PV, by "minority groups" who have no loyalty to the moral values of the qualitatively representative majority and "fail to recognize that every right carries with it a corresponding responsibility" (PV 20b).

For these and similar reasons, says PV, these two models of "ethical" thought should be considered "bad libertarian arguments" (PV 20b). PV correctly asserts that the right to "freedom of expression" does not exist "in a vacuum," but carries with it a public and a personal responsibility. It reiterates in slightly different words what was said earlier: Anyone who has sound reason is publicly responsible for at least the following four trusts:

---

[13] See F. Molinari, "Tolleranza," in *Dizionario enciclopedia di teologia morale*, diretto da L. Rossi & A. Valsecchi, 4a ed., (Paoline, Roma, 1974) 1123-41.

[14] See "Tolleranza," in Centro di Studii Fil. di Gallarate, *Enciclopedia Filosofica*, Ristampa, vol. VIII, ed. Lucarini, (Firenze, Le Lettere, 1982) 263-66; "Tolleranza," in G. C. Sansoni, ed., *Dizionario delle idee* (Firenze, S.P.A., 1977) 1189-99; O. Hoeffe, "Tolerance," in O. Hoeffe, ed., *Dictionnaire de Morale* (Univ. Fribourg Suisse - Cerf, Paris, 1983) 202-03; K. Demmer, "Der Anspruch der Toleranz. Zum Theme 'Mitwirkung' in der pluralistischen Gesellschaft," *Gregorianum* 63 (1982) 701-20.

the promotion of the moral good of the young, respect for women, protection of "privacy," and the maintenance of public decency. One could also speak in this connection of contributive or legal justice, and even of social justice. In summary, the conclusion reached by PV appears logical and ethically right insofar as it affirms that the freedom of humanity and of the citizen "cannot be equated with license" (PV 20b).

2.3 Conformism and Pleasure

Ethical conformism is a tendency that levels the axiological problem in such a way that all human, ethical, and religious values are dumped together into a grey zone. Conformism, in its failure to have a right and adequate appreciation of these values, makes no attempt to raise the level of moral behavior. On the contrary, it sacrifices values for a very pragmatic reason—to avoid all objections and ethical questions directed at the media programs. If nonetheless these problems come to be discussed by the media they are cursorily treated in such a superficial manner that every person, intellectually gifted or not, is constrained to accept a standard of values which is quite shapeless, devoid of any real "bite," at an intellectual level that lacks any understanding of media culture.

Conformism in itself is not unrelated to erotization, i.e., the ideology which seeks sensual pleasure in the present moment.[15] False values are also set up—as in the case of those who allow themselves to be seduced by the media into unrealizable desires for utter luxury and riches, as if these were the epitome of genuine human fulfillment. The craving produced by such images can only end in frustration for those worse off, for the immature, and for "impressionable persons, especially those who are young" (PV 12b).

This touches another side of ethical conformism: It makes no distinctions on the cultural level, as if everyone possessed the same degree of preparation, intuition, discernment, and ability to form a right ethical judgment and, consequently, to make life-choices in a mature and responsible manner. This is implied when PV speaks of the "effects of pornography and violence." Years earlier, writing on the same problem, Augustine Cardinal Bea was already posing the pertinent question: "As long as human beings exist who, in virtue of their cultural level, are hardly capable of an independent judgment and who, due to the low level of morality, are scarcely capable of controlling their own instincts—should this not demand a more accurate examination of the consequences that these instruments provoke on people?"[16]

---

[15] Augustine Cardinal Bea, "Gli strumenti di communicazione sociale," in ID., *Unità nella libertà* (Morcelliana, Brescia, 1965) writing on the danger of conformism, calls it "the leveling influence of these instruments, that is, their tendency to unite moral values, the cultural level and their assumption, which often starts from the presupposition that all, listeners and spectators, may have the same discernment and the same capacity of judgment" (43-44).

[16] Ibid. 45.

Certainly the truly free activity of the human will, which arises only after sedulous personal reflection, stands in danger of being replaced in this environment of conformism by an attitude which looks solely to "what pleases me" and "what doesn't please me"—especially in one whose mind has been completely formed by what it encounters in the media. Such a possibility cannot be excluded when we are dealing with "young and impressionable minds" (PV 20a) which are presented with pornography and violence in an alluring and attractive manner as if this were "normal and worthy of imitation" (PV 12b). According to psychologists, TV and video scenes which are absorbed by children "not yet capable of clearly distinguishing between fantasy and reality" (PV 12a) could cause psychic disturbances of various types.

To sum up, we can say that ethical conformism collapses ultimately into an "ethics of the situation"—deprived of any stable criteria. Relying on the instincts of the moment, it falls back into an ethics of immediate individual gratification which "is fundamentally opposed to integral human growth and fulfillment" (PV 29b). The ethical criteria offered by conformism and the "ethics of individual gratification" cannot be a model to tackle the problem of a conflict of conscience or of its formation because they are devoid of every ethical value.

2.4 The Ethic of Total Opposition

With the advent of science and technologies which have the capacity to be dangerous forces in society, we come across occasionally a new tendency that would seek to eliminate any unforeseen negative effect in the fields of kinetics and genetics, for instance, by simply calling a halt to it all. Thus, this "new ethics" demands simply the prohibition of any kind of experimentation, inquiry, or application of the above-mentioned techniques, unless a nearly airtight guarantee against negative effects can be given. Such a model of ethics can provide this generation, involved as it is in an unprecedented manner in experimentation, with just one answer that is hardly plausible: that of abnegation, self-limitation, total opposition. Only such a drastic step, it is argued, can prevent the impending universal catastrophe which will be brought about by mindless manipulation of nuclear energy and human genes.[17]

---

[17] H. Jonas, *Technik, Medizin und Ethik. Zur Praxis des Prinzips Verantwortung* (Frankfurt: Insel, 1985); W. Daele, van den, "Technische Dynamik und gesellschaftliche Moral. Zur soziologischen Bedeutung der Gentechnologie," *Soziale Welt* 37 (1986), Heft 2-3, 149-72; C. G. Christians, "Ethical Theory in a Global Setting," in *Communication Ethics and Global Change*, ed. T. W. Cooper, C. G. Christians, F. F. Plude, R. A. White (New York: Longman Inc., 1989) 3-19; M. Honecker, "Verantwortung für die Zukunft. Die Ethik im Dialog der Wissenschaften," *EvKom* 19 (1986) 506-09.

We do not consider here the specific merits of possibly applying such an ethical model, with its essentially negative criterion. But it is clear that a policy of total renunciation cannot be applied to our problem of pornography and violence in the media—nor to the problem of conflict in general. Throughout the history of Catholic morality, prohibition through condemnation and anathema have been aimed at individual cases of conflict; taken in themselves, however, they seem never to have contributed any positive results. In this connection, PV seems to be ethically very progressive because it opts wisely and justly for another way, very laborious but all the same very human, underlining that "a merely censorious attitude on the part of the Church toward the media is neither sufficient nor appropriate" (PV 30). This point would be valid even in the fantastic case that we could get everyone to agree to the application of an ethics of total renunciation, for this criterion does not correspond to the dignity of the human person. The freedom of moral action must develop humanly, according to principles and ethical criteria that are carefully weighed and therefore applicable in concrete cases.[18]

We have, thus, examined the unsuitable ethical models and now turn to a scrutiny of the more expedient ones. PV offers real steps that are helpful in successfully tackling the problem of conflict influenced by pornography and violence in the media. It recommends one principle and two ethical criteria: the principle of continuous dialogue with the media, and the basic ethical criteria of the good of the human person and of the common good. These proposals carry us beyond the ambit of traditional ethics, both philosophical and theological, but at the same time they are in line with its fundamental and social implications. What is offered here is a modest proposal to articulate an ethics of conflict in the media. Far from being merely negative, this proposal draws from PV decidedly positive elements, both on the personal level of conscience and on the social and political level of the common good, connected as it is to the common ethical sense and protected by the dictates of legal and social justice.

3. The Principle of Dialogue

The ethical principle which PV treats is as old as humanity itself. Authentic dialogue between two or more people involves communication in which each of the partners wholly involves him or herself. It is the sharing with simplicity and sincerity of one's own ideas, opinions, experiences, and emotions, while simultaneously receiving the same from one's dialogue part-

---

[18] Giving a directive on how to educate children, PV does not advise total opposition but dialogue that serves as an approved medium of "persuasion": "In the field of formation, more is obtained with persuasion than with prohibitions" (no. 24b) and cited in note 6: *Communio et Progressio* 67.

ner, as these are reciprocated with equal sincerity and truth. Both parties are fully respected and accepted. The objective is to continue modifying, as is necessary or practical, these same ideas, opinions, etc., in order to arrive at results deemed acceptable to both parties. Dialogue is an ethical principle with a certain flexibility because it embraces all and excludes none, is attentive to every problem posed and does not close itself up when faced with serious and purportedly insurmountable difficulties. It neither manipulates nor pins anyone down, unless by means of persuasion. Dialogue promotes mutual understanding and coming together, with respect both to objective and subjective factors. By itself, it does not provide euphoric or hasty solutions; it is rather a convenient method for delving into problems in all their dimensions, relations, and possible consequences in such a way that the proposed solutions can have the most positive acceptance.[19]

Over the course of history, the method of dialogue has been employed both in everyday life and in the literary world: by pagan philosophers (Socrates, Aristotle, Cicero), by early Christian writers (Justin, Minicius Felix, Augustine), and by the scholastics (Anselm, Hugo of St. Victor). It is found in the poetry, didactics, drama, and art of every epoch. It is also used by the new sciences (Galileo, etc.). Today, the concept of dialogue as a method in human sciences and in all enterprising initiatives finds an echo in the teaching of the Church, beginning with the encyclical *Ecclesiam Suam* of Paul VI (1964) and continuing with the Vatican II documents, *Dignitatis Humanae* and *Gaudium et Spes*. PV, pursuing these same lines of Church teaching, praises the ethical principle of dialogue and highly recommends it as the best way of tackling pornography and violence in the media: "The Church should be engaged in continued dialogue with responsible communicators to encourage them in their work and to provide assistance where it is needed or requested" (PV 30).

The dialogue partners in PV are "the Church" and "the communicators." On a theoretical and qualitative level, "the Church" means "Catholic communicators" and their professional organizations with their special insights and experience in the subject (PV 30). These specialists are "invited

---

[19] See Bernard Marx, "Dialogik als ethisches Prinzip," *Evangelische Theologie* 49 (6/1989) 537-50; J. Moltmann, "Dient die 'pluralistische Theologie' dem Dialog der Welt-Religionen?" *Evangelische Theologie* 49 (6/1989) 528-37; J. Heinrichs, "Dialogik—Philosophisch," in *TRE* Bd. 8, 697-703; G. Sauter, "Dialogik—Theologisch," in *TRE* Bd. 8, 703-09; A. B. Hasler, "Dialogo Interconfessionale," in *Sacramentum Mundi* vol. 3 (Italian), 32-46; R. White, "Mass media and culture in contemporary Catholicism: The significance of Vatican II," in R. Latourelle, ed. *Vatican II Assessment and Perspectives: Twenty-five years after (1962-1987)* (New York: Paulist Press, 1989) Vol. 3: 580-611; A. Schoeph, "Communication," in *Dictionnaire de Morale* 24-25; A. Molinaro, "Responsibilità," in *Dizionario Enciclopedico di teologia morale* 892-901; A. Mercatali, "Dialogo," in *Dizionario di Spiritualità dei Laici* (E. Ancilli dir.), vol. 1 (Milano: O.R., 1981) 211-16.

to play a key role in this continuing dialogue" (PV 30). Among the "communicators" are represented every shade of opinion, attitude, and sentiment, any religion or ideology. On the practical level, PV offers a wide dialogue, a dialogue of all with all. It urges all those who are involved in or concerned about pornography and violence—communication professionals, parents, teachers, youth, the general public, civil authorities, the Church, and the religious (PV 21-29)—to enter into dialogue. To all people of good will, including institutions and structures that could come into contact with pornography and violence in the media, PV speaks of the "urgent need for continuing a dialogue" (PV 27).

PV proffers four interdisciplinary and strategic themes that provide a good deal of material for reflection and discussion. Under the psycho-social aspect, it favors two lines of thought in the form of theses that were studied and confirmed by "ordinary experience" (PV 9), leaving them to the consideration of the partner in dialogue: "No one can consider himself immune from the corrupting effects" of pornography and violence or "safe from injury at the hands of those acting under their influence" (PV 10).[20] Under the aspect of depth psychology, two dangers in dialogue are presented. The first is the possibility of impressionable people being "conditioned" by pornography and violence in the media. The second is the inner disturbances in children who may not be able "to distinguish readily between fantasy and reality" (PV 12). The so-called behavioral sciences also are in accord with the above and offer two ideas. First, healthy people who "view or read" pornographic and violent productions run the risk of carrying over such dangerous attitudes and behavior into their relations with others. Second, "the link between pornography and sadistic violence brings with it particular implications for those suffering from certain forms of mental illness" (PV 13).

Further, PV discusses the theme of lived sexual ethics and mentions four problems. The first is the influence of pornography and violence through soft core and hard core pornography in the media: This renders individuals "morally numb," is "habit-forming" like exposure to narcotics, and increases the likelihood of "anti-social behavior" (PV 14). The second problem is that pornography and violence foster "unhealthy preoccupations" and interfere with "personal moral growth" especially in marriage and family life (PV 15).[21] Third, pornography and violence in the media can threaten family life "in its totality," inasmuch as it contradicts the social and familial character of sexuality by portraying human sexuality "as a continuing fren-

---

[20] Among other things, the text says: "Pornography and sadistic violence debase sexuality, corrode human relationships, exploit individuals, especially women and the young people, undermine marriage and family life, foster anti-social behavior and weaken the moral fibre of society itself" (PV 10).

[21] Without citing the pertinent authors, allow us simply to say that it is well-known that today sexual violence is growing in marriage and in the family. The experts are asking why.

zied search for personal gratification rather than an expression of enduring love in marriage" (PV 16).

The last problem PV discusses concerns the social consequences of pornography and violence in the media. "In the worst cases, pornography can act as an inciting or reinforcing agent, a kind of accomplice, in the behavior of dangerous sex offenders—child molesters, rapists and killers" (PV 17). The document mentions these and other themes certainly with a view to an open and broader dialogue on problems not easily resolvable, but nevertheless real, as attested by studies "conducted around the whole world" by the same media "specialists" and "confirmed by ordinary experience" (PV 9).

In every case, it is of prime importance that the principle proposed by PV of continuous dialogue be confirmed and proposed as the first ethical principle with which to tackle prudently the contemporary problem of conflict. There is no doubt that the need for dialogue transcends the limited concern of pornography and violence in the media.

3.1 The Criterion of the Personal Good

All the parties—Catholic media specialists and non-Catholic alike—are at the service of the same media system and speak the same language. But do they *mean* the same thing when they speak?

The example of pornography and violence is based on facts, studied and proven by experience. Do both partners acknowledge these facts in the same way? Is the dialogue proposed by PV carried out on the basis of suppositions equally accepted by both partners? In the context of dialogue, are ethical values (justice, honesty, chastity) and human good (life, marriage, family) understood in the same manner by both parties? Do the concepts of conflict, conflictual reality, and conflictive mentality have the same content and meaning for both dialoguing parties? If these and similar epistemological questions render any dialogue on these matters complex enough, so much more so will be any dialogue between non-Catholic communicators and Catholic moral theologians, all of whom have different methods, language, and methods of reasoning, as well as different anthropological presuppositions, epistemologies, hermeneutics, and so on. Could and should the moral theologians enter into dialogue solely through an "intermediary," that is, through Catholic communicators who are both experts in the science and technology of the media and in theology at the same time? Doubtless, such highly qualified experts in various fields are needed today more than ever.

Given, then, the general ethical principle that a well-planned dialogue is desirable, there still remains the problem of the ethical criteria necessary to tackle the conflicting phenomenon of pornography and violence in the media. Is there, then, a "metaethical norm" acceptable to all which could measure the morality of the various media programs? Such a standard is what we must seek. Despite conceptual difficulties and ambiguities which can stand in the way of possible mutual understanding, some key concepts (such as "person," "conscience," "dignity," "right," "value," "human good") are held in common—or, at least, come close to the intuitions of the majority of media experts. Such common acceptance could form the basis of a further discussion characterized by mutual understanding and trust.

Given that PV repeatedly asserts that the human person is the key ethical measure on which a correct judgment towards a positive solution to these problems created by the media should rest, it would appear that we can presuppose that the contents of this criterion are understandable by at least the greater majority of the dialoguing partners. In an analogous fashion, documents originating in the United Nations and other high-level international organizations affirm that the foundation of human rights (that is, their ethical basis) is the "dignity proper to every human being" (PV 2), "human dignity" (PV 3), "the authentic dignity...of the human person" (PV 7), "the dignity of the person" (PV 9)), "the dignity of every person" (PV 24). In perfect harmony with these expressions contained in the international documents and in PV is the basic postulate of contemporary moral theology which states that "the decisive criterion is the comprehensive good of the person in the totality of his relationships to fellow human beings, society in general, and to the world."[22] At center stage, therefore, is the human person (transcendental, metaphysical) with all his or her fundamental relations (social, cosmic, transcendental), who in his or her corporeality is the apex of the material world (K. Rahner), but in his or her interiority "transcends the universe."[23] Thus, the unity and dignity of the human person, the two pillars of a common anthropology that admits a duality of body and spirit in the human person while rejecting a primitive dualism,[24] are affirmed.

It is also necessary to note that there is a double hierarchy of "human good." The first presumes a transcendental anthropology of "constant criteria" (the dignity and unity of the person); the second is pragmatic and presupposes a strategy of "what is possible here and now." "Needed will be a rigorous analysis of the respective good to be pursued, conducted however, in the light of this double criterion of the comprehensive good of the human person and that of the 'possible here and now'."[25]

"The comprehensive good of the person" (the dignity of the person) is the first and basic ethical criterion. The good referred to as the "possible

---

[22] K. Demmer, *Christi vestigia sequentes. Appunti di Teologia Morale Fondamentale* (Roma: PUG, 1988) 72.

[23] Vatican II, *Gaudium et Spes* no. 14.

[24] Ivan Fuček, "L'Unità e la dignità della persona nell' antropologia sessuale" 465-89.

[25] Ibid. 73.

here and now" is neither detached nor different from the criterion of the dignity of the person. It is simply the same criterion applied to concrete situations. It is necessary to have a detailed analysis of the concrete situation in order to find that "good" and that "right" that is present in the action that is realizable here and now and which will correspond as much as possible to the criterion of the "comprehensive good" of the acting subject. To effect such a process, it is necessary to apply the appropriate hermeneutic. There is clearly a need to "find the equilibrium between both the criteria." The criterion of action is the intermediation between the metaphysical (transcendental) category and the historical (categorical) category, a mediation that underlies every considered moral judgment.[26]

We will not examine here various other questions, such as for example what is to be done when human goods, considered in the long run and in the short run, come into conflict with each other (D. Mieth); our attempt is only to affirm the ethical criterion of the comprehensive personal good as the basis of dialogue. This principle is consonant with international documents that recognize the "dignity of the human person" as the basis for every human right and, consequently, of every autonomous and non-heteronomous ethics, leaving aside for now the consideration of other philosophical and ideological nuances.

3.2 The Criterion of the Common Good

After the discussion on the "personal" criterion, logically the next question is that of the "social" criterion. The human person grows up in a family, in a social group, in a community. The person matures, as the Vatican II document *Gaudium et Spes* puts it, contributing to the "common good," which today "becomes universal, involved with rights and obligations in relation to the entire human race." Thus, it describes a concept, not quite unambiguous, of the common good as "the sum total of social conditions which allow people, either as groups or as individuals, to reach their fulfillment more fully and easily."[27]

PV commends the media that develop among people the positive conviction "of a radical interdependence [and] solidarity" (PV 2), and communicators who "are animated by a great respect for the common good" (PV 23a). However, the document criticizes legislators for the lack of necessary laws "for the protection of the common good, especially the morals of the young" (PV 20), and emphasizes "the protection of the common good as

---

[26] Ibid.

[27] *Gaudium et Spes* no. 26. The whole paragraph speaks of the promotion of the common good, standing however firmly on the following thesis: "The social order and its progress should always leave the good of the person to prevail, since the order of things must be subordinate to the order of persons, and not the other way around."

their most sacred duty" (PV 28b), especially when "common good is called into question and threatened with these productions" (PV 28c). Required, above all, are "ethical codes inspired for the common good" (PV 23b), and originating *within* the media, which would serve the "development of the entire human race" (PV 23b). Such an insistence on "common good" shows that the criterion of social ethics is precisely the common good which is universally recognized and easily verifiable and protected by law. By means of this criterion there is possible a normative ethic, applicable to the media, especially with regard to the regulation of pornography and violence in the media. But dialogue begins with the question: In what way? By what method might a prudent consensus be reached on the matter of "human good" ("pre-moral good") which participates to some extent in the common good and at the same time is expressive of the human good upon which moral values are shaped? For example, the moral value of chastity is shaped by a certain order of ethical behavior which protects the goodness of a true and authentic human love before marriage, in marriage, in widow-hood, as well as in celibacy. It protects the good of education given to the young to effect a harmonious integration of love and sexuality. It safe-guards the good of marriage with its mutual and complete surrendering of the partners in love that extends to responsible parenthood. In widowhood, it is the guardian of the good of the marriage that has, happily, already been. It protects and fosters the good of celibate love which is the complete gift of self in love for the sake of the "kingdom of heaven." Thus, the meaning of "moral values" is translated in terms of the safeguards of human goods which, in their turn, are "the goods that condition the meaning of values."[28]

But in a pluralistic society, how does one arrive at a consensus regard-ing the goods and values which form part of the common good? A similar course has to be followed here too: How do people in a pluralistic state arrive at a law that is positively honest, just, universally practicable, and useful? At one time, positive law was considered the result of natural right (Thomas Aquinas). Today, however, the ethical foundation for just legisla-tion is the "common consensus." In every society, there is at least a "mini-mum" lived ethos and considered ethic: This "considered ethic" manifests itself theoretically in convictions, in the "lived ethos," in everyday practice. This means that even in a pluralistic society there exist human goodness and moral values: in the moral options expressed as convictions (the minimal moral ethos) and lived praxis (the minimum practical ethos). Such goods are then "collected," studied, and expressed in concrete laws for the society. By now in almost every state there is a political creed which is codified into a constitution. This controls political power, protects the citizen, respects the dignity of the person in the freedom of conscience and of religion, and

---

[28] Ibid. 71.

expresses the minimum of common moral consensus. While it watches over the rights of each and every individual, it also operates upon the principle of common good and is always open to new changes brought about by the same criterion of common good.

There is also possible, of course, within a society, ethical dissent. This dissent might be merely theoretical in nature: Everyone might agree, for instance, that human life should be protected, but disagree about how this should be done. Or it may be practical: Different segments of a society may ascribe to incompatible ethical systems (Christian, secularist, or Marxist systems, for instance). The legislator in drawing up laws should follow the course which is ethically more reasonable, as PV says, in light of the human good and the moral values of the qualitative "majority" (PV 20b). The legislator is the guarantor of the individual's freedom, and should limit the exercise of his or her office to what is necessary for safeguarding and protecting the common good. The law must be capable of being practiced by all.

Analogously, this method could be applied to the general problem of conflict in the media, as well as to particular cases like pornography and violence. Those responsible for the media are charged with the task of seeking out and respecting the common ethical consensus, both practical and theoretical, as well as dissent. On the basis of a common good into which every particular human good of a society converges, they also must decide prudently how to tackle the conflict of conscience of the many and the reality of conflict in general. In short, there is required a strong ecumenical attitude which embraces all and does not offend the good moral sense of anybody.[29] The particular competence of a Christian consists in reconciliation, peace, and in leading people towards more human goals "in which differences are not glided over and the elements of tension are brought to bear on each other's productivity."[30]

---

[29] The term "ecumenical" as we have seen is applied to the collaboration of all, while the same Pontifical Council for Social Communications, "Criteria for Inter-religious and Ecumenical Collaboration in the Field of Social Communications" (Oct. 4, 1989), *L'Osservatore Romano*, no. 253 (39.283), Oct. 1989, 9, has given some important norms for ecumenical collaboration among believers. The scope of the document is described by the President of the above-mentioned council in this way: "These criteria, indications given to Catholics, as much as it concerns ecumenical and interreligious collaboration in the means of communication become, by their nature, an invitation to other religions to unite themselves with us to guarantee that religion has a voice in the media, and to obtain that the values of mutual respect and moral integrity may be promoted" (J. P. Foley, "The Influence of the Media in the Formation of Human Values," Ibid. 9).

[30] D. Mieth, "Conflitto" 106.

4. Conclusion

In summary, we have read and studied in detail the text of the Document on Pornography and Violence in the context of the phenomena of "conflict" and "conflictual reality." Our objective was not to provide an answer to this phenomenon, nor even to define it with precision (which looks to be almost impossible, except for some particular cases of conflict of conscience). Examining the phenomenon of pornography and violence presented by the recent PV, it was our intention to look for realistic possibilities of tackling this problem and lessening its impact. Our study shows, we believe, that PV in a certain sense transcends itself. Given the explanations of the elements which are contained in the document, it could become the model for an understanding of the problem of conflict. Further inquiries into the same document led us to the identification both of unacceptable ethical models as well as one model which may be feasible. The discussion of the latter highlighted four significant points: (1) the principle of continuous dialogue which is ecumenically urgent and goes beyond interreligious collaboration; (2) the fundamental criterion of the dignity of the human person; (3) the social criterion of common good; and finally, (4) some tentative solutions to the question of "how," which may provide the ethical instrumentality to launch a fruitful dialogue, most importantly, among the partners of the media.

Although these results are rather modest, they could nevertheless inspire fresh and ambitious studies that would focus on how moral theology could sharpen its conceptual and methodological tools in confronting the problem of conflict. Towards this end, the unbiased and careful reader of PV will find its importance more than apparent.

15

The Church as Moral Communicator

Paul A. Soukup, S.J.

What role does the Church—as a *communicator*—play in shaping the moral imagination of society? The question itself poses further questions. What is the Church, *as a communicator*? How does the Church act as a communicator of morals? What should the Church do to shape morals? Briefly, I will argue that the Church functions as a moral communicator at several levels, that the Church works best as a moral communicator when the Church shapes the imagination, and that such shaping occurs when the Church is most honestly the Church at the local level.

1. The Church's Moral Communication

Consider the following examples of the Church's moral communication:

- The American Bishops worked through several two-to-three-year processes and issued, after much consultation and debate, a series of pastoral letters or drafts on peace and nuclear weapons, on the economy, and on the role of women in the church.
- Mary Smith, a catechist, teaches a fifth grade class about the life of Jesus and asks the children to draw pictures of different scenes from the Gospels. The process of education, with its thousands of variations, is repeated in parochial schools, Sunday schools, and Catholic high schools across the country.
- Pope John Paul II flies across the globe on pilgrimage to the countries of Africa and Asia, to Canada, to the countries of Europe, to the countries of North and South America. In each place Catholics gather for huge outdoor Masses with numbers reaching into the hundreds of thousands.
- Pope John Paul II publishes an encyclical on social justice, running 50 pages in length. The *New York Times* publishes an excerpt, but the full text doesn't reach the people for several weeks.

- John Jones, an "ordinary Catholic" tries to live his life faithful to the Gospel. He helps with the St. Vincent de Paul Society in his community. Those who know him think he is a decent man.

These form just a few of the ways in which the Church communicates messages and morals in the world today. The list certainly doesn't exhaust the possibilities but does suggest some conclusions. If we add the mass media in the United States into the picture, it would surprise none of us that the actions of Pope and bishops might make the six o'clock news or the morning edition. What we should try not to forget is that the actions of Mary Smith and John Jones play just as vital a role in shaping the moral communication of the Church.

2. Formal Channels

The moral communication of the Church takes two forms. On the one hand lies formal moral teaching: This results from an ongoing reflection on key situations and issues according to the methods of moral theology and philosophical ethics. The bishops' pastorals on war and peace and on the economy are good examples of this process. Papal or Vatican statements on social justice and medical ethics are other examples of the same thing. On the other hand lies an informal moral teaching, a common sense morality, the way we Catholic Christians do things.[1]

Applying any kind of communication analysis to the first type of moral teaching leads to considerations of effectiveness, information, and public relations. Here is the message, the Church seems to say; now how can we best communicate it? In this instance, the Church as a communicator doesn't seem all that different from the White House, General Motors, or Jello—despite the differences in message content. The persuasive form of communication looks to source, message, and audience. Following an Aristotelian scheme of rhetoric, one would evaluate moral communication in terms of source credibility, logic and clarity of topic, and attention to audience characteristics.[2] In most instances this analysis suggests that the nature of the audience powerfully determines the methods of persuasion. Does the Church address the world? If so, in what forum? Does the leadership of the Church address its members? If so, how? The presentation of the credibility of the communicator and, to an extent, the message itself will change according to which group the Church addresses. Traditionally, the formal moral teaching of the Church stresses a hierarchical source and a carefully crafted message directed first to Church members who, it presumes, wel-

---

[1] See Henk Hoekstra and Marjeet Verbeek, Chapter 16, below, for more on this.

[2] Stephen W. Littlejohn, *Theories of Human Communication* 2nd ed. (Belmont, CA: Wadsworth Publishing Company, 1983) 134.

come the message. Only secondly does this formal teaching office address non-members; when it does, it must choose a more explicitly persuasive rhetorical style. In both instances, however, the canons of rhetoric and public relations apply because at this level the Church seems not to differ at all from any other organization.[3]

Of course, many members of the Church and its hierarchy think that the Church does indeed differ significantly from other organizations; that may well be true in terms of the nature of the Church, but that distinction does not apply in terms of the Church's communicative behaviors. The fact that Church officers often accept neither the similarity of the Church to other organizations nor the necessity for audience discrimination has far-reaching effects, often frustrating for those who work for the various communication offices of the Church. Many of these communication professionals chafe at not being allowed to do what they consider standard procedure. For example, I recall an official in the Vatican's Communication Office remarking that he was not allowed to prepare a press release highlighting the important sections of a papal encyclical because, he was told, all the sections of an encyclical are equally important. He was unable to convince the others that the press pool itself—not trained in theology, church history, or philosophy—would prepare such a digest before reporting the encyclical. They did. And in that moment the Church lost any control over how the encyclical was reported around the world. In a similar way, the Vatican has in the past refused to distribute advance copies of its publications even to the bishops, thus preventing leaks but also leaving the local bishops unprepared to comment on Church moral teaching. Thankfully, this practice has changed.

A full discussion of the Church as a moral communicator in the formal sense would have to include the whole range of ways in which the church approaches the communication media. These channels through which the Church speaks include the press, the wire services, the publishing industry, electronic news agencies, and even the local parish where papal and episcopal statements trickle down in the forms of homilies and bulletin inserts. Immense problems plague this kind of communication, not the least of which has to do with who interprets the messages. Related to this, too, is the temporal bias of the media used to communicate. Everything slides towards immediacy in the news business: A moral statement might make page one, but only for one day.

Despite the significance of these formal channels and methods of communication and despite their problems, they are not necessarily the most important kinds of moral communication in the Church. The encyclicals

---

[3] It is interesting to note, too, that with the possible exception of the American Bishops, the Church remains solidly print-oriented in its communication of moral teaching. Perhaps the subject-matter and the methods of moral teaching demand the logic of print, but that rhetorical approach limits the availability of the message.

and pronouncements are interesting; they are vital in shaping the outlook of the Church; but they do not occupy the places in which people live their lives. For this, let us turn to the other realm: the day-to-day, the common sense Catholic living.

3. Informal Channels

Without pretending any of the refinements of moral theology, I would like to suggest that moral action, for most people, emerges from a kind of taken-for-granted framework. People simply presume that they act morally, usually without thinking about it, until they find themselves either in a moral failing or in a complex situation. This model here borrows from Aristotle's thought on moral habit and Hopkins's "The just man justices," but basically it is a communication model: We presume language works, taking all manner of things and processes for granted, until communication fails or a situation demands some kind of planned discourse. In normal conversation we simply presume we understand, using a kind of taken-for-granted rule. When we discover that we really don't understand, we might ask a question.[4] In more complex settings—in a long-term interpersonal relationship, for example—we plug on ahead until we notice a communication breakdown. At that moment we look to theory and seek out a kind of guiding principle for the next step. We might consult with friends or even call upon an expert for advice. Then, generally, we do the best we can.

Granted that the stakes are higher and the issues more profound, I think that the moral life of most Church members follows a similar pattern. Most married couples do not wrestle with whether or not to remain faithful to one another; they just do so. Only in moments of stress or failure do questions arise about what one consciously ought to do. Similarly, most people live their lives with a kind of taken-for-granted respect for human life. The majority of us do not confront issues of medical ethics (when does life begin? when does life end? must extraordinary measures be taken in this situation?). If those issues arise, then we look to the moral theologian or the expert for help.

In this situation of taken-for-granted acting, the role of the Church as moral communicator becomes extremely important. How do people learn those daily behaviors? Standard communication theory borrows from sociology and psychology here. The work of George Herbert Mead examines the function of society in teaching language and other roles to its members.[5]

---

[4] Robert Hopper, "The Taken-for-Granted," *Human Communication Research* 7 (1981) 195-211.

[5] George Herbert Mead, *Mind, Self, and Society from the Standpoint of a Social Behaviorist*, ed. Charles W. Morris (Chicago: University of Chicago Press, 1934). See, too, Jürgen Habermas's reinterpretation and extension of Mead in his

The social use of language comes first; the individual uses only later. Individuals, like baseball players (Mead's example), must learn all the roles of the group in order to successfully enact their own. In this view, to become a moral actor means to become a full member of the group. Similarly, Albert Bandura's social learning theory sketches out a model of how individuals learn behaviors from their society.[6] In his view, they combine informational (cognitive) and motivational (emotional) reinforcement with modelling and role playing: A potential action must first seem desirable. To become a moral actor means imitating what one loves.

Therefore, the morally communicating Church in this instance of the day-to-day is the community of the Church. And, at rock bottom, that community is the local community which communicates through interpersonal dealings and personal discourse. That community is the chief place where people can "see how they love one another." That community puts into action whatever moral tradition might take on life for its members.

In an ideal world the local community forms the place where the people gather to listen to the Word of God, to let that Word touch their hearts, and to share the Eucharist. The local community becomes, after the family, the school of love in which people learn to reach out to one another and to civil society. The local community forms the environment in which people experience love, forgiveness, trust, and support as they seek to put the Gospel into action in their lives. To the local community—first of all but not exclusively—apply the admonitions of the Church's documents on communication that the Church as communicator take Christ as a model:

> While he was on earth Christ revealed himself as the perfect communicator. Through his incarnation he utterly identified himself with those who were to receive his communication, and he gave his message not only in words but in the whole manner of his life. He spoke from within, that is to say, from out of the press of his people. He preached the divine message without fear or compromise. He adjusted to his people's way of talking and to their patterns of thought. And he spoke out of the predicament of their time.[7]

It is this kind of environment that leads to the moral sense which works on the day-to-day level.

Three aspects of the communication process on the local level lead to the kind of moral communication suggested here. According to both Mead

---

wide-ranging sociological theory of human activity: *Theory of Communicative Action*, 2 vols. Thomas McCarthy, trans. (Boston: Beacon Press, 1984 & 1987).

[6] Albert Bandura, *Social Learning Theory* (Englewood Cliffs, N.Y.: Prentice-Hall, 1977).

[7] Pontifical Commission on the Instruments of Social Communication, "Pastoral Instruction on the Means of Social Communication" *(Communio et Progressio)*, in *Vatican II: The Conciliar and Post Conciliar Documents,* ed. Austin Flannery (Collegeville, MN: Liturgical Press, 1975). no. 11.

and Bandura, people learn behaviors from role models which they find attractive, salient, and understandable. Past Church history shows an intuitive recognition of the need for role models in our human living: The cult of the saints (even with all of its abuses and hagiographic excesses) provided a strong set of characters for every moral occasion. The local community needed only to use its wisdom to draw on the appropriate model. The Church's moral teaching, then, depends greatly upon the people who make up the community, upon how they live their lives, and upon their collective memory of holiness. This implies three conclusions. First, granted we are all sinners, we still live under an urgency to model moral behavior for one another. This means that no one in the Church can be content with a spiritual laissez-faire but must model forgiveness as well as holiness. Second, every local community maintains some degree of the tradition of role models since each contains some individual women and men whose lives are noteworthy. I wonder, however, how often we as a Church explicitly recognize these people for who they are. Third, it seems to me that this modelling is not something just for children; we adults equally need it. The strongest encouragements to my own moral living have come from the witness of the lives of others.

The moral communication of the local church also comes through teaching. This most properly links the local church with the Church universal. The Church possesses a tradition of the Scriptures, the Councils, doctrinal pronouncements, moral conclusions, theology, and philosophy. The teaching role of the local church makes this material known to people, not necessarily in all its detail, but at least well enough so that individuals realize that a tradition exists and that they can go to that tradition when the need arises. Education in the local church—whether on the grammar school, high school, university, or adult level—teaches this tradition and, according to the students' age level, the methodology of the tradition. The tradition gives not only a sense of what the Church has thought over the centuries; it also sketches boundaries by teaching what has not worked and identifying what has led to evil rather than to good. Because most of us immediately think of teaching when we reflect on the moral tradition of the church, less needs to be said here about it.

The third aspect the Church's moral communication falls under the heading of imaging or imagining. Imagination leads us to new possibilities for faithful living and moves the notion of moral reasoning from the "is this allowed" stage to the "what ought one to do" stage. In other words, imaging opens to the future. The imagination also provides a link outside of the community; its very nature leads it forth to make use of the images of society and to address society in terms of those images.

The local Christian community supports imaging by providing the safety or stability that allows the individual imagination to try out many different prospects. Imagination needs the ability to make mistakes. Some moral argument will not work but people cannot discover that until someone tries to phrase or, more likely, to image the argument. Since imagination functions with images rather than with acts, it allows a freedom for exploration.

The local community provides not only the security to take the risk of imagining; it also gives the attitudes and material necessary to nourish the imagination. The community affords an environment that can allow and encourage its members to dream. Moreover, by featuring images and the arts, it supplies the materials for that dreaming. A community whose worship, for example, is rich and sensuous gives its members the incentive to combine those images into new ones. Storytellers and artists come from places where words, music, and images matter. The Catholic tradition has generally proven itself abundant in its use of the arts and the imagination. These came from local communities but found encouragement, too, in a sacramental theology which clings to the visible, which takes an understanding of the Incarnation into every aspect of church life.[8]

The ability to image the faith of the community in various situations deepens the community's moral sense. Much the same way that television, for example, allows us as a culture to try out different behaviors and personae vicariously, faith imaging allows the believer to see what would happen if some situation or other were to occur. This is very much a "fleshed-out" case study approach to moral discourse.

In order for the community to take its place as a moral communicator, people must identify with that community, finding it attractive and salient. This happens first at the local level when individuals experience the community's life. How can the Church become a better moral communicator? I would propose the deepening of all levels of the local community first: providing models of Christian living, teaching the Church's tradition, nourishing the imagination. Some argue that the best way to do these things comes through parish renewals; others, through a re-affirmation of the parochial school system. Both parish and school shape the individual; the Church should pay attention to both.[9]

---

[8]William Lynch in *Images of Faith* (Notre Dame, IN: University of Notre Dame Press, 1973) explores the relationship between the images of the believing community and those of secular society: Faith images the world in particular ways, providing that Christian insight into moral action that I have described here. At the same time, secular society too has its images of faith which influence how it deals with the believing community.

[9]James R. Kelly, "Does the *Renew* Program Renew?" *America* 156:9 (March 7, 1987) 197-99; Andrew M. Greeley, "Community as Social Capital: James S. Coleman on Catholic Schools," *America* 157:5 (September 5, 1987) 110-12.

4. Church Universal and Local

This does not eliminate the universal Church or the hierarchical Church from the picture. Given the local situation, the larger Church offers a powerful focus for personal identification, compensating for weakness, and remembering the tradition independently of local circumstances—a sometimes necessary corrective. The larger Church can also provide resources unavailable to the local community. Think again of those papal Masses attended by thousands: The artistic tradition of the Church became evident there on a scale impossible for a parish. Think for a moment of the papal encyclicals or Vatican declarations: These reaffirm the teaching tradition of the Church in a transnational way that moves beyond individual cases to more general principles. Think for a moment of the calendar of saints: Here are models for every life. The parish community, then, does not stand alone but forms the particular locus for the Church as moral communicator. One cannot separate the church from the Church or the Church from the church.

At the same time one cannot separate the interpersonally experienced church from the mediated church. One can draw distinctions between formal and informal communication, as I have tried to do. However, in the lives of individuals, such distinctions soon become slippery. Each of the examples which began this chapter illustrated a particular kind of communication. The interpersonal examples of the catechist and the works of charity communicate something of the life of the Church in a way that nothing else can. The mediated cases illustrate other aspects of the Church as moral communicator. The American Bishops' pastoral letters—formal moral teaching, using the mass media—placed the Catholic Church in the United States squarely in the spotlight of a national policy debate. The bishops caught the public interest, not only of Catholics but of men and women of every kind of belief. Significantly, their method of proceeding (hearings, discussions, drafts) probably conveyed as powerful a message about the Church as did their conclusions.

In a similar way, the pilgrim Pope catches the imagination of the world. Whatever the messages and whatever the motivation of the crowds, people gather to express a celebration of the Church. This is the Church of the imagination; this is the Church which holds up models of holiness. This Church—whether experienced in person or through television—proves attractive to many, even those inactive in local parishes. The teaching Pope (the Pope of the encyclicals) proves less popular, probably because such teaching demands too much of its medium. A sound bite, even a 5,000 word story simply cannot summarize a moral argument.

This particular model of the Church as moral communicator poses some serious questions to the Church. I have already briefly indicated something of the consequences for the parish and for the universal Church: How does it become more perfectly Church, more a community of love, more a place that fosters models of behavior, a place that teaches the tradition, a place that is an environment for imaging? The other serious questions result from the fact that the Church is not the only community to which individuals belong. In a pluralist society like that of the United States, people have multiple memberships: families, work groups, neighborhoods, political affiliations, fan clubs, network loyalties, and so forth.[10] Each of these also provides images, models, and a tradition. How does one determine which images or models will shape people? Does exposure time accurately measure influence? Does brand loyalty have anything to say about religious practice? Ultimately, what determines what people take for granted? What constitutes an individual's or a society's moral universe? The same model which applies to the Church could well apply to these other communities as well. That model may help in an understanding of the communication patterns in our world and their influence in shaping a moral discourse.

This essay has proposed an outline for a model of the Church as a moral communicator. Formal and informal moral teaching and practice develop in radically different ways, but the Church encompasses both. Both formal and informal styles affect and are affected by the communication industry and its products. Perhaps this model will help us to understand a bit more clearly how some of the factors in the moral life interact so that we can more clearly express who we are and who we wish to be as a Church.

---

[10] George Wilson, "Where Do We Belong? United States Jesuits and Their Memberships," *Studies in the Spirituality of Jesuits* 21:1 (January 1989).

III

Using the Media for
Moral Development

III

Introduction

Using the Media for
Moral Development

Moral formation encompasses many dimensions; among the more important ones we can include the home and family which shape early perceptions of good and bad, the surrounding culture from which we pre-reflectively assimilate values and norms for conduct, the formal programs of moral education which institutions such as church and school organize and sponsor, the conversations and discussions we have with trusted friends about important decisions, the public debates which engage us as participants or spectators on matters of personal rights and societal responsibilities, and the critical and scholarly study which examines the practices, images, concepts and arguments embodying and supporting specific patterns of moral life. These dimensions neither stand in isolation from one another, nor do they form a fixed hierarchical pattern; instead, they interact with each other in multiple and varied ways. In the environment of a mass-mediated culture, however, the interaction of these dimensions has become even more complex: Not only have media and their presentations come to penetrate and pervade the dynamics of the other dimensions of moral formation, they seem also to constitute a new, separate and powerful dimension of that formation.

It has not been uncommon for educators, politicians, and ordinary citizens to express concern about the power which mass media have to influence moral formation and to wonder about the extent to which this power threatens the effective working of the other dimensions. In the media we encounter much that is morally charged. It is easy to see, moreover, in media presentations that display images and narratives of violence, convey messages eliciting new consumer needs, or frame complex personal and societal issues into simple argumentative polarities some disturbing paradigms of attitudes and behavior which appeal to the less morally praiseworthy elements of our human makeup such as unrestrained power, acquisitiveness, and self-satisfaction. One can legitimately speculate about the extent to which skillfully packaged appeals to these levels of our human reality have the potential for clouding moral vision and disorienting the processes of moral imagination.

The essayists in this section are not unaware of the potential which mass media have for disrupting other dimensions of moral formation. Exclusive focus on the negative impact which mass media may have upon this process, however, overlooks the potential they also have for enhancement and reenforcement of the dynamics that enliven the various dimensions of moral formation. It also reduces the possibility of discerning in the dynamics proper to mass media new avenues and approaches for effective moral formation. The overall focus they provide, therefore, is upon the identification and exploration of those dynamics of mass media which have potential for enhancing the processes of moral growth.

Henk Hoekstra and Marjeeet Verbeek identify and analyze the dramatic and narrative features of audiovisual media as distinctive sources for ethical reflection. These features, which Hoekstra and Verbeek consider to be central to the communicative form of audiovisual media, offer a basis for the development of models for moral education in which mass media play a positive, energizing role. Processes of moral education which build upon the dramatic and narrative features of audiovisual media make "dialogical communication" their focus—and that focus is particularly apt for persons living in mass-mediated culture. For Hoekstra and Verbeek, moreover, the dialogical communication which enables persons to achieve their ethical identity through the exchange and interpretation of narratives, is not simply one more technique for moral education; it is "the key concept for the formation of a Christian community." They draw upon their experience in using audiovisual media at Catholic Media Center in the Netherlands to provide three examples illustrating principles and methods for effective use of audiovisual media, such as video and film, in processes of moral education to foster dialogical communication.

Elizabeth Willems examines media's power to unsettle current perceptions and ways of thinking; she sees this power serving as an important positive element in moral education. "Disequilibration"—a state of tension in the psychological structure of our cognitive and moral judgments—can result when media present us with information, images, and perspectives that do not fit with our current moral attitudes, sentiments, and judgments. Willems points out that such "disequilibration" and its resolution are central to all learning. Moral learning progresses not by avoidance of this cognitive and affective tension but by resolution of the tension in the direction of moral growth. Willems offers a framework, based upon cognitive development theory and a theology of basic human freedom, to identify two ways in which media can effect moral growth; she contends that media provide two conditions—education and focus—that influence the human freedom which is basic for moral growth. Within this context, she particularly notes how media touch the imagination through which we envision the destiny within God's kingdom to which our freedom is ordered.

Myrna Grant's essay considers mass media's potential for fostering religious as well as moral growth. She discusses two films, *The Mission* and *Repentance*, to illustrate her hypothesis that movies are significant vehicles for the experience of transcendence in contemporary life. Grant notes how the situations and images from these films present to viewers an "experience of otherness" with power to move them beyond their current awareness of the moral and religious significance of their lives. Film is a particularly apt medium for conveying the experience of transcendence because, in Grant's view, it offers space for metaphor, which is "the vehicle by which people experience transcendence." Grant notes that a culture "muffled in a global technological age" provides people with "little experience in handling metaphor" because it gives priority to unambiguous communication. In contrast to this "utilitarian mandate" that "decodes symbols into negotiable communication" film has the possibility for conveying a vision of reality that can "evoke a response of awe and wonder before ultimate mystery."

Anne E. Patrick's essay provides a theologically focused criterion by which to assess the extent to which mass media foster moral development through the enlargement of our moral sensibility. This criterion emerges from the biblical injunction to love one's neighbor; this injunction measures "our basic stance toward ultimate reality" by reference to "where we draw the boundaries between the persons who really count as neighbors and those who are more or less irrelevant." This criterion challenges the tribalisms by which we humans have stubbornly resisted the inclusive and universal demands of love and justice. Patrick turns a critical eye to the question of whether mass media, particularly television, can be enlisted as a trustworthy ally in efforts to break down our society's persistent tribalisms of racism, sexism, and anti-Semitism. Her answer to that question appeals to a singularly instructive exchange from literary history—one between Mary Ann Evans Lewes and Harriet Beecher Stowe, who both sought to make the mass media of their day, the novel, "exercise power over the social mind for good." This exchange suggests that in the complex dynamics of human moral life, no single factor can be expected to serve as the exclusive catalyst for moral enlargement. Patrick notes, moreover, that there are structural elements of commercial television—self-censorship, concern for audience share, the psychologizing of social issues—which inhibit its potential contribution to the task of moral formation. Patrick would have us temper our hopes about the positive moral power of the media; at the same time, she would not have us lose any urgency about the pressing need to devote the full array of our imaginative resources to breaking down these corrosive tribalisms.

16

Possibilities of Audiovisual Narrative for Moral Formation

Henk Hoekstra and Marjeet Verbeek

1. Introduction

The very active presence of mass media, particularly the audiovisual media (cinema and television), strongly influences our contemporary culture and plays an important role in creating popular culture. Therefore, when we speak about audiovisual media, we refer not only to instruments or techniques but to important cultural phenomena. In fact, the messages in these media offer concrete models for expressions of behavior and life.

The audiovisual media "speak" a language distinct from the written language in the print media, with their own specific symbolic communicative code. This specific language is dynamic, concrete, physical, dramatic, and narrative and results from the mixing and editing of moving colorful images, speech, noises and music, organized and supervised by electronics.[1] It has therefore first of all an emotional and affective logic and effect. This language has a certain congeniality with the Christian tradition, which has its own narrative and symbolic language of Scripture and Tradition. The audiovisual language however is a new phenomenon and has its origins in relatively recent technology and developments in electronics.

In this essay we will give some outlines for moral formation in our mass mediated world, focusing especially on *narrative communication* and *morality*. In the formation of the ethical identity of a person or a group of persons, a receptive and dialogical attitude in narrative communication processes, mass-mediated and interpersonal, is fundamental. A story needs to be heard and watched at as a drama: The story reveals meaning to the viewer only in receiving an answer from the viewer. Moral formation in a mass mediated world, which starts with the ethical and aesthetic analysis of

---

[1] Pierre Babin and M. F. Kouloumdjian, *Les nouveux modes de comprendre: La génération de l'audiovisuel et de l'ordinateur* (Paris: Le Centurion, 1983).

audiovisual stories, finally focuses on the formation of the communicative person who communicates with the audiovisual story and moves towards an exchange of stories among the members of a group. In the end the audiovisual product has primarily functioned as an inspiration for dialogical communication about moral issues.

We see narrative communication as the first objectification of the moral experience. And since we judge audiovisual media as primarily dramatic and narrative, we see them as objectifications of moral experiences and therefore as sources for an ethical reflection, which occurs not primarily in argumentative rational discourse but in narrative communication. Specifically, a narrative ethic can integrate aspects of acting and of granting identity in spoken, written, and audiovisual stories. This essay begins with an awareness of the mass mediated culture as a mainly audiovisual culture, in which narratives dominate and exercise influence on the moral formation of people, often quite unconsciously.

2. The actual situation concerning mass media and morality

2.1 Our changing communicative environment

Morality and mass media have a tangled relationship. The mass media form the symbolic environment we tend to drown in more and more. These audiovisual media create a symbolic universe, a media culture, with of all kinds of messages, communications, information, announcements, and invitations concerning life and society. "People are necessarily living in three worlds at the same time," Thayer writes: "the world of their natural environment, the world of their social and cultural environment, and the world of their communicative and symbolic environment. One doesn't deny the ultimate reality of the two other worlds, when one is recognizing that [the hu]man can only understand and survive in those worlds in terms of [their] communicative and symbolic world."[2]

The prevalence of audiovisual language makes it harder to abstract from the phenomenon in order to determine how mass media and morality interact in our society. Audiovisual media do change society. The arrival of a new communication technology has always changed culture. Introduce the alphabet or typography into society and you will change perceptions, social relationships, history, religion, etc. Introduce the moving images of cinema and television and you provoke a communicative revolution.[3] However, judging a contemporary development like this one runs the risk of becoming negative from a fear for the "new."

---

[2] Lee Thayer, "Massamedia in de moderne samenleving," *Massacommunicatie* (1973) 147ff.

[3] Neil Postman, *Amusing Ourselves to Death: Public Discourse in the Age of Show Business* (New York: Viking, 1985) Ch. 5.

2.2 Moral fragmentation versus moral coherence

The mass mediated world has coincided with an increase of moral fragmentation, which sometimes develops towards moral relativism. Such moral attitudes can easily result from an ideologically pluralistic society[4] that has grown out of the historical development called secularization. In general, secularization rejects the normative model of ethics, which was based on obedience and was strongly influenced by the dominant ideology of the Christian Churches and Traditions. This has left us without a suitable model for moral coherence in our contemporary mass mediated society.

The information culture itself partially accounts for moral fragmentation. It is difficult to get a coherent image of human life and the world when too much (un)truthful and often conflicting information comes across the screen. But the mass media are not the only institutions that create fragmentation. They also give, like a mirror, expression to fragmentation due to other institutions in society. The mass mediated presentations of society and the pluralism in society seem to reinforce one another.

Let's take for example the average news broadcast which carries perhaps 10 events in about a half an hour. Usually, these events express distinct and often competing underlying moral values and standards. The news reader tries to present the events in an objective way in order not to manipulate the viewer too much into a certain opinion about the event. This results in a fragmented and pluralistic presentation of the "news of the world." But does not the viewer expect this?

Fictional programs have a slightly different effect. In 60 minutes they present a more or less coherent view on a certain matter. Series usually give expression to concepts or images about good and bad, right and wrong. So, if viewers watch five fictional programs on one night they receive at least five moral concepts. Furthermore, series, which use a multiperspective discourse (*Hill Street Blues, L.A. Law, St. Elsewhere, Miami Vice*) end up creating doubt through the refusal to present coherent moral concepts . These series move towards the expression of moral dilemmas[5] and probably present today's feelings about moral issues: They are complex and not easy to solve.

---

[4] M. Christiaens, "De moraal van de zelfontplooiing: een illusie," *Kultuurleven* (1985) 824ff.

[5] C. Deming, "Hill Street Blues as Narrative," *Critical Studies in Mass Communication* 2 (1985) 1-22.

2.3 The triviality of television

Roughly speaking, two contrasting viewpoints and attitudes exist today towards the audiovisual media, a positive and a negative one.[6] Each of them has its own consequences for the view on moral formation in a mass mediated world.

The negative evaluation holds that mass culture is without value and is dangerous. The traditional view regards the audiovisual media as ephemeral and superficial. They are oriented towards sensation, suspense, violence, and sex, which they present in an exaggerated and spectacular way, manipulating the feelings and emotions of viewers. The producers try to attract huge audiences by adapting their products to the popular taste. Because audiovisual culture represents the culture of the masses, few who take this negative view reflect on it thoroughly.

Such a viewpoint and evaluation make it impossible to value audiovisual culture as other than cheap entertainment, which hardly gives possibilities for moral formation. Instead this view chooses to formulate sharp negative criticism: Audiovisual mass media are culturally worthless but at the same time dangerous; responsible institutions should protect and educate the masses. A specific model for moral formation, the obedience model,[7] corresponds with this negative evaluation. The principle of the obedience model implies that institutions and their representatives have to formulate how one has to judge reality. The model starts from an objective doctrine, an ideology, a system of interpretation. One first learns this doctrine and then follows it. Formation by authority arises from the model: a formation in order to obey, follow others, and ignore personal feelings and thoughts.

2.4 Television as a cultural forum

We don't agree with this negative view on the mass mediated world and the corresponding obedience model in moral formation. Its opposite, the positive evaluation, provides a different start on the subject of moral fragmentation versus coherence. Horace Newcomb and Paul Hirsch[8] place fragmentation in the perspective of "television as a cultural forum." They lay stress on the "collective, cultural view of the social construction and negotiation of reality, on the creation of what Carey refers to as 'public thought.' Communication is then 'a symbolic process whereby reality is

---

[6] Robert A. White, "Mass Media and the Religious Imagination," *Communication Research Trends* 8 (1987).

[7] Dorothee Sölle, *Fantasie en gehoorzaamheid: Toekomst en christelijke ethiek* (Baarn: Bosch & Keuning, 1970).

[8] Horace Newcomb and Paul M. Hirsch, "Television as a Cultural Forum," in *Television: The Critical View*, ed. Horace Newcomb (New York: Oxford University Press, 1987) 455-470.

produced, maintained, repaired and transformed.' "[9] Television plays a key role in this process.

> In its role as central cultural medium it [television] represents a multiplicity of meanings rather than a monolithic dominant point of view. It often focuses on our most prevalent concerns, our deepest dilemmas. Our most traditional views, those that are repressive and reactionary, as well those that are subversive and emancipatory, are upheld, examined, maintained, and transformed. The emphasis is on the process rather than on the product, on discussion rather than indoctrination, on contradiction and confusion rather than coherence. It is with this view that we turn to an analysis of the texts of television that demonstrates and supports the conception of television as cultural forum.[10]

The concept of television as cultural forum reveals four characteristics relevant to fragmentation and coherence. First, in popular culture, "the raising of questions is as important as the answering of them." Second, television does not present firm ideological conclusions but comments on ideological problems. Third, "the rhetoric of television drama is a rhetoric of discussion" which seeks to balance ideological positions within the forum by others from a different perspective. Fourth, the pluralism of the forum corresponds to the pluralism of the wider culture and "monitor[s] the limits and the effectiveness of this pluralism."[11] For moral formation it has the consequence of working to bring about a "*range* of response, the directly contradictory readings of the medium, that cue us to its multiple meanings."[12] Groups may object to the same program for entirely opposing reactions (for example in the 1970s *Charley's Angels* triggered objections based on theories of sexist repression, moral decay, and feminist liberation). Interpretative strategies vary from dominance to opposition to negotiation.

The idea of the cultural forum gives us the possibility to situate and frame fragmentation in our culture. Its characteristics allow us to acknowledge both active interpretations and moral activities of the viewers. We can now raise the question, how moral formation in a mass mediated world might be realized in order to gain increasing moral coherence. Instead of searching for an answer in a normative ethic, we will take for granted the pluralism which is a value in our democratic western culture. We will elaborate a narrative-hermeneutical ethic, which reflects on values, which fulfill the human desire and form part of culture. A narrative-hermeneutical ethic aims at critically comprehending the story that people are.[13] Perhaps

---

[9] Ibid. 457.

[10] Ibid. 459.

[11] Ibid. 461.

[12] Ibid. 465.

[13] J. H. Dijkman, "Integratie van het verhaal in de ethiek: Mogelijkheden en grenzen van het narratieve binnen een theologischethische handelingstheorie," *Tijdschrift*

from this point of view, moral formation can lead to moral coherence in a mass mediated world (even if this includes the recognition of a certain fragmentation as part of the coherent moral concept).

3. Towards a narrative-hermeneutical ethic

We wish to stress the ethical meaning of narratives, in both interpersonal and audiovisual (mass)communication. People achieve their ethical identity through oral, written, and audiovisual narrative. Concrete life demands a story and a story teller. Reflection on the audiovisual narrative forms the foundation for a new ethic because of their influence on today's society.

The main characteristics of the audiovisual media–narration and drama–are not new for the Christian tradition. The gospel and parable, as well as symbolism in icons and liturgy, have always taken an important place, one that the Church has increasingly recognized since Vatican II. The strong influence of the audiovisual media in our society invites theologians to confront the value of both old and contemporary stories. Dialogical communication forms the key concept for the formation of a Christian community.

3.1 The meaning of narratives

Communicative acting as narration, when it is spoken, written, or audiovisualized, can always be read and watched as a life story, a drama. Through all centuries people and nations have felt the need to tell stories, in which they formulated their experiences and expressed their life stories in order to create an identity of their own and of the following generations. In the heart of all these stories, folk tales, and myths, central events and fundamental experiences break into existence, cross the daily routines, and cause turning points in life: We call them liminal experiences or moments of (self)transcendence. These stories deal with phenomena greater than humanity by using symbols, archetypes, mythical figures, and images to express the experiences since narrative discourse more adequately tells these life stories than does argumentative discourse.[14]

A story personifies on a private level what argumentative language proclaims as an abstract ideal. Rather than asserting it (as would argumentative discourse), a good story concretely and visually presents a new view on the world as a possibility for realization. This implies, first, that a story can offer a new understanding of reality to the person willing to perceive its meaning and, second, that this quality gives a dialogical character to the

---

voor Theologie 28 (1988) 50-73.

[14]Martin Esslin, *The age of television* (San Francisco: Freeman & Company, 1982) 17ff.

communication between receiver and story. Further, through dialogue the story becomes meaningful for the community.

Within narratives imagination plays a dominant role, provides image to an idea, and it brings together ideas or meanings in order to give new meaning to the world to which the story refers. By metaphorically and symbolically realizing the world these stories aim not so much to truthfully reproduce reality but to express a specific attitude towards reality. Every program wants to communicate a learning process, a fable, or myth.[15] In audiovisual programs this occurs through the heuristic function of fiction: a presentation of new concepts that challenge our normal ways of thinking.

3.2 The interpretation of narratives

In the interpretation of the audiovisual stories viewers hermeneutically and dialectically move between the objective otherness of the audiovisual program and their self understanding.[16] Audiovisual media, seen from this point of view, can reveal hidden aspects of both world and self because they consist of closed sign systems that ask questions to which viewers get the opportunity to formulate answers. These answers, in turn, the viewers transform and express in their communicative acting. This implies that audiovisual media can have a mediating function in the development of a community.

Since the audiovisual media play an important role in the personal life experiences of people, we subscribe to the thesis that the audiovisual media can act as sources of inspiration as well as fora for religious imagination and spirituality. The audiovisual narratives reveal both good and bad values of our contemporary society. In order to be able to reflect critically upon these values we think advisable an explicit moral formation which is oriented towards understanding and towards a meaningful and creative use of the mass media. In place of the obedience model of doctrine and dogma, we propose "the fantasy model" which orients people to the revealing function of narrative and drama by appealing to the imagination and creativity in the hermeneutical process. In this model people can experience audiovisual narratives as possibilities or chances for exploring new situations, relationships, and ways of life.

4. The relationship between aesthetics and ethics

For people today, television messages function increasingly as narrative reference and interpretation systems about what occurs in their environment.[17] These messages express our actual values and form the main

---

[15] T. Kuchenbuch, *Filmanalyse: Theorien, Modelle, Kritik* (Köln: Prometh Verlag, 1978) 130-169.

[16] S. Schwartz, "Hermeneutics and the Productive Imagination: Paul Ricoeur in the 1970s," *Journal of Religion* 63 (1983) 290-300.

sources for meaning, references for orientation, and guides for choosing a life style. What makes the audiovisual media so attractive and fascinating and with what result? In order to formulate answers to these questions we elaborate on the specific symbolic code, or aesthetic of audiovisual language.

4.1 The audiovisual discourse

Earlier we defined audiovisual language as the mixing and editing of colorful moving images, speech, noises and music, supervised by electronics. Audiovisual images prolong or extend the two sense organs, eyes and ears. Therefore they easily compare with everyday perception. However, unlike perception, they have their origin in electronics: television screen, sound instruments, edit machines, cameras, etc. Combining speech and moving images they tell stories in a distinct symbolic code. The audiovisual media, mainly television, have created a new communicative environment—the audiovisual culture. This culture implies two developments: one concerning the composition, the other concerning the content of the audiovisual messages.

Audiovisual media require no special training as does argumentation or abstract reasoning. They address the majority of people because they use a concrete and emotional "speech."[18] These audiovisual media tell stories or mini-dramas in documentaries, serials, news broadcasts, sports, advertisements, or religious programs. They provide compositions of moral lifestyles and ways of life, of options, viewpoints, doubts, and dilemmas in a concrete, physical, presentational way. Content matters but so does manner of presentation and source of action. The nonverbal communication tells us *how* we have to understand and to interpret *what* has been said and done. Furthermore, the audiovisual language of camera and montage (close up strategies, camera perspectives, editing techniques etc.) communicates moral attitudes and viewpoints.

According to Silverstone[19] the dramatized narrative belongs to every genre in television. Living in the media means living in drama.[20] Every genre contains an intrigue or a conflict. Protagonists and antagonists battle between good and evil; obstacles, crises and solutions appear. Audiovisual narrative challenges viewers to identify themselves and to choose sides: good or evil, beautiful or ugly, agreeable or disagreeable. This style of storytelling, this immediate directing towards emotions typifies audiovisual communication.

---

[17] R. P. Snow, *Creating Mediaculture* (Beverly Hills: Sage, 1983).

[18] L. van Poecke, "Het neo-alfabetisme en de crisis van het geletterd discours," *Kultuurleven* (1987) 9, 811ff.

[19] Roger Silverstone, *The Message of Television: Myth and Narrative in Contemporary Culture* (London: Heinemann Educational Books, 1981).

[20] Babin and Kouloumdjian 38.

4.2 The centrality of aesthetics

Since the invention of printing, politicians, authorities, educators, and church leaders have tried to reach people through written and printed media. Until recently people judged the truth of their speech only by the credible construction of their texts. Now that audiovisual media accompany the print media the truth of the judgments depends on the credible presentation of the authority: the television camera uses close-ups in order to picture the emotions of the person. The picture gives meta-information about the extent to which somebody is real. This development creates a change in the relationship between verbal and nonverbal: The nonverbal (picture) tells us how the verbal (content) should be understood. When a person's behavior tells the viewer something other than the words, the viewer tends not to take the person too seriously. This has huge consequences for all communication and for the understanding of leadership and authority in our culture.

In the audiovisual context the composition of a message matters at least as much as its content. The composition may represent the content but will at the same time affect the receptivity of the content. The audiovisual media put aesthetics strongly ahead of text or content, so strongly sometimes, that the aesthetics themselves become messages. Whatever the quality of the content, it is not advisable to use a program that is not attractive enough to involve viewers emotionally.

5. Spiritual growth as fundamental for a moral attitude

As we have pointed out all television programs present today's values in a narrative communication. In order to be able to critically reflect on these values we now have to decide on some principles of narrative ethic. This involves a certain image of human life and the world.

5.1 Morality in audiovisual culture

Morality and moral formation can take two forms. First, it can be unintended and implicit, almost unconscious. Most of parents' moral formation of their children follows the implicit pattern as they transmit unreflective moral values and norms to their children. Moral formation, however, can also be intended, explicit, reflected upon, and structured, as for example in courses and seminars.[21] Thus we can divide morality as such into (1) morality as a way of life, habitual and implicit; and (2) morality as a result of explicit reflection, based on more abstract ideas and values. In our soci-

---

[21] H. Fleischer, *Ethik ohne Imperativ: Zur Kritik des moralischen Bewusstseins* (Frankfurt a/M: Fischer Wissenschaft, 1987); see also Paul Soukup's essay in Chapter 15.

ety we have concentrated so strongly on this second level of morality that we have forgotten that morality starts implicitly in the concrete life stories of people, that life stories are the first objectifications of moral experiences which come before the rational reflection on values. We have to take these life stories—including those which, for example, the media widely represent—seriously as one of the main sources of moral formation.

There are different levels on which audiovisual media implicitly present morality in their programs and on which viewers interact and negotiate with the audiovisual messages:[22] (1) television structures reality; (2) it gives orientation, not in a systematic, but in a fragmented way (by giving signs and symbols for communicative speech; rules for communication; models for behavior; and criteria for the true, the real, and the normal); (3) it reinforces acting space of the viewer through enlarging or diminishing it; (4) it confirms the feeling of identity by presenting models and identification figures; and (5) it creates plausibility structures and collective meanings.

When we take the above mentioned functions of television and cinema seriously, we can begin to talk about a more explicit reflection on values. This more explicit moral formation occurs in groups through narrative dialogue which requires a certain moral attitude of the group members. We will try to define the required moral attitude by elaborating on the subject of spirituality.

Individuals experience life long dramas of integration.[23] During their lives people try to realize their ideal image of wholeness but cannot because an idealized image remains imaginary. It drives and inspires people who experience this limitation permanently yet still cling to the desire to dissolve the fragmentation of existence. The way they try to do this determines the drama of integration. The desire for integration leads people to start a dialectic with the world. This dialectical movement always puts the idealized unity in the future: In order to dissolve this fragmentation, people projects their desire into the future.

There are three important moments of the drama of integration: people facing towards their own limitations, towards the others that surround them, and towards the world that reaches them through symbols. Narrative communication plays an important role in the "non-imaginary" (symbolic) realization of the idealized unity.

◆

---

[22] J. van der Lans, "Zingeving onder invloed van het televisie-medium: een conceptueel kader," in *Televisie en zingeving* (Nijmegen: Katholiek Studiecentrum Nijmegen, 1989)

[23] B. Bro, "De mens en de sacramenten: De antropologische onderbouw van de christelijke sacramenten," *Concilium* (1967) 35-52.

5.2 *Spirituality and the spiritual dialogue*

The drama of integration however is not so "tragic" as it seems at first sight. Binding desire to the historical, contingent situation has a positive side, namely the transcendence of the self.[24] The human desire to transcend oneself has two poles: self-transcendence and transcendence. Self-transcendence occurs when the individual has a liminal experience and creates a new situation, searching for (M)mystery. Transcendence, on the other hand, is the experience of the unapproachability of the other, the (M)mystery, inside and outside.

The conscious integration and ordering of liminal experiences is called spirituality[25] and it always takes place from a certain perspective–female, secular, atheistic, religious, Christian, catholic, or originated by certain religious traditions as Dominicans, Franciscans, Carmelites, etc. Spirituality cultivates a mental attitude towards life, emerging out of a certain view of human life and world. Christian spirituality aims at the integration of the two poles, Self-transcendence and Transcendence. This integration determines the structure of the spirituality: transcendence which at the same time binds desire to finiteness in order to reach acceptance and responsibility for the other. Theology expresses self-transcendence positively in images of people, others, and God. On the other hand, it expresses transcendence negatively as absence or longing. Films, for example, often express this as abandonment by God or as conversion of the self: One hardly recognizes the others and God anymore. The self turns to a receptive emptiness and experiences grace.

When the spiritual integration of the self occurs in a group, we speak of a dialogical spirituality. Speech has everything to do with the development of spiritual and moral identity of the speaker but also of the listeners because speech wants to be heard, asking for recognition and an answer. When it concerns a life story, this narrative speech goes beyond the rational. Communication is the key word here. Through narrative speech people try to achieve unity with themselves and with others. Rational speech is not enough to create dialogue or community. Narrative communication is more than speech because it also implies action.

Where action enters, so too do values. The normative aspects of narrative communication include what De Reuver[26] terms some theological key words with which we can judge communication. A first set is wholeness, guilt, love, and solidarity. All of these manifest an image of human beings

---

[24] W. G. Tillmans, "Theologische impulsen voor een werkzame samenhang van spiritualiteit en tv/film," in *Over religieuze films gesproken*, ed. Johan G. Hahn, Henk Hoekstra, and Frits Tillmans (Hilversum: Gooi & Sticht, 1987) 76ff.

[25] J. Peters, "Religie en spiritualiteit," *Speling* (1977) 18ff.

[26] G. J. de Reuver *Schoolkathechese en communicatie* (Kampen: De Reuver, 1987) 400-405.

and the world that aims at self realization or freedom. These attitudes open up an individual towards others in solidarity and love and give meaning to human action. They give an integrated identity, a wholeness. De Reuver's second series is hope, reconciliation with death, and anamnetic solidarity. People must actively reconcile themselves with their fragmentation and failing, including death. Only having done this can they realize a free communication, a communicative acting guided by the conviction that the lives of those who have suffered under injustice in history can have a meaning. This implies not only solidarity towards the present and the future, but also towards the past. This movement is called anamnetic solidarity. One has to be aware of the conflictive reality that realizes evil and suffering and one has to protest against this in a creative way. Communicative acting requires an ongoing learning in which identity continually emerges from a fighting loose of the many forms of pressure and fear that hold the individual small and prevents an open communication with others and with the world.

Group use of audiovisual media can aid this process. This is what we mean by media and spirituality: A group looks at an audiovisual program and communicates interpersonally about the program from and towards the perspective of dialogical spirituality.

Now we can define the moral attitude required for the explicit reflection on audiovisualized morality in group dialogue. The spiritual growth of a person, which depends on a symbolic integration of life experiences, can grant a moral attitude through which the individual can realize a moral coherence based on solidarity and love towards others, without denying the fundamental fragmentation in personal existence. Dialogical spirituality, as a conscious dialogical reflection on the moral experience, grounds the development of a moral identity and a moral coherence. Sölle[27] has defined this attitude as a free, imaginative morality, that starts from the concrete values and needs in the historical situation. She stresses the importance of a conscious and imaginative decision-making that responds to needs in the concrete situation, instead of obedience to static norms. Free and imaginative people have a morality guided by the principle of care for others. It originates from a feeling for justice and solidarity.

Our view on the moral attitude required in group dialogue also gives us the opportunity to look again at audiovisual narratives as sources for morality. Often they present personalities that are involved in a spiritual process concerning ethical issues. They also constantly seem to deal with evil forces in history. By offering meaning to these and many other themes they mediate the development of a person's moral identity. As expressions of narrated values in today's situation, they can reveal meaning in our contemporary society. Audiovisual media provide a moral opportunity. But the

---

[27] Sölle 60-65.

recognition of this opportunity requires of the viewers a creative, imaginative morality.

We hope to start a learning process aimed at making people aware of this opportunity through explicit moral formation in a mass mediated world, based on dialogical spirituality. The next section describes how this conscious, goal oriented, and systematic moral formation in groups might take place.

6. Explicit moral formation in a mass mediated world

6.1 Objectives for explicit moral formation

Our approach to the development of the Christian community in a mass mediated world implies (1) the value of explicit moral formation of the reflection on the audiovisual stories that reveal the moral values in the life styles of our contemporary culture and (2) the value of discussion in groups about the morality in these stories and their implications for the morality of the group. Through such group dialogue, where a confrontation with media messages takes place, a new ethical identity can grow. Moral educators can only guide, confront, and question. We want people to develop a creative and active perception of what comes to them in audiovisual messages so that they become more free and imaginative. We seek a morality that is initiated from solidarity and care for others, that comes into existence as a dynamic process, not as a static, ahistorical set of values.

From this background we formulate the following objectives for explicit moral formation in a mass mediated world:

- to teach viewers to understand audiovisual language and its aesthetic and ethical implications (colors, music, symbols, nonverbal expressions);
- to sensitize viewers to the forms of implicit or explicit morality in the mass mediated culture (through the analysis of the audiovisual program);
- to develop a moral judgment about morality in different audiovisual programs;
- to stimulate and cultivate dialogue about the audiovisual programs and morality in general;
- to stimulate the development of a moral judgment on the mass mediated world.

The development of moral attitudes and judgments depends on spiritual growth. But not every group has the same spiritual and moral "level." Therefore, the group leader has to deal with the actual conditions of the spiritual and moral stage and development of the group members. The capability to reflect on and discuss moral issues and dilemmas depends on age, education, profession, social status, and the personal biography of the group members.[28] Therefore the choice of films and television programs for purposes of moral education should take these conditions into account.

The group leader should also choose films and television programs for a seminar according to the "audiovisual taste" and "audiovisual competence" of the group. Without trying to be complete on this subject we point out that for example programs like *Miami Vice* or music videos are hardly appropriate in a course for elderly people. The dramaturgical composition is often too complex (quick editing, harsh colors, loud music) and the story is usually too difficult to follow. When such aesthetic products in a course for elderly people are used, even on the subject of moral formation, misunderstanding and disgust often results. The same thing applies—in reverse fashion—with groups of young people.

But whatever audiovisual programs used, the group leader must make a thorough analysis of the program before the seminar starts. Here we give two examples of how an analysis of the moral values in audiovisual narratives can be made.

In analyzing fiction it is important to distinguish the ideological and aesthetic moments. An audiovisual product communicates individual and collective relationships towards reality, together with emotions connected with these relationships. In fiction the characteristic dramatic performance dissolves the viewer's determination of the program's "reality" and instead presents a conceptual image of reality: a conscious reduction or styling of reality in order to effectuate a learning process.

6.2 *Example I:* An Officer and a Gentleman
(Implicit morality as a way of life)

In the analysis of the film *An Officer and a Gentleman* (Taylor Hackford, 1981) we focus on the ideological moments and on the concrete lifestyles that young people embody. The main characters perform the moral attitudes, behavior, conflicts, and dilemmas, incarnated in these life stories.

6.2.1 The story. Remembering his childhood as a sailor's son, Zack Mayo decides that he wants to become an pilot in the American navy, although his father doesn't agree with his plans. Nevertheless, Zack enrolls at the training school under the sometimes harsh and humiliating leadership of Sergeant Foley. During the weekends the recruits meet with local girls to relax and celebrate. Many of these girls dream of marrying an aviator pilot, but the recruits usually just want to have fun with the girls. Sometimes a girl gets pregnant, hoping that the concerned recruit will marry her.

Zack and his friend Sid meet Paula and Lynette, who both work in the local paper factory. The relationship between Zack and Paula evokes feelings they don't always have under control: Paula obviously falls in love.

---

[28] Lawrence Kohlberg, *The philosophy of moral development: Vol. 1. Essays on moral development,* (San Francisco: Harper & Row, 1981) 409-412.

Lynette sees Sid as a good prospect and their relationship as an investment for a better life in the future.

Meanwhile, the training continues. Friendships develop in the midst of failures, accidents, and conflicts; even Zack and Foley develop a kind of mutual respect. At the end of the course, Zack has the clear intention not to take Paula with him and has stopped meeting her. Sid still visits Lynette, although he intends to marry Susan, a girl from his hometown. Lynette tries to gain Sid with the help of a story of pregnancy. Sid quits his training in order to marry Lynette; however, this frustrates Lynette because she wants to become the wife of a pilot. She refuses to marry him. Sid, who realizes that he loves Lynette, hangs himself. Because of this suicide Zack and Paula meet one another again. Zack tells Paula again that there is no future for them as a couple. The training is finished and there is nobody to congratulate Zack. He is alone, without family and friends. Then he takes his motorcycle and drives to the paper factory where he takes Paula in his arms and leaves the factory with her.

6.2.2 Reflection on the implicit and explicit morality. This film proved very popular in cinemas and video rentals all over the world. The story features moral conflicts and dilemmas; In fact the moral attitudes, implicitly embodied in the main characters, represent various kinds of moral archetypes. Although their life stories determine the moral behavior of these main characters, a development in their moral attitudes occurs. Each of them faces situations involving moral dilemmas where decisions have to be taken.

Zack is morally inner-directed but egocentric. Convinced that people are responsible for their own lives, Zack doesn't think he has any moral obligations. He also does not have much sense of them, because he was not raised with altruistic values. His strong identity, guided by an egoism based on bad youth experiences leaves him little trust in other human beings. Therefore his friendship with Sid has high value for him. Because his main goal in life is to succeed in his training, he judges his relationship with Paula as accidental, as something to finish when his training ends. Confronted however with the suicide of Sid, the love that Paula feels for him, and his growing awareness of his own loneliness, he ultimately decides to give up his former moral self-centered attitude towards others and he chooses the love of Paula.

Sid is the opposite of Zack. His traditional parental background has strongly influenced Sid; moral rules come from the outside and tradition dictates his feeling of responsibility, leaving him naively altruistic. His moral behavior and thinking are only directed to moral obligations and altruism. Unlike Zack he has a weak identity. In many ways, he is a tragic figure. During the film he finds out that other people determine his life: first his parents (he has to become an aviator pilot as a replacement for his dead brother) and later Lynette (by fooling him with her pretended love).

He has never chosen for his own life. Lynette's refusal to marry him triggers his suicide because he has never learned to solve his life problems otherwise.

Paula judges her love for Zack as her most important value and she shows her love in spite of all the consequences. She takes responsibility for herself and does not allow history to determine her morality (she wishes to avoid what happened to her mother when her mother once was in a similar situation). She cares for other people, like Sid. And she also respects the choices of other people, like Zack. In her moral judgment concerning the egoistic behavior of her friend Lynette, however, she is very negative. In this film Paula's moral attitude develops most strongly. Involved in a spiritual process where self transcendence plays a major part, she reaches a certain coherence between altruism and egocentrism.

Lynette, like Paula, comes from a lower social class and has few prospects for her future but thinks she can change her situation through Sid. All her strategies are oriented towards this option. Her strategy changes, however, when Sid decides to leave the training school. Because opportunism guides her, she instrumentalizes her moral attitudes to reach her goals. All her moral decisions, her relationship with Sid, her pretended love and pregnancy, have to be seen in this egoistic perspective. In the end she (together with Sid) loses all. She is the most unsympathetic character.

The film in general works out two themes: the love story, including its moral dilemmas, and the pilot training which highlights options for authority, discipline, and competition. (This story, which we do not discuss here, takes personal form in Sergeant Foley and his group of recruits.)

6.3 Example II: Bronski Beat, "Small Town Boy" (Audiovisual aesthetics as carriers of moral values)

In this music video the symbolic character of the nonverbal expressions, the music, and the *mise-en-scene*–in other words, the audiovisual language and the aesthetic moments–determine the ideological moments and the moral values presented. We will start, therefore, with an analysis of the aesthetics in order to determine the ideological moments.

6.3.1 *The story.* A boy in a train remembers events from the recent past which the video clip dramatizes: his situation at home, where there is a lack of understanding; his situation on the streets where he has been beaten up and which leads to his decision to leave home. In the end we see the train going further.

6.3.2 *Symbols.* The boy sits in a train that passes through switching points. This symbolizes that the boy faces choices; he is on his way, but still searching. At the end of the video the train leaves the switches behind: The boy continues on his way, but not searching nor as confused as he was five minutes before. He now has a new perspective for his future. By going through his memories again, he has integrated his past. The camera symbolizes the reminiscences through a close up of his expressive eyes. We then see the events passing through his memory. At a breakfast at home hardly any communication takes place between the members of the family. Next we see a scene in the local swimming pool where he watches some boys that are diving. From the slow motion pictures of one particular boy he watches extensively and from the scene where the same boy beats him up it becomes clear that the main character is a homosexual. Later on a police officer brings him home. His father wants to hit him; his mother is crying. In the next scene the boy leaves home: His mother embraces him, his father just gives him some money. The bird's eye camera shows a lonely, small boy in a rainy street on his way to the railway station.

From the analysis of the symbols in this music video the content becomes clear. The message consists of the problems homosexuals encounter when they are confronted with heterosexuals, like the parents and the local boys. The video uses cliché images and symbols so that it can present the story without speech beyond the text of the song.

6.3.3 Ideological aspects. At first sight the video deals with homosexuality and the problems heterosexuals have with them. This does not mean that only homosexuals can identify with the story. Young people in general can project themselves in the video because the deeper structure of the story carries the message that young people have to say goodbye to their childhood. Each young person must search for autonomy. From the point of view of spirituality, as the conscious integration and ordering of life experiences, this video is very interesting. In the compartment of the train the boy integrates his experiences through reminiscing. But his end remains open because his future is still unclear. The viewer gets a place in such an ending because the viewer, too, must decide what the future can be. A dialogue about such a music video can reach the soul of viewers.

Audiovisual programs like *An Officer and a Gentleman* and "Small Town Boy" influence indirectly and implicitly moral thinking and moral attitudes of viewers. They offer concrete moral models that can give meaning to receptive viewers. Similar programs offer lots of possibilities for identification on a more emotional and affective level. Motivated viewers interact with the stories and the main characters and relate them to their own concrete life situations. Of course, different people will have more or less intense reactions, depending on their life situations. The process we have described can guide individuals or groups in a more explicit moral formation dialogue.

Our discussion of these audiovisual products illustrates the possibilities for a dialogue with the mass media. Although interpersonal communication has a strategic priority over mass communication for moral formation, mass communication offers narratives to the viewers and draws attention to them so that the viewers dialogue about, reflect on, comment on, evaluate, and decide about the audiovisual narratives. A media dialogue can offer moments of (self)recognition through identification or alienation. In this sense audiovisual narratives can initiate a dialogue with the viewpoints, options, and preferences of the producers. Second, audiovisual narratives can provoke interpersonal communication between the receivers in a group, engaging them in a dialogue about their own viewpoints, options, preferences. The group dialogue about their own morality grows from the audiovisual narratives. Third, the group can (re)order and integrate their life experiences, see new perspectives, and find new orientations. In this sense audiovisual narratives can develop a reorientation of life.

This dialogue about audiovisual narratives has importance for moral formation in a mass mediated world because it is possible to organize in a goal-oriented and systematic way what quite often happens spontaneously between people. Furthermore, it is possible to realize these narrative moral dialogues about audiovisual narratives from a Christian viewpoint. Anything (news programs, advertisements, documentaries, drama series, films, talk shows, video clips, religious programs etc.) can function as a starting point.

People might tell about the way they feel and experience these messages. They can discuss the content and composition of the audiovisual narratives. They might search for and reflect on the implicit or explicit viewpoints, values, norms, options, lifestyles in the audiovisual messages. They can analyze the intentions and interests of the producers. And last but not least, they might reflect on all these questions from the Christian point of view.

7. Two models for explicit moral formation

Finally we present two models for moral formation as we use them in our Catholic Media Center in the Netherlands. One model we usually name "Media and Spirituality," because we see spiritual growth as the fundamental for the development of the free and imaginative moral attitude. In this kind of moral formation we start with audiovisual programs, analyze them in terms of spirituality and morality, exchange experiences we had with the program in the group, and exchange life experiences of the group members in order to initiate dialogical spirituality and morality. The second model we present focuses on values that the group has already determined beforehand. We give, for example, a course that focusses on the theme "Media and Conciliar Process about Peace, Justice, and Preservation of Creation." In this course the group investigates how the audiovisual media present and reflect on these themes.

7.1 Model 1: Audiovisual narratives that inspire moral attitudes

All media narratives create a kind of ordering and integration of life experiences from a certain point of view. In this sense all media narratives have a certain spirituality. As viewers we look with our own spiritual eyes and hear with our own spiritual ears. The media dialogue becomes an expression of dialogical spirituality: the spirituality *in* the media narratives and *in* the viewers.

To illustrate this, we now give a third example of an television film, a docudrama, in which spirituality and moral growth predominate. We often use this film with success in our explicit moral formation courses.

7.2 *Example III:* Choices of the Heart

7.2.1 The story. Choices of the Heart (Katz/Callin/Half Pint Productions, 1983) tells the true story of the fundamental moral dilemma a young woman, Jean Donovan, encounters. The docudrama starts with foggy images, a kind of dreamworld. The film also ends with these images of her and the other women in the film. Then it becomes clear that Jean and the others are giving a post-mortem speech.

The actual story begins with the end. Jean and her colleague, a nun, pick up two colleagues, nuns, at the San Salvador airport and leave the airport in a van. The military police stop the van. The film ends with the same scene when it has become clear what actually happened to the women.

Two levels in the film move through one another. One tells the story after the murder in the van: The United States ambassador tries to locate the missing women and finally finds out that the soldiers raped and killed them. The other story tells about Jean's life: What made her decide to go to El Salvador, why she didn't want to return to the States when things got dangerous, and why she was murdered.

Jean's life story starts in the States, where, as a student, she lived with a girl friend. Together with her girl-friend she moves to Ireland, where she meets a priest with whom she can discuss her moral dilemmas. Jean is not satisfied with her life: She wants to experience more, to feel more, to do something for others. But she is not yet ready to give up family wealth and her materialistic life. She returns to the U.S.A. where she starts to collect materialistic things, like motorcycles, cars, etc. However, one evening, alone in her room, she makes a decision to go to Latin America as a lay missionary. From this point on she starts to feel happy. But her girlfriend loses contact with her. Just before she leaves for the training school, she meets the new roommate of her girl friend, a medical student and a friendship develops to a relationship.

After her training in the States she leaves for El Salvador where in the beginning she feels quite useless. She hardly speaks any Spanish and she has the feeling she doesn't make any difference. But after a while she realizes that she makes a difference. She delivers food and medical supplies to villages in guerilla territory in the mountains. She takes care of and teaches homeless children about the political situation. She also helps refugees. The military obviously do not like these activities of Jean and the nuns. In the meantime her boyfriend visits her and wants her to return with him because he is worried for her, but she decides that she cannot go back to the States anymore.

Sometimes Jean is lonely and feels helpless. She grows quite fond of a Salvadorian seminarian. One night, just after Bishop Romero is murdered, soldiers visit the campus and murder the seminarian. After that Jean is really disillusioned. She is almost to the point of collapse, especially when it becomes clear that the boy was murdered as a warning for her. Her colleagues try to help her the best they can and they advise her to go to Ireland for a vacation.

In Ireland, the priest asks her to tell her story to his students. There she explains that, although the situation is dangerous, she has to return to El Salvador. She cannot choose anymore between the life of children over there and her own life. The priest and her boy friend try, unsuccessfully, to bring her to other thoughts. She is determined to return.

Back in El Salvador she continues her activities. The last night of her life she visits the American ambassador and tells him that the U.S.A. is selling arms to the Salvadorian government. The next day she and her colleague go to pick up the nuns from the airport. On their way back they are raped and killed.

The foggy images return. There Jean tells about one dream she had. Walking along a deserted beach, she looks behind her and sees footprints in the sand, first of two persons, later of one. She concludes that the single pair of footprints occurred at the hardest moments, when God was carrying her.

7.2.2 *Symbols.* Because the film is filled with symbols, we will only point out some important ones. Harmonious music supports every positive event. When the women work with the Salvadorians and when they are happy, Latin American, romantic music accompanies the action. When situations become dangerous or the military is in sight, the music changes to very threatening marching music.

Jean's materialism at the beginning of the film also has a symbolic function. She tries to masquerade her loneliness and dissatisfaction with life in her possessions. Later on, in El Salvador she uses some of these possessions to make herself helpful. The symbolic meaning of the two worlds–the Western, wealthy and safe, but unsatisfying world, and the Latin American, poor and dangerous, but for Jean at least, "real" world–is obvious. There is a very important scene when Archbishop Romero gives a speech and helicopters fly over. He inspires the women, but he also symbolizes the danger that is threatening them. Another very important scene comes when Jean speaks to the students in Ireland. There it becomes clear that she had to choose in favor of the Latin American world, a choice others from the Western culture cannot understand.

One can judge the film as an example of spiritual growth that leads to an imaginative moral attitude of the main character, Jean. Some moments in the film mark this process: when she hears of the cancer of her brother, when she sees the photos the priest shows her about the poverty in Ulster, the discussion she has with the Irish priest, the decision she makes in the States to go to Latin America, the death of the seminarian, and her decision in Ireland to return to El Salvador. At first she lives for her own interests: *She* wants to do by self, *she* wants to give love, *she* wants to change the world, etc. She is unable to give herself to something she can live for. In El Salvador she discovers real life in the children she works for because these children know that "in September the roses will bloom again." Suddenly she is not the center any more. She needs to let go of the "do by self." Through Romero she discovers the value of prayer and love for others. This love by which she can lose her life causes a moral change in her. She wants to grow to the attitude "receive me Lord, here I come." It is the total surrender of her own life and death.

7.3 Model 2: Moral values as sources for audiovisual narratives

A second option for explicit moral formation starts from existing values in our society. In such a course we try to find the presentation of these values in the audiovisual media. An example of this course in moral formation is "Media and the Conciliar Process concerning Peace, Justice, and Preservation of Creation." In the Dutch churches an ecumenical discussion has developed about the threat to peace and justice in, and the creation of our world. Through this "Conciliar Process" the Church wants to make a difference in the world. But the churches are not the only institutions concerned about these moral values. The mass media constantly report about these values, from a religious as well as a secular point of view. These values concern the whole society.

We are convinced that the mass media usually report progressively on these matters and we think that they can help in the ecumenical discussion. In small groups we try to continue this discussion with the help of audiovisual programs, which address the theme. This explicit moral formation in the mass mediated world allows audiovisual narratives like documentaries, docudrama, series, films, talk shows etc. to function as an inspiration for a moral dialogue. We use audiovisuals because we are convinced that through their emotional effect, they can deepen the morality of the group and that they can make the group aware of the place the mass media take in the mediation of our contemporary values.

8. Conclusions

We wish to summarize the main thoughts of this chapter in the form of some theses.

(1) The audiovisual media and culture can work as a site and source for religious inspiration and imagination, for morality and spirituality.

(2) In terms of moral formation, the audiovisual media should not be isolated from the communication of people with themselves (intrapersonal) and with their fellows (dialogical communication). Interpersonal communication has a strategic priority over mass communication.

(3) The intended, goal oriented, and systematic dialogue about audiovisual narratives in a group can lead to an explicit moral formation. Audiovisual narratives initiate this moral formation which interpersonal communication sustains and deepens. This media dialogue implies an active and creative interaction of the viewers with the mass mediated messages.

(4) This dialogue about media messages is or should be at the same time a spiritual dialogue which deals with the ordering and the integration of life experiences from a Christian viewpoint.

(5) Media dialogue and spirituality function as answers to the questions of moral coherence/fragmentation and pluralistic cultural forum and help create moral coherence in the mass mediated world.

(6) In the development of moral coherence through dialogical spirituality, the acceptance of a certain fragmentation in our world and in ourselves nevertheless is inevitable.

(7) The cultivation of the media dialogue should have a priority in the perspective of the development of the Christian community in a mass mediated world.

17

Formation of Moral Life in a Mass-mediated Culture

Elizabeth Willems, S.S.N.D.

1. Introduction

The media are unsettling. They have the ability to stir the waters of the mind and the emotions into a hurricane or to unsettle one with a moral windstorm. Recently the media created a moral windstorm in me.

In late September while I was preparing for school and keeping one eye on the national TV news, I was jerked to attention by the broadcaster reporting murders and racial violence in Shreveport, Louisiana. Shreveport is just north of New Orleans—rather close to home. I was again jerked to attention one Friday afternoon last December, when the news reported the brutal murder of Fr. Pat MacCarthy, a white priest whom I knew. Pat had been murdered just blocks from my home, by a black man whom he had befriended. More recently, I have been attending Sunday liturgy at different parishes in New Orleans. All of the 15 or so parishes I visited were racially mixed, yet most liturgical music was white-oriented. On a recent weekend, there was a KKK demonstration in Biloxi, Mississippi about one hour's drive from New Orleans. There were more whites opposing the demonstration than there were demonstrators, evidence that there had been growth toward the equality of races. The media were: TV, radio, music, and crowds. All had unsettling effects on me. I thought racism had ended in the 1960s. It was disturbing to feel it was alive and well even today, in my city and in my neighborhood. I had not addressed the issue of racism with our seminarians even though I was the Director of Pastoral Field Education. The media bothered me, nudged me, startled me into the reality of my surroundings. That is disequilibration.

One of the pioneers in developmental psychology, Piaget, believed that organisms continually strive to reach equilibrium. The state of equilibrium is shaken when opposing forces are at work; these forces create a state of disequilibration. At those times a person will attempt to reach equilibrium

and engage in what Piaget calls the process of equilibration to reduce tension or disequilibration. To regain a state of equilibrium, a person chooses
new psychological structures that best suit apparent needs. According to
some psychologists, equilibration is the primary force behind human development because of its motivational and integrative power for change.[1]

The media's messages about Blacks helped me feel disequilibration
and set up the process of equilibration. I could reduce the tension by somehow rejecting the challenge through some rationalization, by taking a compromise position, or I could reintegrate my moral values through an examination of
my stands on racism and then take a new moral position in my work.

Some examples for each of these positions might be: a decision not to
disturb one's neighbors, family, or friends by saying little about the racism
in one's own neighborhood. Churches that do not recognize black members
may resist singing African-American hymns by reasoning that "one must
take people (whites) where they are"; or, I could say that raising the racism
issue at the seminary might alienate me from some students. My work is
too valuable to be put into jeopardy. An approach to reintegrate my values,
however, would be to address the issue both in myself and in my professional interactions with students and colleagues. I could raise the question of
racism in the classes I teach, in preparation sessions for ministry, and at appropriate moments in faculty discussions. Each of the three positions, i.e., rejection, compromise, re-integration, is a move to a new moral position.

However, not every new position is a position of greater moral integrity. The new position may indeed offer some comfort to ease moral tension
but is it the most moral position to hold? The moral challenge then becomes, "How does one determine whether the new state is an advance or a
decline in moral growth?" "Is the new state more closely aligned with the
message of Jesus and his view of the Kingdom?" To answer these questions, I will first make four assertions, then discuss two concepts about the
media as a force of disequilibration, and finally examine the role of basic
freedom in moral growth.

2. Four Assertions

(1) Formation of the moral life thrives under certain conditions which
the media provide.

---

[1] Jean Piaget, "Equilibration and the Logical Structures in the Moral Development of
the Child" in *Discussions on Child Development*, Vol. IV, ed. J.M. Tanner and B.
Inhelder (London: Tavistock Publications, Ltd., 1960); Herbert Ginsburg and Sylvia
Opper, *Piaget's Theory of Intellectual Development* (New Jersey: Prentice-Hall,
Inc., 1968) 172-75. Neil J. Salkind, *Theories of Human Development* (Cincinnati:
D. Van Nostrand Company, 1981) 186-87.

(2) Education and focus are paramount conditions the media provide for formation of the moral life.

(3) Human freedom, an essential element of the moral life, is significantly influenced by the conditions of education and focus.

(4) Mass-mediated culture can contribute positively to formation of the moral life in the western world.

2.1 Definitions

Before I substantiate my assertions, I would like to define mass media and education. Mass media include all those means used by human beings to communicate with each other and their world, particularly those means that are intended to communicate with masses of people. These means include everything from the written word in magazines to electronic/laser colors and sound/vibration systems employed by technologists to communicate on a subliminal level. (My consideration of mass media in this essay is primarily from a western world view and reflects their use in the culture of the USA.) Education is any process that enables people to become their unique and best selves.

2.2 Explanation of Assertions

(1) Formation of the moral life thrives under certain conditions which the media provide.

The mass media create two conditions that can stimulate moral development: education and focus. While many sociological studies have proven the importance of education in changing society, cognitive developmental psychologists have shown how cognitive structures influence the psychological and moral development of the human person. Education, they contend, is a crucial element in forming one's conscience and values.[2] Piaget, Kohlberg, Gilligan, Loevinger, Oser, and others have convincingly demonstrated stages of cognitive development, moral reasoning, and moral judgment.[3] Cognitive development and affective development, they tell us, mature in a parallel fashion and shape our attitudes, values, choices, and lifestyle.[4]

---

[2] William G. Perry, *Forms of Intellectual and Ethical Development in the College Years: A Scheme* (Chicago: Holt, Rinehart and Winston, Inc., 1970).

[3] Ibid.; Jean Piaget, "Equilibration and the Logical Structures in the Moral Development of the Child"; Carol Gilligan, *In a Different Voice: Psychological Theory and Women's Development* (Cambridge: Harvard University Press, 1982). Jane Loevinger, *Ego Development: Conceptions and Theories* (Washington: Jossey-Bass Publishers, 1982).

[4] Lawrence Kohlberg, *Essays on Moral Development*, Vol. 1 (San Francisco: Harper & Row, 1981).

2.2.1 Education. New cognitive structures emerge when old ones are no longer serviceable. As one becomes educated, new information, situations, dilemmas, relationships, and values cannot be adequately processed and integrated in the present system. In psychological terms, one experiences disequilibration in the cognitive structures. One is forced to seek new ways and new systems of thought to process the multitude of situations in order to restore psychological equilibrium. Perry has shown how education perhaps most powerfully causes disequilibrium and a break down of old psychological structures. Education motivates and points the way to new cognitive structures, thereby leading the seeker to new planes of equilibrium in the moral life.

Mass media can be educators for they teach; they can be a powerful means of learning. As educators, mass media play a significant role in disequilibrium within our psychological and moral structures. They teach convincingly by using the lives of people; as we identify with the characters and their life situations, whether in the news or in a soap opera or a movie, we vicariously sort out our own life dilemmas. By capturing our senses in every conceivable way, mass media stretch our imaginations and imperceptibly make certain decisions appealing and convincing. Since they are mass media, one has the feeling that the masses, everyone, thinks and feels as the characters do.[5] "A picture is worth a thousand words" has been proven true by advertising companies who use the media to educate people about their product. The masses and the culture are shaped by the purveyors of communication whether in billboard commercials, soap operas, Spielberg fantasies, texts of rock music, electronic sound, or *Wall Street Journal* reports.

In terms of cognitive development, mass media have the potential to increase awareness, expand intellectual horizons and provide experiences beyond the present stage of understanding. When the viewer can emotionally and psychologically enter the world of another culture, another person; when values and attitudes are questioned; when new information is shared, the media can educate and can promote formation in the moral life. The news media are particularly adept at educating one to other cultures, lifestyles, and viewpoints.

One must also acknowledge the limitations of the media. They are selective in their presentations of cultures, lifestyles, and viewpoints for they must keep a watchful eye on viewer responses. Selectivity operates through positive viewer ratings that determine the economic feasibility of the media.

---

[5] Note the essay by David Eley, Chapter 9, above. Eley believes the elements of pleasure enable us to identify with media figures and events. In Chapter 4, Thomas Shanks acknowledges the power of media over personal and public opinion. Shanks finds that "people who perceive from media reports that trends of opinion are running against their views, fearing social isolation, will refrain from expressing these opinions (except to those who share them)." Michael Real addresses the issue of imagination and focus through structuralism; see Chapter 2, above.

As noted by Real,[6] the media are geared toward the "promotional culture of narcissism and consumption" that caters to the self and personal satisfaction. This norm of selectivity, narcissism and consumption, can be in direct conflict with moral development and Christian living. According to Real, the media are likewise restricted in their portrayal of stereotypical roles in terms of gender and race. That which is least disturbing of the social system can be subtly portrayed as most acceptable.

When the media educate people to the true, the good, and the beautiful, to justice and to communal values, the culture is enhanced and moral formation is advanced. When the media promote disequilibrium and dissatisfaction with the status quo, with the present stage of moral reasoning, they are encouraging growth in moral development. A few examples of this are certainly evident in media presentations surrounding summit meetings, the elections, treatment of minorities, military conflicts, the AIDS epidemic, and help for the homeless. After learning more about each of these situations, one's perceptions are shifted, attitudes and judgments are transformed, and moral reasoning can become more inclusive. Disequilibrium has occurred and a new way of thinking emerges. Because of their educational function, the media are largely responsible for these changes and for accelerating formation in the moral life.

While the media have the great potential to stimulate growth, one must acknowledge the fact that often the status quo or the least disturbing stage of moral growth is portrayed by the media. Disequilibrium can be sacrificed to equilibrium at all costs thereby sanctioning, even anesthetizing, the public to seek the most comfortable and easy means of living the moral life. This can be true when the mass media cater to the comfortable values of the powerful, to isolationist views, and to an immoral majority.

2.2.2 Focus. The focus of a camera has the power of becoming our eyes to the world. The media can bring the world to our living rooms where tragedy is personalized as we see floods, poverty, drought, and famine in the faces of its victims; we hear the explosion of bombs in the Near East; we feel the anguish of hostage families; we strain with Olympic competitors; and we watch the stock market crash. Movement, coloring, lighting, music, and perspective all sharpen an image and give focus to a message both subliminally and explicitly. By focusing, the eye of the camera can imperceptibly force us to look at the most spectacular, gruesome, frightening, daring, beautiful, and extraordinary sights; it can also force us to see new ideas and information. The focus of the media can challenge our thought systems and bend our minds down new avenues of thought. At times we can be too captivated to look away or not listen, thereby losing our personal sense of perspective; we take on the perspective of the focus, the eye of the communicator. The personal view within our mind's eye cannot be easily balanced

---

[6] See Michael Real's essay, Chapter 2, above.

with the graphic focus of a camera's eye. These experiences cause disequilibrium, a state of unease, that relativizes one's present stance in the light of other views and by exposure to another more appealing, convincing, and satisfying stance.

The media mediate values to the masses, values which are frequently imbibed uncritically partially due to the power of focus. Those people who see beyond the popular vision, whose focus transcends the immoral, cause disequilibrium in the culture. They are usually found newsworthy, however, only because they are unique and different rather than valued as pioneers of moral development. Too often their potential to educate is lost because of a "mis-focus" or misinterpretation of their message. With a morally correct focus, the media can form people in the moral life.

The focus of a media purveyor is contingent on his or her moral values and belief system, for one can explicate only what is internalized. By enabling us to see through the eyes of another, we assume their focus and are being formed and educated into the other's way of thinking and viewing the world. Modern media do much of this subliminally in a manner that somewhat dupes and seduces the viewer since the techniques bypass conscious awareness. This process affects free choice and our freedom. Insofar as we become willing participants, we must know we are also unconscious participants in the power of the media to form and inform us, and eventually to be formed by the moral standards of the media.[7]

On the basis of the arguments I have just presented, my second assertion follows:

(2) Education and focus are paramount conditions the media provide for formation of the moral life.

3. Freedom

(3) Human freedom, an essential element of the moral life, is significantly influenced by the conditions of education and focus provided by the media.

Morality is about values, attitudes, and norms that lead and free people to become themselves. True freedom enables people to flourish as whole and sound human beings who are proud to be themselves and rejoice in being alive. According to Rahner and Fuchs, freedom is the ability to create oneself, to create something eternal, unlimited by the finite, creaturely dimensions of the human. Rahner calls this type of freedom "transcendental freedom" while Fuchs describes this as "basic freedom."[8] In basic freedom

---

[7] See Thomas Shanks's essay, Chapter 4, above. Shanks delineates the interdependent nature of the communication process as found in the relationship of audiences, media, and the larger social system.

[8] Karl Rahner, "Man's Freedom and Responsibility" in *Foundations of Christian*

I create myself through free decisions about personal goals and actions, and the ultimate determination of my life. Under basic freedom, one creates oneself using the God-given gift (grace if you prefer) of freedom. This is not a freedom we achieve simply through discrete or categorical acts although acts of choice are involved. Basic freedom involves our entire being for the whole person participates in this freedom through a commitment to live as Jesus did. Rahner and Fuchs hold that human beings are free but the exercise of that freedom is our responsibility. We are free to shape ourselves with God's grace, into persons who are fully human, fully alive, fully loving, fully integrated: These are free persons. In basic freedom we can transcend ourselves and participate in the divine spirit that is infinite. How does the media foster growth in this kind of basic freedom?

To help answer this question, I will use Fuchs's distinction between psychological freedom and moral freedom. With psychological freedom, one makes particular choices between numerous options. Moral freedom is more encompassing for in its exercise one strives to lead a good life, not simply to perform good actions. Certainly the media enhance psychological freedom by increasing the options from which one can choose. But the media can also promote moral freedom by motivating one to lead a good life. However, neither psychological freedom nor moral freedom encompass basic freedom. The type of human freedom of which Rahner and Fuchs speak, transcendental freedom or basic freedom, is more than particular choices or leading a good life. It is a life-time project of creating a free person who is eternally free, a project that transcends the boundaries of human existence and extends into eternity. The media can be instrumental in this creation particularly through the formation of one's imagination.

The media touch one's imagination through images and sound and evoke an image of the ideal we each carry of ourselves. In our imagination, I contend, we have a vision of Christ's Kingdom and of our own final destiny. Our frustrations and strivings are daily (perhaps negative) evidence of that final (positive) vision both for ourselves and our world. By engaging our imagination wisely and well, the media participate in and have the potential to assist us in creating ourselves, in making something infinite with our lives. Creating the free person is a lifetime work that occurs within ourselves and is also achieved through activity outside of ourselves. The media reflect to us the nature and quality of that outside, external activity. We then have the opportunity to exercise psychological and moral freedom to decide about specific actions, values, motives, and structures that will promote basic freedom. The media can be a powerful force for they can

---

Faith (New York: The Seabury Press, 1978) 93-97; Josef Fuchs, "Basic Freedom and Morality" in *Human Values and Christian Morality* (Dublin: Gill and Macmillan, 1970) 92-111.

utilize imagination, freedom and reflection to promote growth of the free person. I can thus justifiably make my fourth assertion:

(4) Mass mediated culture can contribute positively to formation of the moral life in the western world.

4. Conclusion

The media unsettle but they can also resettle. They can resettle one in a more mature level of moral conviction. Going through disequilibration to equilibration is difficult, uncomfortable, vexing but the process of equilibration can yield the morally mature adult who is more at peace. Through education and focusing, the media can be powerful catalysts to formation in the moral life. The media have the power to resettle one, to create out of a moral hurricane or windstorm a new place of equilibrium that is free in the spirit of Jesus and in the spirit of one becoming a fully alive human person.

18

Mass Media and the Enlargement of Moral Sensibility

Myrna Reid Grant

I propose two hypotheses in this essay: Mass media, and specifically movies, are significant vehicles for the experience of transcendence in contemporary life and metaphor is the vehicle by which people experience transcendence. This assertion should be of interest to media scholars and workers and to moral and religious educators. It suggests why some forms of content (texts) in the film medium will be more rhetorically effective in the task of moral enlargement than others.

Neil Hurley in his book, *Theology Through Film*, asserts that movies are for the masses what theology is for an elite.[1] The statement is impressive for the important place it gives to secular motion pictures as the locus where common humanity goes to study God.

Why is film and not television such a place? It is true that in Europe, religious radio and television broadcasting departments in national public service media systems such as the BBC in the U.K., have made a significant and appreciated impact on general audiences.[2] However, with few exceptions, in the United States, the banality and the abuses of "Christian" television have been well documented. The electronic church has attracted the attention of communication scholars on both sides of the Atlantic, including William Fore, Stewart Hoover, Peter Horsfield, Neil Postman, Quentin Schultze, and others. They have chronicled the history, audiences, uses of evangelical programming and have shown that the stated objectives are to evangelize, teach, encourage, and aid in worship. Scholars have also examined the entrepreneur aspect of evangelical programming as the prime method of financing the programming. This dependence on donor/viewers for money has been a significant factor in the failure of Christian

---

[1] Neil Hurley, *Theology Through Film* (New York: Harper and Row, 1970) ix.

[2] *BBC Religious Broadcasting* (London: British Broadcasting Corporation, n.d.) 11.

media workers to create television programs and films that stir the religious imagination.

In this essay I examine film as a vehicle of transcendence also because the creative work of the film maker and the film viewer are more discrete activities than their opposite numbers in television. The television product is most often a highly diffuse team effort and the viewing of television is frequently a group experience. In contrast, a motion picture can be the work of a single artistic vision and its theatrical presentation comes to the viewer as a solitary experience. Amedee Ayfre says, "Film does not give a translation. The cinema is an instrument of discovery."[3]

Sallie TeSelle writes of the exercise of the "theological imagination."[4] Yet precisely how is the theological imagination stimulated by film? What happens when such stimulus occurs? Anecdotal accounts indicate that dramatic moral, theological, or spiritual insights can take place in movie theaters. Yet little has been done to study the dynamics of these encounters.

This is not to suggest that identification of relevant variables within such cinematic moments will guarantee that film makers employing such variables will succeed in fashioning a film that will evoke a "transcendent response" within some viewers. Such moments may be facilitated by understanding the interplay between craft and metaphor. However, in the long run, the mysteries of faith are inaccessible to human analysis and contrivance, certainly within the technological domain of celluloid and tape.

Dictionary definitions of transcendence include, "To pass beyond a human limit," "To exist above and independent of material experience of the universes."[5] Hurley speaks of "this strange force, conscience...that form of transcendent determination."[6] TeSelle describes the parabolic tradition as "the transcendent (which) comes to ordinary reality and disrupts it."[7] Mircea Eliade coins the term "hierophany" to signify "the act of manifestation of the sacred."[8] These writers agree that a true transcendent moment arrives by means of the natural, known, profane world. Dufrenne adds a provocative detail to the definitions, suggesting that transcendence is not passive: "It expects its meaning to be spoken."[9]

Recently a young evangelical businessman recounted a film experience of a moment of spiritual discovery that occurred while viewing David Put-

---

[3] John May and Michael Bird, *Religion in Film* (Knoxville: University of Tennessee Press, 1982) 17.

[4] Sallie Teselle, *Speaking in Parables* (Philadelphia: Fortress Press, 1975) 8.

[5] William Morris, ed., *The American Heritage Dictionary* (Boston: Houghton Mifflin, 1981) 1362.

[6] Neil Hurley, *Theology Through Film* 57.

[7] Sallie Teselle, *Speaking in Parables* 2-3.

[8] Mircea Eliade, *Myths, Dreams, and Mysteries* (New York: Harper, 1961) 11.

[9] John May and Michael Bird, *Religion in Film* 8.

nam's film, *The Mission*. He described the scene in which a man who has killed his brother is climbing up a high precipice. He expressed a feeling of surprise to see the character of the murderer dragging his whole heavy coat of armor behind him, tied onto his body. A Jesuit, also climbing with him, and not being able to bear the agony and danger of the murderer's ordeal, cuts the rope to free him from the armor. Immediately the murderer retrieves the rope and continues his tormented climb pulling the armor with him. At this juncture, the viewer experienced a flash of insight. "I never understood penance before. I saw what was going on for him was personal. He had a deep spiritual need to right the wrongs he had done. Asking for forgiveness means there are things you have to *do*. Nothing in my evangelical subculture had ever taught me that."

Here is a second and more sweeping example of a transcendent response. The film, *Repentance*, directed by the Georgian film maker, Tengiz Abuladze, was completed in 1984, but had to wait until *glasnost* to be shown in the then Soviet Union. It won a prize at the Cannes Film Festival in May, 1988. In its first two months, more than 4 million people saw the film in Moscow, breaking the box office record.[10] According to the Voice of America, over 90 million Russians and other nationalities have seen the film which is a satirical anti-totalitarian protest. By means of symbol and metaphor, the most improbable scenes become painfully relevant. In one scene two people buried up to their necks in a shallow grave are forced to listen to the mayor of their town sing happy operatic arias from his limousine. Yet it is not only the indifferent mayor—the main figure of the movie, a combination of Stalin, Hitler and Mussolini—who is implicated. All Soviet citizens are guilty of evil by complicity. Christian forgiveness, the forgiveness of the film's title, becomes the only recourse. In the last scene, an old peasant woman stops by an open window and asks, "Is this the road to the church?" When the answer, "There is no church on this road" is given, she replies plaintively, "What is the good of a road that doesn't lead to a church?"

Reports on the effects of this film on then Soviet viewers were startling. "I have been turned inside-out," is a typical response. "Everything I tried to think before has been reversed. I am a different person."

Identifying transcendent experiences and dynamics in film is particularly significant today because the piercing experience of "otherness" in contemporary culture is muffled in a global, technological, information age. Increasingly, people have little experience in handling metaphor. The bustle of everyday living has no symbolic significance and the world of fantasy has no practical significance. In spite of the "religiosity" of American life, there is little sensitivity to the Divine Presence and little experience of awe and wonder before ultimate mystery. Part of the blame can be directed at

---

[10] Sophie Quinn-Judge, "The Man Behind the USSR's Most Popular Film," *Christian Science Monitor* (August 7, 1988) 19.

our dominant computer technology which has made unambiguous communication of ultimate priority. Even "the hot line" between Moscow and Washington, which most of us take to be a red telephone for the countries' leaders to speak person to person should an international crisis arise, is not a telephone at all. Mere human speech would be too open to error. The hot line is a computer system in which messages from one leader to the other are transferred in writing so that no possibility of misunderstanding the words can exist.

To speak clearly, to write clearly, to communicate with accuracy and brevity are skills greatly valued in our culture. When symbols occur, they are rapidly decoded into negotiable communication. Metaphor wastes time and can be ambiguous. It is preferable to say directly what you mean.

There is a problem with this utilitarian mandate because the language of symbol and metaphor is the language by which the deepest understanding of self and God is expressed. Metaphor is not merely the means by which the transcendent is communicated. Other than the miraculous spiritual event, metaphor *is* the communication of transcendence.

In *Anne of the Thousand Days*, playwright Maxwell Anderson gives these lines to Henry VIII: "There is a load every man lugs behind him, heavy, invisible, sealed, concealed, perfumed, a package of dead things he drags along, never opened save to put in some horror of the mind, some horror of his own doing...."[11] This vivid image of sin was actualized in the filmic metaphor of the murderer lugging along his armor—symbol of unforgiven violence and blood, of most horrible sin—that he literally ties to his body with a rope. By making concrete and visible these invisible sins that weighed so heavily on the murderer, David Puttnam creates a powerful metaphor that strikes into viewers' consciousness with the urgent awareness that is a characteristic of revelation. TeSelle says, "Metaphor is *the* way of human knowing. It is not simply a way of embellishing something we can know in some other way. There is no other way."[12]

In the last 15 years I have spent in academia, I have listened to the questions and yearnings of graduate communication students in Radio/TV/Film. Many long to learn how to create media products that will be vehicles of truth and moral substance. By no means is this interest limited to Wheaton College students, where I teach. As I have had opportunity to interact with Christian media students in other colleges and seminaries in North and South America, and in Europe, I have heard the same searching concern for the communication of meaning. There is a passion to explore

---

[11] Maxwell Anderson, *Anne of the Thousand Days* (New York: W. Sloane Associates, Inc. 1948) 82.

[12] Sallie Teselle, *Speaking in Parables* 4.

the possibilities of television and film as vehicles by which they can express their vision of reality.

Certain questions inevitably arise: How best can that vision be expressed? What filmic genres produce what results? Are there facilitating techniques that can be learned? These students hope to succeed where others have failed. They wish on the most genuine and deepest levels to use their art in the service of moral enlargement and religious growth. At the same time they recognize that their dilemma is two-sided. If they are to achieve their goals, (supposing they have the vision and talent) they are aware that they need the moral and financial support of funding sources. Will future employers or backers give their ideas a chance to materialize? Their visions of subtlety and metaphor, evocative rather than proclamatory truth are difficult enough to articulate and more difficult to demonstrate in a script or script proposal. They recognize the risk of innovation in a medium that is voraciously expensive and where failures are financial as well as artistic disasters.

There are three areas in the matter of media education that are useful to consider. The first concerns the aspirations and visions of students. Students need to be confirmed in their sense that artistic and literary devices offer tremendous potential for communicating truth and facilitating moral growth. Their aspirations are not merely "artsy" self-indulgence but are foundational to visual quality and depth. As well, students need the encouragement and savvy of working professionals in their field. The bridge between the classroom and the industry is critical to the development of student talent. There has to be a grounding for the dreams of students who need to incorporate the practicalities and pressures of this complex and competitive profession.

To build such bridges between academia and the professional film world calls for the vulnerability of educators. Film and television-makers are by definition driven by intense time constraints. It takes patience and sensitivity on the part of the educator to develop and nurture contacts and to make such relationships reciprocal. How can academics serve professionals? One way is to take the time to study the work of the professional and to offer knowledgeable encouragement and appreciation for what he or she is achieving. This obviously goes beyond simple compliments and enters into an understanding that may offer a useful perspective to the artist. At the least it can raise the relationship above that of a harried academic grasping at the chance to "use" a professional to shore up his or her teaching.

A second area concerns the need of students to have a reservoir of examples of the work of film makers particularly concerned with communicating their individual visions of reality. The analysis of such films is not the same as the traditional "history of film" course, useful as this is for media students. Certainly the celebrated films of Bergman, Dreyer, Bresson, and Tarkovsky are classic examples. Closer at hand, the English film maker, David Putnam is a contemporary film maker of passion and commitment. In a PBS interview with Bill Moyers, (World of Ideas 1989) Puttnam stated, "I do plead guilty to strong beliefs, to faith in the individual vision informed by craft and purpose." His films (including *Chariots of Fire*, *The Killing Fields*, *The Mission*) are examples of his vision.

The third concern of educators extends into the area of the church and/or the religious audience. Christians are not necessarily visually literate. The church historically has stressed and continues to emphasize the centrality of the printed word. The church-going public may have little understanding of how the visual arts contribute to the modern person's "quest to find God." Christian film and television makers frequently lack the emotional, spiritual, and financial support of their families and local congregations. What they are doing may seem frivolous to the church.

The development of the Christian Arts Group movement, which started in London in the 1960s and which has spread to major cities throughout the Western world, is a response to the need for support for young Christian artists who were rejected by their churches. Often, the Christian community needs help in understanding the moral potential of mass media. Today, some Christian scholars and media specialists are providing popular analyses of mass media for Christian readers. May and Bird's *Religion in Film*, William Fore's *Television and Religion*, and Quentin Schultze's *Television, Manna From Hollywood* are notable titles available to congregations. Educators should consider taking the time to write articles for denominational or religious publications, offering to speak on television/film for local church groups, encouraging film discussion groups in local congregations. Pastors can be encouraged to incorporate narrative and parabolic form in sermons, to establish an arts committee within the church, to suggest discussion groups in which transcendence in Scripture, literature, and film are examined, to encourage creativity throughout the church in all its functions. In these and doubtless many other ways, academics can contribute to preparing audiences for the Christian film makers of tomorrow.

The tasks before educators may often seem daunting; the flow of progress, upstream. Christian films of the past have not been distinguished by quality or evocative meaning. The economic nature of the industry is compellingly biased toward entertainment, even religious entertainment products. There is little precedent or encouragement for our students to champion quality and moral standards.

The late Peter Brooks was a well-known BBC religious TV producer who worked in the religious TV department of the BBC from 1966 to 1983. Before moving over into television he had been an effective BBC radio producer for many years. Both his radio and especially his television programs were distinguished by their simplicity and effectiveness and by the striking success many of them achieved in communicating meaning and a sense of awe and wonder. Brooks frequently lectured on the subject of the nature of Christian communication and wrote two small books on the subject.[13]

He was unshakable in his conviction that the visual arts (even television) have extraordinary potential for the transfer of meaning. The body of his work abounds with metaphor, simile, the subtleties of creation, human love, and human struggle. His untiring television work opened the hearts and inner eyes of a cumulatively huge audience to see splendor behind the mundane activities and relationships of this world. What he achieved was the work of one quietly purposeful person, highly skilled in his craft, who consistently offered his audiences religious television as a means to moral enlargement.

In the last analysis, great though our task as media educators may seem to be in these closing days of the 20th century, perhaps ours is not really a heavy yoke at all. Perhaps it comes down to each of us, one by one, holding to the possibilities of media transcendence ourselves, communicating the vision to, and encouraging it in, our students and, as clearly as possible, sharing it with our Christian contemporaries. In his book, *Communicating Conviction*, Brooks says: "As communicators we have to learn for ourselves as well as teach others, the essentially symbolic and indirect nature of our language. We have to think in that way and we have to live in that way."[14] It is possible that this personal mandate is a less complex task, a simpler vision, and a more effective pedagogy than we educators and practitioners had thought.

---

[13] *Person to Person* (London: Epworth Press, 1964) and *Communicating Conviction* (London: Epworth Press, 1983).

[14] Peter Brooks, *Communicating Conviction* 37.

19

Mass Media and the Enlargement of Moral Sensibility: Insights from Theology and Literary History

Anne E. Patrick, S.N.J.M.

The theme "Mass Media and the Enlargement of Moral Sensibility" invokes a metaphor of size, asking us to think about moral development in terms of a widening scope of ethical concern. We might have spoken instead of a "heightened moral awareness" or, in a context emphasizing electronic communications technology, of a more "finely tuned" conscience. But the metaphor of size does serve well, and it suggests that the influence of the American theologian H. Richard Niebuhr (1894-1962) in setting the task for this section of essays is not insignificant. For Niebuhr has shown in a much-studied book from 1960, *Radical Monotheism and Western Culture*, that where the ethical obligation to love our neighbor is concerned, the boundaries we draw separating those who really count as neighbors from those who are more or less irrelevant or expendable when we make decisions are of utmost moral and religious importance.[1]

1. Theological Context

Niebuhr recognized that despite professing faith in one God, most Christians tend to slip from the ideal of radical monotheism. We center our lives not on the "One beyond the many" but on such finite values as success, knowledge, wealth, or what he termed "social gods." Niebuhr believed that the chief obstacle to authentic faith is our tendency to put boundless trust and loyalty in finite objects, groups, and causes instead of in the principle of Being-itself. Placing the family, the nation-state, or even the

---

[1] H. Richard Niebuhr, *Radical Monotheism and Western Culture* (New York: Harper & Row, 1960).

church at the center of life is a subtle form of idolatry, he emphasized, for only God is worthy of absolute trust and loyalty. Niebuhr affirmed that there is value in family and country, in science and technology, and in organized religion, but he insisted that such value is relative to the ultimate Source of value. What this entails for ethics is that the perspective of *universal* love and justice must supersede narrow self-interest or group-interest.

These theological points are fundamental to the topic of this essay, for moral sensibility in need of enlargement is sized according to our basic stance toward ultimate reality. Because none is God but God, moral sensibility must be enlarged to include concern for the entire community of being. The lectures that became *Radical Monotheism and Western Culture* were delivered at the University of Nebraska in 1957, but Niebuhr's critique of the morality of religious and secular persons in America remains valid today. The commercialism, consumerism, and idolatry toward the nation-state, which other essays in the present volume have recognized as prominent in the practical use of media, are very much related to Niebuhr's point about social gods. So also are such evils as racism, sexism, and anti-Semitism, which have long marked American society despite our protestations of belief in human dignity and equality. Affirm as we might that all persons have rights, we still operate much of the time according to a mentality that does not consistently regard those outside the tribe—whether of family, gender, nation, race, religion, or other category—as neighbors in an ethically meaningful sense. Some might find Niebuhr too harsh a critic of western culture. After all, western culture has given us the notion of universal human rights, not to mention considerable insight into universal human dignity, a recurring theme in modern Catholic social teaching. Nonetheless we do not need to look far to find instances where racism, sexism, and anti-Semitism affect our society today; we continue to be guilty of exactly the sort of tribalism Niebuhr described.

I have begun with a theological foundation for ethical universalism because the enlargement of moral sensibility is connected with deep religious matters, including the mysterious phenomenon we term *conversion*. For this reason it would be naive to suppose that sophisticated new media formats can package the gospel in a way that makes enlargement of moral sensibility automatic. Classical notions of sin and grace have bearing on the question of how the media influence our consciences, and the long history of Christian reflection on the theological and psychological ramifications of these doctrines is relevant here. If we have learned anything from centuries of debates about Pelagianism, for example, we should be aware that we are never in full control of such phenomena as conversion. That having been said, it still seems reasonable to think that media can sometimes influence the human mind and heart in such a way that conversion to more authentic forms of faith and morality becomes more likely than would otherwise be the case. Grace can surely operate in cultural forms as well as in natural ones—indeed, culture itself is an aspect of human nature. And whether or not they would express it in Christian language, many artists have worked with media in the hope of casting a critical light upon excessive self-interest and group-interest, seeking by whatever tricks are up their sleeves to enlarge our moral sensibilities.

The tribalistic attitudes selected for attention here—racism, sexism, and anti-Semitism—support relationships of injustice because they presume, often beneath the level of awareness, that some people are more fully human, have greater dignity, and have interests that count more than others. Moreover, our very theories of ethics have at times reinforced these skewed perceptions, for example, by stressing property rights in a slavery-based economy, or to take a current example, by teaching about woman's so-called "special nature" and thereby legitimating sexism.[2] Certain individuals have been aware of these problems for quite some time, but more generalized awareness, with the behavior changes that flow from such awareness, has been mighty slow in coming. What we are asking, then, is whether the judicious use of mass media can hasten this growth in awareness and thus contribute to moral progress in our society.

2. Insights from Literary History

Before turning to the question of television's possibilities in this regard, it is good to recall that cultural elites have been worrying and wondering about the moral influence of mass media ever since the printing press made it possible to spread ideas and attitudes through appealing narratives that could be widely distributed at little cost. The questions we ask today about mass media and enlarged moral sensibility, as well as the question folks are always pursuing about how media damage moral sensibility, are direct descendants of questions posed in the 18th and 19th centuries about the positive and harmful effects of reading novels.[3] We might remember that novels became high culture only in the 20th century, about the time network radio began to reach large audiences, and that movies began to be studied as a serious art form only when television had become the dominant popular expression of culture. Some of the best minds of the last century

---

[2] For discussions of this anthropological question, see Dorothy L. Sayers, *Are Women Human?* (Grand Rapids: Eerdmans, 1971); Mary Aquin O'Neill, "Toward a Renewed Anthropology," *Theological Studies* 36 (1975) 725-36; Sara Butler, ed., *Research Report: Women in Church and Society* (Bronx, NY: Catholic Theological Society of America, 1978) 32-40; and, Mary Aquin O'Neill, "Imagine Being Human: An Anthropology of Mutuality," in *Miriam's Song II* (West Hyattsville, MD: Priests for Equality, 1988) 11-14.

[3] For a discussion of evangelical perspectives on fiction, see Samuel Pickering, Jr., *The Moral Tradition in English Fiction, 1785-1850* (Hanover, NH: University Press of New England, 1976).

were occupied with using novels, the mass media of their day, to exert moral influence, and we can learn from what happened to their efforts.

Harriet Beecher Stowe's *Uncle Tom's Cabin* (1852) was the biggest media event of the 19th century in this country, with arguably the greatest influence on the moral sensibilities of white Americans. As Jane P. Tompkins has remarked, "*Uncle Tom's Cabin* was, in almost any terms one can think of, the most important book of the century."[4] Thanks to Stowe's skilled use of sentimental conventions involving the symbolism of religion and the family, the consciences of thousands of white readers were substantially enlarged, at least for a while. Bonds of sympathy were created between white readers and fictional black characters, who were seen, perhaps for the first time, to have human qualities and human needs. We can learn much from the Stowe example. We should note in the first place that although the book put in question some aspects of racism, it hardly eliminated it. Victims were romanticized, and the story's "happy ending" involved not the incorporation of Blacks as full citizens of the United States, but rather their return to a mythically idealized Africa. Today many readers find Stowe's handling of racism flawed; indeed, there are grounds for calling the novel itself racist. But also to be borne in mind is the fact that this powerful story is absent from the standard lists of American classics. The prevailing excuse for this omission is that *Uncle Tom's Cabin* lacks whatever "great art" requires, as defined, of course, by those whose social location of power and privilege allows them to control definitions of what art should and should not involve. Fortunately critics are now reevaluating *Uncle Tom's Cabin* and other "sentimental novels" of the last century, and offering good reasons to include some of them in the American literary canon. Tompkins, for example, argues convincingly that modernist assumptions of the literary establishment are to blame for the neglect of this important book:

> In modernist thinking, literature is by definition a form of discourse that has no designs on the world. It does not attempt to change things, but merely to represent them, and it does so in a specifically literary language whose claim to value lies in its uniqueness. Consequently, works whose stated purpose is to influence the course of history, and which therefore employ a language that is not only not unique but common and accessible to everyone, do not qualify as works of art. Literary texts such as the sentimental novel, which make continual and obvious appeals to the reader's emotions and use technical devices that are distinguished by their utter conventionality, epitomize the opposite of everything that good literature is supposed to be.[5]

---

[4] Jane P. Tompkins, "Sentimental Power: *Uncle Tom's Cabin* and the Politics of Literary History," in *The New Feminist Criticism: Essays on Women, Literature, and Theory*, ed. Elaine Showalter (New York: Pantheon Books, 1985) 83.

[5] Ibid. 84.

Of the many 19th-century readers affected by Stowe's book, there is one I want to single out for attention here because *Uncle Tom's Cabin* was among the factors that led her eventually to choose popular fiction as the medium for communicating her own religious and moral vision. Mary Ann Evans read the novel in September 1852, and four years later began to write fiction herself, which she published under the name "George Eliot." Her letters leave no doubt that Stowe's books influenced her decision to write novels designed to enlarge the moral sensibilities of literate citizens of England. Her last two novels, *Middlemarch* (1871-72) and *Daniel Deronda* (1876), in fact, challenge sexist and anti-Semitic attitudes directly. Writing to Stowe shortly after the latter book was published, George Eliot put her hope thus:

> There is nothing I should care more to do, if it were possible, than to rouse the imagination of men and women to a vision of human claims in those races of their fellow-men who most differ from them in customs and beliefs.[6]

Middlemarch has been regarded as a classic for half a century, but the seriousness of its critique of sexism is only recently beginning to be recognized; *Daniel Deronda* is a rarely read effort of nearly 900 pages that influential critics have dismissed as too moralistic in tone on the Jewish question, with art thereby suffering.[7] The extent to which these texts enlarged the moral sensibilities of Victorian readers is difficult to gauge, and neither was a "media event" comparable to *Uncle Tom's Cabin*. My own informed guess is that sexist and anti-Semitic assumptions did suffer erosion in the minds of some readers, though the process was generally subtler than what went on with the Stowe novel.[8] In any event, the author's recognition of the limits

---

[6] M. E. Lewes to Mrs. Harriet Beecher Stowe, 29 October 1876, in *The George Eliot Letters*, vol. 6, ed. Gordon S. Haight (New Haven: Yale University Press, 1955) 301.

[7] In a December 1876 review for *The Atlantic Monthly*, Henry James dismissed the Jewish section of *Daniel Deronda* as "cold," and in the highly influential study *The Great Tradition* (1948) (Garden City, NY: Doubleday, 1954), F. R. Leavis went so far as to suggest that this Jewish half (which he found "fervid" rather than "cold") be excised and the remaining novel entitled *Gwendolen Harleth* (150). The James review, "*Daniel Deronda*: A Conversation," is published as an Appendix to this edition of the Leavis book (300-19). Some years later Leavis withdrew his suggestion about cutting away the "bad part" of *Daniel Deronda* in the essay, "George Eliot's Zionist Novel," which appeared first in *Commentary* 30 (October 1960) 317-25, and subsequently as an introduction to a 1961 edition of *Daniel Deronda* published by Harper Torchbooks. But this late acknowledgment that the "flawed" sections of the novel were too tightly bound up with its "greatness" to be removed did little to offset the influence of the original suggestion, which was much more widely circulated than the retraction.

[8] The ethical dimensions of these novels are discussed in Anne E. Patrick, "Rosamond Rescued: George Eliot's Critique of Sexism in *Middlemarch*," *Journal of Religion* 67 (1987) 220-38; "George Eliot's Final Experiment: Power and

of her own highly intelligent work, crafted in a medium that addressed the most thoughtful of readers, tells us something about how hard it is to enlarge moral sensibilities. For one thing, it is clear that few efforts will escape criticism, either on ethical or artistic grounds. For another, there is reason to suspect that ideological factors affect judgments about art as well as about morals.[9] And for a third, even relatively good efforts to enlarge moral sensibility succeed only in a slow and incomplete fashion. Even assuming that popular art can have some influence for enlarging moral sensibility, the words George Eliot wrote to the author of *Uncle Tom's Cabin* in 1869 remain true today:

> ...I dare say you have long seen, as I am beginning to see with new clearness, that if a book which has any sort of exquisiteness happens also to be a popular widely circulated book, its power over the social mind, for any good, is after all due to its reception by a few appreciative natures, and is the slow result of radiation from that narrow circle. ...[O]ne must continually feel how slowly the centuries work toward the moral good of men [sic].[10]

3. Prime-Time Television

As we leave this popular author of the last century, who functioned as both Sybil and Dear Abby of her day, and consider contemporary efforts to deal with racism, sexism, and anti-Semitism on television, we can only ask: If George Eliot is describing what happens to the green wood, what can we hope for in the dry? Turning to prime-time TV, let us bear in mind some-

---

Responsibility in *Daniel Deronda*," in *Morphologies of Faith*, ed. Mary Gerhart and Anthony C. Yu (Atlanta: Scholars Press, 1990) 319-42; and in a forthcoming volume entitled *Faith, Ethics, and Fiction: The Case of George Eliot's Last Novels*.

[9] Although the James-Leavis objections to *Daniel Deronda* have to some extent been accepted by many Christian and secular interpreters, Jews have from the first tended to read the novel in a much more favorable light. In *George Eliot: The Jewish Connection* (Jerusalem: Massada, Ltd., 1975), Ruth Levitt traces the influence of this text on figures including the influential Zionist, Henrietta Szold; the first president of the Jewish Theological Seminary, Solomon Schechter; and, the American poet Emma Lazarus. Levitt asks, "Did George Eliot...not influence Zionism in [Theodore] Herzl's time by preparing the very air which Herzl breathed in England, by planting the seeds of his acceptance with her idealistic hero and her unforgettable and prophetic words?" (74). More recently, Irving Howe describes the character Deronda as "abundantly virtuous but only intermittently alive" in his "Introduction to *Daniel Deronda*," (New York: New American Library, 1979). Howe insists, however, citing the opinion of Lionel Trilling, that the idealization needs to be understood in light of the need to oppose the Fagin-stereotype of the Jewish villain with a "counter-myth," a necessary step toward allowing a "fully shaded humanity to characterization of Jews" (xiii).

[10] M. E. Lewes to Mrs. Harriet Beecher Stowe, 8 May 1869, in *The George Eliot Letters*, vol. 5, 30-31.

thing implied in George Eliot's rather discouraging—she would say, realistic—observation, namely that it is a mistake to assume that change for good or ill is a monocausal phenomenon. The factors that influence human beings are complex, and images on a screen or words on a page are only *some* of the factors that affect moral sensibility. This insight has practical implications for parents and educators. What people see on TV does exert influence, no doubt about that. But far more powerful are the *real* persons who sit around the living room with the viewer, or who use or lose the chance to bring social analysis and ethical wisdom to bear on classroom discussions of what has been seen and heard.

Certainly there are many differences between prime-time TV and the media situation 100 years ago, one of the most important of which concerns authorship. Whatever distinctions literary critics may want to draw about authors, implied authors, or intentional fallacies, we are in a different ballpark altogether when we start to talk about who is responsible for programs that succeed or fail in treating social issues on television. These programs are not the work of individual authors, but rather are "committee products," developed by teams who work with a constant sense that producers, sponsors, and network executives are looking over their shoulders.

Media expert Todd Gitlin provides an informative and fascinating account of what goes on behind the scenes of commercial television in the 1985 volume *Inside Prime Time*. The most disconcerting fact he points out is that the whole television production system practices a more or less automatic self-censorship, refusing even to get near questions that would make sponsors nervous. After describing how pressure from the Kimberly-Clark Corporation led in 1982 to the cancelling of the Lou Grant show (which had featured Ed Asner, an actor known for his political activism), Gitlin observes that this case was unusual because it involved *direct* pressure from a program's sponsor: "Normally there is not even the suggestion of overt political concern at the networks, and normally advertisers do not intervene so directly in network affairs. Their interests form the context that decision-makers take for granted."[11]

To put matters another way, it is usually unnecessary for a sponsor to intervene because the production team anticipates the concerns of those who finance their efforts; the "normal network mentality" involves indifference to anything but ratings, and so the aim becomes to displease as few viewers as possible in order to keep them all watching.

If what Gitlin says about automatic preconscious self-censorship is true, then the shows that come to mind as efforts to enlarge moral sensibilities, and, in particular, to challenge racist, sexist, or anti-Semitic attitudes, are just flukes. They do not come along very often, and when they do they are certainly limited, one might well say flawed. But rarities like *Roots* or

---

[11] Todd Gitlin, *Inside Prime Time* (New York: Pantheon Books, 1985) 11.

Holocaust and successful series like *The Cosby Show* or *Murder, She Wrote* are about as good as it has gotten recently. During the conservative '80s, networks did not hope for the audience shares that *Roots* and *Holocaust* surprised them with in the preceding decade, and for all the good the Cosby show accomplished by providing images of a successful African-American family, can anyone recall an episode where a Huxtable child (or adult, for that matter) had to wrestle with racism?

There needs to be more ethical analysis of the issues involved in the shows that do deal with the areas of moral growth singled out for attention here. Recall, for instance, the debates that went on around the *Holocaust* mini-series in 1978. Many Jews and others argued that it was essential to portray something of the event, and tolerable to use melodrama for the sake of holding a mass audience that needed to know, at a minimum, that the Holocaust occurred. On the other side Elie Wiesel was insisting that, of course the Holocaust must be remembered, but for goodness sake, *not as a TV show.*[12] The question of what means are capable of holding audiences at the same time as viewers are challenged or informed on difficult topics is by no means an easy one to settle.

Another area for investigation concerns the advantages and limits of the programs that try out newer approaches to representing female characters (such as *Cagney and Lacey*) or that make tentative forays into disputed areas such as sex-roles or surrogate motherhood. It also is worth pondering why prime-time shows seem oblivious to Christian anti-Semitism in America, as well as to the now prevalent bigotry toward Arabs and matters Islamic. I cannot address such questions here, but simply put them on the agenda for future consideration. Clearly we are only beginning to do the work that can lead to more effective use of the media in enhancing ethical awareness. To conclude, I would stress three points to bear in mind as this work proceeds, two based on Gitlin's research and the last on my own experience as an educator.

In the first place, we should recognize that network paranoia about audience ratings and advertising contracts sharply reduces the likelihood that challenging social material will make it to prime-time viewers. Gitlin reports that one network executive told him that " '[t]he networks are always mistaking real social issues for little human-condition stories.' " The tendency to ignore the sociopolitical dimension of problems is so well-entrenched, Gitlin notes, that "[f]or weeks, whenever I told executives I was trying to understand how television dealt with social issues, they proceeded to tell me about movies dealing with alcoholism, cancer, drugs, crippling

---

[12]In an essay that appeared in the *Chicago Tribune* for April 19, 1978 under the headline "Trivializing the Holocaust: Semifact and Semifiction," Wiesel called the film, "untrue, offensive, cheap," and maintained that "the witness does not recognize himself in this film." He concluded: "The Holocaust *must* be remembered. But not as a show."

illness, death and dying." Personal stories are "routinely depoliticized," he emphasizes, and "stories about racial conflict get sidetracked or bleached."[13] There is an especially great reluctance to treat material involving racism or anti-Semitism, for sponsors are very nervous about anything that puts in question the myth of a united America. According to Gitlin, the airing of the film *Masada* was unusual, and his comment on its success is telling: "*Masada*—about 'Jews and history,' two 'downer' subjects in industry terms—could nonetheless be a hit because, despite rising anti-Semitism, there was no national constituency for the Romans."[14]

A second and more subtle finding from Gitlin is that in those cases when social issues do get an airing, they tend to be psychologized rather than analyzed in social and political terms. His discussion of the ABC drama, *Inside the Third Reich*, which is influenced by writings of T. S. Adorno objecting to "'the spurious personalization of objective issues,'" illustrates the problem well. Observes Gitlin:

> The high-rated May 1982 *Inside the Third Reich* was based, of course, on the memoirs of Hitler's architect and minister for war production, Albert Speer, supplemented by hundreds of hours the writer-producer spent interviewing Speer. The movie's vision retained the blinders that led Speer into the Nazi movement and kept him there. Speer's motives were pared down to the television-sized staple of Faustian ambition, revealing nothing of Nazism's historical mainsprings: inflation, nationalist panic, anti-Semitism. For the sake of balance, Speer was issued an anti-Nazi wife, but by Part II she had degenerated into the familiar nagging *Hausfrau* whose principal objection was that political meetings were pulling her husband away from his family nest.... *Inside the Third Reich* did open with newsreel footage including the dread images of heaped corpses found in the death camps at the end of the war. The movie proper included some valuable reminders that Hitler's rants and Goering's bluster were responsible for mass murder. But the bulk of the movie was family angst, petty palace intrigues, and pageantry passing for historical understanding. ABC's expensive European locales simulated authenticity without challenging Speer's worldview, which was that he was mysteriously trapped by Hitler's charisma.[15]

These two problems identified by Gitlin, the avoidance of controversial social topics and their reduction to personal-psychological problems instead of socio-political ones, deserve thoughtful probing by all who are interested in media and the enlargement of moral sensibility. A third matter concerns not so much the decisions of those who produce prime-time shows or educational videos, but rather the educators who make use of filmed material as aids to teaching about social issues in the classroom. Educators

---

[13] Ibid. 179-80.

[14] Ibid. 198.

[15] Ibid. 190-91.

who care about overcoming social injustice must beware of what I call the "displaced guilt flick syndrome." Otherwise we who are bothered by injustice may fall into the trap of dealing with our own feelings of guilt and powerlessness by using documentaries or half-way decent TV programs simply to tell our students how bad things are. It is a kind of lazy way out. We suppose that since we can't be Martin Luther King or Oscar Romero, maybe this video will inspire one of these young persons to go out and change the world. I am *not* saying we should never show films like *Hunger in America* or *Bitter Harvest*, or video clips reporting the latest atrocity in some war-torn part of the globe, but unless we provide our students with analytical tools and avenues for taking action, not to mention some grounds for hope, our socially relevant films may be more paralyzing than empowering. We may, in other words, be using media more for our own comfort than for changing anything in the world, which I take to be the point of enlarging moral sensibility in the first place.

IV

Philosophical and Theological Reflections

IV

Introduction

Philosophical and Theological Reflections: The Importance of Moral Imagining

A fundamental source of the power of mass media lies in their ability to engage our human imagination. In consequence, any effort to understand and to evaluate the role which media play in the moral dynamics of contemporary culture must examine media in relationship to the multivalent human capacity we call "imagination." Such an examination must not only take account of the array of appeals which media make to human imagination, it must also reflect upon the fundamental importance of imagination in shaping our moral life. Because media can present imaginative appeals of great power, we may all too readily grant to media the primary initiative in directing the focus of our imagination. We may lose sight of the active imaginative power which is central to our moral personhood and agency and only see, instead, our imagination becoming more passive and more helpless against an overwhelming onslaught of media images over which we have little control.

The essays in this section remind us, however, that imagination is far more than a passive capacity to receive images which others have shaped. It is, more fundamentally, an active capacity that is most potent when it is attentive to the call implanted in our human nature to participate in community. Each essay explores ways in which our moral imagining is ordered to and serves our ties to one another in the human community. As a result, they all argue that media engage our imagination in the most morally significant ways when they present us with possibilities for enlarging—or for constricting—the breadth of our identification with our fellow human beings and the depth of our understanding of the humanity we have in common.

Philip Rossi thus examines the possibilities which media offer for moral enlargement when they enable us imaginatively "to stand in someone else's shoes." This ability to take the perspective of another and, even, to take the perspective of *all* others, is a fundamental first step to thinking, feeling, and acting morally. This first exercise of moral imagination, however, is not sufficient to render us moral or to bring moral growth all by itself; we also need the imaginative ability to place the full range of such seeings into the ordered totality of a moral "world." Rossi reiterates Paul Philibert's claim that such a moral world is co-constructed and thus public and shared. He then argues that, despite the media's evident power to bring us to "stand in the shoes" of many others, the structural dynamics of commercial media act in complicity with our own unwillingness to see other than what we like and want to see; as a result, we narrow and restrict the range of other "shoes" from which we are prepared to see the horizons of moral life. If media fail to engage our moral imagination and to enlarge our moral horizons, the fault is thus as much ours as theirs. Such narrow imagining indicates a need to pose fundamental questions, both to media and to ourselves, about the extent of our commitment to image and to co-construct a moral world inclusive of all that is human: "Who is to take part in the co-construction of the moral world and...whose world is it to be?" In the light of these questions, one measure emerges for evaluating media's role in shaping our moral imaginings: Do they "stretch our imagination beyond the boundaries of our exclusivities" by which we divide the world into "us" and "them"? Rossi concludes by noting a fundamental condition for media successfully playing their role in the enlargement moral imagination: We ourselves must be already engaged in the work of dismantling, "stone by stone," the boundaries that divide the world into "us" and "them."

James Pollock evaluates the role of media in shaping our moral imagination from the moral perspective on authentic development human offered by Pope John Paul II's encyclical, *Sollicitudo Rei Socialis*. Particularly important in this perspective, in Pollock's view, are its rooting in human solidarity and the special option it entails for "the weakest and most powerless of our brother and sisters." Seen this way, media have a role not only as instruments to "foster our humanity and its authentic development," but they also stand "rooted in the foundational image of our humanity." This so because their imaginative power can "invite us to deepened self-knowledge and self-understanding." Pollock argues that "the power and the truth of mass media lie precisely in their ability to render us more faithful to our calling and to our reality." Central to this calling is participation in the paschal mystery of the death and the rising of Jesus; in such participation we encounter the deepest levels of our human solidarity. Pollock reminds us, however, of John Paul's warning about another, darker side of our human reality. Expressed in "the desire for profit and the thirst for power," these sinful powers stand in opposition to authentic human development. Media, as part of our human reality, thus have power both to serve and to hinder authentic human development. Media coverage of the Olympics provides an illustration of their ambivalent potential "to provide us, at the same time, with images of paschal excellence and dehumanizing consumerism."

In the context of media's complex power to engage our potential for authentic development, Pollock sees particular significance in the option for the poor and powerless; in them we see "most starkly and clearly" our common human reality: "the image of human persons bonded together in our common slavery to sin and selfishness, our common need for redemption, and our common capacity to be graceful signs of the loving God who communicates God's own life and love to us and invites us continually to become more godlike."

Enda McDonagh's essay explores the extent to which communication can itself serve as the fundamental imaginative framework for guiding moral reflection. He maintains that the dynamics of communication, particularly in its ordering toward the building of community, can be articulated as foundational for moral life and its guiding norms. McDonagh then examines "the central social symbol of Jesus's preaching, the Kingdom of God" in the light of the dynamics of communication. Although he acknowledges that "a theology of receiving and achieving the Kingdom is basically Christian theology of morality in both personal and social idioms," he also claims that "it does...like most analyses of morality, religious and secular, ignore the destructive side of moral life." For McDonagh, this destructive side originates in the fact that, in our human condition, "we are trapped between consumption and communion." While most evident at the biological level, the tension between consumption and communion extends to all levels of our existence: "The ambiguity of all human relationships centers on the dilemma of communing and consuming." Yet this tension does not require that destructive consumption prevail over communion because "Jesus made God present at the very heart of the human dilemma." McDonagh directs our attention to the "consumption events" in Jesus's life and indicates how the Eucharist brings into clear focus their significance as the "triumph of communion not just over consumption but in and through consumption." This vision of the scope of genuine human communication as open to the gift of "holy communion with neighbor and God" thus provides a challenging conclusion to these explorations of the role of media in the moral dynamics of contemporary culture.

20

Moral Imagination and the Media: Whose "World" Do We See, Whose "World" Shall It Be?

Philip J. Rossi, S.J.

The past 15 years have seen a growing body of work reassessing the role that the complex intellectual and cultural heritage of "the Enlightenment" has played in shaping our contemporary world.[1] Much of this discussion has been quite critical: The grand expectations for human scientific, moral, and cultural progress set forth by the Enlightenment rested upon foundations which the subsequent course of history has shown to be quite unsteady. Not wholly undeserved, these criticisms have made manifest how much of the moral fragmentation of our contemporary culture is the ironic result of the Enlightenment's hope for a secular, wholly immanent moral coherence: the expectation that human beings could successfully construct a coherent pattern of moral life without recourse to a transcendent grounding for the authority of that pattern. Despite the validity of this criticism, I would like, nonetheless, to focus this essay upon two of the ideas about our human moral capacities that were brought to prominent expression in the era of "Enlightenment": first, the insight that before we can make moral claims on one another, we must be able "to stand in one another's shoes"; second, the requirement of "universality" for our moral judgments. I hope to show that these ideas retain significant power even in a post-Enlightenment, "post-

---

[1] Among the most notable are Robert Bellah et al. *The Good Society* (New York: Knopf, 1991); *Habits of the Heart: Individualism and Commitment in American Life* (University of California Press: Berkeley, 1985); Christopher Lasch, *The True and Only Heaven* (W. W. Norton: New York and London, 1991); Alasdair MacIntyre, *After Virtue* (University of Notre Dame Press: Notre Dame 1981; second edition, 1984); *Three Rival Versions of Moral Inquiry* (University of Notre Dame Press: Notre Dame, 1988); *Whose Justice? Which Rationality?* (University of Notre Dame Press: Notre Dame, 1990); Charles Taylor, *Sources of the Self* (Cambridge University Press: Cambridge, 1989).

modern" world; in particular, I plan to argue that they can help us see better how mass media function in the interplay of the forces that make for moral coherence or for moral fragmentation in our contemporary culture.

Alasdair MacIntyre's *After Virtue* was one of the earliest of the works critical of the Enlightenment to gain attention. Although MacIntyre's treatment of the Enlightenment needs qualification (some of which he has himself provided in subsequent works), it still offers a particularly helpful starting point for my discussion of the role of media in shaping our moral world precisely because the issue of moral coherence and moral fragmentation is central to his interpretation. From MacIntyre's perspective, the Enlightenment "project" for moral philosophy focused on providing a coherent rational justification for morality.[2] This project, at least in its early and formative stages, presupposed the coherence of morality itself: Philosophy could give a coherent rational justification for morality because moral life is itself a coherent enterprise. For more than one Enlightenment philosopher, indeed, morality gave human life its overarching form of coherence. On MacIntyre's judgment, this project has failed: Every justification of morality proposed as coherent and rational, even by the recognized "greats" of Enlightenment and Post-Enlightenment philosophy, can be found wanting, often on internal grounds most damning to claims for coherence. More significant than the now centuries-long failure of this project, however, is the fact that confidence in the presupposition at its base—the coherence of moral life itself—has effectively been eroded. Although the erosion of confidence first took place among philosophers themselves, MacIntyre indicates that it has also taken place within the culture at large.

I would not strenuously dispute MacIntyre on that last point. Some of the other essays in this volume, notably the ones in Part I, have pointed to one of the clearest signs of this erosion: a growing inability, at least within the United States, to conduct "civic argument." William Sullivan quite rightly notes that behind this inability lies a lack of sureness about what, if anything, we hold as truths in common: We seem increasingly unable to resolve matters of public concern about which we disagree in consequence of being less and less sure about those substantive matters of principle on which we do agree.[3] In the public arena, shared beliefs about what justice and equity substantively require have had to give way more and more to regulations and rules that direct the observance of proper procedure and that become law to insure that all will observe them. The private arena leaves each of us to build moral coherence for our individual selves.[4] A residue of

---

[2] *After Virtue*, 39.

[3] See William Sullivan, Chapter 3, above.

[4] Robert Bellah, et al., *Habits of the Heart: Individualism and Commitment in American Life* offer useful descriptions and analyses of the forces at work in American culture that lead us to believe that personal morality is a "do it yourself" project. See, for instance, the section "Leaving Church."

belief in the coherence of moral life remains in the hope that, as each of us individually constructs a morally coherent pattern for living, we will see to it that our pattern does not interfere with anyone else's.

I think it useful for us to consider briefly that residue of belief in moral coherence, not in its all too common form of uncritically tolerant relativism, but as a very dimmed reflection of a crucially important insight the Enlightenment had about what makes a perspective worthy to be considered a *moral* perspective. In simplest terms, it is the insight that before we can make moral claims on one another, we must be able "to stand in one another's shoes." This insight, by no means a new discovery made by the savants of the Enlightenment, has a venerable heritage that stretches back at least as far as the biblical injunction to do unto others as we would have them do unto us. The moral philosophers in the Enlightenment could make this insight properly their own precisely because its force seems not to rest upon an appeal to transcendent authority. As a result, it even lies behind two Enlightenment perspectives on morality—Hume's and Kant's—that philosophers ordinarily take to stand in polar opposition. For beneath some very real differences, each recognizes that moral life cannot occur without some human ability to take the perspective of others—and, indeed, even to take the perspective of *all* others. Each assigns this ability to a different part of the human psyche: Hume sees this as an affective ability, "sympathy," while Kant sees it as an intellectual one, "reason." Even so, they both take it for granted that we need such an ability and, in fact, that we have it, even though we may not always use it or use it well.

I think one could argue that the age of Hume and Kant differs crucially from our own contemporary world in that we no longer see very clearly the connection between the ability to stand in one another's shoes and the principles and practice of morality. It may be that an image of the self as so incommunicable, as so private, that we cannot even conceive of our having such an ability has captivated us; even less can we conceive of such an ability enabling us to bring moral principles to bear constructively on matters of public import. Constructing such a case would have philosophical and theological interest, but it is not my aim here. Instead I wish to suggest that one crucial function for media in the interplay of the forces that make for moral coherence or for moral fragmentation lies in the possibilities they offer for engaging our ability to stand in the shoes of one another.

Before we look at some of the possibilities media offer for engaging this ability, however, I think we need to specify this ability "to stand in one another's shoes" a bit more, as well as to diagnose its decline into what I earlier termed "uncritically tolerant relativism." We need to specify this ability more precisely because it forms only part of a larger complex of abilities that we need in order to think, feel, and act morally. Moral life gets both started and sustained through our ability to envision someone else's perspective so that we can say, "Yes, I now see what you see and see as you do." That is a start, but by itself, it does not suffice for several reasons. First, the standing in another's shoes has to be reciprocal: The other also has to stand in my shoes, and I must allow her to do so. (This last, we should note, is not always easy to do, since it makes it possible for another to see our own self-deceptions.) Second, and of even greater importance for our discussion of the role of the media, such seeing by itself does not show us how to relate the two "seeings," if and when they differ. Even less does it help when the seeings are multiple and, on the face of it, incompatible.

I believe another insight crystallized in a certain way by Enlightenment philosophers can help us see what we need to take the step beyond mere "seeing." That insight holds that whatever each of us is "seeing" must take its place within a "world"—it must be placed, at least potentially, as part of a ordered totality. Kant's work makes this insight prominent; H. Richard Niebuhr, in this century, has developed it in a way particularly helpful for both the moral philosopher and the moral theologian. A "world"—some form of totality—provides the most fundamental backdrop for our efforts to make sense of our existence. We make sense of each and every item encountered in our experience by placing it over against a "horizon" of elements that already stand in some kind of ordered relationship to each other and to ourselves. For both Kant and Niebuhr, there is a "givenness" to such ordering even though we also participate in its construction; Kant marks "reason" and Niebuhr marks "language" as the human capacity through which this order occurs and through which we participate in the ordering. They both note that, to the extent that such a "world" is given, it tends not to be the object of our explicit attention, and makes us liable to misunderstand the very elements and process of our own understanding which are involved in its constitution.[5]

One of the forms such misunderstanding takes in our contemporary age results from our psychologizing the "seeing": We take note of the "seeing" being "my" seeing to such an extent that we neglect it as a seeing of a "world," or of at least part of a "world."[6] We see this process of "making sense" in individualized and atomistic terms, and learn to regard "given" meanings, particularly moral meanings, with suspicion. We psychologize our making sense of the world to such an extent that we find it easy to speak of it in ways that would be oxymoronic to an Enlightenment thinker

---

[5] See H. Richard Niebuhr, *The Responsible Self: An Essay in Christian Moral Philosophy* (New York: Harper and Row, 1963) pp. 88-89; 98-100; Immanuel Kant, *Critique of Pure Reason*, trans. Norman Kemp Smith (Toronto: Macmillan, 1929) A 415-420/B 442-448.

[6] Paul Philibert, Chapter 6, above.

such as Kant: We find it easy to think of individuals each having their "own" worlds, and even their own "private" worlds.[7] This psychologized perspective loses the insight that "worlds" are public, not private; they are meant to be shared. Paul Philibert puts well this insight into the shared nature of a "world" when he notes that we best understand autonomy in terms of our entering into relationships that enable us "to co-construct...a world." To this I would add that a "world" comes into being *only* by co-construction.

This public and co-constructed nature of a "world" immediately suggests one important step that we need to take so that our "seeing" from one another's shoes moves us towards moral coherence: We must see these vantage points as places from which to start the work of co-construction so that they may finally be brought to stand as perspectives on the same, shared world. Dialogue defines an important element of that co-constructive work: We must be willing and able to talk with one another about our different "seeings" so that we can locate those parts of such a world that we can or do share.[8] In contrast to this, an uncritically tolerant relativism carries an implicit confession of despair in the possibility that we can share a moral world. It entails abandonment of the dialogue by which we initiate and enable the co-construction of a shared moral word. An uncritically tolerant relativism, moreover, is unwilling to confront the possibility that the work of co-construction may at times require that we tell someone else, or that we be told, that the world is not as they (or we) have seen it to be. Because the world is public and shared it requires that what we tell of it be true.

Considerably more could be said regarding these Enlightenment ideas about our ability to see from another's perspective and about the public and shared character of the world—including the fact that they grow out of elements of even longer standing traditions of Western philosophical and theological reflection on our human situation. We have said enough about them, however, to allow us to use them to examine how the mass media function in the interplay of the forces within contemporary culture that make for moral coherence or for moral fragmentation. This examination seeks to formulate and raise the kinds of questions that we can put to the dynamics, the presentations, and the representations of media in order to evaluate their role in helping or hindering our human task of co-constructing the moral world. In the context of these insights, I will focus my examination of mass media

---

[7] Leibniz, two generations before Kant, provides a particularly instructive contrast to this contemporary view. Although his doctrine that every substance [for our purposes, mind] mirrors the world might suggest a plurality of "worlds"—indeed, as many "worlds" as there are minds—he maintains the unity and coherence of a single "world" by his coordinate doctrine of pre-established harmony: God provides the guarantee that what we all mirror is one and the same world.

[8] See Henk Hoekstra and Marjeet Verbeek, Chapter 16, for a longer discussion of moral dialogue in relation to the mass media.

upon their power to present "seeings" of the world, to invite us to see from the perspective of "someone else's shoes," and to engage ourselves with others in dialogue that tests the truth of our seeings and in other activities that make possible the co-construction of the moral world.

Since the invention of the printing press, mass media have made it possible for many more of us to share more quickly in the "seeings" of others. This, indeed, may constitute the mass media's most particular and important power, even though human culture has had, for far longer, public gatherings of ritual and festival to present the very "seeings" that hold a particular people together in a shared world. Mass media's power, more-over, need not work in only the one direction that makes us recipients of someone else's "seeing." It has also become increasingly possible for more and more people to present their own "seeings" more rapidly and to a larger circle of others: from the printing press and the ditto machine we have moved to copy machines and telefaxes, conference calls and teleconferenc-ing, desktop publishing and tape recorders, video cameras and computer net-works. A very legitimate and important concern to examine and evaluate the role of media when we stand before them as recipients of the "seeings" of others should not cause us to neglect a coordinate examination and evalu-ation of the possibilities we may have or be offered to use the means of modern communication to present and share our own "seeings" with others. Yet, as analysts of the media have pointed out, various dynamics, particu-larly economic ones, seem to narrow the range and the variety of "seeings" that print and television present;[9] in consequence, it seems all the more ur-gent to attend first and foremost to an examination and evaluation of the "seeings" that get presented to us, willy-nilly, by those whom Gregor Goethals has very telling described as the new patrons of our skilled symbol makers.[10] Though there can be little doubt of the media's power to present us with a wide—perhaps unlimited—range of "seeings" of the world, we need to examine how and why only, in fact, a limited range of them come before us.

Media limit their power to invite us to see from the perspective of someone else's shoes, to the extent that they provide only a narrow and selective range of "seeings." This suggests that we need to ask the media a double question: In whose shoes are we being asked to stand? Second, how did *these* "shoes" get selected as the perspective from which we are invited to see? These are not easy questions to answer for a medium such as televi-sion which requires collaborative production. Producer, director, sponsor, writers, editors all play major roles in fashioning the "seeing"—but whose "seeing" is the program that finally appears on our screen? In dealing with these questions, I think we need to take careful note of the dual face the

---

[9] Thomas Shanks, Chapter 4, above.

[10] Gregor Goethals, Chapter 1, above.

collaborative process itself presents. On the one hand, the process can and should be open to the mutual testing of different "seeings" and even to the invitation of yet other "seeings"; as a result, it can eventuate in a "seeing" shaped and enriched by the different perspectives of all who co-construct it. Such a co-constructed "seeing" would truly be the responsibility of all who took part in its making and could be acknowledged as such. On the other hand, the process falls subject to the dynamics of dominative power, in which the "seeings" are not so much tested against one another as they are shaped by concerns extrinsic to their authenticity and truth: Will it sell? Will it shock? Will it "fit" our image? Will it promote an agenda? Will it promote a career? In these circumstances, the process is more likely to result in a "seeing" made blind to other perspectives and for which collaborative responsibility can easily be sloughed off: It's what "the public" wants—after all, it sells, doesn't it?

The bite of that last retort—"it sells, doesn't it?"—can't be completely ignored, for successful presentations of the media, the ones we do watch and watch again, become, in an important sense, *our* seeings.[11] There is thus more than a little truth to our having complicity in those "seeings" media present which show only what we like and want to see. They reassure the comfortable majority of us that we are a majority and that we are comfortable. On the other hand, media can and do present "seeings" which are not our own and which have the power to correct our seeing of the world and to enlarge its horizon.[12] This power to unsettle indicates that we do not always want to look at the world from a vantage point other than our own. Thus the question posed to media must also be a question to ourselves: In whose shoes other than our own are we *willing* to stand? Since, moreover, these "seeings" are to be a starting point for the work of co-construction of a moral world, both the question we pose to the media and the question we pose to ourselves turn out to be questions about who is to take part in the co-construction of this world and, finally, about *whose* world it is to be.

These latter questions, I believe, get us very close to central issues, not just to the role media play as forces for moral coherence or moral fragmentation but also to the moral dynamics of an increasingly interdependent global culture. These questions probe the ability and the willingness, both of media and of ourselves, to engage ourselves with others in the dialogue that tests the truth of our "seeings" and in the whole range of activities that make possible the co-construction of the moral world. The questions that we need to pose to the media and to ourselves will not be all that different from those that we also need to pose to the other institutions and forces that shape culture. These questions ask chiefly about the mutually related realities of participation and power. We must ask questions that will enable us

---

[11] See Michael Real, Chapter 2, above.

[12] See Anne E. Patrick, Chapter 19, above.

to find out what particular kind of power the media and each of these institutions and forces have to shape culture; we must also ask questions to find out who takes part in the exercise of this power—and who and what determine who takes part. The latter question is a particularly crucial one because through it we can begin to unmask what I have termed above the dynamics of dominative power: institutional arrangements that do not permit co-constructive exercise of that power by all whose lives and reality are shaped by it.

It is especially important, moreover, to pose these questions to the mass media because their particular powers bear with special potency upon the shaping of our imaginations. Media have acquired the symbolic and mythic power that enables them to play a role not only in shaping culture but also in shaping our perceptions both of culture and of our own identity within culture. In such matters, there is more than a little truth in Berkeley's dictum, *esse est percipi*. Questions about whose "seeings" media present and about whose "seeings" we are willing to bring into our own purview, are questions about the breadth and the depth of imagination—both the media's and our own. To evaluate adequately the media's role in the dynamics of moral coherence and moral fragmentation we need ways to take moral measure of the media's shaping of our imaginations. Some help in doing so can be found, I believe, in yet another Enlightenment idea, universality, refined by H. Richard Niebuhr into the inclusivity of universal community. A consideration of this idea will appropriately bring this discussion full circle and thus to conclusion.

"Universality" is an Enlightenment idea that has received bad reviews from a number of quarters. Some philosophical and theological circles have long suspected it for its formality and abstractness. That, in itself, seems to disqualify it from standing as a moral measure of imagination, which is made of the very stuff of particularity. More recently it has been seen as a mask for dominance: Claims made its name turn out to be infected with a partiality that serves first the interests of the socially and culturally dominant—most especially their interest in remaining dominant. Much of this criticism is well taken; it is, however, directed at an understanding of "universality" viewed through an ahistorical optic. From that vantage point, universality brings all into unity at the price of leveling all differences. H. Richard Niebuhr was certainly neither a partisan nor friend of a universality that had been turned into such a gray and lifeless shadow. Yet, when he viewed universality from the concrete and historical optic of Christian faith, he effected its transformation into the overarching moral ideal of the inclusivity of universal community. That ideal, I believe, can function well for taking moral measure of the presentations and representations of our human imagination. It suggests ways to specify the task of imagination in the dynamics of moral coherence and moral fragmentation and, thus, provides a basis on which to evaluate how adequately media serve to shape imagination for this task.

Niebuhr bases his transformation of universality on the Christian doctrines of Creation and Redemption that reveal the inclusive nature of God's providence and love. For Niebuhr, the ordered totality that constitutes the "world" is the focus for God's providence and love. The moral and religious life of humankind, on his view, has its beginning in an acknowledgment of the inclusivity of God's love. This immediately sets down imagination's fundamental moral and religious task: to function as the power that enables us to see more and more of the world as open to God's providence and love. Although the task of imagination here is fundamentally one of "seeing," it is a task also ordered to "doing": In seeing more and more of the world as open to God's providence and love we see more places in which God's sustaining activity invites our response as well. These are no easy tasks because we so readily set our human exclusivities over against God's inclusivity. We mark off boundaries—most often the boundary of "we" and "they"—beyond which we see no possibility for God's grace to do its transforming work; more subtly, we see just those possibilities which will protect us in our exclusivity: To be touched by God's grace and love "they" must first become like "us."

I believe that we now have reached at least one touchstone by which to measure the way that the media shape our imagination when they invite us to stand in the shoes of another. Does that seeing of another's world open up the possibilities by which our own world can become more encompassing, more inclusive of perspectives not our own? Or does it serve, instead, to raise higher between "us" and "them" the boundaries and barriers already in place, or even lay down the foundations for new ones? From the evidence in so far, there are still far too few presentations of mass media that seem likely to meet this measure for the expansion of our moral sensibility. We surely should treasure those that do and encourage more like them. But all too often economic, racial, or social divisions get reinforced, or papered over, rather than faced and overcome. That fact, however, need not counsel despair—save that in this regard media neither do nor fare all that better, or worse, than the rest of our culture. The mass media cannot solve a problem that is fundamentally a problem for us all and which is bound up with the brokenness of our human condition. The media can help us, however, to stretch our imaginations beyond the bounds of our exclusivities, but they can do so successfully only in coordination with our own labor to dismantle them, stone by stone by stone.

21

Power, Truth, and the Flow of Information

James R. Pollock, S.J.

Oftentimes it is assumed that the characteristic role of moral theology revolves around distinguishing good from evil, promoting the former, of course, and condemning the latter. In a way, this observation is true; but more fundamentally, it obscures the truth of the human moral life. When there are relatively evident goods and evils which face us, the choice of the good is typically not so difficult to make. If abortion, for example, were simply in all circumstances a choice between preserving innocent life and committing murder, there would be far fewer abortions. The more characteristic task of moral theology, particularly in our exceedingly complex world, is to discern between competing goods and values, and often in a context of accompanying evils and disvalues. This process of discernment, furthermore, requires serious effort to maintain harmony between individual choices and overall life patterns, attitudes, and convictions. Similarly, for the Christian, the need for harmony between faith's demands, rooted in our personal and communal experience of God's presence, and the fundamental demands of our common humanity urges us to continue our discernment process faithfully and often painstakingly and in a somewhat groping fashion. An additional fact that we must contend with is that frequently what is a value for me may be a disvalue for you—or, even more, the reality we encounter is ambivalent and ambiguous.

Consider the words of our title. "Power" evokes images and feelings, I suspect, that both thrill and disquiet us. "Truth" seems unambiguously desirable and good, until we recognize that it is not principally conceptual, but onerously personal and interpersonal and always, for human beings, partial and relative to other truths. Jesus's "I am the Truth" suggests both its delectability and its incompleteness or ultimate uncontainability. "The flow of information" is similarly polyvalent, suggesting both increasing possibilities and the potential for being inundated by a lack of differentiation—it seems conflictive, both valuable and value-free.

Since I have described a reality that is at once processive and insoluble, I feel free from a need to try to offer solutions and free to explore imaginatively some of the issues our topic raises. I will try to offer some reflections, from the viewpoint of moral theology, which might stimulate dialogue and discussion in a search for understanding.

I would like to set the context for this discussion in the notion of development as discussed by John Paul II in *Sollicitudo Rei Socialis*. It seems to me that, for a moral evaluation of the possibilities inherent in mass media, authentic human development, rooted in solidarity and an option in a special way for the weakest and most powerless of our brothers and sisters, provides an interesting optic.

John Paul's encyclical is not intended to be primarily about mass media—it is not, for example, another *Miranda Prorsus*—yet, many of his themes address particularly germane elements of our own problematic. He says, "It is important that as far as possible the developing nations themselves should favor the self-affirmation of each citizen through access to a wider culture and a free flow of information. Whatever promotes literacy and the basic education which completes and deepens it is a direct contribution to true development...."[1] Mass media certainly enjoy a privileged position today precisely in terms of their capacity to create and disseminate not only information but also the broader phenomenon of public culture. That they have a role in relation to the promotion of authentic human development should be clear.

John Paul has taken great care in the fourth chapter of *Sollicitudo* to define authentic human development in terms much broader and more profound than simply economic categories.

> Development, which is not only economic, must be measured and oriented according to the reality and vocation of man seen in his totality, namely according to his interior dimension. There is no doubt that he needs created goods and the products of industry, which is constantly being enriched by scientific and technological progress. And the ever greater availability of material goods not only meets needs but also opens new horizons. The danger of the misuse of material goods and the appearance of artificial needs should in no way hinder the regard we have for the few goods and resources placed at our disposal and the use we make of them. On the contrary, we must see them as a gift from God and as a response to the human vocation, which is fully realized in Christ.[2]

---

[1] All references to *Sollicitudo Rei Socialis* by Pope John Paul II are from *Origins* 17:38 (March 3, 1988) 641-60. This first is found in no. 44, 656.

[2] Ibid., no. 29, 650-51. For purposes of accuracy, I cite the official English translation of *Sollicitudo*, which regrettably employs sexist language. This itself, of course, works against authentic human development. In this context, see the article referred to in footnote 7.

In this context, it is valuable to point out that mass media, in themselves, are gifts from God. Dangers of their misuse do not justify turning away from God's gifts. They are also a "response to man's vocation," that is, a means for human beings to expand and grow in their capacity to mirror forth the loving, fundamentally communitarian God in whose image all are created. They will aid us in this task precisely as they foster our humanity and its authentic development. We are called to be agents of love and solidarity, agents of a love that is creative and empowering, as creation itself testifies to God's own motives. Mass media, then, are part of the on-going process of creation and redemption. They evidence our capacity to be co-creators with God and further testify to ways that God's grace is structured in our lives.

Another way of looking at this is to see the imaginative power of mass media as rooted in the foundational image of our humanity, that is, the image of God that Christian faith sees in each and every human being. If mass media can expand our horizons, the point of reference in this expansive process is the image of mystery that we incarnate. Expanded horizons, then, in a real sense, invite us to deepened self-knowledge and understanding. We become more truly ourselves at the very moment in which we transcend ourselves, becoming more like the one whole image we body forth. In this sense, then, the power and the truth of mass media lie precisely in their ability to render us more faithful to our calling and to our reality. Generally speaking, increased self-understanding stands in a reciprocal relationship to our capacity to reach beyond ourselves, to transcend our individuality and loneliness, to love. Naturally, this process is not automatic and is susceptible of frustration in many ways and for many reasons. Nonetheless, if it remains true to itself, even suffering the occasional setback, if it remains open-ended, increasing awareness of self and one's possibilities necessarily leads to growth in love.[3]

Authentic human development, then, to recapitulate, is not principally a process whose goal is the amassing of more material goods, certainly not for their own sake. This is to truncate the image of humanity—in mass media terms, it is to see ourselves continually out of focus, to hear ourselves and our possibilities with so much static that as we speak and listen, distortion of our truth begins to seem normal. Authentic human development accentuates, rather, the purpose and potential of our lives because it highlights the moral and spiritual dimensions of our existence, our freedom and responsibility, our capacity to become Godlike in bringing forth life instead of death, love instead of hatred or indifference, good instead of evil.

---

[3] John Paul speaks to this in a related sense: "Development is not a straightforward process, as it were automatic and in itself limitless, as though, given certain conditions, the human race were able to progress rapidly toward an undefined perfection of some kind." Ibid., no. 27, 650.

Let us return more explicitly to the ambivalence I earlier noted. In a controversial element of *Sollicitudo*, John Paul says that "what is hindering full development is that desire for profit and that thirst for power already mentioned."[4] These factors block particularly the reality of interdependence whose "correlative response as a moral and social attitude, as a 'virtue,' is solidarity...a firm and persevering determination to commit oneself to the common good...to the good of all and of each individual because we are all really responsible for all."[5] Ultimately, of course, the good of each and of all refers to the image of humanity we have been discussing, an image that is profoundly personal and communitarian because of its roots in the God who is Love.

John Paul identifies the desire for profit and thirst for power in ways that relate to ideological conflicts between East and West. More fundamentally, however, he is describing sinful attitudes and actions that distort humanity by opposing ourselves to God's will, which can only be, in this context, authentic human development. Furthermore, he characterizes these desires and thirsts as particularly evil when pursued "at any price."[6]

Mass media, in their ambivalence, demonstrate that these destructive possibilities transcend the boundaries between East and West because they bear within themselves the seeds of this harmful harvest. The desire for profit and the thirst for power at any price can be subtly manipulated and practiced by those who control and produce mass media. It is, however, after all, only a capacity for evil that throws the reality and possibility of good into effective and noticeable relief. It is important to remember in this context that potential dangers should not dissuade us from recognizing and using God's gifts. It should be superfluous at this point to acknowledge how congenially the desire for profit and the thirst for power fit into our individual psyches as well.

The power of the media is awesome. Similarly awesome is their capacity to promote what is truly profitable for humanity, namely, authentic human development. It is, of course, precisely this development that can provide human and moral parameters for the exercise of power and the pursuit of profit.

I have elsewhere tried to suggest moral dimensions of the phenomenon of human communication, described as a process of establishing union with the self, others, God, and the world.[7] In this context, I have developed particularly some of the specifically Christian elements that can throw light on the significance of human communication—elements such as the dignity of

---

[4] Ibid., no. 38, 654.

[5] Ibid.

[6] Ibid., no. 37, 653.

[7] An example of this is found in my "Human Rights, Communication, and Morality," *Milltown Studies* 18 (Autumn 1986) 1-17.

human persons, those persons' vocation to love, and the roots of this vocation in God's trinitarian reality. I would here, however, like to take this process a step further and develop it in a way that relates the process of human communication, and more specifically mass media as typically communicative, to the paschal mystery that is at the heart of Christian faith. I do this for a number of reasons. The paschal mystery, with its stark insistence that we are baptized into the suffering and death of the Lord, so to rise with him to new life, is a highly ambivalent reality. Christianity does not promise life without our undergoing, in countless ways, the experience of death. We do not seek suffering and death, but we recognize that any significant human growth will entail its bitter taste. Self-transcendence itself, so characteristic of authentic human development, is a necessarily painful phenomenon. As exciting and rewarding as love is, it is not without its necessarily painful dimensions, though the new life that is love makes it immensely profitable and desirable for us.

This dimension of love, namely its curious combination of death and life, highlights the fact that the union which is the ongoing goal of communication is not conflict-free, is not sentimental, is not automatic. Clearly, it is reminiscent of John Paul's description of solidarity—"a firm and persevering determination to commit oneself to the common good...to the good of all and of each individual."

Perhaps reflecting on a concrete example will help to clarify this point. Consider the Olympic Games which every four years dominate the media and enter thereby into our own lives. Let me suggest some ways in which the Olympics may promote authentic human development and at the same time manifest its paschal dimensions, its moral and spiritual characteristics. In addition, let me suggest the ambivalence of the media event and our interiorization of it.

The Games are highly competitive events, and competition is a word that often has negative connotations in moral discourse. The ugly underside of a competitive spirit in athletics leads us to consider what people will do or contemplate doing just to make a team or to qualify for an event, let alone to win it. Competition on this worldwide scale can become ideological and chauvinistic, and not just on the part of athletes, but on the part of trainers, judges, coaches, spectators, commentators. Patriotism itself can be trivialized in an atmosphere that promotes winning at any cost. The crass, competitive commercialism that vies to honor winners as it seduces them with the promise of profit and gain threatens to cheapen the true value of gold, silver, and bronze.

What is celebrated at the games, however, first and foremost, is simple excellence. The discipline, pain, and hard work involved in preparation for an event and its execution are a part of the competitive phenomenon whose purpose is to promote and reward achievement and excellence. Athletes compete against their own limits in order to carve out new possibilities for themselves and for all of humanity, new images of what human beings can accomplish when their energies and force are centered upon the transcendence of ordinary limits.

This is taken a step further in the team events because other, often hidden, skills are called upon where one's contribution depends on those of others. No one athlete can win a team event, without becoming a part of something bigger than himself or herself. This reality changes the way a person will respond or play in a particular situation. My excellence may be most noteworthy to the trained eye of one who sees me pass a ball to someone else rather than jockey myself into the limelight. The excellence of one motivates and enables and even empowers excellence in others. This echoes the firm and persevering determination to commit oneself to the common good that John Paul called solidarity. In the Games we see multiple examples of excellence, in the individual and group levels and we see its absence.

We are justifiably proud when our compatriots compete and excel and win, especially when they are doing this among a field of winners. Our loyalties, however, may transcend mere national boundaries for a variety of reasons. Most especially, we see the humanity of other competitors, we respect and recognize their accomplishments and their excellence. We are engaged and move beyond national isolation in awe and wonder at the talents of those who represent our own human finest in some particular way. It is true that our loyalties are and remain complex—this is faithful to the reality of our lives, to the ambiguity of our existence. We are given, however, the opportunity to recognize ourselves truly as members of the human race, to recognize common bonds of humanity that may lift us beyond the isolating absorption of everyday existence and rhetoric and propaganda.

Clearly, the ordered flow of information across our television screens, and screens throughout the world, is a great gift. It may be abused, it is true. But gift it is nonetheless, and we can see our potential interdependence, our solidarity with one another—we can see it and interiorize these values and sense what authenticity might mean when we speak of human development.

The advertising on American screens demonstrates the capacity of power and profit to distort human truth. On one level, of course, we are continually being presented with images of how the good life is conceived. We are drawn to consider human possibilities, and we may well be drawn to desire many things that are, for us, unattainable. Whether they should, in fact, be desirable or attainable for anyone is often an open question. Our longings, however, are frequently stimulated powerfully and manipulated with one goal in mind, the selling of products. Here too the force of competitiveness can easily lead to the shading and nuancing of truth claims that render truth itself a reality without much meaning. Although there is a heightened sensitivity today to the presence of violence in mass media, how many of us object to the more subtly dehumanizing influence of a culture bent more and more on the final comfort, consuming its own humanity along with countless other "goods."

In this light, and from a specifically Christian point of view, the option for the poor and the powerless takes on added significance. The poor and the powerless, in fact, are rich and powerful in their capacity precisely to help focus for us all the real truth of profit and power, "a commitment to the good of one's neighbor with the readiness, in the Gospel sense, to 'lose oneself' for the sake of the other instead of exploiting him, and to 'serve him' instead of oppressing him for one's own advantage."[8] For the real truth of profit and power is found in the real truth of our humanity, the image discernible in all of the loving mystery we call God. Opting for the poor and powerless, is, in the last analysis, opting for ourselves, because in them we see most starkly and clearly our own image—the image of human persons bonded together in our common slavery to sin and selfishness, our common need for redemption, and our common capacity to be graceful signs of the loving God who communicates God's own life and love to us and invites us to become ever more godlike.

Propaganda of whatever type—be it misplaced patriotism or jaded consumerism—by its nature distorts truth, robs human beings of their humanity, and works against authentic human development. The ambivalence of mass media lies, among other places, in their ability to provide us, at the same time, with images of paschal excellence and dehumanizing consumerism. The truth about humanity encompasses elements equally diverse, of course. An option for the poor and the powerless, however, while reminding us that no one's rights are safe or secure when someone's rights are not, on an even deeper level points us in the direction of our own humanity and its nobility. In fact, the poor and the powerless have dignity—we do not bestow it on them by opting on their behalf. Indeed, on the moral level, those who seem most poor and powerless often manifest a sense of value, of goodness, of dignity that is every bit as awesome as Olympian excellence. Our option for them must not be motivated by a demeaning sense of pity but by the respect and care that recognize in all our brothers and sisters the dignity of the children of God. This optic reminds us of the basic ambiguities we have been exploring. Is there power in images that convince us of our desperate need for the very latest? Most decidedly so! Is there truth in that view of humanity? Again—yes. What are the possibilities for mass media, however, in a recognition of the fact that truly creative and life-giving power find their roots in the one in whose image we are all made? This is our most foundational truth—each of us is born to love, to "develop" through often painful processes to a recognition of our need for God and for one another. We are called to recognize the significance of the many competing

---

[8] John Paul II, *Sollicitudo Rei Socialis* no. 38, 654.

goods in our lives according to the ways in which those goods fulfill us authentically, revealing and enfleshing the image of our worth.

I have not tried to resolve the dialogue between moral theology and mass media. I have tried to suggest moral parameters for dealing with these gifts from God so marked by the ambivalence and ambiguity of our lives. Their ongoing contribution to authentic human development will be a function of our lives and our convictions and our choices. Finally, who we are and who we want to be will determine how our creations serve us, represent us, and continue to image forth ourselves and the One whose image is the ground of all truth, power, and goodness.

22

Moral Theology as Communication

Enda McDonagh

Given the obvious limitations of an individualist approach to morality and moral theology with its emphasis on individual fulfillment and neglect of community goals, the move to a more social communication model for morality has philosophical and theological support. Such a move and model must connect with communication and communication models as they seek to uncover social structures and dynamics. In this context moral theology as communication, or at least as a communications theory, is not such an unlikely proposal.

The first temptation in using such a model may be to seize on some of the more sophisticated systems theories associated with communications in a computer mode and offer a complete, almost infinitely subtle but finally determinist model of society, its moral structures and dynamics. A more persistent temptation is to use the model of human language itself as the social system of a living community. Into this system each human being is born and by this system he or she learns to communicate, relate and serve to the point where he or she has freedom within the system to communicate freely out of the self and even to extend creatively the system. The final originality of each one's linguistic communications and their dependence on the shared language, offer many illuminating insights into the originality and communality of their whole lives including their moral dimension.

Language as a communication system, a community and personal possession, allowing for personal originality and bound by community goals, may provide the most fruitful links between communications and morality or moral theology. This essay will be driven back to examine these links to support parts of its own thesis. The restrictions of the language model, where it is allowed to dominate, and the interests and limitations of the author suggest a somewhat different approach. Language parallels will at times be necessary and obvious.

A more comprehensive view of humanity as moral, free, and responsible attends to its inescapable and inseparable, personal, relational, and communitarian dimensions. Persons in relationships in communities counterpoint communities of relationship of persons. Persons only come into existence, survive, develop, and die in relationships in communities. By relationships I mean named face-to-face historical connections between people. A set of these such as a family or a neighborhood might be called a community. At any rate such relationships belong in a series of communities which is eventually world-wide. In terms of inheritance, debts, and resources these communities have histories, are in communication with and (morally) responsible to predecessor communities. A further dimension of their time-laden character is their connection with and responsibility to future communities. The ozone layer crisis is only one powerful reminder of future humanity speaking to, communicating with, and establishing community with the present.

Persons-in-communities and communities-of-persons, to abbreviate for the moment, must retain their biological rootedness. To be true to the given of themselves as cosmic, material, and biological beings persons and communities have to use and respect the food and water, air and heat available to them and, by Christian understanding, entrusted to them as well. The moral responsibility of persons and communities must pay reasoned and responsible attention to the development and distribution of the natural resources of the planet they share. Reason and responsibility require human structures in the organized communities called societies. In some discourse this distinction of community and society requires fuller consideration. And there may be occasions when it will be useful to return to it. At present community and society will be taken as the counterpoint to person, with relationship as a mediating term.

The brief sketch of the human background to moral and theological discussion needs some further moral detailing. Person, relationship, and community are already suggestive of morality; reason and responsibility even more so. However, the vision and the ought of moral discourse require fuller refinement. I say "vision" and "ought" to convey something of both the grand text or design of the human moral enterprise and its small print or particular rules of grammar. The imagery, and such imagery is inescapable in moral discourse, seeks to combine final goal and immediate duty as characteristic of a complete moral life, at least for Christians, before any analysis into warring teleological and deontological dimensions.

The vision and the ought for persons-in-communities and community-of-persons focus on the deeper differentiation of the persons, the increasing development of their personal gifts and resources in increasing solidarity with the community, in fuller communion. This formal description of the thrust of human morality towards deeper differentiation or personalization in fuller communion must be set in the context of biological need, temporal finitude, and human destructiveness before facing translation into more concrete values and norms.[1]

---

[1] A more developed account of all this may be found in my *Social Ethics and the Christian: Towards Freedom in Communion* (Manchester: Manchester University Press, 1978).

1. Community, Communication, and the Kingdom of God

Before attempting fuller theological analysis it may be useful to summarize. Persons in community are persons in communication. This communication operates in a number of different forms of which linguistic communication is only one, if a critical one. Attempts to treat all communication in linguistic terms can be illuminating. It can also be restrictive. It does illuminate the essentials of being born into a community and of the developing in community of the person who shares a common language, appropriates it as her own, and through that common language makes a personal, distinctive contribution to the community and its conversation. The interaction between person and community, their essential interdependence is, as I said earlier, powerfully illustrated by language and linguistic communication.

Other dimensions of communication and community require other models. Communication as building community, as dynamic development of unity of peoples in promotion of common goals, needs language of course, but is not illuminated by an exclusively linguistic mode. The personal self-giving and personal development which communication as both relationship- and community-building may involve may be illustrated linguistically but not finally analyzed. The overall moral dialectic then of deeper personal differentiation and further developing community transcends the usual terms of the linguistic model. Theological interpretation of person-in-community and community-of-persons may center on the central social symbol of Jesus's preaching, the Kingdom or Reign of God. This transforming presence and power of God was announced by Jesus as the fulfillment of the prophetic and messianic promises of a new covenant and a new Israel. The gift of the Kingdom was the gift of a new people and a new world which was first of all to be received and then to be achieved. Jesus's Kingdom ministry and Kingdom teaching in parable and preaching emphasized both this gift and response character and the personal and communal dimensions.

The gift was the Word of God made flesh. God's self-communication to humanity and cosmos had reached the point of ultimate unity in incarnation, in the man Jesus in whom God dwelt. He was called and was Son of God. His presence was also the presence of Abba. Differentiation with intimate unity within God was revealed through God's self-involvement with humanity. Further reflection discerned a three-fold divine differentiation in unity and equality with Abba, the Word, and the Spirit.

The very God whose presence and power was to heal and transform humanity and cosmos with its God-given differentiation (Genesis 1:2) and grace and call to unity, already enjoyed this differentiation in unity. In Johannine terms, the model of our final unity and differentiation is that of Jesus and Abba (see John 14-17). A phenomenology of human morality and moral possibilities in person and community may be interpreted in ways converging with a model of the Jesus event and its communication of God and of God's purpose.

Moral vision and ought in those broad lines cohere with theological vision and ought in New Testament outline. The communion of saints to which all people are called and empowered will ensure their personal fulfillment or final differentiation in ultimate unity. The vine and its branches and the Body of Christ are other New Testament symbols for the flourishing in communion of all, perhaps the best paraphrase of the great Kingdom gift of Shalom.

A theology of receiving and achieving the Kingdom is basically Christian theology of morality in both social and personal idioms. It does, however, like most analyses of morality, religious and secular, ignore the destructive side of moral life. It is true that Christian and sometimes secular moralists go on to take account of the destructive or evil side of the human moral animal but as an extra, however inevitable or inextricable. There is here a close parallel to the difficulty most moral philosophers and theologians have in integrating the personal and social dimensions of morality. The social is necessary, even essential but, it is extra. Destructiveness and evil also come later, in analysis certainly, and for some in experience. The story of the fall in Jewish and Christian theology is one such paradigmatic account of the advent of evil to the fundamentally morally good of humanity. In this context this implies the fundamentally good communication between human beings. In a discussion of morality/moral theology as communication such a paradigm has enormous implications. The analysis of communication is clearly involved, as a good which may be corrupted. The real difficulty here is, as the conventional wisdom has it, simply with the abuse of communication and abuse of the media. Media ethics follows directly from this kind of analysis.

Such analysis, despite all its reputable forebears in philosophy and theology, seems to me to be fundamentally flawed. And this becomes more evident in discussing the relationship between morality and communication or still more in discussing morality in its secular or Christian forms as communication. One of the critical elements of this is the material and more particularly the biological condition of humanity. In a shorthand that will I hope become intelligible the crucial terms are communication or communion and consumption.

2. Consumption and Communion

The dilemma of humanity, tragic or no, is that we are trapped between consumption and communion/communication. As a biological being we have to consume to survive. This makes us a user-destroyer of other cosmic, indeed of other biological, beings. This consumer condition of human beings is at once shared with other biological beings and a threat to them.

One of the obvious obstacles to our friendship with the animals is the fact that we eat them or, if not them, certainly other living organisms such as vegetables. Talking to one's plants and so establishing "community" with them must always operate under the shadow of our consuming human needs. Consumption is at least as intrinsic to the human condition as communication if humanity is to survive. It already sets the terms for the challenge to humanity presented by the needs of consumption and of communion.

This challenge operates at the human as well as the biological level. The ambiguity of all human relationships centers on the dilemma of communing and consuming. The tragic side of the human story rests on a combination of the inevitable and willful mutual devouring to which humans have been prone in their search for human survival and for flourishing in community. In their relationships and communities humans are both consumers and communers. Their needs for the same kinds of food, shelter, security, intimacy, partnerships, jobs, prestige can set them in competition which may be destructive of one or both. Struggles for essential consumable goods readily develop into life and death struggles for people. Human beings are consumed to satisfy the need or greed of other human beings. In the contemporary world the profound disparities in possessions and power show two-thirds of the world suffering hunger, thirst, illness, and oppression while one third displays so many symptoms of overconsumption. The global communications which reveal this to whomever wishes to read and act on it, also provide a basis for action to promote fairness and equality en route to replacing disordered consumption by at least basic communion. The consumption of the poor, their premature deaths, and other privations are directly related to the possessions and powers of the over-consuming or consumerist wealthy. Like the fool in the gospels (Luke 12:17-21) the wealthy are diminished and finally destroyed by their own selfishness. They in turn are victims of consumption.

While all this can and should be recognized for the global evil that it is, the challenge to overcome it can appear impossibly daunting and dispiriting. The very means of communication with their thrust to establishing community are increasingly controlled by a powerful elite, frequently too powerful for national governments, even strong ones and certainly too powerful for the governments of poorer countries or embryonic international organizations. The Churches as communities of believers in the gift and challenge of the Kingdom of God have a particular responsibility to analyze these difficulties and to enter fully into overcoming them on a planet-wide basis.

The consumption-communion tension is not simply global or narrowly social. It enters sharply into our most intimate relationships in marriage and the family, in neighborhood and work place, in religious house and university college. In our personal searches for communion we find ourselves frequently playing a consuming role. If we do not always kill the thing we love, we are inevitably in our very dependent years, in infancy and old age, consumers of care and careers. This can also characterize our more mature years. The possessiveness, power-seeking, jealousy, and paranoia which can afflict any human relationship are drives to consumption of the other which usually end in consuming the self also. Communion may look more attainable on this smaller scale and consumption may look more avoidable, but looks frequently deceive.

3. Jesus: Hope of Communion

Human history bears the unmistakable traces of consumption triumphing over communion in war and in famine, in affluence and in poverty, in national, international, and domestic contexts. For Israel, the hope of a Messiah, of a New Covenant, was a hope of a New Creation in which love of neighbor and love of God would be the real axis of relations between humans themselves and between God and humanity and so transform human relations with cosmos. For Christians these hopes were fulfilled in Jesus. For too many of Jesus's compatriots the fulfillment was incredible, indeed for some blasphemous, in its paradoxical character. That a mere man should claim such intimacy, unity, even identity with God! That, in the Johannine vision, God should be made flesh, destined to consume and with all human flesh to be consumed! That the messiah should be a consumer and in the end consumed by the rejection of his enemies and desertion of his friends! *Consummatum est (tetelestai).* It is finished. Jesus's life is complete. He has in the historical sense been consumed and for us and for our sins—our destructive consumption of others and of ourselves. The human consumption which prevents communion had finally destroyed the man from Nazareth, who preached the Kingdom of ultimate unity, who prayed that we might be one as he and the Father were one (John 17:21).

Had destructive consumption prevailed? Had Israel's and humanity's last best chance perished on Calvary? To appreciate the force of the Christian answers to these questions it is necessary to reflect again on certain events in Jesus's life and on their significance. These events are consumption events. Jesus's feeding of the hungry multitudes and his insistence on feeding the hungry as a test of faith (see Matthew 25:31-46) reveal his authentic sense of human beings as consumers of the earth's goods. This is part of their God-given nature and an essential part of their being human together. Consumption must be a sharing of the earth's goods with the neighbor. Only the fool, in divine perspective, fills his barns and settles for selfish enjoyment (Luke 12:17-21). The rich man in his castle ignoring Lazarus at the gate is revealed as ultimately self-destructive (Luke 16:19-31). In this setting Jesus made God present at the very heart of the human dilemma. God was in Jesus's consuming as a real human being but with the further purpose of reconciling humanity (2 Corinthians 5:18-19), of establishing true community, real communion. In Jesus as consumer, God became human and so as consumer was engaged in the saving, liberating task of drawing consumer humanity into communion with and in the manner of the God of communion, who could not be finally consumed.

4. Jesus's Communion through Consumption

The preparatory teaching and ministry reached their climax in the passion story, its transforming prelude and postlude.

> Now as they were eating, Jesus took bread, and blessed and broke it and gave it to his disciples and said, "Take, eat; this is my body." And he took a cup and when he had given thanks he gave it to them saying, "Drink of it, all of you; for this is my blood of the covenant, which is poured out for many for the forgiveness of sins" (Matthew 26:26-28).

> On the first day of the week, Mary Magdalene and the other Mary went to see the sepulchre...And behold Jesus met them and said, "Hail!" Then Jesus said to them, "Do not be afraid; go and tell my brethren to go to Galilee, and there they will see me" (Matthew 28:1, 9-10).

> That very day, two of them were going to a village named Emmaus.... While they were talking and discussing together, Jesus himself drew near and went with them. But their eyes were kept from recognizing him...And they said to him, "Concerning Jesus of Nazareth...a prophet...and how our chief priests and rulers delivered him up to be condemned to death and crucified. But we had hoped that he was the one to redeem Israel."...And he said to them, "O foolish men, and slow of heart to believe all that the prophets have spoken! Was it not necessary that the Christ should suffer all these things and enter into his glory?" And beginning with Moses and all the prophets, he interpreted to them in all the scriptures the things concerning himself...they constrained him, saying, "Stay with us...the day is now far spent." So he went in to stay with them. When he was at table with them, he took the bread and blessed and broke it, and gave it to them. And their eyes were opened and they recognized him; and he vanished from their sight (Luke 24: 13-31).

The night before he suffered and the first day of the week belong together as anticipation and fulfillment of the triumph of communion not just over consumption but in and through consumption. In Jesus God had entered the consuming world to be consumed as the basis for the most intimate and permanent communion. The sovereign, creator God of Israel had shared the consumer fate of humanity to show the inexhaustibility of divine love and life, the inconsumability in which we might all share. The terrifying bondage of consumption has given way to the possibility of communion for all and with all. Even the final consumption of death has been transcended including death through the consuming others.

The grace of communion through consumption established in Jesus Christ finds its obvious symbolic expression in the Eucharist, as the scripture stories from Thursday evening and Sunday indicate. The intimacy of relationship, the equality in sharing and the inexhaustibility of the resource render this communion truly holy and utterly distinct, in *qadosh* terms, from any merely human and cosmic union.

The grace is gift and empowerment. It is also challenge. Eating and drinking unworthily is now, as it was among the early Christians of Corinth, a continuing temptation and threat (1 Corinthians 11:27-29). The destruction of communion by unworthy consumption summarizes contemporary human failure to accept God's offer in the least ones (Matthew 25:31-46). And the invitation to communion, to the marriage feast of Jesus's parable, requires a freedom from personal, selfish preoccupations and entry into the world of the others. Along this way lies authentic communication or community making. Only so do persons begin to achieve their full differentiation and communities their deeper unity.

5. Our Communicating World

In the intensely communicating world in which we live, the possibilities for destructive consumption and liberating communion are enormous. These possibilities are now planetwide with other spatial boundaries diminishing. Domestic communication has as already mentioned the same essential difficulties as the planetary. How people consume one another is part of everyday family experience. Yet communion in one flesh is a reality for many loving couples and reaches out to include children in genuine communion also. Sexual and family morality might be at once more realistic and inspiring if it were developed on a communications model, taking account of both consumption and communion and their Christian meaning and power.

The larger canvas of social morality could be depicted in the same broad strokes with considerable fresh insight. In that picture the communications media could find their own place as part of a wider communication with both moral and Christian dimensions. Moral theology as communication could in this fashion be elaborated in ways that were true to human communication, genuinely moral, and finally Christian. The way could be opened for an understanding of and engagement with the achievement of communion through inevitable but properly human consumption. Eucharist becomes the central symbol as consumption for holy communion with neighbor and God.

Index

Abbott, W. 53
ABC 131, 140, 257
abortion 103, 273
Abuladze, T. 244
Adams, W. 148
Adoni, H. 182
Adorno, T. 257
advertising 5, 22, 23, 29, 31, 43-45, 80, 104, 121, 124-127, 129, 138, 141, 156, 158, 172, 237, 256, 278
aesthetics 32, 129, 218, 220, 227
Africa 139, 197, 252
aggression 85, 91, 94, 95, 133, 151
AIDS 238
Alcala, M. 183
alcoholism 256
aletheia 77
Alphonsus 181
Altheide, D. 138
Amadeus 32
Ambrosiaster 54
Ancilli, E. 189
Anderson, M. 245
Andolsen, B. 131
androgyny 132, 160
Andy Griffith Show 110
Ang, I. 108
Angelou, M. 134
Anselm 189
anthropology 58, 183, 192, 251
anti-Semitism 211, 249-251, 254, 256, 257

Appelo, T. 132
Aquinas, T. 62, 73, 94, 194
architecture 26, 128
Aristotle 27, 75, 189
Arlen, M. 153
Asia 37, 197
Asner, E. 255
Aspitarte, E. Lopez 183
Athens 24, 27
audience 6, 19, 28, 31, 43, 44, 46, 49-51, 55, 63, 80, 84, 125, 129, 135-138, 140, 143, 147, 150-152, 154, 159-161, 167, 172, 198, 199, 211, 215, 239, 242, 247, 248, 251, 256
audiovisuals 210, 212, 213, 215, 217-221, 223-225, 227-229, 232, 233
Auer, A. 56, 165, 174
Ayfre, A. 243

Babin, P. 212, 219
Bacon, F. 57
Bagdikian, B. 23, 45, 46
Baird, Z. 131
Baker, R. 150
Balicki, J. 105, 162
Ball, S. 150
Balthasar, H. U. von 63
Bandura, A. 92, 93, 154, 201, 202
Barnett, I. 134
Barthes, R. 120, 122

Bastianel, S. 181
Baum, G. 112
Baur, K. 133, 134
BBC 242, 247
Bea, A. 186
Becker, S. 47
behavior 3, 29, 50, 134, 141, 149, 151, 153, 154, 158, 163, 172, 173, 181, 186, 190, 191, 194, 202, 205, 209, 212, 220, 221, 225-227
Bellah, R. 128, 151, 264, 265
Benet, J. 157
Bennett, W. 148, 151
Berg, C. 158
Berger, C. 48, 182
Berger, J. 121
Bergman, I. 246
Bettelheim, B. 95
Biffi, F. 181
bioethics 103
Bird, M. 243
Bleistein, R. 56
Boorstin, D. 151, 153
Bosch, H. 31
Boventer, H. 172, 174
Bremer, A. 30
Bresson, A. 246
Britain 125
Bro, B. 221
broadcasting 126, 140, 148, 156, 158, 166, 167, 170, 182, 242
Brokaw, T. 20
Bronowski, J. 27
Bronski Beat 227
Brooks, P. 247, 248
Brothers Karamazov 61
Bucceroni, G. 181
Bush, G. 19, 44, 137
Butler, S. 251

Cagney and Lacey 256
Calvary 286
Camacho, I. 183
campaign, presidential 5, 19, 28, 35, 39, 41, 153
Campbell, J. 127-129
Cantor, M. 158

capitalism 7, 47, 99, 110, 113, 141, 144
Capo, J. 105, 146, 152, 153
Captian Kangaroo 129
Carey, J. 147, 215
Carlen, C. 171
Castro, J. 131
catechists 197, 204
Cathcart, R. 26
CBS 21, 140, 153
celibacy 194
Chaffee, S. 48, 149, 182
Chakrapani, S. 148
Challenger 120
Chariots of Fire 247
chastity 191, 194
Chave, A. 12
Chavez, D. 158
Cherlin, A. 156
Chernobyl 105, 162-171, 177
Chiavacci, E. 179
China 34
Choices of the Heart 230
Chomsky, N. 46, 141
Christ 11, 27, 54, 58, 61-63, 152, 201, 274, 284, 287, 288
Christianity 3, 128, 277
Christians, C. 49, 51
Christic Institute 46
Church 11, 12, 14, 22, 26, 54, 58, 63, 64, 66, 67, 98, 103, 105, 121, 124, 129, 138, 155, 166, 188-190, 197-205, 209, 217, 220, 232, 242, 244, 247, 250, 251, 265
Cicero 189
cinema (see also film) 121, 212, 213, 221, 243
Clark, K. 22
Coelho, G. 154
Cohen, A. 182
Coleman, J. 203
Collingwood, R. G. 11
comedies, situation 94, 104, 108-110
commercialism 250, 277
commercials 14, 15, 17, 20, 22, 24, 31, 119, 124-127, 150, 158, 237

communio 59-65, 67, 174
Communio et Progressio 52, 55, 61-
  63, 67, 188, 201
communism 19, 141
Comstock, G. 48, 149, 154
conflict 50, 65, 92, 104, 105, 128,
  148, 151, 158, 160, 178-183,
  185, 187, 188, 191, 193, 195,
  196, 219, 238, 257, 277
Congar, Y. 54
conscience 26, 65-67, 82, 86, 94,
  131, 174, 178, 180, 181, 187,
  188, 194-196, 236, 243, 249
Constitution, U.S. 43, 44
consumerism 22, 31, 104, 114, 125,
  126, 128, 154-156, 250, 262,
  279
consumption 22, 31, 60, 64, 65,
  104, 114, 123, 124, 150, 156,
  158, 160, 185, 238, 263, 284-
  288
Cooley, C. H. 26
Cooper, D. 183
Cooper, T. 187
Cosby, Bill 21, 29
Cosby Show 21, 29, 30, 110, 111,
  256
Coverdale, L. 122
Cronkite, W. 20
Crooks, R. 133, 134
Czitrom, D. 26

Daele, W. 187
Dahlgren, P. 148
Dalfert, I. 59
Dallas 17, 108, 151, 156
Daly, L. 104, 107, 116
Daniel Deronda 253, 254
Daniels, A. 157
Davis, A. 134
Davis, K. 156
Deming, C. 47, 214
Demmer, K. 185, 192
democracy 26, 34-37, 40-42, 46, 47
DeNiro, R. 29
Depression, great 38, 40
Descartes 72, 73
development, moral 85-88

Dewey, J. 5, 26, 36-41
diakonia 63
dialogue 188-191, 268-270, 274,
  280
Dibb, M. 121
Diener, E. 182
Dignitatis Humanae 189
Dijkman, J. 216
discernment of spirits 64-67
discourse 5, 6, 31, 39, 41, 60, 61,
  66, 73, 79, 80, 83, 84, 103,
  119, 200, 201, 203, 205, 213,
  214, 217, 219, 252, 277, 282
disinformation 173
Dittmar, P. 165
docudrama 27, 230, 232
documentaries 27, 130, 219, 229,
  232, 258
Donaldson, S. 20
Donovan, J. 230-232
Dostoevsky, F. 61
Douglas, A. 142
Drewermann, E. 58
Dreyer, C. 246
Dufrenne, M. 243
Durbin, P. 73
Dynasty 151

Ecclesiam Suam 189
ecclesiology 63, 64
education 37, 38, 41, 44, 51, 55, 57,
  74, 76, 80, 92, 93, 99, 103,
  107, 109, 112, 117, 130, 137,
  145-147, 149, 150, 152, 153,
  156, 176, 177, 194, 197, 202,
  209, 210, 224, 225, 234, 236,
  237, 239, 241, 246, 274
Eillensky, H. 55
El Salvador 230-232
elections 131, 136, 177
Eley, D. 104, 116, 237
Eliade, M. 243
Eliot, G. (see also Lewes, M.) 253,
  254
Ellul, J. 152
Emde, R. 87
Enderle, G. 184
Enlightenment 57, 264-268, 271

entertainment 15-18, 21, 50, 55, 57, 58, 60, 80, 82, 91, 98, 104, 116, 118, 120, 121, 124-126, 130, 136, 138, 144, 150, 158, 159, 215, 247
epikeia 65
epistemology 74, 76, 93, 178
Erikson, E. 78
Esslin, M. 217
ethics 3, 31, 49, 64, 65, 80, 96, 110, 116, 120, 121, 128, 131, 152, 164, 165, 171, 173-175, 179, 187, 188, 190, 193, 194, 198, 200, 214, 218, 250, 251, 253, 282, 284
ethnocentrism 47, 158, 179
existentialism 179

fantasy 21, 27, 74, 75, 87, 88, 90, 96, 127, 187, 190, 218, 244
FAZ 167
Felton, G. 125, 126
feminism 39, 131, 137, 156, 158, 216, 252
Ferrante, C. 158
film (see also cinema) 210, 211, 222, 225-227, 230-232, 242-247, 256, 257
Fiske, J. 120, 147
Fleck, F. 175
Fleischer, H. 220
Foley, J. 179, 195
Folger, J. 182
Fore, W. 157, 242
Forschner, M. 181
Fox, C. 121
Fox, R. 124
Freud, S. 86
Fuček, I. 105, 178, 182, 192
Fuchs, J. 239, 240
Fujita, P. 158

Gadamer, H.-G. 116
Galbraith, J. K. 46
Galileo 189
Gallup organization 20, 21
Gannett 140

Gans, H. 47, 148
Garanzini, M. 6, 85
Gassner, J. 22
GAU 167
Gaudium et Spes 53, 54, 61, 189, 192, 193
gender 29, 104, 105, 121, 130-136, 138-145, 147, 155, 158, 161, 238, 250
gender justice 105, 130, 132
gender socialization 134
genetics 187
Gerbner, G. 153
Gerhart, M. 254
Ghandi 96
Gilgamesh 128
Gilligan, C. 75, 94, 236
Ginsburg, H. 75, 76, 235
Giovanni, N. 134
Gitlin, T. 148, 255-257
Glasnost 165, 244
Glueck, G. 13
Goethals, G. 4, 11, 27, 53, 148, 154, 269
Goethe, J. 57
Goldman, K. 131
Gorbachev, M. 165
Goslin, D. 93
Grand Inquisitor 61
Grant, M. 211, 242
Greeley, A. 203
Green Acres 110
Green, P. 141
Greshake, G. 59, 62
Gross, L. 153
Guatemala 46
Gudorf, C. 104, 105, 130, 158, 160
Gumpert, G. 26
Guth, R. 65

Habermas, J. 12, 66
Hackford, T. 225
Hahn, J. 222
Haight, G. 253
Hall, A. 29
Hall, P. 174
Hamer, F. 134
Hampshire, S. 178, 181, 182

Hargrove, B. 150, 161
Harrison, K. 158
Hartley, J. 147
Hasler, A. 189
Haynes, A. 158
hegemony 31, 51
Heidegger, M. 56
Heinrichs, J. 189
Henley, N. 133
Herman, E. 141
hermeneutics 178, 191, 193, 218
Herzl, T. 254
Hess, T. 12
Himmelstein, H. 108-110
Hinkley, J. 29
Hirsch, P. 215
Hitler, A. 244
Hoeffe, O. 181, 185
Hoekstra, H. 198, 210, 212, 222, 268
Hollis, R. 121
Hollywood 150, 247
Holocaust 256
homosexuality 103, 228
Honecker, M. 187
Honeymooners, The 110
Hoover, S. 242
Hopper, R. 200
Horsfield, P. 242
Hübner, K. 58
Hungary 34
Hunold, G. 57
Hurley, N. 242, 243
Hurth 181
Huter, A. 54

ideology 31, 34, 35, 56, 112, 160, 186, 190, 214, 215
Idigoras, J. 183
imagination 3-7, 27, 33, 44, 58, 67, 73, 74, 95-97, 103, 104, 106-108, 115, 121, 123, 126-129, 150-153, 197, 202-204, 210, 211, 215, 218, 233, 237, 240, 241, 243, 253, 261, 262, 264, 271, 272
injustice 134, 143, 166, 223, 251, 258

Innis, H. A. 26
Innuit 117
Innuks 117
Iran 21, 44, 46
Iran-Contra scandal 21, 44, 46
Irenee de Lyon 58

Jackson, Jesse 28
Jenkins, C. 46
Jennings, P. 20
John Paul II, Pope 60, 104, 108, 112-115, 181, 197, 198, 262, 274
Johnson, D. 120
Jonas, H. 165, 187
journalism 37, 38, 46, 138, 151, 170, 171
journalists 5, 37, 38, 152, 167, 171, 174, 175
Jungel, E. 59
justice 31, 62, 93, 94, 105, 113, 128, 130, 132, 143, 146, 186, 188, 191, 197, 198, 211, 223, 229, 232, 238, 250, 264, 265
Justin 189

Kagan, J. 87
Kandinsky, W. 12
Kant, I. 57, 79, 266-268
Katzman, N. 149
Keane, P. 96
Kegan, R. 75, 94, 96
Kellen, K. 152
Kelly, J. 203
Kennedy, John 17, 32
Kennedy, W. 150, 153
Kenny, A. 73
Kern, W. 53
King, M. L. 96, 258
Kingdom of Heaven 54, 61, 63, 66, 194, 211, 235, 240, 263, 283-286
Kingsley, S. 158
Klaus, E. 170
Klein, J. 86
Knickerbocker, B. 46
Kohlberg, L. 78, 93, 94, 225, 236

Koppel, T. 31
Kouloumdjian, M. 212, 219
Kuchenbuch, T. 218
Kuhmerker, L. 92
Kuhn, D. 75

Laborem Exercens 112-114
Langer, S. 124
Lans, J. van der 221
Lasch, C. 153, 264
Lasswell, H. 146
Latourelle, R. 189
Lazarsfeld, P. 28
Lears, T. 124
Leavis, F. 253, 254
Leibniz 268
leisure 117-122
Leonard, J. 131
Levitown 38
Lewes, M. 211, 253, 254
liberation 158, 159, 179, 181, 216
Lickona, T. 80
Liebert, R. 153
Linsky, M. 21
Linz, G. 167
Lippmann, W. 5, 26, 36-41, 45
Littlejohn, S. 44, 198
liturgy 217, 234
Lodziak, C. 119
Loevinger, J. 236
Lonergan, B. 122
Louth, A. 73, 77
Luhmann, N. 164
Lumen Gentium 63
lying 54, 175
Lynch, W. 27, 203

MacIntyre, A. 264, 265
MacNeil/Lehrer News Hour 18
Madsen, R. 128
magazines 22, 23, 25, 36, 45, 124,
    126, 136, 140, 145, 156, 167,
    236
Maletzke, G. 163
Manspeak 133
marriage 190, 191, 194, 285, 288
Marx, B. 189

Marx, K. 31
Marxism 165, 179, 195
Masada 257
May, J. 243, 247
McCarthy, J. 35
McCarthy, T. 201
McCombs, M. 48, 149
McDonagh, E. 59, 263, 281
McLaughlin, C. 46, 47
McLuhan, H. M. 26
Mead, G. H. 200, 201
Merkelbach, B. 181
Merton, R. 28
Metromedia 140
Meyrowitz, J. 26, 151, 163
Middlemarch 253
Mieth, D. 181, 193, 195
Miller, R. 120
Miranda Prorsus 171, 274
Mission, The 211, 244, 247
Mitchell, E. 131
Mittelstrass, J. 184
Molinari, F. 185
Molinaro, A. 189
Moltmann, J. 189
Mondrian, P. 12
Moore, S. 147
morality 12, 47, 79, 82, 84, 90, 94,
    95, 103, 104, 110, 124, 128,
    164, 177, 178, 179, 181-183,
    186, 188, 191, 198, 212, 213,
    220, 221, 223-227, 229, 232,
    233, 239, 250, 263, 265, 266,
    276, 281-284, 288
Morris, C. 200
Morris, W. 243
Moyers, W. 128, 247
Mudd, R. 18
Murphy, J. M. 75
Murray, J. C. 41, 103
Mussolini 244
Muzak 149
Myerhoff, B. 147

narcissism 86, 153, 238
narrative 7, 19, 24, 29, 64, 97, 99,
    100, 106, 118, 119, 149, 180,

210, 212-214, 216-222, 229, 247
Nazi 257
NBC 44, 140
Newcomb, H. 149, 215
Newman, Barnett 12
Niebuhr, H. 249, 250, 267, 271, 272
Niehbur, R. 103
Noelle-Neumann, E. 48, 162
Noldin, H. 181
Novak, M. 149
NPR (National Public Radio) 138

O'Neill, M. 251
Officer and a Gentleman, An 225, 228
Olympics 31, 124, 131, 160, 238, 262, 277, 278
Opper, S. 75, 76, 235
Oser, F. 236
Ozzie and Harriet 30, 109

parables 65, 243, 245
Parker, E. 150
Parks, R. 134
Parthenon 23, 24
Pascal, B. 53
Patrick, A. 211, 249, 253, 270
PBS (Public Broadcasting Service) 21, 77, 247
peace 133, 166, 195, 197, 198, 229, 232, 241
Pelagianism 250
Perry, W. 236, 237
Peru 139, 148
Peters, J. 222
Philibert, P. 6, 26, 30, 31, 71, 267, 268
Phillips, J. 74, 75
Piaget, J. 6, 74-79, 82, 84, 93, 234-236
Pickering, S. 251
Plato 24, 77
Plude, F. 187
Poecke, L. van 219
Poland 34
Pollock, J. 13, 66, 262, 263, 273

pornography 179, 180, 183-191, 194-196
Pornography and Violence 179, 180, 183-196
Porter, W. E. 43
Postman, N. 60, 121, 213, 242
Price, V. 48
privacy 150, 185, 186
privatization 144, 161
Progressive party 40
Prokop, D. 55
Prümmer, D. 181
psychology 6, 30, 78, 85, 173, 190, 200, 234
Putnam, D. 245, 247
Putnam, L. 182

Quayle, D. 44
Quinn-Judge, S. 244

racism 39, 56, 211, 234, 235, 249-252, 254, 256, 257
radio 21, 22, 25, 26, 52, 53, 116, 124, 125, 136-138, 140, 144, 145, 149, 168, 170, 234, 242, 245, 247, 251
Rahner, H. 58
Rahner, K. 192, 239, 240
Rakow, L. 155
Rather, D. 20
Reagan, R. 17-19, 21, 29, 44, 137
Real, M. 5, 25, 48, 53, 67, 83, 148, 237, 238, 270
Real McCoys, The 109
redemption 6, 54, 57, 61-63, 124, 263, 272, 275, 279
relativism 31, 160, 214, 266, 268
religion 5, 12, 14-17, 19, 22, 27, 89, 136, 137, 141, 144, 146, 147, 149, 185, 190, 194, 195, 213, 218, 243, 247, 250, 252, 253
Renaissance 121, 126
Repentance 211, 244
Reuver, G. de 222
Revers, W. 56
rhetoric 19, 40, 41, 152, 198, 199, 216, 278

Ricoeur, P. 218
rights 93, 103, 113, 124, 128, 139,
  192, 193, 195, 209, 250, 251,
  276, 279
Rilke, R. 116
RKO 140
Robb, C. 131
Roberts, D. 48, 149
Roberts, J. 156
Robinson, M. 151, 153
Roegele, O. 162, 172
Rogers, F. 129
Roloff, M. 182
Romero, O. 231, 232, 258
Roots 73, 86, 255, 256
Rosenberg, B. 28
Rosenberg, H. 13
Rossi, P. 66, 185, 262, 264
Rothko, M. 12
Rowland, W. 179
Rubin, A. 50
Rubin, B. 44
Rühl, M. 175
Rust, H. 174

Sagan, C. 27
Salkind, N. 235
salvation 12-14, 58, 66, 124
Sansoni, G. 185
Sarnoff, C. 87
satellites 26, 50, 62, 119, 166
Sauter, G. 189
Sawyer, D. 20
Sayers, D. 251
Schabl, H. 184
Schaef, A. 142
Schechter, S. 254
Schiller, H. 30, 162
Schnabel, J. 13
Schoeph, A. 189
Schramm, W. 43, 146
Schropp, M. 148, 151
Schultz, H. 174
Schultze, Q. 242, 247
Schulz, W. 162
Schwartz, S. 218
Schwartz, T. 149
Schwedt, H. 166

Scorcese, M. 29
semantics 73
Sesame Street 25, 153
sex 60, 82, 91, 95, 98, 99, 107, 126,
  127, 131-137, 139, 156, 158,
  191, 215, 256
sexism 114, 133, 155, 158, 160,
  211, 216, 249-251, 253, 254,
  255, 274
Shanks, T. 5, 43, 67, 237, 239, 269
Shaw, D. 48
Sheehan, M. 153
Showalter, E. 252
Silverstone, R. 219
Simpsons, The 139
Small Town Boy 227, 228
Smith, H. 134
Smith, N. 267
Snow, R. 138, 219
soap opera 120
socialism 113
socialization 79, 93, 130, 132, 134,
  135, 148, 154, 155
Sojourner Truth 134
solidarity 66, 82, 113, 193, 222-
  224, 262, 274-278, 282
Sölle, D. 104, 108, 112-115, 215,
  223
Sollicitudo Rei Socialis 60, 181,
  262, 274, 276, 279
Soukup, P. 52, 105, 197
Spielberg, S. 237
Spigel, L. 155, 156
Stalin 244
Steenland, S. 158
Sterling, C. 140
Stevens, W. 96
Stoeckle, B. 181
storytelling 220
Stowe, H. 211, 252-254
Strachey, J. 86
structuralism 29, 30, 237
Sullivan, W. 5, 26, 34, 83, 128, 265
Super Bowl 14, 18, 31, 160
Swidler, A. 128
Szold, H. 254

Taft 140

Tanner, J. 235
Tarkovsky, A. 246
Taxi 110
Taylor, C. 264
Teichert, W. 167-170
telephone 145, 155, 245
television 4, 14, 15, 17, 18-23, 25-
    28, 30-32, 35, 38, 45, 48, 50,
    52, 53, 56, 58, 64, 71, 80-85,
    90-92, 94, 95, 97-100, 104,
    107, 108, 114, 115, 116, 118-
    121, 123-127, 129-132, 135-
    141, 144, 145, 147-154, 156-
    158, 161, 167, 168, 170, 179,
    182, 187, 203, 204, 211-213,
    215-222, 225, 230, 234, 242,
    243, 245-248, 251, 254-258,
    269, 278
Teresa, Mother 96
terrorism 144
TeSelle, S. 243, 245
Thayer, L. 213
Thom, B. 133
Thomas, S. 22
Thorburn, D. 149
Thyen, E. 167, 170
Tichenorr, P. 182
Tillmans, W. 222
Timm, H. 104, 123
Timm, J. 104, 123
Tipton, S. 128
Tompert, H. 174
Tompkins, J. 252
Toqueville, A. de 128
tradition 5, 6, 43, 54, 64, 65, 73, 77,
    83, 96, 99, 106, 131, 148, 201-
    205, 212, 217, 226, 243, 251,
    253
Traube, K. 167
Trilling, L. 254
Tuchman, G. 148, 157, 159
Turiel, E. 94

Ukraine 163
Uncle Tom's Cabin 252-254
Underwood, D. 46
United Nations 137, 174
USSR 35

Valsecchi, A. 185
values 5, 11, 13-17, 23, 24, 28, 31,
    32, 40, 44, 46, 47, 50, 53, 54,
    60, 63, 66, 74, 79, 81-84, 86,
    98-100, 104, 105, 109-111,
    124, 129, 132, 142, 146-152,
    154, 155, 157-161, 169, 172,
    175, 176, 179, 183, 185, 186,
    191, 194, 195, 209, 214, 216,
    218-227, 229, 232, 235-240,
    249, 273, 278, 282
Verbeek, M. 198, 210, 212, 268
Vidal, M. 183
violence 3, 27, 28, 85, 91, 98-100,
    133, 144, 150, 153, 158, 179,
    180, 182, 183, 185-191, 194-
    196, 209, 215, 234, 245, 278
Virt, G. 6, 52, 65
Voegelin, E. 24

Wagner, H. 55
Wallace, G. 30
Wallace, M. 20
Warren, M. 107, 108, 112, 150, 154
Weaver, P. 153
White, D. M. 28
White, R. 160, 161, 187, 189, 215
Whittemore, L. 158
Wiesel, E. 256
Wilke, J. 162
Willems, E. 83, 210, 234
Williams, F. 163
Williams, J. 140
Wilson, B. 14, 15
Wilson, G. 205
Wilson, J. 15-17, 131
Windahl, S. 50
Winnicott, D. 87, 90, 96
Womanspeak 133
Wood, Kimba 131
Woody, L. 182
work 107-115
Wosnessenski, A. 165
Wunden, W. 105, 162, 174

Youniss, J. 79
Yu, A. 253

Zaretsky, E. 144
ZDF 167
Zeitgeist 57
Zionism 253, 254
Zogin, R. 21
Zorro 32

About the Authors

Janusz Balicki is a priest of the Diocese of Gdansk in Poland. Since the change in government, he has added to his pastoral responsibilities oversight for and work in church radio and broadcasting.

James A. Capo directs the Public Communications Graduate Program and serves as the Associate Director of The Donald McGannon Communication Research Center at Fordham University. Former chair of Fordham's Communications Department, he holds a doctorate in Ethics and Society from the University of Chicago. His analyses of media and values have been published in *The Catholic Encyclopedia, Media Development, Critical Studies in Mass Communication, Journalism Quarterly, Journal of Communication Inquiry,* and *Religious Education.* Capo also serves as a telecommunications activist consultant and currently convenes the McGannon Center's public interest and media professionals conference panel. He directs the Center's research stipend research awards programs.

Lois K. Daly is Associate Professor of Religious Studies and Director of the Reinhold Niebuhr Institiue of Religion and Culture at Siena College in Loudonville, New York. She tries to use videos, especially recent commercial television programs, in as many of her theology and ethics courses as she can.

David Eley, S.J., is an Associate Professor in the Department of Communication Studies at Concordia University, Montréal, Quebec, Canada. He is also the assistant director of The Loyola Peace Institute and the chair of the publishing committee of *Compass* magazine.

Ivan Fucek, S.J., is Professor of Moral Theology at the Pontifical Gregorian University, Rome; former member of the International Theological Commission; present member of the Societas Ethica: Europäishe Forschungsgesellschaft für Ethik, member of the Comitato Direttivo del Centro di Bioetica (Università Cattolica del Sacro Cuore, Rome), member of the association Scienziati e Tecnologi per l'Ethca dello Sviluppo (STES). He contributes frequently to journals, dictionaries, and other professional publications, in various languages. Of his 12 published books, his most recent are *Il peccato oggi* (1991) and *La sessualità al servizio dell'amore* (1993).

Michael J. Garanzini, S.J., serves as Acting Academic Vice President and Professor of Counseling Education at Saint Louis University. Holding a Ph.D. in Psychology and Religion from the Graduate Theological Union and the University of California at Berkeley, he has taught at the University of San Francisco, the Gregorian University, and Saint Louis University. In addition to articles on moral development and child therapy, he has published *The Attachment Cycle* and has *Child Centered Schools: An Educator's Guide to Family Dynamics* currently in press.

Gregor T. Goethals, Professor of Art History at the Rhode Island School of Design and a free-lance designer, received an interdepartmental Ph.D. from Harvard University in Art History and Philosophy of Religion. She wrote *The TV Ritual: Worship at the Video Altar* (1981) and *The Electronic Golden Calf: Images, Religion and the Making of Meaning* (1990). Besides various articles and guest lectures, her designs have appeared through a variety of media over the last thirty years in all parts of North America.

Myrna Reid Grant is Associate Professor of Graduate Communications at Wheaton College. She has worked professionally as a writer in radio, television, film, and print and holds a Ph.D. in Radio/TV/Film from Northwestern University. She is currently completing a book on religious television programs and producers in Britain and is the author of 12 trade books as well as scholarly journal articles. She is a published poet and lectures internationally on mass media and writing.

Christine E. Gudorf, Associate Professor of Religious Studies at Florida International University, received her Ph.D. from Columbia University. Her most recent books are *Victimization: Examining Christian Com-*

plicity (1992) and *Reconstructing Christian Sexual Ethics* (1994). She has published other books and numerous articles on Latin American liberation theologies, feminist ethics, Catholic social teaching and controverted questions in the Catholic Church.

Born in the north of Holland in 1932, **Henk Hoekstra** is a Carmelite priest. He studied philosophy and theology in Holland and communication sciences at the Catholic University of Louvain (Belgium). Now a member of the Catholic Theological Faculty of Amsterdam teaching mass media and group dynamics, he has served as a member of the Study and Research Department of the KRO (Catholic Broadcasing in Holland) and as senior staff of the KMC (Catholic Media Center, Holland). He is president of OCIC (Organisation Catholique Internationale du Cinema et Audiovisuel), member of the Pontifical Council for Social Communications in Rome, and president of CAMECO (Catholic Media Council). He teaches and conducts training courses at several Universities and Institutions around the world. He is the co-author of *Media and Religious Communication, The Media Dialogue about Film and Television*, and many articles about media education.

Enda McDonagh is Professor of Moral Theology at St. Patrick's College in Maynooth, Ireland. His books include *Invitation and Response* (1972), *Doing the Truth: The Quest for Moral Theology* (1979), *The Making of Disciples: Tasks of Moral Theology* (1982) and *Between Chaos and New Creation: Doing Theology at the Fringe* (1986). Christian social ethics, biomedical ethics, liberation theology, and pneumatology and anthropology have been topics of his various other scholarly articles.

Anne E. Patrick, S.N.J.M., is Professor of Religion at Carleton College in Northfield, Minnesota. A recent President of the Catholic Theological Society of America, she earned an M.A. in English from the University of Maryland and a Ph.D. in Religion and Literature from the University of Chicago. She has also served as a Director of the Society of Christian Ethics and an editor for the Religious Book Club. She is now completing the volume *Liberating Conscience: Feminist Explorations in Catholic Moral Theology* for Crossroad Publishing Company.

Paul J. Philibert, O.P., is Director of the Institute for Church Life of the University of Notre Dame. He was recently provincial superior of the Order of Preachers in the southern United States and before that president and professor of Christian Ethics at the Dominican School of Philosophy and Theology in Berkeley, California.

James Pollock, S.J., (†1990) was Associate Professor of Theology at St. Louis University. His S.T.D. in moral theology was granted by the Gregorian University in Rome. He was Chair of the Board of Advisors of *Theology Digest* and the author of articles in such journals as *Milltown Studies* and *Chicago Studies*.

Michael Real is Professor of Telecommunications and Film at San Diego State University. He is the author of *Mass-Mediated Culture, Super-Media: A Cultural Studies Approach*, and many other books and articles. He holds a Ph.D. in Communication from the University of Illinois, has directed a variety of local, national, and international research projects, and has produced television programming on current issues and for underserved populations. He lives with his wife and daughter in Del Mar, California. The focus of his writing concerns media, culture, and social relationship.

Philip Rossi, S.J., Professor of Theology at Marquette University, Milwaukee, Wisconsin, and editor of *Philosophy & Theology: Marquette University Quarterly*, holds a Ph.D. in philosophy from the University of Texas at Austin. He is the auhtor of *Together Toward Hope: A Journey to Moral Theology* (1983) and co-editor of *Kant's Philosophy of Religion Reconsidered* (1991). He has published articles on the role of imagination in moral life, the moral and religious philosophy of Immanuel Kant, and is currently working on a monograph on the role of religion in Kant's philosophy of history and culture.

Thomas E. Shanks, S.J., is currently associate dean of the College of Arts & Sciences and Director of the Center for Applied Ethics at Santa Clara University. The founding chair of the University's Communication Department, he received his Ph.D. in communication from Stanford University with a special focus on audience analysis and media effects.

Paul A. Soukup, S.J., an associate professor in the Communication Department of Santa Clara University, has explored ways of integrating theology and communication study since 1982. He is a research associate of the Jesuit-sponsored Centre for the Study of Communication and Culture in St. Louis and has worked with the World Association for Christian Communication (London) and the Communication Committee of the U.S. Catholic Conference. He is the author of *Theology and Communication: An Introduction and Review of the Literature* (London: WACC, 1983) and *Christian Communication: An Annotated Bibliography* (Westport, CT: Greenwood Press, 1989) as well as a number of articles on the topic. More recently he has edited several books, including (with Thomas J. Farrell) *Communication and Lonergan* (Sheed & Ward, 1993).

William M. Sullivan is Professor of Philosophy at La Salle University. He holds a Ph.D. in Philosophy from Fordham University and has published in the areas of political and social philosophy and the philosophy of the social sciences. Sullivan is the author of *Reconstructing Public Philosophy* (1982) and co-author of *Habits of the Heart* (1985) and *The Good Society* (1991) as well as author of the forthcoming *A Question of Integrity: The Crisis and Promise of Professionalism in America* (1994).

Joan S. Timm graduated from Wellesley College and holds an Ed.D. from Harvard University where Lawrence Kohlberg was her dissertation adviser. She currently serves as Associate Professor at the University of Wisconsin Oshkosh. With Henry Timm she is the author of *Athena's Minor: Moral Reasoning in Poetry, Short Story, and Drama.*

Henry C. Timm graduated from Hamline University and holds a Master's degree from the University of Minnesota. As a playwright, he has written over 50 plays and has adapted extensively for theater productions. He is currently a free-lance writer.

Dr. Marjeet Verbeek studied pastoral theology and mass communication (film and television) in Amsterdam, the Netherlands. Since 1986 she has worked in media education, specifically addressing the question of how to intergrate the audiovisual media into religious education and spiritual guidance. Her main activities in this area include training theology students, catechists, and lay people on the subject; lecturing; writing journal articles; and writing handbooks for using specific film and television programs in teaching. From 1986 to 1992 she worked at the Catholic Media Center in Amstermdam; since 1992 she has continued her teaching and writing on a free-lance basis.

Ordained in 1965, **Günther Virt** holds a doctorate in theology from the University of Vienna. He serves as chaplain in various parishes in Vienna and as Assistant Professor at the Institute of Moral Theology at the University of Vienna. In addition, he earned his post-doctoral lecturing qualification at the University of Tübingen, Germany in 1981 and has held the position of professor of Moral Theology in Padeborn, Germany (1981-1982) and in Salzburg, Austria (1983-1986). Since 1986 the director of the Institute for Moral Theology, he has recently been appointed to chair the Institute of Medical Ethics at the University of Vienna.

Elizabeth Willems, S.S.N.D., a native of Cologne, MN, is a professor of moral theology at Notre Dame Seminary in New Orleans, LA. Her doctoral degree from Marquette University is in moral theology and psychology. Besides teaching courses in principles of moral theology, sexual ethics, and social ethics, Sr. Willems has been a speaker and author on interdisciplinary topics.

Wolfgang Wunden, who holds a doctorate of theology, has worked at Süddeutscher Rundfunk in Stuttgart, Germany, since 1973. He currently serves as head of the Radio Department for planning and coordinating radio programs; in addition he has served as assistant to the Director General, as producer of educational radio programs, and as assistant to the head of the radio department. Some of his publications include *Das Recht des Intim* (1975), *Medienpädagogik—Führerschein fürs Ferhsehen?* (1984, 2nd ed.), *Medien zwischen Markt und Moral* (edited, 1989), and *Öffentlichkeit und Kommunikationskultur* (edited, to appear in 1994).

"*Communication, Culture & Theology*" is a series jointly sponsored by The Centre for the Study of Communication and Culture, St. Louis University, St. Louis, Missouri and The Center for Interdisciplinary Study of Communication, The Gregorian University, Rome, Italy. General Editor for the series is Robert A. White, S.J., of the Gregorian University Centre.

The present book is the fruit of the international "Cavalletti" Conference on Theology and Communication. Beginning in 1981, this series of conferences in Rome and in other parts of the world has been jointly sponsored by the Centre for the Study of Communication and Culture formerly in London and now in St. Louis, Missouri.

The Center at the Gregorian University was formally established in 1978 by Carlo Maria Martini, S.J., now the Archbishop of Milan and then the Rector Magnificus and already deeply interested in the Church and communication. Since 1981 the Gregorian University has offered an interdisciplinary licentiate and doctoral degree in theology and communication as well as philosophy and communication. As a basis for creating this interdisciplinary research and degree program, the members of the theology faculty and the Center for Communication Studies at the Gregorian University began a series of internal seminars that were later expanded into the international seminars inviting major theologians interested in the interaction of theology, philosophy, the media and arts, and communications.

The Centre for the Study of Communication and Culture (CSCC) was closely linked with the Gregorian University from its inception in 1977, but was established to foster research on the church's mission in the world of mass media and communications. From the beginning, one of the priority research projects of the CSCC has been theology and communication, especially from the perspective of research on how to integrate communication education in the formation of pastoral personnel in the post-Vatican II church.

The significance of the Cavalletti conferences on Theology and Communication is highlighted by the emphasis that major theologians such as Bernard Lonergan, Avery Dulles, Karl Rahner and, more recently, David Tracy have given to communications in theological studies. Christian theology is a theology of "communication" between God and human communities and among human communities. Theologies of the Trinity, the Incarnation, Revelation, Sacraments and the Church have always drawn on the communication concepts at a philosophical/scientific level and at a popular level. The Center for Inderdisciplinary Studies in Communication at the Gregorian University originated as a response to theologians' questions about communications. But the church's communications directors are also constantly seeking a foundation in theologies. This mutual interest of theology, philosophy and communication has been the raison d'etre of communication studies at the Gregorian University and the ongoing conferences on theology and communication that have been the source of the books in this series.

Other titles in this series:

Communication and Lonergan: Common Ground for Forging the New Age, Thomas J. Farrell and Paul A. Soukup, eds., 1993.

The Church and Communication, Patrick Granfield, O.S.B., ed., 1994.

Communicating the Faith: New Light on Fundamental Theology, Robert A. White, S.J., ed., 1994.

Theology and the Religious Film, John May, ed., 1995.